'This is a particularly innovative book on international marketing, focusing on original thought and stimulating ideas. Such high goals are achieved through a deliberate mix of research and practically oriented chapters, including, appropriately for the new global landscape, two chapters each on pricing and branding, while other topics are given a new twist.'

Professor Bill Merrilees, Griffith University, Australia

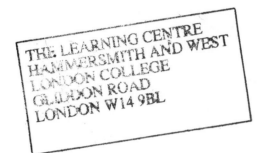

STRATEGIC INTERNATIONAL MARKETING

AN ADVANCED PERSPECTIVE

EDITED BY

T. C. MELEWAR
SURAKSHA GUPTA
BRUNEL UNIVERSITY, UK

palgrave
macmillan

First published 2012 by
PALGRAVE MACMILLAN

Palgrave Macmillan in the UK is an imprint of Macmillan Publishers Limited,
registered in England, company number 785998, of Houndmills, Basingstoke,
Hampshire RG21 6XS.

Palgrave Macmillan in the US is a division of St Martin's Press LLC,
175 Fifth Avenue, New York, NY 10010.

Palgrave Macmillan is the global academic imprint of the above companies
and has companies and representatives throughout the world.

Palgrave® and Macmillan® are registered trademarks in the United States,
the United Kingdom, Europe and other countries.

ISBN: 978–0–230–58024–4

This book is printed on paper suitable for recycling and made from fully
managed and sustained forest sources. Logging, pulping and manufacturing
processes are expected to conform to the environmental regulations of the
country of origin.

A catalogue record for this book is available from the British Library.

A catalog record for this book is available from the Library of Congress.

10 9 8 7 6 5 4 3 2 1
21 20 19 18 17 16 15 14 13 12

Printed in China

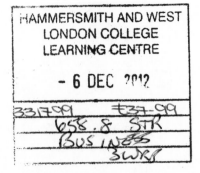

Contents overview

We dedicate this book to
Encik Saedah binti Idrus and
Prabodh Bhushan Gupta

Contents

List of figures

List of tables

Notes on contributors

Suraksha Gupta is Lecturer in Marketing at Brunel Business School, Brunel University, UK and is responsible for pathway leadership of the MSc marketing degree. She has taught at various institutes in the UK and abroad, such as Essex Business School, London School of Economics, Middlesex University Business School, Grenoble Business School and Beijing Institute of Post and Telegraph. She has over 15 years' industry experience, latterly as a director of Systems Research Pvt Ltd in India. During her academic career, she has published in various journals, such as *Industrial Marketing Management* and *Journal of World Business*.

T.C. Melewar is Professor of Marketing and Strategy at Brunel Business School, Brunel University, UK. He has previous experience at Zurich University of Applied Sciences, Switzerland, University of Warwick, De Montfort University, Loughborough University, UK and MARA Institute of Technology, Malaysia. T.C. teaches strategic marketing management, corporate brand management and international marketing on a range of undergraduate, MBA and executive courses. He has published in many journals such as *Journal of International Business Studies*, *International Marketing Review*, *International Journal of Management Reviews*, *Industrial Marketing Management* and *Journal of World Business*. T.C. has taught MBA in countries such as Sweden, Germany, France, Georgia, Moldova, Russia and Indonesia. He is currently a visiting professor at the University of Malaya, Malaysia.

Amanda Broderick is Dean and Chair in Marketing at Salford Business School, University of Salford, UK. An award-winning researcher, she consults widely for business, commerce and public policy and is a representative on a variety of national and international bodies and committees. Her research expertise lies in the field of marketing psychology, with particular application to the electronic and international marketplaces.

John W. Cadogan is Professor of Marketing at the School of Business and Economics, Loughborough University, UK and Honorary Professor and Docent at Lappeenranta University of Technology, Finland. His primary research interests are export marketing, marketing strategy and sales management.

Verolien Cauberghe is Assistant Professor at the Ghent University, Belgium, where she teaches courses on marketing communication, corporate communication and social marketing. Her PhD, obtained in 2008, was on the impact of new advertising opportunities on interactive digital TV. Currently, her research interests are advertising effectiveness and new media, gaming, social marketing, health communication, risk communication and crisis communication. She has published in several journals, including *Journal of Advertising*, *Journal of Interactive Marketing*, *Journal of Business Research*, *Journal of Advertising Research* and *Journal of Social Marketing*. She serves as a reviewer for *Journal of Marketing Communication* and *Journal of Computer-Mediated Communication*.

Tendai Chikweche has worked in academia and the corporate sector primarily in marketing in four different countries. He has taught at universities in Zimbabwe, South Africa and Australia and completed his PhD at the University of Western Sydney. His research interests are primarily on inquiry on the bottom of pyramid and small to medium-sized enterprises. His PhD thesis was on marketing to the BOP and he has published in refereed conference and journal papers on the subject area.

A. Coskun Samli is Research Professor of International Business and Marketing at the University of North Florida. Born in Turkey, he was one of the first business scholars to come from that country to the US. He has published 24 books and more than 100 articles. He was chairman of the board of governors of the Academy of Marketing Science and holds that association's Harold Berkman Award.

Michael R. Czinkota is Associate Professor at Georgetown University, Washington DC and Birmingham Business School, UK. He was raised and educated in Germany, Austria, Scotland and Spain and completed his PhD at the Ohio State University. He has written a number of books, including *International Marketing* (with I.A. Ronkainen, 9th edn, 2010, Cengage) and *International Business* (8th edn, 2011, Wiley). He has also published in *Journal of International Business Studies*, *Journal of International Marketing*, *Journal of World Business* and *Management International Review*. His main research areas are export development, export promotion, trade policy and international marketing.

Keith Dinnie is director of the Centre for Nation Branding, and the founder of Brand Horizons consultancy. He is also Senior Lecturer in International Marketing at NHTV Breda University of Applied Sciences in the Netherlands. He is the author of the world's first academic textbook on nation branding, *Nation Branding: Concepts, Issues, Practice* (2008, Butterworth-Heinemann), and editor of *City Branding: Theory and Cases* (2011, Palgrave Macmillan). He has published in various international journals, including *Place Branding and Public Diplomacy*, *Journal of Brand Management*, *Journal of Consumer Marketing* and *International Marketing Review*.

Richard Fletcher is Adjunct Professor of Marketing at the University of Western Sydney. Since becoming an academic in 1989, Richard has authored 91 refereed publications and is the instigator and lead author of the largest selling textbook in international marketing in Australia and New Zealand, now in its 5th edition, *International Marketing: An Asia-Pacific Perspective* (with H. Crawford, 2011, Pearson). Prior to 1989, he was an Australian trade commissioner for 25 years and represented Australia's commercial interests while variously based in New Delhi, Mumbai, San Francisco, Jakarta, Teheran, Libya, Los Angeles and Bangkok – hence his academic specialization in international marketing.

Mark J. French is a director of Evolve Marketing (http://evolve-marketing.co.uk/), a marketing consultancy providing services to small and medium-sized businesses. His first degree was from Swansea University, and he has a PhD from Loughborough University's School of Business and Economics. His prior industry experience was in the drinks and media industries, where he held analysis and strategy roles. His primary research interest is business strategy.

Mark S. Glynn is Associate Professor of Marketing in the Faculty of Business and Law at Auckland University of Technology, Auckland, New Zealand. He has a PhD from the University of Auckland. In 2006, Mark won the Emerald/EFMD Best Thesis Award for outstanding doctoral research in marketing strategy. His research areas are branding, business-to-business marketing and retail channels and his research has been published in *European Journal of Marketing, Industrial Marketing Management, Journal of Business Research* and *Marketing Theory*. He also serves on the editorial boards of *Industrial Marketing Management* and *Journal of Business & Industrial Marketing*.

Jurg Hari is Professor at Zurich University of Applied Sciences. He holds a PhD from the Federal Institute of Technology in Zurich, Switzerland, and an MBA from Cornell University, Ithaca, USA. He has worked in various sales and marketing positions for several major pharmaceutical companies, for example Merck, Roche and Pharmacia, and as an international strategy and marketing consultant. His research focuses on personal selling, market research methodology and pricing.

Zlatko Jančič is Associate Professor, Head of Marketing Communications and Public Relations Chair at the Faculty of Social Sciences, University of Ljubljana, Slovenia. He teaches advertising strategy, marketing management, marketing relationships and strategic marketing courses. Prior to his full engagement at the University of Ljubljana in 1994, he had a successful career in the biggest advertising agency in the region. He has written several Slovenian books on marketing, and has also published internationally in various journals, such as *Journal of Advertising Research, Journal of Marketing Management, Journal of Marketing Communications* and *European Journal of Marketing*.

Eva Kipnis is Senior Lecturer in Marketing at Coventry Business School, Coventry University, UK and a chartered marketer. She has over 10 years' experience as a practising and consulting marketer, working with a number of international brands. Her teaching responsibilities include international marketing strategy, advertising psychology and research methods at undergraduate and postgraduate levels. Her research interests focus on consumer identities, consumption and branding strategies in multicultural marketplaces, with a particular focus on the impact of multicultural consumer identities on consumption.

Andrej Kohont is teaching assistant at the Faculty of Social Sciences, University of Ljubljana. As a researcher at the Organizations and Human Resources Research Centre, University of Ljubljana, he has been involved in a number of research projects on international HRM, competence management in companies and public organizations, labour market and public employment services, VET in the automotive sector and various higher education projects. He collaborates with the Cranet network and lectures on HRM, organizational behaviour and the theory and practice of leadership. He is a vice president of the Slovenian HR Association.

Kirsti Lindberg-Repo is Adjunct Professor at the University of Vaasa and Aalto University of Industrial Arts and Design. During 2007–11 she was in charge of an international academic research project called BIG at Hanken School of Economics, Helsinki, cooperating with Emory University, Atlanta, IIFT, Delhi and SMU, Singapore. The BIG project was funded by TEKES (Finnish Funding Agency for Technology and Innovation) and was based on the themes of branding, innovation and globalization. The BIG aim was to generate growth and competitiveness through improved value generation of new business models. The BIG project successfully culminated in the book *Titans of Branding*.

Jyoti Navare is Head of Department (Marketing and Enterprise) at Middlesex University Business School. She holds a PhD from Southampton University and is a fellow of the Higher Education Academy. She has a number of years' experience as an international risk manager and underwriter based in London and Sweden, working closely with financial services organizations and governments internationally. In academia, she undertook several senior management roles and held visiting professorships in Germany, Poland and Iceland. Her key research activities are in risk management, financial institutions, innovation, marketing, business sustainability, corporate social responsibility and professional education.

Sak Onkvisit is Professor of Marketing at San Jose State University, USA. He has authored several textbooks and has published in leading journals. An internationally known scholar, he has taught in several countries and has served as a Fulbright Senior Scholar and a Fulbright Senior Specialist. His textbook, *International Marketing: Strategy and Theory* (with J. Shaw, 2008, Routledge), now in its 5th edition, is one of the most authoritative textbooks in the field of international marketing.

Adrian Palmer is Professor of Marketing at University of Wales, Swansea. His first career was in tourism marketing and management. Since joining academia, he has researched and published extensively on the subject of services marketing and the efforts of service organizations to create memorable experiences. His book *Principles of Services Marketing* (2011, McGraw-Hill), now in its sixth edition, is widely used throughout the world to provide a grounding in the challenges and opportunities of marketing services.

Patrick De Pelsmacker is Professor of Marketing at the University of Antwerp and part-time Professor of Marketing at Ghent University, Belgium. He teaches marketing communication, marketing research and consumer behaviour. His research interests are in advertising effectiveness, advertising and consumer behaviour in new media, branding, health communication, social marketing and ethical consumer behaviour. He has published in, among others, *Journal of Advertising, International Journal of Advertising, Journal of Advertising Research, Journal of Interactive Marketing, International Marketing Review, Journal of Business Research* and *Journal of Business Research*.

Klement Podnar is Associate Professor and Vice Dean for Public Relations and Development at the Faculty of Social Sciences at the University of Ljubljana. He teaches corporate communication, basics of visual communication and marketing. His research has been published in journals such as *European Journal of Marketing, Journal of Public Policy & Marketing, Corporate Communication: An International Journal, Journal of Communication Management, Corporate Reputation Review* and *Journal of Marketing Communications*.

Rosmimah Mohd Roslin teaches at the Faculty of Business Management, Universiti Teknologi MARA, Malaysia, and is chief editor of the *Journal of International Business and Entrepreneurship,* published by the university. She holds a PhD from Keele University, UK, an MBA from Western Illinois University and a BSc from Indiana University, USA. Her research interests are in the areas of marketing channels, channel relationships, relationship marketing, qualitative research and retail development. She has published in several journals, including *Journal of Global Marketing, International Journal of Retail and Distribution Management, International Journal of Interdisciplinary Social Sciences, International Journal of Arts and Sciences* and *Journal of Asia-Pacific Business*. She was the academic adviser for the Institute of Marketing Malaysia.

Don E. Schultz is Emeritus Professor of Integrated Marketing Communication, Northwestern University, Evanston, USA. He is also president of the global marketing consultancy Agora, Inc. He is the author/co-author of 18 books, plus numerous book chapters, prefaces and forwards for some of the leading books in the field. He has published over 100 articles on marketing, advertising, branding, sales promotion and integrated communication in most of the leading trade and academic journals around the world. He is a regular columnist of *Marketing Management* and *Marketing News* and is the founding editor of the *Journal of Direct Marketing*.

Janet Shaner is Director of Program Design and Delivery at IMD, Lausanne, Switzerland, where she is responsible for running the operations of the MBA programme. She earned her PhD at the University of Lausanne, researching the relationship between external business networks and performance in foreign investments. Her current research interests are related to managing young talent and managing the millennials.

John J. Shaw is Professor Emeritus at Providence College, Rhode Island, USA. He has co-authored over 80 papers in journals and at conferences. He is the co-author, with Sak Onkvisit, of *International Marketing: Strategy and Theory*, a textbook that is used internationally at all education levels – undergraduate, MBA and PhD.

Jean-Claude Usunier is Professor at the Faculty of Business and Economics of the University of Lausanne, Switzerland. His research interests are cross-cultural consumer behaviour, cultural and linguistic aspects of international marketing, comparative management and international business negotiations. His recent research was published in *International Journal of Research in Marketing, Journal of Research in Personality, Time and Society, Journal of International Marketing, European Management Review* and *International Journal of Electronic Commerce*.

Foreword

It takes an admirable act of courage to compile a new text on international marketing. To further add to the challenge, the authors of this book sought to publish the 'best' articles in circulation. To provide the expected synthesis of current practice and critical discussion is always going to be difficult, because the world is changing in so many ways – politically, economically, commercially, culturally and socially. There are so many variables to control, so many areas to cover, so many new ideas and theories to incorporate that the decision boils down to whose perspective among the many possible stakeholders should be incorporated, and what material should they cover, given the constraints around the extent of the book set by the publisher? What is consistent with the target audience? What is most relevant to the readership without adding needless pages and costs? Overall, it is a difficult judgement to have to make. The task has been lightened here by approaching the pre-eminent researchers and writers in the field today and asking them to provide commentary on the current trends, theory and practices across global markets.

The framework adopted here is the 7Ps, borrowed from services marketing (Booms and Bitner, 1981). Yet, typical of marketing itself, we have no further consensus on the final definitive number of Ps to include for international marketing. Many years ago, a small, slim textbook, now out of print (Paliwoda, 1994), featured nine Ps, which were then expanded to ten (Paliwoda and Ryans, 2004), but the issue should not be how many Ps are necessary, rather, what will fulfil the need for adequate coverage of the international marketing field, which in itself is vast? Here, the 7Ps intersect with the 3Cs (changes, challenges and contributions) of markets and marketing strategies to provide a good, global overall perspective. One point that should be borne in mind is that the market potential of commercial precedents found in one market may be replicated in others – and not necessarily by the same company. Today, we live in what was foreseen by Marshall McLuhan in 1964 as a 'global village'. Everything we see and do is capable of being transmitted to audiences worldwide in real time. In the same way, any new or unusual practices might be seized upon by competitors for use in other markets in an extension of the 'demonstration' effect, which we have always known to exist.

One major change that has affected our lives irredeemably is globalization, which was discussed in a seminal article in 1983 by Theodore Levitt in the *Harvard Business Review*. Since then, we have learned to come to terms with new globally available standardized products and the ubiquitous multinational corporation, but here important misconceptions can arise. While popularly acknowledging the advance of globalization, we also have to signal the work of Professor Alan Rugman (2005), whose research found that among the Fortune 500 listing of the world's largest multina-tionals, only nine were truly multinational, in that they were not dependent upon sales in their home region. This, then, establishes a new rationale and purpose for such companies, as well as a new, more limited, orientation of regionalization as opposed to globalization. Aligned with this, there is the debate about standardization and localization, or adaptation, which is represented in a chapter here devoted to that other but newer hybrid word, 'glocalization', which is used increasingly frequently in offering advice to international companies, with the dictum: 'go global in as many ways as possible but be prepared to adapt and to localize a product where necessary'. Today, not only are products and services more and more standardized but so, too, are the media that are used to communicate these products and services. In the same way, new perspectives in looking at the practices of international marketing are offered across these chapters. Chapter content includes some of the traditional mix that we might expect to see in considering international marketing variables, but, in addition, there are also more unusual headings to be found here, such as spelling, sounds and pronunciation, which have direct relevance and validity.

Clearly, there are always going to be new paradigms emerging. We all have to recog-nize that what constitutes market acceptability for a product today is different from what was acceptable 20 years ago. People change and their tastes change; technology push creates new products and new applications and this then creates new markets. Mobile phones, especially 'smart' phones, have created new forms of communication, enabled advertising and promotion direct to the phone, and developed new forms of use, for example airline boarding passes and credit card payments.

Markets everywhere today cry out for what I call 'low cost excellence': not only are products expected to meet the best prevailing industry standards, but they must also be produced and provided to the final consumer at low cost. The market requirements for success always seem to have to consider cost minimization on the one hand, while ensuring value maximization for the final consumer on the other.

Who, then, are the actors who occupy this space? The actors in the arena of inter-national marketing have changed over the years and become more sophisticated and demanding, as credit and information have become more freely available. Alongside this, there has been diminishing regulation, since the rules for trading are increasingly now being created at a level higher than the nation state, such as the European Union or the World Trade Organization. At the same time, convergence has increasingly taken place in technology and in the agreement of international standards. This has further reduced trade barriers, as has the harmonized system of tariffs, the agreed nomencla-ture of products, and countless advances in both transportation and telecommunica-tions. These developments have implications for the carriage of goods and customer handling but, more importantly, for finance. We have a single European market and across its markets more sophisticated buyers and sellers than ever before because today everyone has access to the same information. Concealment is difficult, if not impossible, with the internet offering auctions for consumers and suppliers, as well as price comparison sites. The BRIC countries (Brazil, Russia, India and China), known for their fast growing markets, are surpassing growth elsewhere around the globe and demand special attention.

The 15 chapters in this book are aimed at a final year undergraduate and post-graduate readership. I think the market has been well judged and the book has been well conceived to deliver to this market. Regulation is expected to continue to fall unless the present recession becomes really entrenched and intellectual property is likely to be the key challenge in years ahead. But many other factors are likely to present challenges, including:

- the increasing sophistication of consumers
- sociodemographic changes, such as the greying of consumers in developed economies, such as Japan, the USA, Canada and Western Europe, in which the largest and most affluent section of the population is moving into retirement and dependent for their pensions on the minority working population
- outsourcing and offshoring, the trend towards which will continue with the drive to minimize costs.

Meanwhile, we can expect to see more change in the Fortune 500 multinationals listing, with more companies emerging from the developing world. The international trading infrastructure will continue to expand. The euro appears to be fairly well established, despite the economic scares of 2011 prompted by the weaker EU members such as Greece, Italy, Spain, Portugal and Ireland. The internet will continue to facilitate trade for good and bad among companies large and small, experienced and inexperienced, honest and criminal.

References

Booms, B.H. and M.J. Bitner (1981) 'Marketing strategies and organizational structures for service firms', in J.H. Donnelly and W.R. George (eds) *Marketing of Services*. Chicago: American Marketing Association.

Levitt, T. (1983) 'The globalization of markets'. *Harvard Business Review*, 61: 92–102.

McLuhan, M. (1964) *Understanding Media*. New York: Mentor.

Paliwoda, S.J. (1994) *The Essence of International Marketing*. Prentice Hall: Hemel Hempstead.

Paliwoda, S.J. and Ryans, J.K. Jr (2004) 'Landmarks in the mapping of international marketing', in P.J. Kitchen (ed.) *Marketing Mind Prints*. Basingstoke: Palgrave Macmillan.

Rugman, A.M. (2005) *The Regional Multinationals, MNEs and 'Global' Strategic Management*. Cambridge: Cambridge University Press.

Stanley J. Paliwoda
Professor of Marketing
University of Strathclyde

Acknowledgements

Personal acknowledgements

It has been a challenging task preparing and completing this book. We have managed to pool together academics from the four corners of the world to share their research insights into the field of international marketing. We hope that we have successfully imbued energy, enthusiasm and encouragement in this highly volatile and changeable arena of international marketing. We would like to say thank you to all our esteemed colleagues who have contributed chapters to this book. Special thanks to Martin Drewe at Palgrave Macmillan, whose persuasion and encouragement have helped us in producing this book. Lastly, let us move the frontier of academic knowledge and practice of international marketing into areas that have been left untouched.

Publisher's acknowledgements

Journal of Marketing Communications for Usunier, J.-C. and Shaner, J. (2002) 'Using linguistics for creating better international brand names'. *Journal of Marketing Communications*, 8: 1–18.

Thunderbird International Business Review for Czinkota, M.R. and Samli, A.C. (2010) 'The people dimension in modern international marketing: Neglected but crucial'. *Thunderbird International Business Review*, 52(5): 391–401.

Cengage Learning for Damar International case study from Czinkota, M.R. and Ronkainen, I.A. (2010) *International Marketing with InfoTrac*, 9th edn.

Every effort has been made to contact all copyright holders, but if any have been inadvertently omitted the publishers will be pleased to make the necessary arrangements at the earliest opportunity.

Introduction

Strategic International Marketing: An Advanced Perspective provides an essential text for international marketing and management students. Existing theories focus on the consumer and reflect upon the application of simple and general marketing tools in global markets. This book evaluates the changes and challenges in the international business environment, which are discussed by both practitioners and academics. Recent developments impose a greater need to understand the differences in behaviour of international consumers. In this book, we highlight the challenges within global markets and the need for strategic capabilities when promoting products across geographic and cultural boundaries.

Global issues have been explored by academics in various associations including the Academy of Marketing, the European Marketing Academy and the Industrial Marketing and Purchasing Group. There has been a substantial rise in research activity in this domain. Highly reputed journals that have contributed to this field include the *Journal of Marketing*, the *Journal of Academy of Marketing Science*, the *Journal of Strategic Marketing*, the *Journal of Marketing Management*, the *European Journal of Marketing* and the *Journal of Brand Management*. Research has been conducted by reputable business schools such as Brunel University, Zurich University of Applied Sciences, Northwestern University, University of Lausanne, San Jose State University, University of Ljubljana, Ghent University, University of Antwerp, Georgetown University, University of North Florida, Hanken School of Economics, Loughborough University Business School, Temple University and Swansea University. These institutions have specialized research groups focusing on developing cutting-edge tools that deal with shifting global landscapes.

Practically all sizes of firms at both national and international level have encountered changes and challenges due to globalization. Today, international boundaries are not considered to be barriers for trade. Most economies have opened their doors to international products and services. These developments put global marketing tactics in the category of sweeping, broadbrush strategies. Globalization has turned markets into highly volatile places where customers are more aware of alternative products across borders. Competition extends over wider territories, offering customers a vast choice. The situation calls for a more complex decision making when it comes to purchasing and product adoption. In order to meet these challenges, companies rely on the field of marketing to address and develop competitive advantage for strategic growth.

During the past few years of economic recession, the world economy's perform-ance indicators, such as gross domestic product, employment, inflation and household income, were all in decline. Marketing helped businesses to sustain themselves by understanding the psychological aspects of consumer behaviour and strategizing accordingly. Marketing insights and commercial results provided new confidence to managers, who, by the beginning of 2010, witnessed a recovery in domestic and inter-national markets. Post-recession, the economic environment rekindled the corporate thirst for market share growth and investor value. This reflects the need for further discussion and the development of a stronger theoretical and practical infrastructure.

Inspired by McDonald (2010), this book provides a series of guidelines written by top marketing experts in the world. It addresses the opportunities and threats in today's volatile markets, with examples provided in the form of case studies to rein-force readers' understanding of such complex concepts. It sheds light on contempo-rary ideas and trends in relation to original research on the theory and practice of global marketing strategy. This book presents different international perspectives concerning planning, organization and marketing in global markets. Knowledge in these areas is presented in a concise manner and is derived from the contributions of expert academics working in the field.

The book aims to strike a balance between three elements within global markets: change, challenges and contributions (3Cs). The text covers the knowledge that falls under the scope of the 3Cs and we have presented it in a form that would be accessible to its readers. The authors present different viewpoints of the application of the marketing mix in the form of the 7Ps and the 3Cs. By discussing managerial implica-tions, they attempt to foster new and intriguing ideas and present future research opportunities.

Each chapter represents conceptual and empirical work done by researchers specializing in the respective principles of marketing. The chapters contain summary lists of the key learning points and recommended readings for ease of reference.

Chapter 1 by Usunier and Shaner addresses the relevance of the different aspects of branding products across borders in relation to the creation of global brand equity. It explores the interpretation of brand equity in the home country context for internat-ional marketers.

Chapter 2 by Onkvisit and Shaw provides a discussion of the theories and assump-tions of standardization and localization of products in relation to glocalization. Onkvisit and Shaw offer a global and integrated perspective that can help in managing homogeneity and heterogeneity in the marketing mix. They address efficiency and the overall effectiveness of marketing strategies as part of the adaptation process of campaigns designed for both national and international customers.

Chapter 3 contributed by Mohd Roslin discusses the challenges faced by firms in identifying global pricing strategies. It integrates the pricing techniques with global situational demand and highlights the implications of the global environment on pricing strategies.

Chapter 4 has been contributed by Jurg Hari. Based on an overview of the challenges faced by managers in relation to the pricing for serving consumers in global markets, this chapter provides insights into the role of salespeople particularly in the context of business-to-business markets with a focus on the use of price-quality cues. These cues as per the author are used for assessment of products and services by consumers.

Glynn focuses on the sources and long-term benefits of manufacturers' brand value for retailers in Chapter 5. He specifies how brand strength is transformed into brand value for retailers. He describes its influence when combined with product category changes and the relationship outcomes for both the manufacturer and the retailer.

Chapter 6 by Eva Kipnis and Amanda Broderick identifies key categories of place or country of origin to review their relationship with the behavioural aspect of consumption. The authors have used their understanding of the concepts to explain the use of its dimensions for positioning purposes. The analysis helps readers to understand the role of place association in enabling managers to take strategic and positioning decisions.

In Chapter 7, Schultz attempts to help readers understand the role of marketing communication as a change agent in a global setting wherein customers have taken control of the marketplace. As proposed by Schultz, marketers should recognize the push-pull strategy as a tool for the successful deployment of a horizontal marketing systems and the management of networked sales systems.

The relevance of promotion in the digital era is taken up by Cauberghe and de Pelsmacker in Chapter 8. They explain its logical contributions and limitations in relation to marketing communication based on the theory of planned behaviour. Recommendations made by Cauberghe and Pelsmacker will help the reader adopt and improve the efficiency of the drivers of IDTV advertising.

In Chapter 9, Podnar, Kohont and Jančič recognize the human factor as a specific challenge for marketers in international business. Their contribution highlights the utility of different practices adopted by firms towards career development opportunities for employees in the international domain. They provide insights for international firms into career development methods for the successful management of people in global markets.

The concept of the human dimension in the 7Ps of marketing is extended by Czinkota and Samli in Chapter 10. They explain the challenges posed by the changing dynamics of marketing in the international domain and the role of entities operating in it. They outline different ways to cope with international challenges, with an emphasis on their individual activities.

The dimension of processes is discussed by Lindberg-Repo in Chapter 11, who explains the need for marketers to understand the evolving nature of processes in the world economy. The author develops methods for building different kinds of strong processes that can drive value as the core concept of process innovation aligned to meet the changing needs of customers.

In Chapter 12, French and Cadogan explain the potential role of export market-oriented processes on business drivers such as cash flows and their contribution in shaping the performance of firms involved in exporting.

In Chapter 13, Palmer directs the reader to the service dominant logic to explain the desire of customers to receive hedonistic benefits from their purchases. Palmer also discusses the role of customer experience management in shaping the dominant reality that will enable customers to distinguish between competitors.

Another perspective of physical evidence is presented in Chapter 14 by Dinnie, who explains the importance of public–private sector partnerships as a core component of marketing to an overseas audience in the context of nation brand equity.

This book ends with future directions as envisaged by Fletcher and Chikweche. In Chapter 15, they discuss the gaps in current knowledge and the time needed by marketers to identify and operate successfully in international markets. Fletcher and Chikweche promote the application of an ethical approach in deriving the theories required to understand the 7Ps as drivers of customer purchase behaviour. These are essentially based on the concept that growth in new territories comes from the bottom of the pyramid.

Due to the expanse of the field of international marketing, it has been a challenging task for the editors to include every possible relevant topic in one book. We apologize in advance to readers who may feel that some topics have been overlooked. The book does not attempt to cover all the issues. It fosters enthusiasm by encouraging original thought and stimulating ideas in topics critical to this field. Contributors have duly tried to address the conceptual debate about the marketing mix and its application in industrial practices.

Finally, we would like to thank all those who have contributed to make this project a reality. Any success in this regard is to be credited to the authors. Thanks to these stimulating and contemporary topics, we are certain that this dynamic field of study and practice will continue to change and expand in the future.

We welcome feedback and suggestions, which may be sent to Suraksha Gupta at Brunel University, suraksha.gupta@brunel.ac.uk.

Suraksha Gupta
T. C. Melewar

Reference

McDonald, M. (2010) 'A brief review of marketing accountability, and a research agenda'. *Journal of Business and Industrial Marketing,* 25(5): 383–93.

1

International branding: creating global brand equity through language[1]

Jean-Claude Usunier and Janet Shaner

Learning outcomes

At the end of this chapter, readers should be able to:

1. Understand the linguistic aspects of branding and their relationship to meaning in the home country context and language.

2. Analyse why and how brands as linguistic assets transfer (or do not transfer) to different target linguistic contexts.

3. Identify key obstacles when transferring a brand name from a source to a target context.

4. Build meaningful brand names across languages, thus adding value to global branding.

Key points

- International product sales are increasingly important for most companies. As a result, cross-border brand naming has become a significant international marketing issue.

- A brand name is stored in consumers' minds as a combination of the alphanumeric content of the brand name and its design (logo, fonts and so on).

- Linguistic aspects of brand names such as phonetics, etymology and rhetoric can be used for assessing its original meaning.

---

1. This chapter is partly based on Jean-Claude Usunier and Janet Shaner (2002) 'Using linguistics for creating better international brand names'. *Journal of Marketing Communications*, 8: 1–18. With the permission of *Journal of Marketing Communications*.

- A good name for an international brand involves adequate spelling, consistent pronunciation across languages, and positive meaning that fits with the intended product attributes, benefits and positioning.

- When transferring brands across borders and languages, new meanings may emerge, source meanings may be lost, and unintended, negative meanings may bubble up. How these linguistic assets transfer (or do not transfer) to target linguistic contexts can be assessed through the comprehensive framework presented in this chapter.

- For developing brand names with globally transferable meaning structures, there are three solutions: a blank name (source and target names are blank), focusing on the visual versus the textual aspects of a brand name, and/or choosing a name from the global thesaurus.

- Our recommendation is that managers follow a mix of the 'Juliet principle' and the 'Joyce principle', thereby building strong meaningful brands across languages.

Introduction

Most global brands originate from a particular linguistic context (Shalofsky, 1987) and a significant part of their brand equity is tied to local spelling and meaning idiosyncrasies. For instance, *7-Eleven* conveys a message of extensive opening hours that hardly crosses US borders unless shoppers in target countries have a minimal command of English. This is not a problem as long as brands remain on the domestic market. However, international product sales are increasingly important for most companies and cross-border branding becomes a significant marketing issue that requires considering the linguistic content of brands.

Many authors have researched what makes a good brand name (Shipley et al. 1988; Chan, 1990; Keller, 1993). Most characteristics of a good brand name such as being easy to spell, read and pronounce, suggesting product benefits, and conveying no undesirable imagery tend not to cross borders easily. In fact, most of these characteristics are related to the local language context where the brand name was originally launched. Because brand naming is usually embedded in the source language, brand names have a number of key features, that is, sound, spelling and meaning, that are attractive to local consumers and enable them to invest the brand with particular representations that may not be meaningful to global consumers.

International branding may involve transferring home country brands to foreign markets or creating entirely new brands, designed to be international from the start. In either case, standardized international branding reduces advertising and inventory costs and provides convenient identification for people travelling internationally. Building a global brand is expensive but valuable. For example, the value of the *Coca-Cola* brand is estimated at £43bn, *IBM* at £37.4bn, *Microsoft* at £35.5bn and the *Disney* brand name at £17.4bn (Interbrand, 2009). Language, including the spoken sounds and conventional symbols, is only a part of a brand's book value, but it takes on more importance when crossing national borders. However, companies often do not consider the linguistic context of brands because it seems beyond their reach, especially when corporate names are linked to founders' names and considered 'sacred cows'.

We propose a comprehensive framework for analysing how linguistic assets, built into a brand name in its domestic context, transfer (or do not transfer) to a number of target linguistic contexts. First, we provide insights into how various branches of linguistics are relevant in assessing the linguistic value of a brand in its native language context, with an emphasis on sounds (phonetics and phonemics, phonology), the roots of words (etymology), and the art of persuasive discourse (rhetoric). Second, we describe whether and how these linguistic assets transfer to other languages, and third, we outline key recommendations for managers who want to create effective global brands by optimizing the transferability of brand names across linguistic contexts.

Brands as composite signs

Brands are complex and composite signs based on pictographs (alphabetic or other), on sounds as spelled locally (in each particular linguistic context) and on other visual elements, that is, logos and iconic content. The linguistic content of a brand name has an influence on its verbal, auditive and intellectual meaning, and its interpretation by consumers. The first step in assessing a brand name is to review the various facets of its linguistic content in its source context (see Figure 1.1): text, sound, visual cues and meanings associated with these linguistic cues. As a result, the value analysis of a brand name must be assessed using several different branches of linguistics (phonetics, phonology, semantics, etymology, rhetoric, semiotics). As shown in Figure 1.1, there are both visual and textual components in the brand. A brand is first and foremost a

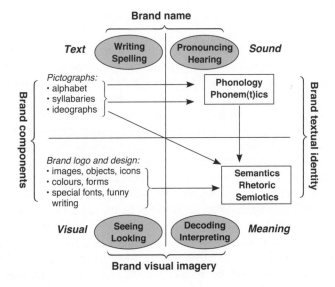

Figure 1.1　A comprehensive framework for assessing the linguistic value of a brand

name, that is, text, based on various kinds of pictographs that may either be read or said by consumers. It is also deeply associated with linguistic codes related to other brand components such as the design of the brand name (special fonts, colours and so on), its logo and the way it has been traditionally presented in marketing communications, especially in advertising. While the combination of the brand's sound with its meaning results in the brand's textual identity, the combination of its visual base with consumers' interpretations results in the brand's visual imagery. Consumer activities leading to the full attribution of meaning are coupled as 'signifier' and 'signified' in semiotics. Reading signs is not fully separated from their interpretation.

Spelling, sounds and pronunciation

One key component of a brand is its textual part, that is, any combination of signs representing both words and numbers – generally that part of a brand that can be uttered. Reading and pronouncing a brand name is easy in its home country. In contrast, pronouncing foreign words may be difficult. Brand names, as they are written on advertisements and product packaging, may be based on a number of different written signs, ranging from alphabets (the set of characters representing basic sounds of speech), syllabaries (the set of characters representing full spoken syllables) or ideographs (signs that directly represent an idea or a thing while often having a sound value as well). The most popular writing system for brand names is the Roman alphabet, which is not fully unified since many languages have a number of special characters. But there are also other alphabets such as the Cyrillic and Arabic. The interpretation of alphabetic writing is mediated by sound, while ideographs have a direct and potentially an indirect interpretation, through their sound as well as through their visual image (see Figure 1.1).

Phonemics, one of the branches of phonology (the study of the sound system of languages), is concerned with the classification and analysis of the phonemes (speech sounds in any given language that distinguish one word from another). Relative to selecting a brand name, a distinction should be made between a purely *semantic* relationship (between the word and the object) and a *symbolic, meaningful* connection (Dogana, 1967). The semantic relationship is based on an associative process taking place over a long period of time, with an arbitrary connection between the word's phonetic structure and its meaning. In some cases, the phonetic structure of a word fits closely with the object it represents and, to this extent, the sound qualities of its phonemes have a symbolic relationship to the object. For example, names starting with plosives (*B, C, D, G, K, P, T*) are easier for consumers to recall and recognize than names not starting with these strong-sounding consonants, and names that start with or contain 'K' and 'P' are often 'funny' sounds (Vanden Bergh et al., 1984). In addition, eight letters (*A, B, C, K, M, P, S, D, T*) represented at least 55% of the initial letters of the top 200 brands for each year since 1975 (Vanden Bergh, 1983), including *Bic, Buick, Coca-Cola, Delta, Kodak, Pampers* and *Toyota*. Front vowels (*i, é, è*) express dynamic concepts (rapidity, vivacity, lightness), while back vowels (*a, o, u*) communicate slowness and heaviness (Dogana, 1967).

Some phonemes are specific to one or a limited number of particular languages, like the English *th*, which is unknown to Italians or Germans but is familiar to Greeks. The use of local phonemes is part of the value of a brand in its home context, since native speakers recognize familiar sounds. In some languages, the discrepancy between writing and speaking is small, for example German and Turkish, but in other languages, such as French, there are major discrepancies between what is written and how it should be pronounced. For instance, French people know that *eau* (water), *eaux* (waters), *aux* (garlic) and *os* (bone) all should be pronounced simply *o*.

Denotative meaning: designating the product or service category

Brand textual identity relates to how written signs translate into sounds and how these sounds in turn translate into meaning. Brand textual identity involves the mental experience created by the textual part of the brand name. However, some cues can be both textual and visual: a Chinese character typically contains both elements. That is why the diagonal arrow in Figure 1.1 goes to the lower right quadrant on semantics and semiotics. Assessing the meaning-based value of a brand name requires a semantic approach, and a brand name has both denotative and connotative meanings. As indicated by Keller (1993, p. 10), brand equity is reinforced if the brand name semantically suggests 'the product or service category' and consequently enhances 'awareness of the brand and identification with the product category'. This *direct* influence is based on denotative meaning, which relates to a brand name's ability to designate and indicate.

For instance, *Nescafé* denotes a coffee-based product. Similarly, *U-Haul* denotes moving and doing it yourself, a service product. And *All-Bran* says that the product is pure, 100% bran. However, these examples of denotative capacity only have value for native English speakers. *Ambre Solaire*, a French brand of sun cream, denotes the product category by using the adjective for 'solar' but, again, this denotative value is limited to a French-speaking context. Etymology (a branch of linguistics dealing with the study of the sources of words) is sometimes used for denotative purposes, although not all consumers understand the roots of words.

Connotative meaning: suggesting key attributes and producing inferences about key benefits

Connotation exists when a name suggests meaning and associates the name with key attributes and benefits. Connotation is more indirect than denotation, and the meaning originally intended by the marketer may not be understood by consumers. As outlined by Keller (1993, p. 10), 'the semantic meaning of a suggestive brand name may enable consumers to infer certain attributes and benefits' and 'facilitates marketing activity designed to link certain associations to the brand'.

For example, *Tide* suggests the strength of the tidal wave and associates it with the cleaning power of a detergent. However, it is probable that not all consumers, even within the native linguistic context, make this association. The connotative value of a brand's name may communicate service attributes and suggest key benefits, such as *Dollar* or *Budget* (car rental for good value), *Palm Pilot* (a computer that organizes your life, sized for the palm of your hand), *Papermate* (a faithful companion for writing) or

Tartinette from *tartiner* (to spread). An important element of connotation is the country of origin suggested by the brand name and its legitimacy as a producer, such as the Swiss origin of *Swatch*, a combination of *Sw*itzerland and *watch*.

The connotative power of a brand's name may also be related to physical and symbolic attributes, such as *Milka* chocolate where the name suggests milk, a natural ingredient, reinforced by advertising copy showing cows in Swiss mountain pastures. Brand names also can reinforce favourable country stereotypes made by consumers (Usunier and Cestre, 2007). However, the border between denotative (designating) and connotative (suggesting) meaning may not always be fully clear. *Weight Watchers*, for instance, lies somewhere between indicating that this brand's products deal with diet food (product category) and suggesting weight loss (inferred key benefit). While the cathead in the *Whiskas* brand is denotative, the phonetic analogy with 'whiskers' is connotative, because it indirectly suggests benefits (after eating a delicious meal, cats often wipe their whiskers) that need more interpretive elaboration.

Brand rhetoric: constructing brand names for persuasion and influence

Rhetoric is the art of using speech to persuade or influence, very much in favour in Ancient Greece and systematized as a field of knowledge. A key issue for a brand name is its ability to capture consumers' attention and convey a persuasive statement as to the credibility and performance of the product. Denotation, connotation and brand rhetoric can be based on the use of figures of speech, such as:

- *metaphor:* a word or phrase is applied to an object or action that it does not really denote in order to imply a resemblance
- *synecdoche:* a part is substituted for the whole or a whole for a part
- *oxymoron:* an epigrammatic effect by which contradictory terms are used together
- *litotes:* using understatement for rhetorical effect.

A brand like *Piz Buin* uses a metaphor, that of a high mountain in the eastern Swiss Alps, which implies burning sun and boasts the high protective capacities of the product against sunburn. Other brands using metaphors are *Aqua-Fresh*, *Longueurs et Pointes*, *Head and Shoulders* and *Tendres Promesses*. Oxymoron, a conjunction of opposites, can be found in brands such as *Easy-Off* or *Crème de Peinture*. Metaphors and oxymorons are very bound to the source language.

The denotative and connotative meanings implied by the brand name are more extensive in an Asian context where the pictographic signs offer a much richer potential for inferential meaning. In East Asia and especially China, calligraphy and meaning become much more important in branding decisions in comparison with Western countries. A brand name must have a positive connotation, a combination of characters with favourable sounds that can be pronounced in almost the same way in as many regions as possible while avoiding the pitfalls due to tonality, characters that convey a favourable meaning, a relationship with the brand's advertised qualities, a favourable content in terms of lucky numbers such as eight, and a balance between yin and yang characters (Schmitt and Pan, 1994; Alon et al., 2009).

Visual cues associated with the brand

The visual elements associated with the brand name, although not based on language, depend on the interpretation of signs and symbols and on the relations between written, spoken and visual signs and their referents in the physical world or the world of ideas (semiotics). A brand name is stored in consumers' minds as a combination of the alphanumeric content of the brand name and its traditional design (type of fonts, funny writing, font colours and so on). The brand name is often associated with a copyrighted design. The graphic composition of the logo conveys as much meaning as the letters of the brand name. They combine into what we call 'brand visual imagery' in Figure 1.1. Brand imagery relates to the mental experience created by the visual part of the brand name, for example how consumers decode the bamboo tree, the Chinese lantern and the rising red sun in the *Suzy Wan* logo (a Mars brand for Chinese convenience food).

For instance, the *IBM* trademark is inseparable from the evocative ability of its graphics. The three letters of the *IBM* logo are obtained by the superimposition of characters known as 'mecanes' and alternate slats of coloured bands or 'blinds'. The mecanes are typesetting characters whose square serif evokes industrial production and roots in the mechanical world. The *IBM* logo, with its combination of mecanes and blinds, conveys an image of binary-based computer language. The imagery of the *IBM* brand logo is largely translinguistic, and therefore offers a truly international ability to convey meaning.

In Chinese characters for brands, visual symbols are translated into meaning. The characters are not just random strokes: each basic Chinese character is originally based on a concrete, simplified picture (for example a tree, a paddy field, a river and so on) and has a meaning based on the content of the picture. Further characters are based on combinations of basic characters (for example, the character for East is based on a compound of the character for tree, meant as root or origin, and the character for sun, resulting in a meaning for East as 'origin of the sun'). Additionally, there should be a balance between *yin* (an even number of strokes) and *yang* characters (an odd number of strokes). And the calligraphy of the brand must convey certain visual signs that fit the brand visual imagery. In the case of the Volkswagen *Cheep*, a character was used that evoked an imaginary slope that the jeep had to climb (Schmitt and Pan, 1994; Alon et al., 2009).

The challenge of transferring brand names to other languages

'What's in a name? That which we call a rose by any other name would smell as sweet.' This is the Juliet principle as first written by William Shakespeare. An opposing view is the 'Joyce principle' from *Finnegan's Wake*, where James Joyce used phonetic symbolism as opposed to words to communicate. Where the Juliet principle says 'a rose by any other name would smell as sweet', the Joyce principle would say 'A rose is a rose is a rose' (Collins, 1977, p. 52). In international branding, both principles apply along a continuum from meaningless brands with simple spelling (Juliet principle) to highly meaningful flags that convey context-bound messages (Joyce principle). However, strong believers in the Juliet principle will put little emphasis on brand linguistics. For them, brand awareness will be based mainly on brand age, cumulated advertising expenses, brand presence and familiarity.

A good name for an international brand from a linguistic point of view involves adequate spelling, consistent pronunciation across languages, and positive meaning that fits with the intended product attributes, benefits, and the positioning of the product. A key issue for target language consumers is that they can easily manipulate the brand name – spell it when they hear it and pronounce it when they see it as text, on a magazine ad, on product packaging or on a billboard. The writing and spelling system must be familiar to them. This may be a problem in China where the Roman alphabet is unfamiliar to many people or in Japan where, although familiar, *romaji* (Roman alphabet writing) is connoted as foreign (*gaijin*) and interpreted as non-Japanese branding (Sherry and Camargo, 1987).

There are a number of phonological features that typically make a name difficult to spell and pronounce in target linguistic contexts. It is the case when some of the phonemes used in the brand name are rather specific to a particular language. Rare combinations of consonants or vowels (called diphthongs and triphthongs) do not easily cross language borders. Long sequences of consonants or vowels (three and more) are impediments for linguistic transferability because certain languages, including Chinese and Japanese, do not have these long sequences.

Generally, simple brand names are most effective. However, brands names should avoid simplicity, spelling and pronunciation ease when there is a clear intention associated with the product that may influence consumers positively in a large number of countries. When people cannot pronounce foreign words, they simply change the pronunciation, that is, the correspondence between spelling and sound, by skipping letters and/or putting the tonic accent on a different syllable. For example, the assemblage *rlb* in *Marlboro* is difficult to pronounce for many people because of the confusion made by a number of languages between *l* and *r* sounds, and because the *r* or *l* sounds before a *b* sound is unfamiliar in many languages. As a consequence, the spoken brand name is often *malboro*. Also, the letter *f* is pronounced slightly differently in Japanese from how it is in Western languages, so the word *coffee* has been adapted to the Japanese palate as *kohi*. However, Japanese people are perfectly able to pronounce the *f* in *Nescafé* because it is understood as foreign.

Orthography, the principles underlying what is considered correct spelling in a writing system, is a key issue in the linkage between pictographs and sounds. One misleading feature is the lags between text and sound, due to orthographic convention. Items such as mute letters and special characters are not translinguistic. The *Peugeot* car brand, with a mute *t* at the end and its *ge* pronounced *j*, reflects the discrepancy in French between writing and speaking, between letters and sounds, with complex diphthongs and triphthongs and many mute letters. As a rule, this should be avoided unless there is an intention as with å in *Haågen Dazs*.

Unfamiliar sounds are not a problem, if they can be positively associated with a favourable origin or when certain sounds typically suggest qualities and benefits especially through onomatopoeia. The *Crunch* brand has some onomatopoeic value similar to the English *crunchy*, the French *croustillant* and the German *knusprig*; the combinations of *c+r+s* or *ch* suggest a food item deliciously cracking under the teeth, in the three languages.

In short, spelling and pronunciation should be rewarding for the speaker. Difficult names often suggest foreignness and difficult spelling may stimulate the attention of local consumers. While the ease of sound and spelling recognition plays an important role in transferring brand names, fascination for the unknown may paradoxically be favourable for some brand names because of positive associations of foreignness.

Problems with transferring brand meanings

When transferring brands across borders and languages, new meanings may emerge, source meanings may be lost, and unintended, negative meanings may bubble up. For example, Kellogg's changed its *Bran Buds* name in Sweden because Swedish people did not want to buy a 'grilled farmer' cereal brand. Other illustrations include the German hairspray *Caby-Net* launched on the French market (cabinet is a toilet in French) or the Chevrolet *Nova*, whose intended meaning was 'new' but translated into Spanish as 'does not work'. In Portugal, the literal meaning of *Nescafé* is 'it is not coffee' (Collins, 1977).

New meanings may emerge in the target linguistic contexts

There are a number of cases where new, positive or neutral meanings emerge in target contexts. Some new meanings may emerge involuntarily, such as for *Makita*, Japanese power tools, which favourably connotes 'make it' and a performance orientation in English. Transferred brand names more often have a neutral or positive meaning than a negative one. In a study of Chinese names of foreign brands, Chan (1990) shows that a positive connotation in Chinese accounted for 50.6% of brand names, neutral meanings in Chinese for 49.6%, and negative, unpleasant meanings for only 0.8%. However, even neutral or positive meanings should be qualitatively analysed because they may not match the product category or the key benefits to be conveyed by the brand name.

Most of the source meaning is lost in the cross-border transfer

Connotative meaning is generally lost when crossing borders. For example, the detergent *Tide* was once used in non-English-speaking countries (pronounced 'teed') where nobody had the slightest idea of the powerful tidal waves washing clothes evoked by the brand. As emphasized earlier, 'global brands' might well be portfolios of local brands, federated under a common, lexically identical name. Controlling meaning is a difficult task even for sophisticated companies. Most of the denotative meaning is lost in the cross-border transfer process because speakers in target contexts simply do not understand the name. Most of the connotative source meaning is also lost because the rhetorical elements generally are not understood across linguistic contexts. Figures such as metaphors, synecdoches, litotes, oxymoron and paronomasia (play on words, such as a pun) require an understanding of the source language. For instance, *Fédor*, an orange juice that is 'made of gold' (*fait d'or*), can be understood only by French speakers (provided they are sophisticated enough to understand, even unconsciously, the play on words). Among figures of rhetoric, metonymies (application of one object or quality for another, such as in *Midas*, *Ajax*, *Uncle Ben's*, *Aunt Jemima* or *Bounty*) are the most transposable type of semantic devices, provided that the semantic support is sufficiently well known worldwide. *Bounty*, a chocolate bar with coconut, evokes the flight of the 'bounty' ship in the South Seas, popularized in films.

Possibilities for transposing a brand name

The key issue in transferring a brand name across linguistic contexts is whether sound or meaning transposition is preferred, since they often conflict. In the case of 'translating' English brand names for the Chinese market, Zhang and Schmitt, B.H. (2001) distinguish three transposition methods: phonetic (that is, by sound), semantic (that is, by meaning), and phonosemantic (that is, sound plus meaning). Sophisticated transposition processes can try to overcome language barriers by reconstructing both the sound and meaning of a brand in the target linguistic context.

Czinkota and Ronkainen (2006) distinguish different avenues for the transposition of a brand name originally created for a specific national context:

1. *translation*, pure and simple
2. *transliteration*, an attempt to reconstitute in the target language the connotative meaning that exists in the source language, that is, Gillette's *Silkience* hair care product sold as *Soyance* in France and *Sientel* in Italy
3. *transparency*, a brand name that is suitable everywhere such as *Sony*.

Translation

There is no reason why the translation process would automatically create in the target language the values found in the source language. For instance, the *All-Bran* brand would translate in French as *Tout Son* and in German as *Alles Kleie*. While the French translated name is rather misleading (because of homonyms, *son* also means sound, his or her, besides bran), the German name sounds very strange, even stranger than the *All-Bran* name may have appeared to English-speaking consumers when it was first introduced. Pure and simple translation is the worst solution for the cross-border transfer of brands because different connotations are applied to lexically similar words. The detergent *Tide* could be translated as *Marée* in French, a term that connotes strong smells and dirt rather than strength, washing power and cleanliness.

Transliteration

A particular brand name, when pronounced in different languages, does not produce equivalent sounds and is not heard in the same way everywhere. The way in which it is said and heard can be critical for voice-based media such as television and radio. Native speakers put accentuation on different syllables in the word, resulting in different sounds for the same combination of letters. *Coca-Cola*, for instance, may be pronounced quite differently according to the syllable accented.

Incompatibility between sound, spelling and meaning may occur when the translit-eration of sounds in a new writing and pronunciation system conflicts with that of meanings. The first attitude of a company is to try and reproduce the brand sound in the target language. For instance, *Philip Morris*, approximated in Chinese as *mo li see*, evoked bad luck. Consequently, it was changed into *mor ha li see*, which suggested good luck for the buyer (Huang and Chan, 1997). Even *Coca-Cola* is not known exactly by this name in China, since the original name has a negative connotation. *Coca-Cola* is transliterated as *kekou kele* (in terms of rough sound equivalence) and conveys the meaning of 'tasty and enjoyable/happy' (Wilke, 1994).

Based on the linguistic differences between Chinese and English, spelling/charac-ters/vision have more weight in forming the brand attitudes of Chinese consumers, while sound is more important for Americans (Pan and Schmitt, 1995). Consequently, a brand like *Pepsi-Cola* is transposed into Chinese characters meaning a 'hundred happy things' and *Mercedes-Benz* changes into *Benchi* with two characters meaning 'striving forward fast'. However, this is not possible for all brands. In some cases, when the transposition of sounds is preferred over the transposition of meaning, that is, when it is difficult to find a chain of characters that transliterate both sound and meaning (not to mention calligraphic elements), the brand name may sound close to the Western version, such as *nifeya* for *Nivea*, while being poor at the meaning level – 'girl-not/Africa and second rank/Asia' (Wilke, 1994, p. 15).

In Japan, the issue is both less and more complicated, since the Japanese are familiar with the Western alphabet (*romaji*), but they also use Chinese characters (*kanji*) and two syllabaries, the *hiragana* for Japanese words and the *katakana* for foreign loan words (the same syllables as *hiragana* but with a slightly different calli-graphic style which signal the foreign origin). These alternative writing systems carry different meaning associations, which must be carefully monitored in order to convey appropriate subliminal messages:

1. *kanji* and *hiragana* will look more Japanese, while *romaji* and *katakana* signal foreignness
2. high-tech products will best be written in *katakana,* which connotes modernity, while traditional products are best served by *kanji*
3. *hiragana* has a feminine image and is frequently used for beauty products and cosmetics (Schmitt and Pan, 1994).

Transparency (blank names)

A blank name is a meaningless word when first launched. However, through the product, the pack, the advertising and the people who use it, the name comes to have a meaning. We have to distinguish between source blank and target blank names. *Sony*, for instance, is source blank because it has no meaning in Japanese, and it is target blank in most contexts except the US. A washing powder name like *Tide* is not blank in its source context (the US) but it is blank in most countries of the world. Another washing powder *Persil* is blank in its German source context but not in the French target context where it means 'parsley'. Strikingly, very few names are really blank across *all* linguistic contexts.

The impact of meaning on building a global brand

In summary, there are different ways to build meaning, and the name itself is not the only cue. It is not easy to globalize consumers' motivations since their attitude towards brands may vary cross-nationally. Consumers always 'construct' the identity of brands, even for 'global products', and they do so on the basis of their local language and culture. Much of the meaning in the original context will be lost in the cross-border transfer process. This leaves room for meaning investment through advertising, enabling a brand to build adequate meaning on a 'blank' meaning base. In this respect, crossing language borders may be seen as an opportunity rather than a constraint.

An overall assessment of brand linguistic value

A brand can be poor on one aspect and stronger on another aspect of linguistics. Only when the linguistic characteristics of a brand have been explicitly assessed in its native context does it become possible to investigate whether each of the components of linguistic value transfer into target linguistic contexts. The first phase is based on desk research and can be done by outsiders who have a fair level of language education in their own language and in at least one foreign language. This involves looking at spelling, writing and accentuation, and checking the semantics in dictionaries, possibly involving the back-translation of a brand name. However, for connotative meanings and rhetorical intents, it is necessary to check with natives in major linguistic contexts, that is, Arabic, Chinese, English, French, German, Japanese and Spanish. A final field research step involves interviewing a representative sample of linguistic insiders in target contexts and/or conducting brainstorming sessions to make sure the name fits when it is decided to alter a brand name in the cross-border transfer process.

In making weighting decisions, managers may consider these guidelines:

Brand name: spelling and sound
- In the West, the text and sound in the brand name and brand identity are more important (Zhang and Schmitt, 2001).
- When the brand is on the radio or TV, the name needs to be frequently verbalized and spelling and sound become more important.
- When a brand only covers a regional area where countries share a similar linguistic background (that is, Latin countries in Europe), spelling is less of an issue because consumers are more likely to be familiar with the words and pronunciation of neighbouring countries.
- When retaining the corporate image or founder's name is important, the speakers should be respected in the ease of name pronunciation.

Brand name: ethnic value
- Brand names should communicate appropriate product ethnicity, that is, the right match between product category and country of origin (Usunier and Cestre, 2007). For instance, *Giorgio di St. Angelo* designer wear is not Italian fashion but the product of US designer Martin Price (Leclerc et al., 1994).

- In Japan, a manager can choose to communicate a foreign or Japanese product identity depending on the language used: *kanji* and *hiragana* look more Japanese, while *romaji* and *katakana* signal foreignness (Schmitt and Pan, 1994).

Brand visual imagery
- In the East, visual cues and therefore brand visual imagery are more important (Zhang and Schmitt, 2001).
- When the brand is global, visual imagery is more important because names cannot convey meaning in all linguistic contexts.
- In the case of product ethnicity, that is, when consumers stereotype links between countries and products such as between Switzerland and watches, the connotative cues in the brand visual imagery are more important to link to the country of origin and the denotation of the product category is less important (Usunier and Cestre, 2007).

So what should a manager do?

Brand names with globally transferable meaning structure

There are three solutions: a blank name (source and target names are blank), focusing on the visual versus the textual aspects of a brand name, and/or choosing a name from the global thesaurus. *Avis* illustrates a blank name that is also bisyllabic and easy to pronounce. Visual elements of the brand name are the most transferable across borders because images require much less interpretation than words. They are generally based on icons (that is, they use visuals that are analogous to the thing they represent) such as *Suzy Wan* (Chinese food by Mars), which, in its visual, uses a combination of a bamboo tree and a rising sun, both icons of the Far East.

The value of a brand based on a global lexicon is that connotations can be transferred internationally. The global lexicon contains words that are borrowed from particular languages including English (*go, lady, job*), German (*kindergarten*), and Japanese (*judo, samurai*). Among this global lexicon, a word like *Magnum* evokes a large item, big like the gun that bears the same brand name. It may be effective despite the limited knowledge of Latin in our global world. (*Magnus* is a Latin adjective that means *big, great* or *large. Magnum* is its neutral and/or accusative form.) This Unilever ice-cream brand generates a feeling of being physically great (there is a lot to eat in this ice cream) and a great experience (it is great to eat). In a brand like *Kinder* (by Ferrero, milk and chocolate-based products targeted at children), both the sound base and the meaning may be shared in a great many countries because *kindergarten* belongs to the global lexicon. *Mon chéri*, another Ferrero brand, belongs to that sort of universe, as does *Taboo*, a Polynesian word popularized by Freud. *Dollar* and *Budget* also belong and will be seen almost everywhere as brands for good value.

Designing completely new names with global spelling/sound capability

A simple rule for completely new names with intended global potential is that they should be easy to spell and pronounce in as many languages as possible:

1. Keep the Roman alphabet because it is the global medium.
2. Names should not exceed three to four syllables.
3. The syllabic structure preferably should be based on basic consonant-vowel units (such as in *Lu*) and assembled sequentially.
4. Avoid syllables with long sequences of consonants and/or vowels.
5. Avoid phonemes that are specific to a particular language.
6. Respect sequences of consonants or vowels that are typically found in most languages, for example *ct* vs. *tk*. Sequences such as the English *ngth* (as in *length* or *strength*) that are language specific should be avoided.

For those products where a global brand strategy applies, the brand must fulfil the following conditions:

1. It must be based preferably on a fairly transparent name, which needs neither translation nor transliteration, such as *Kodak* or *Nokia*, does not produce inadequate meaning associations in certain linguistic and cultural contexts, and conveys an image either related to our modern technological world (that is, *Pentium*) or related to what can be considered as a common cultural heritage (although family related, *Mars* evokes a Greek god and a planet).
2. It must have consistent underlying core themes, serving common functional uses of the product cross-nationally and emphasizing consistent consumer benefits across countries.
3. Consumer needs must be fairly consistent for this product category worldwide.
4. Advertising strategy must have been executed for at least fifteen years in a similar manner across a large number of countries.

It is difficult to achieve full consistency in global brand development since it is done over tens of years and the advertising strategy is rarely fully coherent over time and across countries. It may be done by different companies who are successive owners of the brand name and by different people as brand managers within the same company. A poor name in linguistic terms, that is, with little chance of being used in a large number of language contexts, may have been supported over years by advertising and brand presence in stores, so that it achieves high scores on recall and recognition.

We are entering a new, global world where new brand names can be chosen either from scratch or from a large portfolio of existing brand names within a global company. Like James Joyce, who found echo beyond the confines of his poetic English style, marketers must not renounce the possibility to build strongly meaningful brands across languages. Following the Joyce principle is simply a way to consciously add value to global brand names.

Issues for further discussion

1. Can brands be virtually language free? Can they become language free when transferred internationally?
2. How difficult is it for brands to cross the barriers of writing systems, especially in the case of Chinese and Arabic writing systems?

3. Would you support the 'Juliet principle' or the 'Joyce principle' in international branding?
4. Is product ethnicity likely to become a major issue for creating international brands?

CASE STUDY

Soshi Sumsin Ltd

Sammy Soshi's first assignment for his new job with Soshi Sumsin Ltd was to recommend a new name for the firm's line of electronic products. Sammy had completed his MBA at Emory University in May 2002 and had returned to Seoul, Korea, to work in his father's firm. Soshi Sumsin manufactured a line of electronic products, which included VCRs, stereos and TVs. Mr Soshi (senior) got involved in electronics manufacturing when he agreed to manufacture TV components for a US manufacturer in 1980. Eventually, he was producing a full line of TVs, as well as VCRs and stereo equipment for three American firms. In addition, he had been marketing his own line of products in the Korean market since 1992 under the Sumsin brand name.

Mr Soshi felt that his firm was now ready, both in terms of manufacturing know-how and capital, to enter international markets under his own brand name. The US market was chosen as the first target because of its size and buying power, and an introduction date of April 2003 was tentatively set. Being unfamiliar with the US market, Mr Soshi relied heavily on his son, Sammy, to help with marketing decisions.

The first problem Sammy tackled was the selection of a brand name for the line. His father had planned to use the Sumsin name in the US market. Sammy pointed out that failing to carefully consider the effect of a brand name in a different culture could cause major marketing difficulties at a later stage. He cited the Tatung experience as a case in point. Tatung was a Taiwanese maker of TVs, fans and computer terminals. When the company entered the US market, it did not even consider changing its brand name. The Tatung company had a favourable connotation in Chinese and was known in the company's oriental markets. However, in the US, not only was the name meaningless, but it was difficult to know how to pronounce it. Because of these difficulties, Tatung's US advertising agency finally decided to emphasize the strangeness of the name, and it launched a campaign based on a play on words to help customers pronounce Tatung. Each advert carried the query, 'Cat Got Your Tatung?' Sammy believed that a lot of effort that should have been put into the product itself had been spent on overcoming a bad trade name.

Sammy cited a second example of problems resulting from a poorly chosen brand name. Another Taiwanese company, Kunnan Lo, introduced its own brand of tennis rackets in the US market in 1987. Recognizing that its own name would present problems in the US market, it decided to select a US name. Ultimately, it decided on the name Kennedy; this was quite similar to the company name, and was certainly familiar in the US. However, after initial promotional efforts, it quickly became apparent that Kennedy was not a neutral name. Many tennis players were Republicans, and for them the Kennedy name had negative connotations. As a result, the name was changed to Kennex, a neutral, artificial word that was still similar to the company name. However, Kennex also proved to be unsatisfactory, because of some confusion with the name Kleenex. To eliminate this confusion, the name was finally changed to Pro-Kennex, which provided both a tennis tie-in and retention of a root similar to Kunnan Lo. The waste of resources in the series of name changes could have been avoided.

Determined to avoid the mistakes of these other companies entering the US market, Sammy Soshi carefully evaluated the alternatives available to his company. The first was his father's preference – to use a company family name. However, Sumsin was somewhat difficult for English-speaking people to pronounce and seemed meaningless and foreign. Soshi was equally unfamiliar and meaningless, but he was also afraid that Americans would confuse it with the Japanese raw fish, sushi.

A second alternative was to acquire ownership of an existing US brand name, preferably one with market recognition. After considerable research, he chose the name Monarch. The Monarch company had started manufacturing radios in Chicago in 1932 and Monarch radios had been nationally known in the 1940s. The company was badly hurt by television in the 1950s, which reduced the size of the radio market appreciably. The company was finally wiped out by the invasion of inexpensive transistor radios from Asia in the 1960s. The company filed for bankruptcy in 1972. Sammy found that he could buy the rights to the Monarch name for $50,000. The name was tied in with electronic products in the public's mind, but he wondered how many people still remembered or recognized the Monarch name. He also wondered whether this recognition might be more negative than positive because of the company's failure in the market.

A third alternative would be to select a new name and build market recognition through promotion. Such a name would need to be politically and socially neutral in the US market and ultimately in other foreign markets. It had to be easy to pronounce and remember, with a neutral or favourable meaning to the public. The possibilities might be considered. The first was Proteus, the name of an ancient Greek sea god. This name would be easy to pronounce in most European languages, but was almost too neutral to help sell the product. The other alternative was Blue Streak, again, an easy name in English, but not necessarily in other European languages. Sammy felt that the favourable connotation of speed and progress might provide a boost for the products to which it was applied.

This case study has been adapted from Cundiff, E.W. and Hilger. M.T. (1984) Marketing in the International Environment, *Englewood Cliffs, NJ: Prentice-Hall, pp. 440–2. Reproduced with kind permission.*

Questions

1. Evaluate the alternative names being considered by Sammy Soshi. Which name would you recommend?
2. Whatever new name is chosen, should Soshi Sumsin adopt the same name in the Korean market?
3. What are the advantages of selecting different brand names, as appropriate, in each foreign market?
4. Enumerate the characteristics that a good international brand name should possess.

Exercises on international branding

1. Discuss the international transferability of the following assemblages (product, company, country of manufacture, brand name).

Generic product	Company name	Brand name	Made in
Pizza	Dr Oetker	*Pizza Rustica*	Germany
Computer chip	Intel	*Pentium*	United States
Drilling tool	Bosch	*Fuchsschwanz*	Spain

Generic product	Company name	Brand name	Made in
Internet service	France-Télécom	*Wanadoo*	France
Insulation products	Owens-Corning	*Fiberglas*	United States
Chinese convenience food	Mars	*Suzy Wan*	The Netherlands
Breakfast cereals	Kellogg's	*All-Bran*	Locally made
Car	Daewoo	*Daewoo/Nexia*	South Korea
Tomato sauce	Mars	*Dolmio*	The Netherlands
Insecticide	Bayer	*Baygon*	Germany

2. Discuss the relationship between a country's image (through its people, its history, its political and social situation and so on) and the image of products known to be made in this country. Find brand names that exemplify using a favourable match between the linguistic content of a brand and its country of origin.
3. Discuss the possible international extension of the following companies and/or brand names:
Müller (German yoghurts)
Barilla (Italian pastas and cookies)
Petrobras (oil business)
Teysseire (French syrups)
Kuoni (Swiss tour operator)
Schimmelpenninck (Dutch cigars and cigarillos)
Ishikawajima Harima Heavy Industries (Japanese industrial equipment company)
Roi des Montagnes (French dried mushrooms)
Hewlett-Packard (electronics and IT)
Douwe-Egberts (large Dutch food and tobacco company)
Club Méditerrannée (French tour operator)
Svenska Kullager Fabrik (the world's leading company for roller bearings)
Peugeot (car manufacturer)
Hertz (car rental)
Thrifty (car rental)

References

Alon, I., Littrell, R.F. and Chan, A.K. (2009) 'Branding in China: Global product strategy alternatives'. *Multinational Business Review*, 17(4): 123–42.

Chan, A.K. (1990) 'Localization in international branding: A preliminary investigation on Chinese names of foreign brands in Hong Kong'. *International Journal of Advertising*, 9: 81–91.

Collins, L. (1977) 'A name to conjure with'. *European Journal of Marketing*, 11(5): 340–63.

Czinkota, M.R. and Ronkainen, I.A. (2006) *International Marketing* (2nd edn). Boston: South-Western Publishing.

Dogana, F. (1967) 'Psycholinguistic contributions to the problem of brand names'. *European Marketing Research Review*, 2(1): 50–8.

Huang, Y.Y. and Chan, A.K. (1997) 'Chinese branding name: From general principles to specific rules'. *International Journal of Advertising*, 16(4): 320–35.

Interbrand (2009) 'Top ten brands in 2009', http://www.interbrand.com/best_global_brands_intro.aspx, retrieved May 11, 2010.

Keller, K.L. (1993) 'Conceptualizing, measuring, and managing customer-based brand equity'. *Journal of Marketing*, 57: 1–22.

Leclerc, F., Schmitt, B. and Dubé, L. (1994) 'Foreign branding and its effect on product perception and attitudes'. *Journal of Marketing Research*, 36: 263–70.

Pan, Y. and Schmitt, B. (1995) 'What's in a name? An empirical comparison of Chinese and Western brand names'. *Asian Journal of Marketing*, 4(1): 7–16.

Schmitt, B.H. and Pan, Y. (1994) 'Managing corporate and brand identities in the Asia-Pacific region'. *California Management Review*, 36(4): 32–47.

Shalofsky, I. (1987) 'Research for global brands'. *European Research*, 8: 88–93.

Sherry, J.F. and Camargo, E.G. (1987) '"May your life be marvelous": English language labelling and the semiotics of Japanese promotion'. *Journal of Consumer Research*, 14: 174–88.

Shipley, D., Hooley, G.J. and Wallace, S. (1988) 'The brand name development process'. *International Journal of Advertising*, 1: 253–66.

Usunier, J.-C. and Cestre, G. (2007) 'Product ethnicity: Revisiting the match between products and countries'. *Journal of International Marketing*, 15(3): 32–72.

Vanden Bergh, B.G. (1983) 'More chickens and pickles'. *Journal of Advertising Research*, 22: 39–44.

Vanden Bergh, B.G., Collins, J., Schultz, M. and Adher, K. (1984) 'Sound advice on brand names'. *Journalism Quarterly*, 61(4): 835–40.

Wilke, M. (1994) 'Der Werte Name: Die Marke auf Chinesisch'. *Der Neue China*, 21(3): 15–16.

Zhang, S. and Schmitt, B.H. (2001) 'Creating local brands in multilingual international markets'. *Journal of Marketing Research*, 38: 313–25.

2

The 'glocalization' of product and advertising strategies

Sak Onkvisit and John J. Shaw

Learning outcomes

At the end of this chapter, readers should be able to:

1. Address the standardization–localization bifurcation in terms of the origin, merits, conceptualization and empirical evidence.
2. Advance the standardization–localization debate by focusing on 'glocalization', a dynamic and hybrid concept.
3. Utilize the universal principles of 'glocal marketing' when designing product and advertising strategies.
4. Discuss the conceptual, research and strategic implications of glocalization.

Key points

- Standardization assumes that the world market is homogeneous, and the strategy is efficient but not effective.
- Localization assumes that the world market is heterogeneous, and the strategy is effective but not efficient.
- Glocalization and standardization are two distinct concepts, and a standardized campaign does not become global or international simply because the campaign is employed in multiple countries.
- Glocalization, bridging the gap between standardization and localization, offers a global and integrated perspective that balances market homogeneity and heterogeneity on the one hand and strives for efficiency and effectiveness on the other hand.
- Principles of glocalization provide a framework for the planning of the marketing mix on a global basis as well as at a local (national) level. A glocal campaign is globally and locally relevant, and it is adaptation ready.

Introduction: in retrospect

The first generation of international marketing textbooks was heavily influenced by the economics discipline. Utilizing the institutional approach, the early pioneers identified the various actors (for example marketing intermediaries) and their functions. As a result, these first-generation textbooks basically focused on logistics, transportation modes, facilitating agents (for example freight forwarders) and documentation. The emphasis on the distribution aspect was based on the assumption that the international marketing task primarily involved moving an existing (standardized) product abroad.

Beginning in the late 1960s and accelerating in the 1970s, the second generation of international textbooks emerged, and the coverage shifted towards the decision-making process. This move paralleled the trend of marketing books in general (for example principles of marketing, marketing management and consumer behaviour), which were moving out of the shadow of the economics discipline towards the establishment of marketing as a distinct discipline of study in its own right. Recognition of consumer heterogeneity began to supplant the assumed homogeneity. This paradigm shift moved the discussion from a static perspective towards a more dynamic approach, with the emphasis on decision making. The shift also signalled a more balanced perspective by moving beyond distribution to allocate equal attention to the other aspects of the marketing mix.

The birth of a debate

The early 1960s was the dawn of the standardization–localization debate. The crux of the standardization debate is whether it is appropriate for a company doing business overseas to simply export its marketing mix programme, that is, the 4Ps of marketing – product, place/distribution, promotion and price.

For some reason that has never been elaborated, the standardization debate focuses solely on the product and promotion strategies, while the place and pricing strategies have essentially been ignored. One possible explanation for the low level of attention given to place is that marketing scholars and practitioners, perhaps by default, have accepted the premise that each country or market has its own unique infrastructure that requires some form of local distribution.

Likewise, with regard to price, each market has its own unique cost structure that is derived from the local infrastructure, labour market, local and overseas transportation, among others, as well as currency exchange, tariffs and other trade barriers. Given that it is difficult to have a uniform price on a nationwide basis, it is a foregone conclusion that it is practically impossible for a multinational corporation to maintain a uniform price on a worldwide basis. The only exception perhaps is commodities such as oil and gold (and also currencies) that are consumed and traded on a worldwide basis.

Within the context of product strategies, the standardization proposition first focuses on whether the physical and functional attributes of a product sold abroad should be altered to conform to local market conditions. From time to time, other aspects such as brands or packaging also enter the debate. In the case of promotion strategies, the standardization debate exclusively focuses on international advertising practices. As a rule, for whatever reason, there is not much interest in the other areas of promotion (that is, personal selling, publicity and sales promotion).

This chapter concentrates on product and advertising strategies, the elements of the marketing mix that have gained the greatest degree of attention, but the discussion is relevant to the other aspects of the marketing mix. Additionally, the main purpose of the chapter is to move beyond the standardization–localization bifurcation. The theme of the chapter is 'glocalization', a truly global strategy that aims to combine the efficiency of standardization and the effectiveness of localization. The proposed 'glocalization' principles, neither home country nor host country oriented, provide a framework for the planning of marketing mix on a worldwide basis.

A parallel

In a way, the standardization–localization debate parallels the centralization–decentralization debate. Standardization is a cousin of centralization, which advocates that it is best for the headquarters to make decisions for local, overseas operations. In all likelihood, the centralized approach will mandate the utilization of standardization. Decentralization is the flip side of the coin, and this approach will afford overseas managers the luxury of devising their own marketing plans for their own national markets. Therefore, local managers will probably design their own local strategies. It should be noted that the management literature started the centralization–decentralization debate long before the emergence of the standardization–localization controversy. Even now, after more than half a century of heated debate, conclusions regarding the superiority (or inferiority) of centralization remain elusive. Consequently, some experts have endorsed a management approach that combines both centralization and decentralization, somewhat consistent with the integrated advertising approach.

The original three schools of thought: yes, no and maybe

Conceptual framework

To simplify the standardization–localization debate, the traditional schools of thought can be dubbed: yes, no and maybe.

When asked whether an international marketer's marketing mix should be standardized, one group of scholars and practitioners has replied 'yes'. This school of thought is also known as universality, uniformity, commonality and so on. This perspective assumes that basic physiological and psychological needs are culture free. It further assumes that technology, communication and education have resulted in a convergence of art, literature, tastes and thoughts. Proponents of standardization maintain that, because consumer needs are universal, a particular marketing mix that performs well at home should work equally well abroad. It is thus foolish to incur extra costs and time by needlessly adapting the existing marketing mix.

Opponents of standardization say 'no' to the standardization practice. They disagree with the notion of consumer homogeneity, especially on a worldwide basis. Instead, their contention is that differences abound across countries. As a result, they insist that international marketers must adjust their marketing mix to fit each host country's unique and specific situation. The localization school of thought can also be called nonstandardization, specificity, individualization, adaptation, modification and customization.

Finally, the third school of thought acts as a voice of reason as it attempts to provide a reasonable compromise. Those proposing this perspective explain that standardization, while not always feasible, may be possible and even desirable in certain cases. Therefore, the practicality of standardization is country dependent and situation specific.

Some empirical evidence

One significant reason why the standardization–localization debate remains unresolved is because the standardization concept has not been adequately defined (Onkvisit and Shaw, 1999; Jeong et al., 2002). The merits of product standardization (or localization) have generally been debated in the context of anecdotal evidence. As an example, some countries allow no advertising of cigarettes and thus any standardized (or localized) advertisements are out of the question. Indonesia, while allowing cigarette advertising, prohibits advertisements showing cigarettes or the act of smoking, thus instantly barring Marlboro's US print advertisements that routinely show a pack of cigarettes (*Wall Street Journal*, 2007a, 2007b).

Walt Disney Co., in spite of its world-renowned cartoon characters, is moving away from Americanizing its international audiences, at least in high-growth foreign markets such as India, China, Russia, Latin America and South Korea (*Wall Street Journal*, 2007c). The company's new strategy is to work with local experts to make culturally customized films. In India, Disney collaborates with Yash Raj Films to make Disney-branded animated films, with the voices of Bollywood stars. In fact, films may even have to be specifically made for the southern part of India, an important region with distinct tastes in films. In any case, a film must be released in at least the Hindi, Tamil and Telugu languages.

In contrast to advertising standardization, product standardization has received far less attention in terms of empirical research. There are a few recent studies that investigated the practice of standardization/localization without directly addressing the issue of effectiveness. According to one study, the performance of Korean exporters of electronics is enhanced by the adaptation of products to foreign customers' tastes and the adjustment of export prices to foreign market conditions (Lee and Griffith, 2004). Based on another study, it is not uncommon for exporters or managers to underadapt their host market strategies (Dow, 2006). In the field of information and communication technology, companies that globalize their operations after the domestic period lean in the direction of product standardization (Gabrielsson et al., 2006).

Just like a marketer of a tangible product, a service provider must also consider whether to standardize, localize or glocalize its service offering. According to a study of business-to-business repair service quality for mission-critical equipment, there are remarkable similarities in the US and Europe (Peterson et al., 2005). In the case of financial services firms in Australia and the US, there are some common practices as well as national variations. Depending on market conditions, either standardization or localization (or both) can be utilized (Alam, 2006).

Researchers have employed varying bases to study advertising standardization. The dimensions studied range from consumer homogeneity to comparison of national media and management perceptions. In general, differences across countries have been found, repeatedly and consistently.

A few recent studies offer some limited support for the standardization school of thought. In India, several American firms employ standardized advertising (Chandra et al., 2002). Based on a worldwide survey of foreign advertisers in China, only 10% and 12% respectively utilize localized and standardized strategies:

> A predominant majority of the companies surveyed use the combination strategy, that is, partly standardized and partly localized. Factors that relate to the advertising strategies used in China are the number of subsidiaries, the perceived importance of localizing language and product attributes, and the perceived importance of mostly Chinese cultural values. (Yin, 1999, p. 25)

Both Japanese and American managers employ a moderate level of advertising standardization. While they value cost savings, they also recognize obstacles to the utilization of advertising standardization (Taylor and Okazaki, 2006).

The results of most studies point to the localization school of thought. A study of corporate practices reveals that localization overshadows standardization (Kanso and Nelson, 2002). Appeals, symbols and even themes in the communication content need to be targeted to local culture. Children's TV commercials in China, while showing some evidence of Western values creeping in, reflect China's traditional cultural values and its social and economic development level (Ji and McNeal, 2001). Whereas US advertisements more frequently use the hard sell approach, Chinese advertisements emphasize the soft sell (Lin, 2001). Dutch respondents show a somewhat negative attitude towards TV commercials that use the English language (Gerritsen et al., 2000). Although Americans prefer a utilitarian advertisement to an image advertisement, their Taiwanese counterparts appear to respond equally well to both types of appeal (Chang, 2006). South Korea, when compared to Hong Kong, displays more values of low uncertainty avoidance in TV commercials (Moon and Chan, 2005). In Hong Kong, there is a stronger consumer acceptance for localized advertising (Pae et al., 2002). One literature review has found that the average propensity to adapt advertising theme, creative execution and media allocation in global markets is 49%, 59% and 63% respectively (Theodosiou and Leonidou, 2003).

Recently, content analysis is a preferred method of investigation for a number of researchers. They have investigated the contents of magazine and TV advertisements from the US, Japan, Germany, Russia, Sweden, Egypt, Lebanon, the United Arab Emirates and so on. Images and appeals found in these advertisements vary across countries (Maynard and Taylor, 1999; Milner and Collins, 2000; Al-Olayan and Karande, 2000; Dallmann, 2001). A content analysis of US, British, Japanese and South Korean corporate websites in terms of 25 interactivity functions/indicators has found that Western websites tend to emphasize consumer-message and consumer-marketer interactivity and that Eastern websites are more likely to highlight consumer-consumer interactivity (Cho and Cheon, 2005). Based on a comparison of the visuals of US and Chinese TV commercials, traditional storytelling techniques (for example story line and comparison and identification) are better vehicles for cultural manifestations than cinematographic variables (for example subjective camera, direct address and pacing) (Zhou et al., 2005). A study by Lynch et al. (2001) highlights that, to effectively target international internet shoppers, companies need to tailor their websites for different regions in the world.

A few studies support the compromise school of thought. Although New Zealand firms operating in at least two European Union (EU) countries recognize the varying marketing environments across EU countries, some country pairs (for example the UK and Ireland) offer a degree of similarity that facilitates some degree of standardization (Chung, 2005). Japanese and US subsidiaries in the EU show that corporate performance can be improved if the external environment and internal resources are conducive to standardization (Okazaki et al., 2006). Multinationals can lessen local subsidiaries' resistance to standardization and centralization when they understand market similarities, are familiar with foreign contexts, and headquarters' managers and subsidiary managers have developed shared values (Laroche et al., 2001). Subsidiaries' acquiescence is related to a global company's ability to foster successful relationships between the headquarters and its foreign subsidiaries (Hewett and Bearden, 2001). To implement standardization programmes, a thorough understanding of local market conditions is required (Solberg, 2002). Because beauty products are more likely than cars, food and household goods to utilize the strategy of standardization (Nelson and Paek, 2007), the practice may be product specific.

In conclusion, there is a varying degree of support for each school of thought. A review of the literature of management responses, consumer responses and consumer characteristics indicates that there is no theoretical or empirical evidence to support the standardization approach in its pure form (Onkvisit and Shaw, 1987). According to a more recent review by Theodosiou and Leonidou (2003, p. 141):

> based on an integrative analysis of 36 studies centering around strategy standardization/adaptation, its antecedents, and performance outcomes, this stream of research was found to be characterized by non-significant, contradictory, and, to some extent, confusing findings attributable to inappropriate conceptualizations, inadequate research designs, and weak analytical techniques.

The concept of glocalization: a new paradigm

Glocalization, as a hybrid school of thought, is neither standardization nor localization per se. The tenet of this most contemporary school is that a multinational corporation or person should 'think global and act local' (that is, 'glocal'), thus being both global and local simultaneously. This hybrid model combines relevant aspects of all traditional schools of thought. The goal is to reconcile the various conflicting points of view. As such, it incorporates the strengths of each traditional idea, while minimizing the inherent limitations in the process, with the global framework as a backdrop. For our purpose, the terms 'glocal' and 'global' are synonymous. The term 'glocalization' is, however, preferred because it better captures the essence of the concept by incorporating a local game plan into the overall global framework.

While there is still no agreement on how to meaningfully differentiate standardization from localization, there is much less of an attempt to distinguish a standardized marketing campaign from a glocal or global one. Most authors, advertisers and advertising agencies have been using these two terms loosely and interchangeably. Some even mention a 'standardized global' campaign. Inevitably, confusion abounds when the two distinct concepts are treated as one.

It is important to recognize that a *standardized* product is not the same thing as a *global* or world product. Neither is a *standardized* advertisement the same as a *global* advertisement. A standardized product or advertisement has a domestic origin because it is designed with a particular market (usually a home market) in mind. For this same product or advertisement to be used internationally (that is, in more than one country) does not make it any more international or global than before. In the end, it is nothing more than just a national advertisement being used abroad. It takes more than the number of countries for a product or advertisement to shed its national or standardized identity.

A glocal marketing mix (also known as an international or world campaign) does not have a domestic origin since it is designed with a global market (or multiple countries) in mind from the outset. The strategy attempts to identify intercountry denominators in terms of homogeneity as well as heterogeneity. The common denominators will be used to construct a main theme or other common elements for the global campaign. Simultaneously, the heterogeneous factors will also be considered so as to plan certain modifications that are required for particular markets. As an example, European tour operators within the Nordic region understand the challenge of the philosophy of 'think regional, act local' or 'cooperative centralization'. While managing marketing regionally, they adapt certain activities due to situation-specific factors such as product and industry characteristics (Roper, 2005). This practice resembles glocalization on a smaller scale.

Glocalization does not necessarily shy away from standardization or localization when either one of them is appropriate. Nevertheless, it is generally desirable for multinational corporations to avoid those extreme approaches. Given the inherent flaws associated with either standardization or localization, a strong case can be made for the utilization of a truly global (universal) marketing campaign. The practice of glocalization strives to achieve the efficiency of standardization and effectiveness of localization, while minimizing the disadvantages of both strategies. The efficiency is derived from the identification of a common theme and elements whose appeal is universal enough to serve as the campaign's main theme that can be used everywhere. The effectiveness stems from the recognition and preplanned inclusion of market differences.

Principles of glocalization

Marketing globalists need to have a global framework to guide their marketing campaigns. Toward this end, a number of principles of glocalization (or glocal marketing) should be considered (Box 2.1), and certain mechanisms and requirements must be implemented (see Table 2.1). These principles acknowledge market homogeneity and heterogeneity, and they combine standardization and localization with the goal of simultaneously achieving efficiency and effectiveness (Onkvisit and Shaw, 2002). These principles serve as a blueprint that can be used to judge – uniformly, meaningfully and objectively – whether a certain marketing plan is indeed global in nature.

BOX 2.1 **Principles of glocalization (glocal marketing)**

General principles
Geocentric mentality
Decision-making policy: centralization, decentralization and coordination
Recognition of market homogeneity and heterogeneity
Global and local relevance
Adaptation readiness

Subprinciples: product
Global application
Mass customization
Global engineering, local design
Top management's commitment and conflict resolution system

Table 2.1   A comparison of three international marketing strategies

	Standardization	Localization	Glocalization
Market assumption	Homogeneity	Heterogeneity	Both
Attitude/orientation	Ethnocentricity	Polycentricity	Geocentricity
Country emphasis	Home country	Host country	Whole world
Perspective/philosophy	Think and act home	Think and act local	Think global, act local
Decision making	Centralization	Decentralization	Both plus coordination
Marketing practice	Uniformity (replication)	Flexibility	Both
Pros and cons	Efficient but ineffective	Effective but inefficient	Efficient and effective but complex

Geocentric mentality

Corporate attitude and marketing strategy are related. A multinational firm's standardization effort is in part a function of the corporate orientation of the firm and its managers. Based on the orientation or attitude, a company may be ethnocentric, polycentric or geocentric, which corresponds to the standardized, localized and global marketing strategies respectively (see Table 2.1). These orientations can be described as follows:

- *Ethnocentricity* is a strong orientation towards the home country. Many corporations, managers, consumers and individuals are ethnocentric. Foreign markets and consumers are viewed as unfamiliar and inferior in taste, sophistication and opportunity. An ethnocentric firm, when doing business abroad, is going to 'think home, act home'; thus a US firm might 'think US, act US', while a Japanese manager will 'think Japan, act Japan'. Whatever an ethnocentric manager encounters abroad, they are going to compare everything to what it is like or what it should be at home. As can be expected, the utilization of standardization is pretty much automatic.

- A *polycentric* company, being host country oriented, is going to 'think local, act local' by essentially adopting the host country's perspective (that is, when in Rome, do as the Romans do). Viewing a foreign market as so different to the point that it cannot be understood by an outsider, the firm employs local personnel as overseas subsidiaries' country managers because they are supposed to understand the market's uniqueness. Conceivably, these country managers are so autonomous that they lose sight of the company's global framework. As long as they can meet the profit targets, they are pretty much free to do whatever they see fit. Polycentric firms are much more willing to adopt a localized campaign designed or redesigned for a foreign country.

- When overseeing worldwide operations, a glocalized company needs to have geocentricity as its guiding principle. A *geocentric* firm, being world oriented and even nationalityless, will 'think global, act local'. The company views the world as a total market and allocates resources with no regard to national frontiers. Coca-Cola, as a good example, no longer has 'domestic' and 'international' business units in its administrative structure of worldwide operations. The US business was downgraded to become just one of the six international business units divided by geography.

Decision-making policy: centralization, decentralization and coordination

For an ethnocentric firm, a high degree of centralized decision making is almost inevitable, and standardized international marketing is going to be a consequence. A polycentric firm, in contrast, is most likely to practise decentralization and localization. After many decades of passionate debates, there is still no (and perhaps there never will be) final conclusion regarding the definite superiority (or inferiority) of either strategy. Any claims to support either strategy are based primarily on anecdotes rather than rigorous research methodology.

It is futile to try to prove whether centralization is superior to decentralization (and vice versa), since each approach has its own strengths and limitations. It is thus more desirable to combine their strengths and minimize their disadvantages. Glocalization is a viable solution. On the one hand, glocalization mandates a global game plan that provides a universal framework that must be adhered to by all subsidiaries. This global framework specifies the corporate goals and strategies on a worldwide basis, thus achieving the efficiency of centralized decision making. On the other hand, decentralization also comes into play because it allows local managers or subsidiaries to make their own marketing decisions – as long as such decisions conform to the global requirements. In certain cases, local decisions may even be allowed to deviate from the global framework if a local subsidiary can provide a strong justification.

Glocalization goes beyond the combination of centralization and decentralization to include another essential element – systematic coordination. There is strength in numbers and cohesiveness. A global company's headquarters must coordinate the activities of all subsidiaries across countries so that the company and all its subsidiaries will function as one unit. Useful information (regarding product successes or failures in different markets) should not travel at random. Colgate Palmolive, for example, has a system in place that allows the information to be disseminated in a systematic manner within the entire organization. Likewise, McDonald's headquarters in Illinois functions as an information centre for all franchisees all over the world.

For geocentric firms, while the foreign markets are different, their differences can still be largely understood and reasonably managed. An overseas campaign is therefore treated as part of the company's total worldwide strategy. World-oriented companies are simultaneously tight and loose; they are uniform and yet flexible. They are able to switch from one mode to another when market conditions warrant. The results of one study 'confirm and amplify the need to seek a balance between global efficiency and responsiveness to local conditions' (Gould et al., 1999).

Coca-Cola is a multinational corporation that has gone through all three types of decision making. At one time, Coca-Cola dictated what and how its overseas bottlers should advertise, and it even made TV commercials in Atlanta for China. Later the company realized that it wanted more of localism (Echikson, 2000). As mentioned by Douglas Daft, while he was CEO of Coca-Cola, 'no one drinks a Coke globally' (*Far Eastern Economic Review*, 2000). Based on that belief, the company made a number of key policy changes, including downsizing the marketing staff at headquarters and moving decision-making authority in advertising to local managers. Unfortunately, local advertisements delivered inconsistent marketing messages that hurt the global image of Coke. Now the headquarters has become more active in providing guidance, but local managers can still make advertising decisions within the limits of a broad 'architecture' emanating from the corporate headquarters (McKay, 2002).

Recognition of market homogeneity and heterogeneity

Standardization assumes market homogeneity, while localization assumes heterogeneity. It is inconceivable that the world can be perfectly homogeneous or purely heterogeneous; rather, it is a matter of degree. Therefore, any studies will invariably show some degree of commonality as well as some degree of diversity, thus offering limited support to standardization and localization at the same time. To make matters worse, the proponents and opponents of standardization often rely on anecdotes rather than empirical evidence to make their case.

A standardized campaign can be efficient and effective *if and only if* the various markets are homogeneous. Empirical evidence, however, is overwhelming in the direction of market heterogeneity. One recent study has found responses to be heterogeneous within and among countries (Hofstede et al., 1999). Using US and Korean TV commercials to represent North America and East Asia, another study has yielded the following findings:

> Both countries are present-time oriented, and while individualism and collectivism are prevalent in both cultures, individualism is more dominant in the U.S. Korean

commercials stress oneness-with-nature slightly more than U.S. commercials, and U.S. commercials use more direct approaches. (Cho et al., 1999, p. 59)

It is necessary to make a distinction between vertical (national) and horizontal (international) homogeneity. *Vertical homogeneity* addresses the issue of whether consumers within a particular national market are homogeneous. *Horizontal homogeneity* instead asks whether countries are homogeneous. Alternatively, on a smaller scale, horizontal homogeneity may have to do with whether one particular segment (for example teenagers) in one particular national market is similar to that of another national market. Thus, rather than asking whether a particular country's vertical homogeneity is largely equivalent to the vertical homogeneity of another country, a company may be able to determine that, in spite of the lack of vertical homogeneity, two countries may possess a similar segment of the population.

Given human nature, it is obvious that the various countries are likely to share some degree of commonality. On the other hand, given geographic, religious and cultural differences, some degree of heterogeneity must be expected. Unlike standardization and localization that respectively assume complete homogeneity and total heterogeneity, glocalization readily admits the existence of homogeneity and heterogeneity and attempts to accommodate both. So when the conditions warrant, an international advertiser should be willing to acknowledge their coexistence.

Global and local relevance

A glocal marketing campaign should be both globally and locally relevant. On the one hand, it is culture free, and on the other hand, it is culture bound, when necessary or desirable. Such a campaign should recognize those aspects that are universal and those that are unique to a certain country. In the case of a global product, it should satisfy a universal need while taking local wants into consideration. A wristwatch is used to tell the time anywhere, but the watch's features can be adjusted to accommodate local or religious needs (for example reminding Muslims of the time to pray). Appealing to 1.1 billion Muslims, LG Electronics has introduced a mobile phone that includes an electronic compass (*San Jose Mercury News*, 2003). Muslims pray five times a day facing Mecca, and the phone, equipped with location tracking software, is able to point towards Mecca.

Norelco's target customers are men between the ages of 35 and 54 who want a premium razor (McConnon, 2007). Interviewing 5,000 American, European and Chinese men, the company learned that Chinese men have less hair. Also, Asian hair is stronger but slower growing because it is rounder in shape and thicker in diameter than Caucasian hair. Since Chinese shavers may not need Norelco's high-tech razor with three rotating blades, the company instead offers a double-headed razor.

In the case of a global advertisement, it should adopt a global theme by employing a particular appeal that is universally relevant. For example, it is generally true that people just about everywhere want status, financial success, beauty and fun. These themes can be utilized on a global level. However, the local execution of such a theme may require a different way of expressing it. Certainly, the humour appeal is universal, but what is humorous can significantly vary from country to country as well as within a country. A global theme still must be locally relevant and should be expressed in local or national terms.

United Distillers and Vintners, based in the UK, has introduced a new global advertising strategy for its Johnnie Walker Scotch whisky (Jariyasombat, 1999). Instead of using the traditional product-oriented tactic, it has created the 'Keep Walking' campaign. The theme, focusing on men making progress in life, is based on a research finding that progress is the goal of men worldwide. While each country manages its own advertising, it must utilize the global theme. In Thailand, for example, the campaign started with eight 15-second TV commercials that kept the Johnnie Walker logo inconspicuous. Appealing to male drinkers, each commercial featured a local celebrity in a certain field who gave an account of what inspired him to keep moving ahead. Along the same lines, one Indian version featured a local film producer, while a US version focused on an internationally known film director (Martin Scorsese).

Adaptation readiness

For a global product or advertisement to be cost-efficient in spite of the necessary modifications, the product or advertisement must be *adaptation ready*. Adaptation readiness differs from the modification of a standardized product or advertisement. Once a standard product or advertisement has been designed and engineered with a particular country in mind, any attempt to modify it after the fact for another country involves unforeseen problems and significant costs. Being adaptation ready means that, while designing a product or advertisement for the world, market differences are being accounted for at the same time. During the original planning stage, allowances are made for those differences and subsequent adjustments. When an adjustment has to be later made for a particular country, the preplanned adjustment becomes a simple process.

The car industry provides an example of why global car makers need to be adaptation ready. Due to driving regulations, cars are driven on either the right or left side of the road, necessitating having the steering wheel on a certain side of the vehicle. In the US, a car is driven on the right-hand side of the road, so the steering wheel needs to be on the left. When cars are exported to countries where the traffic is on the opposite side, the steering wheel must be switched to the right-hand side. If the switch has not been considered in the initial stage, the adjustment may run into problems because there is not enough space on the right-hand side to accommodate the steering wheel. A car maker must then go back to the drawing board, and engineers will have to start the design and manufacturing process all over again. If the vehicle were made adaptation ready, a slot on the right-hand side would have been provided, and it is thus a simple process to plug the steering wheel into that slot.

Electrolux, based in Sweden, is the world's largest appliance maker (Rungfapaisarn, 2001). Switching from the 'country-based' approach, the company has set up the 'ASEAN team' so as to unify its marketing strategies in the ASEAN (Association of Southeast Asian Nations) area. The team consists of 15 executives from the various Asian countries and Sweden. The goal is to develop a similar plan to suit ASEAN culture. The effectiveness is accomplished by planning in advance for necessary modifications that will make the advertisement more meaningful to each country's customers.

When preparing an adaptation-ready advertisement, there are 'world-ready' design principles that will facilitate subsequent translation (Bohan, 1994). Any required localization must be considered before – not after – the completion of the English language. A script should seek 'generalized ways of saying things'. It is thus better to use 'a popular place' instead of 'a cool (or hip) place'. Because words in other languages may require more space, there must be enough room for the extra text and voice track length. Moreover, in the area of art direction, a knowledgeable person from the target country must scrutinize the appropriateness of signage, faces, body language, clothing, offices and other symbols or graphic images.

Subprinciples: product

Principles of glocalization apply to both product and advertising strategies and prob-ably to place and price strategies as well. However, due to their specific tasks and functions, global products and global advertisements also have their own separate subprinciples of glocalization that need to be considered. This section discusses how a glocal product should be designed and implemented.

Global application

Sometimes, a national product gets lucky when its origin and standardization do not hinder its international acceptance. Such a product may be fortunate to satisfy a universal need – by accident and not by design. Coca-Cola, originally created for the Atlanta area, owes its global success in part to the setting up of overseas bottling operations during the Second World War to serve American soldiers abroad. Instead of relying on such a fortunate random occurrence, marketers are better off consciously creating a world product that maximizes universal satisfaction and simplifies the production process in the long run.

When it is feasible and practical to do so, it is desirable to offer a world product that satisfies a majority of markets with minimum modification and minimum interruption to production. DVD players sold in the US are a national product that cannot play DVDs based on the non-US broadcast systems (that is, PAL and SECAM instead of NTSC). In contrast, it is not uncommon for DVD players outside the US to be capable of playing DVD movies from all parts of the world, regardless of format. This strategy is desirable because it reduces the complexity of adaptation and maintenance of parts. A world product is not necessarily more expensive than its standardized and localized counter-parts. A company can avoid costly downtime in production that would otherwise be needed to produce the various national versions of the same product. Furthermore, inventory control can be greatly simplified by stocking one universal part instead of many individual parts required for national variations.

In order to provide global application, a product should have a multisystem and multifunction feature. When practical, it should have a universal utility or worldwide applicability in the sense that it can be used anywhere. Laptop computers, as an example, perform a universal function. In particular, the non-profit One Laptop Per Child project, designed for low-income consumers worldwide, offers a brightly coloured, hand-cranked, wireless-enabled portable computer that uses flash memory instead of a hard drive. Its microprocessor requires minimal power. Likewise, an electric shaver with either dual voltage or universal voltage can be used anywhere because its design allows it to be operated with both 110 and 220 volts. Tragically, assault weapons like the AK-47 and weapons of mass destruction are also global products with global application.

The global strategy should stimulate firms to find new ways to satisfy most consumers simultaneously. Whirlpool is a good example of how to design a worldwide or continent-wide product. At one time, its washing machines in Germany and Italy had no common parts whatsoever. Whirlpool wanted to create a European washing machine but was told that it was not feasible because of market differences. French consumers, for example, were supposed to want a narrow, top-loading machine that could fit in a narrow space in a kitchen. Being sceptical of the logic of this argument, Whirlpool conducted a study to identify the universal product features desired by consumers everywhere. According to the results, consumers across Europe want a washing machine that gets clothes clean, is easy to use and trouble free, and does not use too much water, detergent and electricity. If a washing machine can meet these significant criteria, it is then less important with regard to the size and location of the opening of the machine.

While industry differences must be taken into account, it is possible to ascertain the product attributes that have global applicability. One study investigated 16 global product attributes across three product categories in France and Malaysia. It found that product quality and appearance were universal and that they could be standardized. The relevance of the other 14 attributes depended on international market contingencies (Hult et al., 2000).

Mass customization

For many products, a universal product version, which can please all people, does not exist. In such cases, a different definition of the concept of a global product is required. To qualify as a global product (when it is not feasible to offer a single universal version), the product in question needs to possess certain attributes within the framework of mass customization. The product is considered to be global when it has a global platform that can be adjusted to accommodate local use conditions. It is also global when the various national versions are variations that are derived from the same technological or knowledge base.

An international marketer's product strategy is not an either-or proposition in the sense that standardization and localization are the only available options. Neither strategy is capable of being efficient and effective at the same time. Standardization is akin to ready-made and mass-produced suits that offer a lower price but a poorer fit. A tailor-made suit, on the other hand, gives a buyer a perfect fit, albeit at a much higher price, thus being effective but inefficient. In order to have a better fit without a disproportionately higher price, mass customization is a viable solution. Customers of Levi's jeans, for example, can try on a prototype that resembles a reasonable fit. A customer's body (along with the prototype being worn) is then measured in order to see how the prototype can be adjusted for better fit, and the data are transmitted to a production centre. A mass customized pair of jeans, offered at the price that is reasonably higher than the regular price, will soon be delivered to the customer's home.

More and more companies are now experimenting with mass customization. The M&M's Colorworks online site offers 21 colours to coat specially ordered M&M's. While the mass customized version costs significantly more than the regular M&M's, sales have been climbing every year (Keenan, 2002). Likewise, at Lands' End, customers can order customized chinos and jeans online. McDonald's also practises mass customization. Its food items can be made to order. Technology has progressed to the point that it allows McDonald's to have mass customization. A customer's order is instantly displayed on a monitor screen in the kitchen. To speed up food preparation, one worker focuses on toasting buns, while another does the dressings and so on.

When a global product does not have a universal worldwide applicability, the second best strategy is to employ mass customization. This strategy aims to have a global platform for mass production, while it also accommodates local use conditions by incorporating customization within the mass production system. Vaillant, a German boiler company, is the largest maker of central heating boilers in Europe (*Financial Times*, 2002). Because customer tastes as well as building standards vary from country to country, localization results in hundreds of different models. Still it is possible to pursue 'glocalization' to minimize the costs of customization without minimizing customer choice. The company, while focusing on a few common components (for example burners and controls), makes adaptations to meet individual countries' specifications.

An international marketer should consider the creation of a global product by leveraging its technological and knowledge base. *Cosmopolitan* magazine leverages its contents by including them in local editions (which also include local contents). *Business Week* also adheres to the practice of glocalization. The weekly covers for the US, Asian and international editions may be either uniform or different, depending on whether the cover story has a universal or local appeal. The cover story itself may vary from one geographic edition to another. A cover story for the US market may be shortened for Asia if the interest in Asia is not as great. Instead, Asia may have its own cover story, which is covered in much greater depth in Asia but reduced for the US edition. Still all the stories are based on the same database. Children's TV programming is another example that needs to combine both the global and local appeals. Even in the case of the hugely popular *Sesame Street* TV shows, the producers understand that certain contents should be adapted so as to be more relevant to local children and culture. In Egypt, the show's most popular character is a Cairo taxi driver.

Global engineering, local design

A global product should be based on global engineering or technology while allowing local design. Siemens Medical Solutions removes some nonessential features so as to make its X-ray scanners more affordable in India (Ewing, 2007). Lenovo's product design is influenced by culture. By analysing Chinese music, history and objects of desire so as to identify the design elements that had meaning and value to Chinese consumers, Lenovo created the Opti Desktop PC with shapes and colours that appeal to Chinese 'deep immersers' who like to escape by immersing themselves in online games (Nussbaum, 2006). Electrolux sent engineers to make home visits in the US, where its observations of how American consumers loaded their dishwashers let it reposition the baskets and racks of a mini-dishwasher that originated in Italy (Sains and Reed, 2006).

Car makers can start out with a standard model before adjusting it to accommodate local preferences. Foreign car makers understand that American car owners insist on an adequate (or even excessive) number of cup holders. On the other hand, non-American owners of luxury cars have their own requirements. The China-designed version of the Cadillac SLS executive car is four inches longer than the US model. Unlike American owners who drive their own cars, Chinese (and other Asian) owners have chauffeurs and do not want to sit in front with their chauffeurs. To maintain their status, they sit in the back and thus want a roomy backseat (Roberts, 2007).

Top management's commitment and conflict resolution system

To make a global product a reality, it is critical that a multinational corporation's top management team coordinate the cross-border activities. Toyota's Japanese headquarters and its US subsidiary often have conflicting views of design choices. Even interior colour schemes create a dispute (Dawson, 2002). It is necessary for top management to show its commitment to a world product, and there is a need to install a system that resolves the conflicting views of executives working in different countries.

Ford's experience with the Ford Escort provides some insights. The Ford Escort, designed in Europe, was supposed to be a world car. However, American executives were sceptical of the business and engineering judgement of their European counterparts. The car was subsequently thoroughly redesigned, and a tiny water pump seal was the only thing that the US and European versions had in common. To prevent such a recurrence in the case of the Mondeo, Ford required the US and European versions to have 75% common parts. The US division was responsible for automatic transmissions, while the European unit took care of manual transmissions. At the same time, the company's top executives monitored the development.

Conclusion

After almost half a century, although a great deal of knowledge has been gained, the standardization–localization debate is still not satisfactorily resolved. Logically, it is a mistake to use either standardization or localization on a wholesale basis. A well-thought-out product or advertising idea tends to perform reasonably well in multiple markets without a great deal of adjustment. But any flaws associated with a standardized product or advertisement will multiply in tandem with the number of countries. In order to determine whether a company should standardize its marketing mix in the international arena, rigorous research is required to empirically test the effectiveness of product and advertising standardization.

The chapter provides a conceptual framework that describes, justifies and explains the concept of glocalization. A global product or advertisement is a hybrid that strives to achieve the efficiency of standardization and effectiveness of localization, while minimizing the disadvantages of both strategies. The idea is to identify similarities and differences among markets and to coordinate marketing and production activities in order to minimize localization without unduly alienating consumers of certain markets. Multinational corporations need to work out how to adapt while maintaining a global identity. Arguably, the most sophisticated way to arrive at a global campaign is to follow an approach where a product or advertisement is designed after careful consideration of the relevant contextual and strategic factors in all overseas target markets. The campaign does not have a single reference point but is based on conscious analysis of multiple markets with the goal of arriving at a uniform advert, founded on the relevant similarities between these markets.

Based on some limited theoretical and empirical evidence, certain principles of glocal marketing are proposed. In addition, the subprinciples focusing specifically on product and advertising are discussed. However, because the evidence cited is limited and more anecdotal than empirical, it is critical to find additional theories and evidence that support the suggested guidelines. It is also important to study whether the practice of glocal advertising is widespread. To this end, the various principles of glocalization should be precisely stated as research propositions that will allow empirical testing. Once relevant hypotheses are generated, rigorous testing should follow.

Issues for further discussion

1. Can the general principles of glocalization can be extended beyond product and advertising strategies to include place and price strategies?
2. Is there a relationship between a firm's orientation – ethnocentricity, polycentricity or geocentricity – and their marketing strategy – standardization, localization and glocalization?
3. Are the subprinciples of product glocalization universal in the sense that they are also applicable to services, or do services require separate subprinciples?
4. Since product glocalization needs to adhere to certain subprinciples, are there specific subprinciples that are specifically relevant to advertising glocalization?

CASE STUDY

Mcdonald's

Operations

McDonald's is primarily a franchisor. Of the 31,377 restaurants in 118 countries at year-end 2007, franchisees operate 20,505 of them. The business is managed as distinct geographic segments. The US, Europe and APMEA (Asia/Pacific, Middle East and Africa) segments respectively account for 35%, 39% and 16% of total revenues. The 'Other Countries and Corporate' segment includes operations in Canada and Latin America.

Philosophy

The philosophy that drives McDonald's business is 'QSCandV' (quality, service, cleanliness and value). The company aims to be 'forever young', and it is 'shameless to copy' good ideas. It has a global reach with a local footprint. McDonald's is customer focused with a goal of being relevant to its customers in their daily lives.

Customer orientation

Consumer insights indicate that the key drivers of the company's global business are convenience, branded affordability, daypart expansion and menu choice. There are five factors of exceptional customer experiences – people, products, place, price and promotion. Striving to enhance shareholder value, the company's system is aligned towards enhancing the customer experience through a relentless focus on the customer-centred 'Plan to Win'. It keeps all elements of the system (franchisees, suppliers and company employees) working together on behalf of customers worldwide.

Product standardization

Classic menu favourites such as the Big Mac and French fries account for more than 75% of the company's sales around the world. Mystery shoppers are used to ensure uniform service. The utilization of product cut-up guarantees quality consistency. A Big Mac made in the US is flown to a foreign outlet where it is compared to one made locally – layer by layer.

Product localization

In the US, McDonald's has recently introduced the Southwest Salad, in addition to the Southern Style Chicken Biscuit Sandwich for breakfast and the Southern Style Chicken Sandwich for the remainder of the day.

The localized products abroad include Samurai (pork) burger in Thailand, Teriyaki Mac in Japan, variations of the Filet-O-Fish in China, and Lemon Shrimp burger in Germany. In Japan, McDonald's offers Shaka Shaka Chicken, and its McGriddles is billed as the 'breakfast nobody could explain'. McDonald's India is owned and operated by Indians, employs local staff and procures from local suppliers. Its website proclaims that McDonald's India is 'as Indian as you and me'. All vegetarian products are 100% vegetarian, and its mayonnaise was developed specifically for Indian consumers. As a result, the mayonnaise and soft serves do not contain any egg.

Glocalization

The company's ongoing menu innovation is guided by a global food vision that relies on the creativity of the chefs in the food studios in Hong Kong, Munich and Chicago. The Snack Wrap, which is suitable for a light meal or late-night snack, was created in the US. The company's system aims to leverage successes quickly, and the item is now available in 23,000 restaurants worldwide. The system also allows the flexibility to adapt to local tastes, as evidenced by the Ebi (shrimp) Wrap in Japan.

McDonald's has a set of global requirements that localized products must adhere to. Franchisees all over the world have access to the company's information network to learn about other franchisees' product ideas that work or do not work.

Mass customization

Contrary to popular belief, McDonald's allows customers to have 'made to order' items. Technology has made it possible for the company to practise mass customization. When a customer orders a customized sandwich, the order is flashed on a monitor screen in the kitchen. Mass production to speed up the process is achieved by designating a particular person for a particular function (for example toasting the buns, cooking the meat patties and so on). Customization is achieved by having a separate person prepare the dressings for each sandwich.

Promotion and advertising

The 'I'm Lovin' It' campaign originated in Germany and is now used worldwide. The execution of the advertisements, however, is local. Franchisees are free to create their own TV commercials – as long as those localized advertisements satisfy the company's global requirements, for example inclusion of the company's logo, when it must appear and so on.

Place (distribution)

McDonald's prefers franchising to entry alternatives such as company-operated, conventional licence, developmental licence and affiliated. Yet due to the legal and regulatory environment, it believes that it is prudent for the company to own and operate restaurants in countries such as China and Russia.

In Brazil, Indonesia and India, kiosks in high-density locations make it possible for customers to get a quick drink or dessert. The company delivers foods to customers' homes or offices in Singapore, Egypt and several other countries in Asia and the Middle East.

New layouts, service and operating systems are tested in concept restaurants in Romeoville (Illinois), Kirchheim (Germany) and Australia.

Price

To communicate great value to customers, the company offers everyday branded affordability menus. Although products and pricing may vary from country to country, these menus typically feature a mix of eight to ten items including entrees, side dishes, desserts and drinks. The everyday branded affordability menus include Ein Mal Eins in Germany, the Dollar Menu in the US, China's Amazing Value Menu, and Japan's 100 Yen Menu. In Argentina, customers are given greater choice and value via a rotating series of small sandwiches called 'El Placer del Momento' ('the pleasure of the moment').

To offer great food at a great value, McDonald's effectively manages restaurant operating costs. It collaborates with suppliers and leverages economies of scale so as to have a reliable supply of high-quality ingredients at competitive, predictable prices.

Questions

1. Pick one country from each of McDonald's three regions: Europe, APMEA and Other. Study the menus in these three countries and compare them to the menu(s) in the US. Identify the menu items that are universal, and those that are localized products.
2. Based on these three countries and the US, are there any standardized advertisements used in these countries? On the other hand, describe the localized advertisements that are used only in a particular country. Do such localized advertisements make some reference to local customs or cultures?
3. For these three countries as well as the US, are there any aspects of operations that reflect the glocalization strategy?

References

Alam, I. (2006) 'Service innovation strategy and process: A cross-national comparative analysis'. *International Marketing Review*, 23(3): 234–54.

Al-Olayan, F.S. and Karande, K. (2000) 'A content analysis of magazine advertisements from the United States and the Arab world'. *Journal of Advertising*, 29: 69–82.

Bohan, S. (1994) 'Multimedia notes'. *Copy Magazine*.

Chandra, A., Griffith, D.A. and Ryans, J.K. (2002) 'Advertising standardization in India: US multinational experience'. *International Journal of Advertising*, 21(1): 47–66.

Chang, C. (2006) 'Cultural masculinity/femininity influences on advertising appeals'. *Journal of Advertising Research*, 46: 315–23.

Cho, B., Kwon, U., Gentry, J.W. et al. (1999) 'Cultural values reflected in theme and execution: A comparative study of U.S. and Korean television commercials'. *Journal of Advertising*, 28(4): 59–73.

Cho, C. and Cheon, H.J. (2005) 'Cross-cultural comparisons of interactivity on corporate Web sites: The United States, the United Kingdom, Japan, and South Korea'. *Journal of Advertising*, 34: 99–115.

Chung, H.F. (2005) 'An investigation of crossmarket standardisation strategies'. *European Journal of Marketing*, 39(11/12): 1345–71.

Dallman, K.M. (2001) 'Targeting women in German and Japanese magazine advertising: A difference-in-differences approach'. *European Journal of Marketing*, 35: 1320–41.

Dawson, C. (2002) 'The Americanization of Toyota'. *Business Week*, 15 April, 52–4.

Dow, D. (2006) 'Adaptation and performance in foreign markets: Evidence of systematic under-adaptation'. *Journal of International Business Studies*, 37: 212–26.

Echikson, W. (2000) 'For Coke, local is it'. *Business Week*, 3 July, 122.

Ewing, J. (2007) 'The sweet smell of demand'. *Business Week*, 29 January, 46.

Far Eastern Economic Review (2000) 'Coke's new formula'. 20 April, 64.

Financial Times (2002) 'Fired up to introduce new ideas'. 10 December.

Gabrielsson, P., Gabrielsson, M., Darling, J. and Luostarinen, R. (2006) 'Globalizing internationals: Product strategies of ICT manufacturers'. *International Marketing Review*, 23(6): 650–71.

Gerritsen, M., Korzilius, H., Van Meurs, F. and Gijsbers, I. (2000) 'English in Dutch commercials: Not understood and not appreciated'. *Journal of Advertising Research*, 40(4): 17–31.

Gould, S.J., Lerman, D.B. and Grein, A.F. (1999) 'Agency perceptions and practices on global IMC'. *Journal of Advertising Research*, 39: 7–20.

Hewett, K. and Bearden, W.O. (2001) 'Dependence, trust, and relational behavior on the part of foreign subsidiary marketing operations: Implications for managing global marketing operations'. *Journal of Marketing*, 65: 51–66.

Hofstede, F., Steenkamp, J.E. and Wedel, M. (1999) 'International market segmentation based on consumer product relations'. *Journal of Marketing Research*, 36(1): 1–17.

Hult, G.T., Keillor, B.D. and Hightower, R. (2000) 'Valued product attributes in an emerging market: A comparison between French and Malaysian consumers'. *Journal of World Business*, 35(2): 206–19.

Jariyasombat, P. (1999) 'Johnnie Walker seeks rebound'. *Bangkok Post*, 25 November.

Jeong, J., Tharp, M. and Choi, H. (2002) 'Exploring the missing point of view in international advertising management: Local managers in global advertising agencies'. *International Journal of Advertising*, 21(3): 293–321.

Ji, M.F. and McNeal, J.U. (2001) 'How Chinese children's commercials differ from those of the United States: A content analysis'. *Journal of Advertising*, 30: 92.

Kanzo, A. and Nelson, R.A. (2002) 'Advertising localization overshadows standardization'. *Journal of Advertising Research*, 42: 79–89.

Keenan, F. (2002) 'A mass market of one'. *Business Week*, 2 December, 68ff.

Laroche, M., Kirpalani, V.H., Pons, F. and Zhou, L. (2001) 'A model of advertising standardization in multinational corporations'. *Journal of International Business Studies*, 32: 249–66.

Lee, C. and Griffith, D.A. (2004) 'The marketing strategy-performance relationships in an export-driven developing economy: A Korean illustration'. *International Marketing Review*, 21(3): 321–34.

Lin, C.A. (2001) 'Cultural values reflected in Chinese and American television advertising'. *Journal of Advertising*, 30: 83–94.

Lynch, P.D., Kent, R.J. and Srinivasan, S.S. (2001) 'The global internet shopper: Evidence from shopping tasks in twelve countries'. *Journal of Advertising Research*, 41: 15–23.

McConnon, A. (2007) 'Case study: Philips' Norelco'. *Business Week*, June, 18–19.

McKay, B. (2002) 'Coke hunts for talent to re-establish its marketing might'. *Asian Wall Street Journal*, 6 March.

Maynard, M.L. and Taylor, C.R. (1999) 'Girlish images across cultures: Analyzing Japanese versus U.S. Seventeen magazine ads'. *Journal of Advertising*, 28: 39–64.

Milner, L.M. and Collins, J.M. (2000) 'Sex-role portrayals and the gender of nations'. *Journal of Advertising*, 29: 67–73.

Moon, Y.S. and Chan, K. (2005) 'Advertising appeals and cultural values in television commercials: A comparison of Hong Kong and Korea'. *International Marketing Review*, 22(1): 48–66.

Nelson, M.R. and Paek, H. (2007) 'A content analysis of advertising in a global magazine across seven countries: Implications for global advertising strategies'. *International Marketing Review*, 24(1): 64–86.

Nussbaum, B. (2006) 'Annual design awards 2006'. *Business Week*, 10 July, 74–8.

Okazaki, S., Taylor, C.R. and Zou, S. (2006) 'Advertising standardization's positive impact on the bottom line'. *Journal of Advertising*, 35: 17–33.

Onkvisit, S. and Shaw, J.J. (1987) 'Standardized international advertising: A review and critical evaluation of the theoretical and empirical evidence'. *Columbia Journal of World Business*, 22(3): 43–55.

Onkvisit, S. and Shaw, J.J. (1999) 'Standardized international advertising: Some research issues and implications'. *Journal of Advertising Research*, 39: 19–24.

Onkvisit, S. and Shaw, J.J. (2002) 'Marketing/advertising concepts and principles in the international context: Universal or unique?', in C.R. Taylor (ed.) *New Directions in International Advertising Research, Advances in International Marketing*, vol. 12, Amsterdam: JAI.

Pae, J.H., Samiee, S. and Tai, S. (2002) 'Global advertising strategy: The moderating role of brand familiarity and execution style'. *International Marketing Review*, 19(2/3): 176–89.

Peterson, M., Gregory, G. and Munch, J.M. (2005) 'Comparing US and European perspectives on B2B repair service quality for mission-critical equipment'. *International Marketing Review*, 22(3): 353–68.

Roberts, D. (2007) 'Cadillac floors it in China'. *Business Week*, 4 June, 52.

Roper, A. (2005) 'Marketing standardisation: Tour operators in the Nordic region'. *European Journal of Marketing*, 39(5/6): 514–27.

Rungfapaisarn, K. (2001) 'Electrolux eyes "Asean culture"'. *The Nation*, 8 June.

Sains, A. and Reed, S. (2006) 'Electrolux redesigns itself'. *Business Week*, November, 13–15.

San Jose Mercury News (2003) 'LG reaches out to Muslim callers'. 9 September.

Solberg, C.A. (2002) 'The perennial issue of adaptation or standardization of international marketing communication: Organizational contingencies and performance'. *Journal of International Marketing*, 10: 1–21.

Taylor, C.R. and Okazaki, S. (2006) 'Who standardizes advertising more frequently, and why do they do so? A comparison of U.S. and Japanese subsidiaries' advertising practices in the European Union'. *Journal of International Marketing*, 14(1): 98–120.

Theodosiou, M. and Leonidou, L.C. (2003) 'Standardization versus adaptation of international marketing strategy: An integrative assessment of the empirical research'. *International Business Review*, 12: 141–71.

Wall Street Journal (2007a) 'Indonesian tobacco ads pack in humor'. 8 March.

Wall Street Journal (2007b) 'Altria seeks Indonesian smokers'. 2 July.

Wall Street Journal (2007c) 'Disney rewrites script to win fans in India'. 11 June.

Yin, J. (1999) 'International advertising strategies in China: A worldwide survey of foreign advertisers'. *Journal of Advertising Research*, 39: 25–35.

Zhou, S., Zhou, P. and Xue, F. (2005) 'Visual differences in U.S. and Chinese television commercials'. *Journal of Advertising*, 34: 111–19.

3

Setting prices for global markets: global insights and perspectives

Rosmimah Mohd Roslin

Learning outcomes

At the end of this chapter, readers should be able to:

1. Understand the implications of setting prices in global settings.
2. Appreciate the impact of the global environment on strategic pricing development.
3. Comprehend basic techniques of price setting for global markets.
4. Integrate the understanding of basic pricing principles with global situational demands.

Key points

- Setting pricing strategies is more challenging when developing global pricing strategies, as factors that do not appear in domestic markets will need to be considered.

- Marketers understand that consumers will process price information and will interpret these prices in terms of their past experience and their cultural and social environment.

- For marketers exporting into another country, environmental factors, such as economic conditions, technology status and adoption, sociocultural elements and political stability, are crucial in determining pricing strategies.

- Some of the more common pricing strategies are cost-plus pricing, demand-oriented pricing and competition-oriented pricing, but global managers need to assess the country's environmental situation before deciding on the most appropriate pricing strategy.

- Managerial factors such as cost implications, demand fluctuations and competitive pressures must be taken into account when setting a global pricing strategy.

- It is not uncommon to see global marketing strategists adapting the values of the people in a country when planning the best marketing strategies to reach them.
- Globalization has brought about many changes in the way international trade is carried out. Pricing strategies will definitely be incorporated into the strategic formulation of international trade. In essence, consumers across the world should benefit from the price competition brought about by globalization but this has not yet been realized as expected.

Introduction

Price is the most elusive of the marketing mix elements and often difficult to strategize properly especially when marketers lack the ability to see the contribution of an effective pricing strategy. Indeed, pricing strategies must be consistent with the direction of the other elements of the marketing mix and must take into account the various internal and external factors affecting the company. Applying this to the global environment, pricing strategies become more challenging when developing global pricing strategies, as factors that do not appear in domestic markets will need to be considered. This chapter illustrates the importance of pricing as a strategic tool capable of moving a company towards organizational success especially when they are involved in businesses at the global level.

Pricing environment

The competitiveness of today's global business environment demands that firms create effective and creative marketing strategies. Creativity plays a critical role in enhancing the effectiveness of marketing strategies developed by firms. In response to global changes, firms have created many new and innovative pricing initiatives and strategies. For example, Air Asia, the low-cost airline based in Malaysia which has now spread its wings to Thailand and Indonesia, clearly uses pricing strategy as the pull to attract travellers in these three countries. With the tagline 'Now everyone can fly', Air Asia flaunts air tickets priced as low as zero where passengers only need to pay airport taxes and service charges for return flights. Such a strategy has paid off and Air Asia has now extended its wings to include long-haul flights to Australia (Chu, 2008) and soon to the UK.

The pricing environment has changed hugely, to the extent that giving goods away for free is indeed a pricing strategy. Skype's internet phone service is an example where free online services are offered to customers but with a smart twist to this by associating the free service with a premium component, such as group video calling. It is common today to see products with low prices being offered with more expensive components that consumers need to pay for in order to use them. Today's global environment has moved many marketers into creating innovative ways of developing effective pricing strategies.

For marketers exporting into another country, environmental factors are crucial in determining pricing strategies. Environmental factors such as the economic situation, technology status and degree of adoption, sociocultural elements and political stability will affect pricing strategies. In addition, local policies and requirements must be adhered to when exporting into a new market. When pricing products for the export market, various factors have to be considered. Apart from the cost of production, the other costs that must be considered are the costs of packaging, labelling and marketing the product, product certification, domestic and overseas transportation, insurance, import duties and other charges. It is also important to determine which segment of the market the product is for and the prices of similar products being sold in the market before pricing the product for the export market (www.matrade.gov.my). Thus, there is a need to carry out preliminary data collection on the country in which the products are to be exported before developing appropriate marketing strategies.

Price setting

Marketers of today understand that consumers' needs are top priority in price setting. If a price is set that does not meet consumers' requirements, regardless of how low that price is, the marketing strategy of the firm will definitely fail. In an interview with Andrew Stevens, Tony Fernandes, the CEO of Air Asia, remarked that:

> I think when you start a business the most important thing is: does the market want it? And I knew the market wanted it. If that's there, everything is surmountable because people power is strong. (CNN's *The Boardroom*, 23 November 2007)

Regardless of who the consumers are, it is commonly understood by marketers that consumers will process the price information presented to them by marketers and will interpret these prices in terms of their past experience and their cultural and social environment. Therefore, when setting price, the psychology of consumers comes into play as marketers strive to make sense of how consumers perceive their price statements.

Reference price is one element of consumer psychology that affects consumers' perception of price. This occurs when consumers compare an observed price to an internal reference price they recall or an external frame of reference (Mazumdar et al., 2005). Reference prices can stimulate the perception of product position. For example, if a marketer places its products among the expensive competition, consumers may perceive that such products are in the same league and therefore will not mind paying a high price similar to that of the expensive competitor.

In line with this, *price–quality associations* are normal where consumers use price as an indicator of quality. Price acts as a signal of quality when there is no other or very little information about the product characteristics for consumers to use as a basis of evaluation. Therefore, consumers are likely to use price as a cue to indicate quality. Also, with exclusive or luxury goods, the demand for such goods may actually increase with higher prices as customers believe that they are in a small group of people able to afford such luxury (Amaldoss and Jain, 2005).

However, these associations may differ among consumers in different countries. For nondurable goods like food, beverages and household items, price–quality associations can be relatively low, as shown by the study carried out by Faulds and Lonial (2001) across Belgium, the Netherlands, France, Germany and the US. It was found that the correlation of price and quality for nondurable goods across these five nations was relatively low, implying that consumers may be basing their product choices on many other factors such as style and taste as well as other attributes, including store loyalty, availability and vendor locations (Faulds and Lonial, 2001). In Asia, however, the study by Schutte (1998) saw a direct relationship between price and quality among consumers in Southeast Asia. Price, as an indicator of status, is also an indicator of quality. It has been established that 'the price-quality equation serves as a risk-reduction mechanism for the uninformed' (Schutte, 1998, p. 165) and therefore serves as an important cue in influencing consumer buying decisions. Numerous other studies have concurred with this view and therefore have recognized the importance of establishing appropriate pricing strategies for relevant markets in Asia (for example, Probert and Lassere, 1997).

Price–quality associations may also refer to lower price, lower quality. This strategy may, however, have an impact on brand equity in the long run as consumers may view the product as being inferior in quality, which could affect long-term profitability (Kotler et al., 2009). An alternative to using this pricing strategy is to offer warranties, rebates, free maintenance and loyalty programmes that may attract consumers to the product.

Consumer psychology also influences the use of *price endings* where marketers deliberately set price endings with odd numbers. It is common for consumers to see items priced at £99 to be in the 'less than £100' range rather than closer to £100. The use of the number nine as a price ending often conveys the implication of a bargain or discount and this is likely to attract consumers' attention (Anderson and Simester, 2003). Cultural factors also influence the use of price endings. In China and Hong Kong, the number eight is an auspicious number and so among Chinese marketers it is common to use eight as price endings. The number eight is associated with prosperity and has long been a lucky number in Chinese culture because its pronunciation in many Chinese dialects is similar to the word denoting wealth and prosperity. Thus, pricing among Chinese marketers also reflects their belief that the use of the number eight in prices will be well accepted by consumers. In contrast, the number four is rarely or never used, as four denotes 'death' and so will be avoided as much as possible by the Chinese.

Suffice to say, price setting in a global environment requires the marketing strategist to consider numerous factors based on realistic demands and the peculiarities of the culture of the people in the country. It is not uncommon to see marketing strategists adapting to the values of the people in a country when planning the most viable marketing strategies to reach them.

New product pricing

When new products are developed, the pricing decision must be in line with the marketing strategy adopted by the marketer. Initially, a *positioning strategy* needs to be conceptualized so that it is in line with the price and the quality that the product wants to convey. For new products, establishing a firm positioning strategy may require aggressive efforts especially in terms of promotion. Creating awareness is critical at this initial stage and the target market must have enough exposure to the new product to allow consumers to develop an interest for the product or service.

In the global market, new products have to compete with existing products which may vary in terms of their pricing tactics. If a new product is exported into a country, it is pertinent that marketers understand the laws regulating pricing in that country. In the US, for instance, sellers must set prices without discussing issues relating to price setting with their competitors. Consumers are protected by legislation in the US against unethical or deceptive pricing practices that may put the consumers at a disadvantage. Price fixing is not allowed in the US and global marketers must understand the implications of conspiring with other players in the market with regards to the setting of prices.

It is more challenging for new products to develop their pricing strategies as consumer needs and environmental demands must be balanced. Consumers may seek low prices but environmental factors, such as the policies in the country, competitive pressures and economic factors, may hinder the efforts of marketers to meet the demands of the consumers at all times. New products are susceptible to environmental demands. Although it is simple enough to create a pricing strategy that the target market demands, it may not work effectively if the marketer fails to consider these environmental pressures.

The pricing strategy undertaken by a global marketer should take into account external variables such as currency fluctuations, economic conditions and regulatory requirements. At the same time, the direction of the organization must also be considered and the pricing strategy must be conceptualized based on the objectives established by the organization. Generally, new product pricing may adopt three common pricing alternatives based on the strategic orientation of the organization with the incorporation of external variables.

Market skimming pricing

If the objective of pricing is to achieve as much financial gain as possible within a short period of time, then a skimming strategy will be utilized. In *market skimming pricing*, the strategy of high price will be adopted at the initial stage of the new product launch. For market skimming pricing to work, the product has to be unique, innovative and command the attention of the global market. There is a need, however, for the global marketer to be sure that the target market will be sufficiently attracted to the product to pay this high price. Otherwise, market skimming pricing may not work effectively.

Market skimming pricing will ultimately give way to lower pricing as the pool of customers increases and the market expands. This is also the result of competitors entering the market as the innovativeness of the product diminishes and more and more competitors introduce similar products.

Market penetration pricing

If the pricing objective of the global marketer is to gain a wide market acceptance and generate a high volume of sales, then market penetration pricing is likely to be adopted. *Market penetration pricing* will see the global marketer establishing a relatively low price for the new product in the hope of attracting as many buyers as possible. For this to happen, mass markets will be the main target and, to a large extent, these markets are price sensitive and are likely to be captivated by low prices.

In market penetration pricing, the production and distribution costs of the product should reduce as the volume of sales increase. The global marketer must be able to control the production and distribution costs even though the product is entering the global market where a number of environmental uncertainties exist. In essence, the low price of this pricing strategy should serve as a barrier to new entrants and so the global marketer is able to enjoy its position in the market for a relatively long period of time.

Market pricing

A *market pricing* strategy is used by global marketers when almost identical products already exist in the market. The global marketer will be establishing the price of the product based on competitive or market prices. It is pertinent, however, that the global marketer understands the product costs and the implications of distributing the product in the global arena. Often, marketers may not incorporate production costs effectively and will decide the price of the product based solely on market signals. This may lead to problems if volume does not increase to a level that is adequate enough to provide satisfactory returns (Czinkota et al., 1995).

Factors influencing pricing strategy

The global market is a complex environment in which numerous factors influence strategic marketing decisions. Pricing decisions have to take into account the peculiarities of the country in which the product or service is to be marketed. The following discussion outlines several factors affecting global pricing strategy.

Margins required

It is imperative that marketers decide on the margins they want based on the positioning strategy that has been decided. It is highly unlikely that margins in distribution channels will be the same in domestic markets and they will definitely not be identical between different countries. In Thailand, for example, importers of large equipment or machinery charge a commission of 5–10% and allow their customers to open letters of credit themselves. (A letter of credit is a document from the bank guaranteeing that a buyer's payment to a seller will be received on time and for the correct amount. Otherwise, the bank will pay the full payment or remaining payment of the purchase.) Manufacturers or wholesalers normally receive a 5–10% profit margin. Retailers and distributors of local products require a 30–40% margin (*Asian Market Research News*, 2002). The difference in the margin requirements reflects the different costs involved and the value-adding processes as the product moves through the international distribution channel. Transportation costs including insurance and freight charges would add to the pricing structure. Therefore margins in the channels will be influenced by the costs involved in moving the product.

Terms of international trade

Terms of international trade may differ in business relationships among countries trading with one another. There is always the possibility of disagreements among trading parties unless some guidelines exist that will allow trading partners to understand their roles. Thus, the International Chamber of Commerce has set up Incoterms 2000 to specify the terms that will govern the business relationships among trading parties. The purpose of Incoterms is to provide a set of international rules for the interpretation of the most commonly used trade terms in foreign trade, in order to avoid, or at least considerably reduce, the uncertainties of different interpretations of such terms in different countries.

The terms specified in international trade may increase the price of goods in foreign markets. This is because the terms or incoterm (international commercial term) selected by the trading parties will determine which party will bear the cost of each segment of the transporting, loading and unloading of goods and which will bear the risk of losses, which will, in turn, influence the price of the goods traded. Those global marketers accepting the incoterm will normally specify the terms accepted and this will become the terms of trade.

Tariffs and taxes

Tariffs are taxes levied upon goods as they cross national boundaries into global territories by the government of the importing country. The reason for imposing tariffs is normally to generate revenue for the country, although it can also be a form of protective measure to protect domestic industries. The tariffs and taxes imposed are likely to affect the pricing structure of imported goods. In Southeast Asia, members of the Association of Southeast Asian Nations (ASEAN, set up in 1967) established the ASEAN Free Trade Area (AFTA) in 1992, with the intention of lowering intraregional tariffs through the Common Effective Preferential Tariff (CEPT) scheme. More than 99% of the products in the CEPT Inclusion List of ASEAN-6, comprising Brunei Darussalam, Indonesia, Malaysia, the Philippines, Singapore and Thailand, have been brought down to the 0.5% tariff range. Since implementation, the average tariff rate of the ASEAN-6 under the AFTA CEPT has been reduced from 12.8% in 1993 to 0.97% in 2008. Intra-ASEAN trade in 2007 totalled £251.7bn, a 14.5% increase from 2006 (the ASEAN-6 were joined by Vietnam in 1995, Laos and Myanmar in 1997 and Cambodia in 1999). In 2006, intra-ASEAN trade was £219.3bn. Intra-ASEAN trade is 25% of the total ASEAN trade and is fast increasing (www.asesansec.org). Such a move is likely to spur trade movement among the member countries of ASEAN and therefore affect the pricing structure of goods traded in these countries.

Business environmental factors

Environmental considerations as mentioned earlier play an important role in influencing pricing strategies for global marketers. A key business environmental factor that is likely to affect global pricing decision is the impact of *currency fluctuations*. It is important to decide whether to use the seller's own currency or the buyer's currency when quoting prices. Often, a third currency may be preferred such as the US dollar or the euro but it is not uncommon for the supplier to quote the price in its own currency.

By using forward contracts, risk may be removed, which allows the exporter to receive, at the time of the contract with the bank, payment in their own currency (Stone and McCall, 2004). In this situation, the bank handles the exchange risk and the exporter gets funds at a cost that will be taken into account when setting the price. The bank is able to use its knowledge of offsetting risk, and will recover the sales contract value when the money is realized at a future date. For larger organizations operating internationally, the ability to cover exchange rate fluctuations is higher. In many cases, they are likely to use measures such as centralized global hedging.

The fluctuation of *inflation rates* is another business environmental factor affecting pricing strategy. Inflation is an increase in the prices of goods and services that is generally expressed as an annual percentage increase in the Consumer Price Index. The rise of inflation in a country is a reflection of rising prices and rising demand brought about by consumers having money to spend. Inflation can be brought about by the demand or supply side of the economy. For example, prices can be pulled up on the demand side by increases in household spending when there is a greater availability of credit brought about by lower interest rates. Alternatively, on the supply side, inflation can be caused by increases in wages and salaries, which will lead to price increases. In such a situation, the global marketer has to be careful in terms of the form of pricing strategy undertaken as inflation will affect consumer purchasing patterns, which, in turn, will affect the business channels environment in the country.

Managerial decisions on pricing

Marketing managers involved with global pricing development will still be subjected to the common managerial concerns of price development faced by managers dealing with products for domestic distribution. Therefore, managerial factors such as cost implications, demand fluctuations and competitive pressures are factors that must be taken into account when setting a global pricing strategy.

Cost-plus pricing

The simplest format in price setting is when all the cost elements are taken into account. All the known fixed costs will be added to all the variable costs including the cost of distributing products to consumers. Therefore, channel considerations including the profit margins demanded by channel members and logistics costs, as well as tariffs and taxes that will be levied, all go into the pricing development. All these costs will be added up and a required profit margin will be added to come up to the final price of the product.

The advantage of *cost-plus pricing* is that it is simple to formulate, requires minimal information and is easy to administer. However, the simplistic assumption of cost plus pricing brings several disadvantages, such as its inability to take into account consumer demands and competitive pressures, and the fact that it ignores opportunity costs and implications on product performance are often disregarded.

Demand-oriented pricing

Prices set by the marketing strategist will lead to a different level of demand, which will have a different impact on the marketing objectives of the global marketer. In general, demand and price are inversely related, that is, the higher the price, the lower the demand. However, price sensitivity is also dependent on the elasticity of the demand. It is important that global marketers understand how responsive or elastic demand would be to a change in price. Demand is inelastic when a change in price does not lead to a substantial change in demand. The higher the elasticity, the greater the volume growth resulting from a small price reduction (Kotler et al., 2009).

In *demand-oriented pricing*, the global marketer will estimate the volume of sales for different price levels. It will then be possible to calculate the combination of price and volume that will yield the greatest profit contribution. Table 3.1 provides an illustration of a demand-oriented pricing consideration. Based on the computation, a retail price of £1,200 appears to be the best alternative for providing the highest returns, given the cost assumptions and the projected sales at the different price levels.

Table 3.1 Demand-oriented pricing computation example

	Alternative 1	Alternative 2	Alternative 3
Retail price (£)	1,000	1,200	1,500
Unit sales	500	450	300
Sales revenue (£)	500,000	540,000	450,000
Total variable costs (£)	450,000	441,000	330,000
• Manufacturing cost @ £300 per unit	150,000	135,000	90,000
• Marketing cost @ £200 per unit	100,000	90,000	60,000
• Distributor's margin @ 30% of unit selling price	150,000	162,000	135,000
• Entry costs @ 10% of unit selling price	50,000	54,000	45,000
Contribution (£)	50,000	99,000	75,000

Source: Adapted from Stone and McCall (2004)

The price may well be changed for another combination of price and volume depending on the objectives set by the global marketer. In addition, the pricing strategy will also influence the pricing option. For example, a penetration pricing strategy implies a future advantage such as a growing market in which the benefits of the experience curve apply and where costs could drop every time sales increase by a specific percentage (Stone and McCall, 2004).

Competition-oriented pricing

Competition-oriented pricing sets price on the basis of evaluating the offerings of competitors in the global market. The global marketer can choose to sell above or below the competitors' prices based on the evaluation of different product character-istics as well as the environmental factors that may have an impact on product pricing. Competition-oriented pricing is also known as going-rate pricing (Kotler and Keller, 2009). There is a tendency for smaller firms to follow the market leader's price and any changes made to the pricing strategy will be based on the changes carried out by the market leader.

Often when costs are difficult to measure, developing a pricing strategy similar to that of competitors will be a good option because it is considered as following the norms of the international market and the wisdom of the industry players.

Differential versus standardized pricing

Global marketers have the option of offering different prices in different global markets. This is normally used when the marketer wants to get rid of unwanted surpluses or it aims to achieve a specific market share. When low prices are set that differ from the price in the domestic market or at a price below production cost with the intention of getting rid of unwanted surpluses, this is likely to be perceived as *dumping*. To ensure that global marketers are not seen practising dumping, global marketers can focus on value-added products and increase differentiation by including services in the product offering (Czinkota et al., 2004).

Standardized pricing is practised when global marketers offer the same price to all markets, whether international or domestic. Theoretically, standardized pricing is possible but in reality, taking into consideration the global market environment and the regulatory demands associated with marketing across international boundaries, it is impossible to sell at the same price in all markets. Nevertheless, there is pressure on global marketers, especially among consumer goods manufacturers, to standardize prices in the face of the growing number of centrally purchasing retailers and parallel imports (Stone and McCall, 2004). Thus, many global marketers will seek ways of compromising this differential versus standardized pricing approach by following the norms of the host country.

Globalization and pricing tactics

Globalization has brought about many changes in the way international trade is carried out. Globalization has been widely debated, however, especially among developing countries that see the process of globalization as a threat that is likely to slow down their progress. On the other hand, some view it as a beneficial process – a key to future world economic development – and also as inevitable and irreversible, while others regard it with hostility, even fear, believing that it increases inequality within and between nations, threatens employment and living standards and thwarts social progress (IMF, 2000). In spite of all the reactions towards globalization, it is inevitable and its impact has already been felt in some countries.

The globalization of China and India especially has resulted in many positives, which others are trying to emulate. Countries in the Middle East are striving for better economic standing that will allow them to progress in tandem with other countries in the world that share a similar economic background. But the pressure in the global marketplace today makes it increasingly difficult for countries whose economies have yet to reach that level to compete effectively. An element of the marketing mix, pricing strategies will be incorporated into the strategic formulation of international trade. In essence, consumers across the global market should benefit from the price competition brought about by the workings of globalization but this has not been realized as expected.

AFTA, as discussed earlier, is an ASEAN initiative which seeks to increase ASEAN's competitive edge through the impact of trade liberalization. Although it has worked to some extent, especially in the elimination of tariffs and the lowering of import duties of goods traded among member countries, the implementation is still slow and often a subject of much debate even among member nations. The prices of products traded across these ten member nations are assumed to be much lower than those from other countries and this would be the main benefit of having such an initiative. This has, as yet, to be fully realized.

Conclusion

This chapter has tried to establish the importance of effective pricing in a global market environment. A number of factors come into play when international trade is involved. It is clear that setting prices in a global market differs markedly from that in the domestic market. Despite the application of basic pricing tactics used by marketing managers in any type of market, there are peculiarities that must be addressed when developing pricing strategies in the international arena. Environmental influences play a substantive role in influencing the pricing strategy of a global market. In addition, the global marketer may find one pricing approach suitable in one competitive economy, yet this may not be applicable in another economic environment. Pricing options such as cost-plus pricing, demand-oriented pricing and competition-oriented pricing are some of the more common strategies to adopt but often global managers may find that they would need to improvise and, on many occasions, assess the country's sociocultural, economic, technological and competitive situations before deciding on the most appropriate pricing strategy. Such is the challenge of global pricing, and like all the elements of the marketing mix, pricing is indeed challenging when the bottom line is the ultimate consideration.

Issues for further discussion

1. To what extent are the basic principles of pricing applicable to pricing development in the global arena?

2. Marketing strategist operating in the global market must understand the culture and social peculiarities of consumers in the country they are operating in. Is it possible to use uniform pricing strategies for all markets regardless of the location?
3. How has globalization affected strategic pricing development?
4. Why are environmental factors important when developing pricing strategies?

The community airline

The newest airline set up to cater for the needs of a specific target market in Malaysia is Firefly. Firefly was established in April 2007 as a private limited company and is a wholly owned subsidiary of Malaysia Airlines (MAS), the leading national carrier of Malaysia. This new airline operates out of Subang in Kuala Lumpur and Penang, the tourist island located in the northern region of Peninsular Malaysia. The specified routes that this new airline takes are those that are, as yet, untapped by existing carriers. From Penang, Firefly offers the quickest routes to selected destinations within Peninsular Malaysia, as well as to some famous destinations in Thailand like Phuket and Koh Samui.

Initially, the Malaysian government mandated MAS to look for new routes from Penang, while working hard on re-engineering its structure to improve its financial position, which, at that point, was at its lowest ebb. Being a government-backed company, MAS also has a role to play to support the Malaysian government's involvement in the regional coalition between three ASEAN countries – Malaysia, Indonesia and Thailand. This economic coalition, formed in 1993, is known as the Indonesia-Malaysia-Thailand Growth Triangle (IMT-GT). Under IMT-GT, all three countries promised to work hand in hand to stimulate economic growth between them.

Currently, all three countries are members of the ASEAN economic coalition. One of the key issues between them is to enhance connectivity among people in the three countries and this essentially became the main concern in the agenda of promoting economic growth. They believe that good connectivity is crucial not only to provide better economic opportunities but will lead to better regional ties and social integration. Seemingly, any improvement in economic growth between them will have greater spillover effect in the regions when the connectivity is efficient and effective. Hence, Firefly was conceptualized by MAS in April 2007 with the intention that it will become the primary conduit or stimulator to the economic growth in the IMT-GT by providing attractive connectivity for people in these three neighbouring countries.

The parent company

In 1973, Malaysia Airlines (MAS) was born and at present it flies 50,000 passengers daily to some 100 destinations worldwide. In the past 10 years, MAS has won more than 100 awards, among the most notable are the 'World's Best Cabin Crew' in 2007 and the 'Best Airline to Asia' in 2006, while it remains one of only six carriers globally to be accredited as a '5-star airline'. But in the early years of 2000, financial gloom set in when MAS incurred heavy losses due to high operating costs led by huge fuel costs. Poor pricing, rising cost structure, mismatched fleet, weak operational performance, low-intensity performance culture and social obligations worsened the company's performance. The precarious state of its financial performance caused great concern not only to the management of MAS and the Malaysian government but also to the general public.

In view of the crisis, MAS was pressured to implement strategic changes to revive its perform-ance and stem the flow of losses. To make matters worse, the Malaysian government announced in 2006 that it would not bail out its national carrier and urged MAS to work doubly hard towards reviving its performance. Some tough actions had to be taken to overcome the financial and nonfinancial problems faced by the company and this led to the adoption of the Business Turnaround Plan (BTP), a radical plan aimed at reviving MAS.

The BTP sets the new strategic direction of the national carrier towards profitability and conti-nuity of growth. With a clear mission to become a profitable airline, the national carrier pursued a business turnaround strategy that cut losses from RM1.7bn (£0.53bn) (full year) to RM620m (£124m) in 2006, and achieved a profit of RM50m in 2007 and RM500m (£100m) in 2008. MAS has succeeded in doing exactly what it set out to do and, in 2007, achieved a record profit of RM610m (£122m).

With the marked improvement in its financial position, Firefly was proposed by MAS with the support of the government. Firefly is strategically positioned to leverage MAS's existing resources and optimistically, with effective strategies, Firefly has all the potential to generate the expected profit for the company.

The birth of Firefly

When it was first conceptualized, Firefly was intended to be an airline that would attract the untapped market of community travellers – those travelling short distances either on business, on holidays or visiting friends and relatives. Using existing resources that MAS had, Firefly started with the existing turbo propeller aircraft that were ideal for short routes and low-altitude flights. When it was first launched, price was the strategy used to attract potential travellers but as its operation geared up, the profile of the travellers has slowly shifted to middle tier travellers whose main concerns are not necessarily price but services that are good value, although not necessarily full service, and with a strong focus on the time factor. Delays are likely to deter this group of travellers and Firefly was ready to offer them what they needed.

The name Firefly (in Mandarin, *fei ying*) was chosen as this denoted the airline's characteristics of agility, brilliance, charm and fun. To the general public, the name 'firefly' conjures up the insect with a lighted tail, which evokes a sense of uniqueness and of being easily recognized. With its brand name, the company positions itself as a community airline that provides new and exclusive routes to passengers travelling between selected destinations in Malaysia, Thailand, Singapore and Indonesia. Although Firefly's initial business model focused on low-cost structure, its current operation is far from low price. Service is still an essential component of its offerings and Firefly recognizes that its current market seeks value services given the travel environment that Firefly offers.

Firefly's offerings

With a focus on excellent service, the airline's philosophy is that passengers would feel delighted and satisfied and will then always choose Firefly as their airline. Passengers would be provided with a safe, fun travelling experience, since it offers shorter queuing time, assigned seating, first-class service and a practical 20 kg checked baggage allowance.

Undeniably, safety is a crucial factor in the airline industry. To ensure passengers safety, Firefly has invested in a new fleet of technologically advanced European-made ATR-500 aircraft. The ATR-500 aircraft are reputed to be the most economical and environmentally friendly turbo propeller airplanes that are suitable for travelling short distances comfortably. In addition, these aircraft offer the lowest seat-mile cost, are almost vibration free and have low noise pollution.

This is in line with Firefly's green policy of ensuring minimal carbon emissions through flying shorter distances, leading to less air time and less fuel used.

As a young airline, Firefly adopts a rather cautious approach in executing its business model and strategy. This approach is inevitable given that the business is highly risky and dynamic. Contrary to popular investment belief that 'high risk, high returns' are applicable in the airline industry, Firefly's management team believes that an airline business can face the possibility of a 'high risk, low return' situation. Being a government-owned company, Firefly has a social obligation to the country and the management team realizes that this new airline has a long way to go to ensure that it does not fall into financial difficulties.

Competition

As a new community airline serving the region, Firefly faces stiff competition especially from other low-cost carriers such as Air Asia of Malaysia, Tiger Airways of Singapore, Nokair of Thailand and Jet Star of Singapore. To do well in this challenging industry is not easy. Its closest rival is Air Asia, the low-cost carrier that has firmly etched its name across Malaysia, Thailand and Indonesia. Air Asia uses a low-cost, low-fare and low-frills concept and with such an orientation, Firefly does not see Air Asia as a major competitor. On the other hand, MAS, the premier airline in Malaysia, is Firefly's parent and being a 'mother' airline, MAS serves a different pool of customers, specifically, high-end customers both domestically and internationally. The likelihood of taking each other's customers is downplayed by Firefly's targeting strategy, since its pool of target markets is essentially different from MAS and its routes are not necessarily in direct competition with MAS's routes. Firefly's competitive edge lies with its concept of a community airline – an airline that serves communal travellers using turbo propelled aircraft suitable for short flights rather than jets that are not environmentally friendly.

Nonetheless, Firefly's strategists understand that any new changes can pose either opportunities or threats to the industry. The Open Air policy, for example, which came into effect in 2009, may have a drastic impact on Firefly's operational performance. The Open Air policy, as agreed by countries in the ASEAN coalition, will open the ASEAN skies to member countries and therefore diminish regional entry barriers, and more players will penetrate the existing small regional markets. In addition, the fluctuation of fuel prices in the world market poses continuous threats since fuel consumption makes up 40–50% of Firefly's operational cost. The uncertainty in fuel prices and other intervening factors create a game-changing event for this volatile industry.

This case was written together with Puteri Norashikin Mohamad.

Questions

1. As price can be an attractive factor in the airline industry, what kind of pricing strategy will be suitable for Firefly to adopt?
2. Firefly must develop strategies that meet the needs of many customers. Should there be standardized pricing for all? Or is it more viable if a differential pricing strategy is adopted?
3. Are pricing strategies alone enough to address the dynamic needs of travellers. What about service enhancement? Or are there any other elements that should be given attention?
4. Firefly's challenge lies with its ability to meet the demands of its time-conscious travellers, who want their short flights to be as comfortable as possible, while still receiving all the advantages of full service airlines. Is Firefly prepared?

References

Amaldoss, W. and Jain, S. (2005) 'Pricing of conspicuous goods: A competitive analysis of social effects'. *Journal of Marketing Research*, 42: 30–42.

Anderson E. and Simester, D. (2003) 'Mind your pricing cues'. *Harvard Business Review*, 81(9): 96–103.

Asian Market Research News (2002) 'Asians prefer well known brands', 28 April, http://www.asiamarketresearch.com/news/000142.htm, accessed 8 November 2008.

Chu, J. (2008) 'Fast 50 2008: Air Asia', Fast Company, www.fastcompany.com/fast50_08/airasia.html, accessed 23 November 2008.

Czinkota, M.R., Ronkainen, I.A. and Tarrant, J.J. (1995) *The Global Marketing Imperative*. Licolnwood, IL: NTC Business Books.

Czinkota, M.R., Ronkainen, I.A. and Donath, B. (2004) *Mastering Global Markets*. Mason, OH: Southwestern.

Faulds, D.J. and Lonial, S.C. (2001) 'Price-quality relationships of nondurable consumer products: A European and United States perspective'. *Journal of Economic and Social Research*, 3(1): 59–76.

IMF (2000) *Globalization: Threat or Opportunity?* April, http://www.imf.org/external/np, accessed 9 May 2005.

Kotler, P. and Keller, K.L. (2009) *Marketing Management* (13th edn). London: Prentice Hall.

Kotler, P., Keller, K.L., Ang, S.W. et al. (2009) *Marketing Management: An Asian Perspective* (5th edn). Singapore: Prentice Hall.

Mazumdar, T., Raj, S.P. and Sinha, I. (2005) 'Reference price research: Review and propositions'. *Journal of Marketing*, 69: 84–102.

Probert, J. and Lassere, P. (1997) *The Asian Business Context: A Follow-up Survey*, Euro-Asia Centre Research Series No. 4. Fontainebleau: INSEAD-EAC.

Schutte, H. (1998) *Consumer Behaviour in Asia*. Basingstoke: Macmillan – now Palgrave Macmillan.

Stone, M.A. and McCall, J.B. (2004) *International Strategic Marketing: A European Perspective*. London: Routledge.

4

Managerial challenges in setting prices: price–quality cues, role of the sales force and global issues

Jurg Hari

Learning outcomes

At the end of this chapter, readers should be able to:

1. Understand how consumers use price–quality cues when assessing products and particularly services.

2. Gain insights into the important role of salespeople, particularly in a B2B setting.

3. Gain a brief overview of the challenges that managers meet when pricing on a global basis.

Key points

- Price communicates value. Consequently, rebates and discounts will destroy perceived value.

- It is hard for customers to estimate benefits from services and also to compare different offers. Therefore, simple heuristics, such as price–quality inferences, will be used.

- The salesperson seems to be a central element of company (price) communication in many industries and around the globe.

- It is dangerous to include cost information when setting prices.

- Price knowledge is poor and this holds true on a global basis.

- Making a difference between consumers' structured and inherent preferences makes understanding those customers easier.

- Setting prices is still a local matter.

Introduction

Setting the right price is a major challenge in many companies. This is a commonplace statement and almost not worthy to start a chapter. Yet there is a big 'but'. As many consultants and people involved in daily managerial tasks will agree, it is an ambiguous task. On the one hand, managers consider it a high priority, since pricing is the centre-piece of margin creation (or it destroys these margins) and of the 4Ps, pricing is the only one that really creates income. On the other hand, making pricing decisions is viewed as a complex and boring task. It is much more fun to create a new advertising idea or improve product quality or even improve the product itself.

The importance of pricing has been stressed continually (Eugster et al., 2000; Simon and Butscher, 2001; Simon et al., 2003). Trade magazines and management newspapers frequently feature articles on pricing. The following example is easy to follow. An 'average' company has approximately 5% net margin. In other words, for each 100 currency units, the company has the corresponding 95 currency units of costs, leaving 5 units as profit (100 – 95 = 5). A decrease of 1% – in the form of a rebate for example – will decrease the profit by 20% (99 – 95 = 4). A big drop. In many consulting projects and also in educational courses, this illustration is always an eye-opener. The illustrative figures are not that important in this context, rather, it is the mechanism. Many rigorously run companies are surprisingly lax about pricing and managers do not pay enough attention to pricing (Eugster et al., 2000).

At the heart of this debate are usually the rebates and/or the salespeople; 75% of salespeople will cave in to price objections, and they will grant, on average, a discount of close to 7.5% on the selling price (Perriello, 2008). We can compare this with figures for companies listed in the US S&P 500 Index. The pricing leverage is 1 to 8, meaning that a 1% price reduction results in an 8% reduction of profits. Combining the 7.5% with this leverage means that, on average, salespeople wipe out over half the profits.

The basics of price setting are explained in all introductory marketing textbooks and will not be considered here. This chapter will touch on the most important issues in price setting from a manager's point of view (the managerial perspective) and will take an advanced look at those issues. More specifically, the chapter will summarize three concerns in price setting:

- the price–quality cues that consumers use to evaluate products
- the role of the sales force in setting and/or implementing the pricing strategies and tactics
- the global challenges.

Since services are of increasing importance, there will be – whenever possible – a focus on setting the right price for services.

Setting prices for services is a special undertaking and will briefly be considered here, although it is not the focal point of this chapter on price (for a discussion for managers, see Berry and Yadav, 1996). Services are, by their nature, not material, and a buyer owns nothing after the purchase, but has satisfied a need and received some benefit. With a material good like a car, a purchaser at least owns some metal. In a service context, the customer is always part of the transaction or relation. In consequence, there is an inherent quality fluctuation provoked either by the customer or the service provider. As a result of this, it is hard for customers to estimate the benefits from such services and to compare different offers. Therefore, simple heuristics like price–quality inferences will be used.

Price–quality cues

A phenomenon that is commonly termed 'price–quality cue utilization' refers to consumers' assumption that higher priced goods must be of better quality. Normally, higher prices are associated with lower consumer demand. The exception is so-called Giffen goods – inferior goods that experience a rise in demand when prices rise and a fall in demand when the prices decrease. There are, however, few real examples to prove or even illustrate this theory.

In customer satisfaction and other commercial surveys carried out at Zurich University of Applied Sciences in Switzerland, one of the first generic questions that is asked is: 'What comes to your mind concerning company X?' It is a sure bet that the vast majority of survey respondents will reply: 'High priced products with high quality!' This is hardly surprising, given the Swiss background. No one has ever replied: 'High quality at low prices'. This answer does not seem to fit human nature and market experience. Price and quality seem to be linked.

The close correlation between price and quality in most markets presents a formidable challenge for companies. Consumers seek high-quality products for low prices, while implicitly assuming that lower priced products are of lower quality. A higher price will lower demand, but also increase quality perception and vice versa. In the service industry, this phenomenon may be even more challenging. The insurance industry and more specifically the health insurance market in Switzerland may serve as an example. Basic health insurance products are usually highly standardized and yet prices vary considerably. For the same product, a person could pay a premium of CHF 232.55 or CHF 305.0, a difference of 31%. This was also studied in depth in Holland (Van Dijk et al., 2008). As in the Swiss market, basic insurance in Holland is a homogeneous product and yet there is a price difference of 40% between the lowest and the highest premiums. The authors found a small elasticity in basic insurance and no elasticity in supplementary insurance. Young people are a bit more price sensitive than older people. Obviously, competition in these markets is weak and consumers do not switch service providers. In the Dutch market, the authors pointed out that in one particular year (owing to a government rule change), switching rates were as high as 20% and fell back to the normal 5%, a number that is also informally reported for the Swiss market.

From a health insurance company's point of view, this is now really challenging. We also have to keep in mind that the costs per insured person are basically equal, since the product (basic health insurance) is exactly the same for all. Lowering the price should attract more customers, but this may be offset by a lower quality perception and the customer may not want to trade down on quality (after all, health is important). The option to increase price may also be limited, given the many regulations in health markets and the political and media implications this may have.

This example can be replicated in other service markets, for example financial products, phone operator calling plans, electricity and many others (Hari et al., 2008). These markets are characterized by three attributes:

1. They are complex and difficult to understand for the average consumer.
2. They have many difficult to assess quality characteristics, for example 'trust'.
3. Many aspects of the service are to be found in the future (ranging from 'cancer treatment' to anticipated premium increases).

When the information being presented to the consumer is incomplete or overwhelming, consumers will simplify the task and form an overall judgement on the service on the little information available to them and price may be the most prominent attribute of all (see Völckner and Hofmann, 2007 for a summary and meta-analysis of recent studies). It also follows that people focus on relative comparisons among the externally presented options, since absolute attribute values are difficult to assess. This leads to context effects, such as an assortment of written offers. Consumers have an intuitive knowledge of their relative preferences, but they give surprisingly little weight to the options' absolute values or location in the attribute space.

The price–quality link has been studied extensively. Price has two distinctive functions for a consumer: it serves as an informational cue and is a measure of sacrifice (Völckner, 2008). Consumers simplify their cognitive task of evaluating imperfect information on products such as risk (Völckner, 2008; Estelami, 2008).

In a meta-analysis of studies published from 1989 to 2006, Völckner (2008) finds that the price effect on perceived quality has decreased. The relationship is stronger in studies that use a within-subjects design, investigate higher priced products and use samples from European countries. She also finds that the link depends on the product category and is weaker for services, durable goods and when respondents are familiar with the product. Other factors that moderate the link are consumer involvement, purchase frequency, advertising exposure and increased complexity of the service (Estelami, 2008). There are also quite marked differences within services. In Estelami's study, the price–quality link was weakest for cheque accounts and strongest for financial advisory services. Cheque accounts are commodity products, frequently opened and also widely used in financial services in the US. For cheque accounts, consumer price knowledge is greatest. Advisory services exhibit lower levels of consumer price knowledge. Price knowledge may be an explanatory factor (see also Estelami, 2005). An alternative, although less convincing explanation is the cognitive biases and anchoring heuristics that consumers use to assess product values (Laury and McInnes, 2003; Shapira and Venezia, 2008).

For the manager, this raises important questions: Do consumers use this decision-making heuristic consciously or are more subtle mechanisms involved? Are there other attributes of a product/service that moderate the price–quality correlation, for example brand names?

Until recently, the prevailing wisdom was that consumers use the price–quality heuristics, because it worked reasonably well for them in the past (Rao and Monroe, 1988; Rao and Sieben, 1992). Consumers avoided the daunting task of comparing products, each having a bewildering array of potential quality characteristics, by simply using the price/quality cue. This holds true particularly for products with few alternatives on which to assess quality. As a result, this means that they *consciously* choose to rely on the price cue when making purchase decisions. Several recent studies, however, challenge this assumption. For example, Shiv et al. (2005) demonstrated in three experiments that the price of a product (they also included a discount) directly influences its quality evaluation on a *subconscious* level. The first experiment showed that price discounts with or without reinforcing expectations lead to lower performance. When participants were made aware of a potential price–efficacy relationship – the second experiment – the effect did not occur. This suggests that a higher price leads to higher expectations and this causes a more favourable efficacy, and, of course, a better product evaluation. It seems that the pricing effect is strongest when the expectation is not conscious. In their final and third experiment, they showed that advertising reinforces this link between price and performance.

Shiv et al. refer to this effect as a 'placebo effect'. A placebo is often used in clinical trials, when a new drug is being tested (see Shiv et al., 2005 for further references). A new drug is either tested against a commonly used or commonly accepted medical standard and if such a standard is not available, then a placebo (a 'sugar' pill) is used. In these clinical trials, the placebo group will also show changes in subjective parameters such as pain relief or even objective parameters such as liver enzymes. This is why placebos are used in the first place. And this is the surprising finding of Shiv et al.'s studies: price can exert an effect similar to that of a placebo. This means that the messages about a product – in this case pricing and advertising – are more powerful than the product itself. As these findings have huge practical implications for the daily managerial task, the research group conducted more studies to explore this price–quality relationship (for a summary, see Ariely, 2008).

For example, Ariely and co-workers sold what they called 'MIT Brew' beer to university students and the students preferred this brew to the normal beer (Ariely, 2008). This 'MIT Brew' was, however, normal beer with vinegar added to it. When the participants were made aware of the vinegar, then they preferred the normal beer and said that the 'MIT Brew' tasted distasteful. This was not because their experience told them it was bad, but their expectations led them to conclude it tasted bad. Ariely and co-workers made similar observations with coffee. In an upmarket environment, the coffee also tasted more upmarket. And, returning to the pricing issue, they also showed that higher priced painkillers actually lowered pain better when participants knew they were more expensive. A price discount actually lowered its performance significantly.

In another study, researchers asked 20 male subjects to taste five wine samples, which were distinguished solely by their retail price (Plassmann et al., 2008). Unsurprisingly, the subjects consistently reported that the more expensive wines tasted better. During the wine tasting, the participants' brains were scanned and the results showed that pleasantness experienced correlated highly with changes in the brain region responsible for enjoyment. Interestingly and also importantly, there were no changes in the primary taste areas. The price obviously does not influence the basic sensory representation. Rather, the human brain integrates the bottom-up sensory components with the top-down cognitive processes and thus modulates the expectancies and experiences. From this study, it follows that marketing manipulations might affect subjective perceptions.

Plassmann et al.'s study also answers the question that Rao (2005) asked in a commentary on the Shiv experiments: 'If perceptions can influence the performance of objectively identical products, is there such a thing as objective quality?' Objective quality does exist, but the human brain cannot process it (or twists it). Thus, objective quality does not matter for us humans. Psychology and biology are obviously more important than engineering (or wine making). For further insights on this interesting topic, see Gourville and Soman (2002) from a manager's perspective and Rothenberger et al. (2008) for a more theoretical point of view.

For the service industry, the link between price and quality was studied in a university context (library, housing, cafeteria and so on) and also included satisfaction measures (Salvador et al., 2007). The result is in line with other research. Furthermore, the authors demonstrate that the service price–quality link is not universal and that the direction of the relationship varies between services. Bearden et al. (2003) also reached a similar conclusion when studying the framing effect of sale price or invoice amount. The effects of price on quality were complex and varied by market conditions.

All these studies clearly show that expectations are the main drivers of actual product performance and evaluation. In the process of forming this expectation, price (or a discount) is presumably the strongest factor and the psychological mechanism works on the subconscious level.

This leads to the question of how consumers process price in this formation of expectation. Since price is so important, we might assume that people are knowledgeable about price. As will be shown below, this knowledge is surprisingly low. Other factors – probably contextual in nature – come into play. Most probably, the purchasing situation itself will be central in this expectation formation. Let us consider two simple purchases: a hair shampoo and car insurance. Does the reader know the price of these items (any brand may be picked from memory)? Most people fail on this task.

Let us turn first to the example of hair shampoo. We can compare different brands on the shelf and will most probably see a low priced, store brand, a well-known manufacturer's brand and a higher priced, exclusive brand. These clues will serve as external reference prices. The customer may also have an internal reference price in mind, for example store X is more expensive than store Y. This internal reference may moderate the perception of the selection. Based on this, the customer will form an acceptable price range and finally make the purchase decision. If the favoured brand is outside this range, the customer will switch to the alternative brand. This purchasing process was tested and confirmed in an empirical study in Germany (Müller, 2005). In his study, Müller showed that customers use such hybrid reference prices. Customers also adjust the reference prices upwards as price increases occur. The individually perceived price will be adjusted to the objective market price over time. There seems to be a time lag in this adjustment, presumably due to memory effects and also due to stockpiling following market announcements, for example an announced tax increase, as in Müller's case of tobacco products. After deciding on a purchase and putting the item into the shopping basket, an interesting thing is probably going to happen: the customer forgets the price of the chosen product. When supermarket shoppers were asked for the price of the product they had just bought, over half of them had already forgotten (Dickson and Sawyer, 1990).

Indeed, many studies have found that the price knowledge of consumers is rather poor. In a representative study of consumers, Aalto-Setälä and Raijas (2003) asked consumers about the prices of typical items found in a food basket in Finland. Most people gave an answer and made an estimate. The differences in these estimates was quite large, around 19% for coffee to almost 40% for orange juice. On average, consumers as a group were well aware of the market prices. The average estimates were within a 5% range of the average actual prices found in the market.

From these findings, we can conclude that individual consumers are not really aware of prices, but cognitively process them in the context of a purchase situation. In this situation, they will form a price tolerance range and select the products accordingly. This price tolerance range will be moderated by customer satisfaction, the evoked set, switching barriers and involvement (Herrmann et al., 2004). For the manager, this will mean the following. A customer encounters a purchase situation. This customer will have a prior history with this product or brand and therefore have a history of customer satisfaction, also switching barriers are probably a given and so is the involvement of the customer. The only two things that can be influenced at this point in time (the time of the purchase) are the evoked set (alternative offers or the choices on the shelf) and the actual price. This will, by and large, determine the outcome of the product selection process.

We could take this a step further and hypothesize the following. Customers will make the selection even easier by putting the available alternative into three groups: a high price group, a low price group and a medium price group. Unfortunately, this is not convincingly demonstrated in the literature. There is only anecdotal evidence in the Swiss and the UK market. The two big retailers in Switzerland recently introduced a low price line of products and then added a high price product. In a personal communication, managers of both companies stated that this strategy does strengthen the middle part of the assortment. Intuitively, this makes sense if we combine poor price knowledge with the price–quality cues. If a customer is looking for a particular product, they will see some low price products of presumably lower quality and high price products of excellent quality, with all the rest in the middle. The average customer will buy neither the cheap line nor the expensive line, but rather picks the middle price range. Over time, the customer will have a more favourable price perception of the retailer. After all, they can buy the cheap as well as the expensive items if they really need them. And this is exactly what this strategy of offering the three-tier assortment is intended to do.

We now examine the second purchase example of car insurance. The same mechanisms will apply here. The poor customer will probably have little knowledge of the available options in terms of pricing. The customer will probably also use the heuristic rule of the price–quality link. But since insurance is a complicated product, they turn to an independent sales agent, which leads us to the next section that looks at the link between a salesperson and the price.

The sales force and pricing

Mastering the art of 'selling' value is a mantra in all sales training courses (see, for example, Darlington, 2008), and, of course, this is correct. In many businesses around the globe and in service industries in particular, the salesperson articulates the value the company has to offer. This may even be true for low price shopping goods such as laundry detergents and chewing gum. It is the manufacturer's salesperson who explains the details of the product and negotiates an optimal shelf position. The salesperson also coordinates and orchestrates the accompanying promotion of the product. And finally, many if not most products and services are sold with some personal contact. This contact may be a salesperson in a retail shop, a bank teller, an adviser, an agent or other people involved in these transactions. Many of these people would not even consider themselves as 'selling' something.

In summary, the salesperson (or contact person) is a central element of company communication in many industries and around the globe. Some years ago, it was characterized as the 'most important element in marketing communications' (Weitz, 1978) and recently extended to all personnel involved in a relationship with a customer (Calonius, 2006; Grönroos, 2006). It is difficult, however, to actually study those interactions. Every transaction is unique and involves two individuals in a specific environment and many confounding factors. For research purposes, it is hard to identify success factors and make recommendations for managerial practice. This is apparent when we study the top sales literature (Leigh et al., 2001). Not surprisingly therefore, we find little scientific literature using terms related to 'personal selling' and 'pricing'. There are, however, numerous articles in the trade press addressing these issues and they are written for a management audience. Almost universally, these texts emphasize two aspects:

1. The importance of the salesperson in framing and communicating value.
2. The degree of delegating pricing decisions to either a centralized body (often the marketing department) or delegating it to the decentralized sales force.

There is a general mistrust of some salespeople and a fear that they destroy profitability. This mistrust may be justified for some but not for all salespeople.

Let us return to the 'selling value' issue. Specifically, this means that one salesperson is better than another in framing and communicating the value of a product. Intuitively, this makes sense. The message 'This lipstick best suits your colouring' will be perceived completely differently if it comes from the charming, beautiful salesperson than when it comes from the older, more experienced seller. Since this is an underresearched topic in relation to price/value, only one of the pressing challenges will be discussed: the 'free-riding problem'. (For further research into salesperson–customer interactions, see Ambady et al., 2006; Hari and Stros, 2007; Ambady and Skowronski, 2008.)

Free riding occurs when providing advice to consumers can be separated from the actual sale of the product or service. This happens when a customer wants to shop for an expensive product – say, a refrigerator – and seeks advice in one shop but finally buys it in the deep discount store or even over the internet. The first shop incurs all the costs of giving advice. The salesperson spends time and effort helping the customer by listening to the specific situation, carefully demonstrating or even letting them try out different products, and finally recommending and offering the product that best fits the customer's needs. A similar but more complicated case occurs when a customer consults an insurance sales agent and then buys the insurance from a different, cheaper internet retailer. This problem has been studied by Shin (2007). Free riding should hurt the retailer that provides the consulting service, according to common wisdom. Using an analytical model, Shin demonstrates that free riding benefits not only the free-riding retailer, but also the shop that provides this free service. This holds true for two reasons:

1. Customers are heterogeneous in terms of their opportunity costs for shopping. They may not give their custom to a different store or they may feel loyal to the consulting retailer.
2. Free riding prevents an aggressive response from another retailer and, importantly in this context, reduces the intensity of price competition.

Shin's study underlines and confirms the intuitive experience of managers. During the late 1990s, with the advent of selling over the internet, many measures were taken to prevent free riding, for example through exclusive distribution systems or charging certain fees. This has, to a large extent, been abandoned and the value of personal contact is once more emphasized. Customers will self-select the price format that fits them and it is hard for a company to prevent this. Only in the travel industry are fees still being charged for booking commodity products. For managerial practice, this means that frontline people do add value to a product, service or transaction. Free riding and bargain shopping may actually be beneficial, since they steer the discussion away from price towards a deeper discussion on value.

One of the key elements in this discussion is the analysis. Managers often get it wrong and end up making incorrect decisions. During introductory courses, students learn that there are three elements to be considered when setting a price:

1. A customer's willingness to pay for value
2. The prices charged by competitors
3. The cost of the products.

Eugster et al. (2000) suggest grouping sales units not by organizational measures, but by their competitive pressure in the market and then comparing the units and initiating measures to align sales performance. This would leave out the cost and value element. And rightly so. Cost is a figure that should be managed without respect to actual sales prices and sales performance. It is best managed by comparing and benchmarking cost performances across units. The value element (the customer's willingness to pay) is at the heart of the sales job. In addition, attaching objective numbers to this element is very hard. As a result, the value element can also be left aside, which leaves competition. Competitive prices are actually what drive prices down. After all, consumers compare different offers and the more they can compare, the more the prices will come down. In the end, sales units in comparable competitive environments will be able to ask similar prices. Thus, the company comparison tables for sales units will actually compare apples with apples (see Eugster et al., 2000 for the full discussion and methodology).

As already mentioned, the costs of products and particularly services should be carefully considered, when it comes to pricing. There are numerous traps in the accounting of every company; examples include issues such as standardized costing or overhead cost allocations. Every reader can try to calculate the total cost of producing a hot meal at home. Several hard decisions would have to be taken, for example allocating costs for the oven, the electricity, the depreciation of furniture and so on. The cost of producing a service is almost always arbitrary. Costs can be more easily compared using the numbers and figures suggested by Perriello (2008) (with respect to sales performance). Prominent benchmarks include the number of orders per customer, the amount per order, gross profit (with caution), days of sales outstanding, the number of returns and so on. These are useful numbers to compare actual sales performance with respect to costs.

This brings us back the second purchase example of the car insurance. As already noted, a customer will probably have little knowledge of the available options in terms of pricing. The customer will probably also use the heuristic rule of the price–quality link. In this situation they will form a price tolerance range and select the products accordingly. Customer satisfaction, the evoked set, switching barriers and involvement then moderate this price range (Herrmann et al., 2004). In a personal selling situation, this means that the salesperson needs to find out the involvement of the customer, the history of the customer in terms of satisfaction with car insurance and potential switching costs (for example existing contracts). These parameters are external and cannot be changed during a sales encounter. Rather, they will determine the pace of the sales conversation. In a low-involvement situation, the discussion will be straightforward, but more elaborate and detailed in a high-involvement situation.

Again we can combine poor price knowledge with the price–quality cues. The salesperson should now offer three alternatives, with a high, a middle and a low price tag. The customer will see a low price offer as having lower quality and the high price products having excellent quality, with the rest in the middle. An average customer will not sign the cheap or the expensive contract, but rather picks the middle one. A smart salesperson would want to offer an alternative that is at the high end of the price tolerance range of the customer.

Global challenges

Nowadays many companies are internationally oriented and may even operate on a global level. Switzerland is probably a good example of this. Large corporations like Novartis and Roche operate on a global scale and many small and medium-sized companies produce in Switzerland and maybe one additional country and export into the world markets. They are international companies. There are two main concerns for these companies (not only in Switzerland):

1. Country borders offer the opportunity to differentiate prices and, by doing so, reap additional profits.
2. Depending on the legal situation this may provoke parallel imports and/or price comparisons across countries and subsequent pressure to adjust prices.

In recent decades, companies have shifted from the mass marketing of products to the more targeted (market segments) and even individualized (segment-of-one strategy) offering of products and services. The element of the marketing mix that is often neglected in this surge towards designing targeted offerings is the price. Companies acknowledge that different customers place different values on a product, but few actually charge customers individual prices (Simon and Butscher, 2001). This all means that, on the one hand, there should be uniform prices to avoid legal and political action and to avoid parallel imports. On the other hand, there should be individual prices for almost all subsegments of the market. In this chapter the reader will find suggestions on how to deal with this issue.

Global pricing is particularly difficult for companies operating in many countries (Backhaus et al., 2007). Global operations offer many advantages in order to optimize taxes, production and allocation of goods to different markets (Kazaz et al., 2005). All these complications should be acknowledged and there may be many more. In complex situations, a simple solution is often superior to a complex one. The rule proposed above of offering a three-tier structure of products and prices to the market will be applied here as well. From the perspective of the global headquarters, the product and price positioning should be strategically determined and the local organization will either implement the whole strategy or only parts of it, depending on the local competitive environment. A few arguments will support this strategy.

In general, for the European market, research offers mixed conclusions in terms of the presence/absence of cross-country segments, the number, the size and composition of such segments, and the relative importance of various marketing mix elements in describing these (Lemmens et al., 2007). In their study on consumer confidence data, Lemmens et al. find complex varieties in segments. In their summary, they conclude that there is limited potential for pan-European segments. Rather a common European positioning should be found and implemented locally. This means adapting to local market segments, particularly in terms of the pricing element and price promotions. A similar conclusion was reached in Greece (Avlonitis and Indounas, 2007).

The research on price knowledge also provides interesting insights for global pricing. Such studies have been conducted in many contexts and countries (Aalto-Setälä and Raijas, 2003; Müller, 2005; Estelami, 2005, 2008), and almost uniformly show poor price knowledge. A variety of pricing strategies and tactics could therefore be implemented in local markets, as long as the strategy of three-tier product/price positioning is implemented. This three-tier offer is the recommended strategy.

Other observations also lead to the conclusion of local implementation. Revenue management is a commonly observed practice in the US and therefore accepted by US customers. The findings of a recent study show that differences across countries with respect to perceived fairness of such pricing practices is large (Choi and Mattila, 2006). The authors advise caution in implementing such practices across countries. This again calls for a local adaptation of price setting.

Issues for further discussion

1. How can managers act in a situation where customers use the price–quality link ?
2. The relationship between a company representative and a customer acts as a strong moderator of price/value perception. How could this be researched in more depth?
3. What are the managerial implications of the three-tier structure of a choice (in the 'structured preferences' case)?

4. Market research for innovative products and innovative services in particular is challenging. How can customer needs and the corresponding willingness be explored?

ABC Insurance

The medium-sized company ABC Insurance offers a comprehensive range of health insurance
policies for the Swiss market. Being a leader in innovation is an important cornerstone of ABC
Insurance. Its innovation process constantly produces an array of testable and innovative ideas.
Identification of market acceptance and particularly the extent of potential market demand has
proved to be a hurdle in the past. In the health insurance market, this is of particular concern for
two reasons:

1. The process of launching a new service in the market requires approval from a government
   agency.
2. Once a product is on the market, it can only be withdrawn when there are no customers left
   subscribing to the policy.

Both reasons increase the costs for developing the service and also increase the risks. Market
research may therefore offer some help in all four marketing mix variables – product, price,
promotion and place.

For innovative services, the market research institute suggested the focus group format. The
service selected in this case was an insurance product targeted at consumers aged 55 and over.
The insurance company and the research institute were disappointed to recognize, again, that
the focus group results did not match actual consumer behaviour. As a consequence, a deeper
analysis of the experiences with market research for innovative services was launched. Some of
the results are reported here, with a particular emphasis on pricing issues.

The first issue for any focus group interview is the recruiting of participants. On the one hand,
they should be experts in the field, and on the other hand, they should be representative of the
target audience. For some experienced institutes, non-probability sampling offers a way out of
this dilemma. Product and insurance knowledge turned out to be a key aspect of the focus group
procedure. Most consumers acknowledge the importance of health insurance and also recognize
that health insurance is an important expense for them (third only to housing and the private
car). However, most consumers have little knowledge about the disease states they are insuring
themselves against (although consumers perceive themselves as knowledgeable, after all it
concerns their own needs). This is understandable: it is not easy to picture oneself at some time
in the future with a need for a product in the area of nursing homes. The group moderator has
to go a step further and has to describe particular nursing home attributes. Answering these
questions is a formidable challenge for most consumers. Lacking a reasonable answer, they will
want to compare prices for related products. Consumers are thus implying a price–quality relationship, and they are trying to establish some sort of constructed preference in comparison to
related or comparable products.

For a focus group moderator, it is relatively easy to argue the 'constructed preference' issue.
Since the new product is usually an innovation in its field, there are very few products on the
market for comparison, and customers understand this. However, the price issue is much more
difficult to deal with for several reasons. In a normal innovation process, price setting comes only
after having defined the attributes of a new service (except for target costing). As a result, price
should be kept out of the discussion, if possible. For an insurance product, the additional chal-

lenge is that the attributes of the service and the corresponding costs (risk for the insurance company) are tightly linked together. This means that the attributes need to be established first before the calculation of the appropriate risk premium. This leads to a circular discussion or one that skirts around the heart of the problem. In the end, the insurance company, the market research institute and even the customers are disappointed by the results.

Market research for innovative products and innovative services in particular presents a serious managerial challenge for most companies. The scientific literature offers only limited help in this respect. (For further discussion, see Van Kleef et al., 2005; Olsen and Sallis, 2006.)

Questions

1. How can ABC Insurance structure its communications to the market, given the complexity of the service and the low involvement of customers?
2. How should the sales force be trained?
3. Suppose you want to introduce one of ABC's products in another country (maybe your own). What type of market research would you do?

References

Aalto-Setälä, V. and Raijas, A. (2003) 'Actual market prices and consumer price knowledge'. *Journal of Product & Brand Management*, 12(3): 180–92.

Ambady, N. and Skowronski, J.J. (eds) (2008) *First Impressions*. New York: Guilford Press.

Ambady, N., Krabbenhoft, M.A. and Hogan, D. (2006) 'The 30-sec sale: Using thin-slice judgments to evaluate sales effectiveness'. *Journal of Consumer Psychology*, 16: 4–13.

Ariely, D. (2008) *Predictably Irrational: The Hidden Forces that Shape Our Decisions*. New York: HarperCollins.

Avlonitis, G.J. and Indounas, K.A. (2007) 'An empirical examination of the pricing policies and their antecedents in the services sector'. *European Journal of Marketing*, 41: 740–64.

Backhaus, K., Eschweiler, M. and Goette, D. (2007) 'Measuring tendency toward international product arbitrage: Are there differences between high and low value products?' *International Management Review*, 3: 99–106.

Bearden, W.O., Carlson, J.P. and Hardesty, D.M. (2003) 'Using invoice price information to frame advertised offers'. *Journal of Business Research*, 56: 355–66.

Berry, L.L. and Yadav, M.S. (1996) 'Capture and communicate value in the pricing of services'. *Sloan Management Review*, 37: 57–67.

Calonius, H. (2006) 'Contemporary research in marketing: A market behaviour framework'. *Marketing Theory*, 6: 419–28.

Choi, S. and Mattila, A.S. (2006) 'An empirical examination of the pricing policies and their antecedents in the services sector'. *Cornell Hotel and Restaurant Administration Quarterly*, 47: 27–35.

Darlington, H. (2008) 'Mastering the art of "selling" value'. *Supply House Times*, 51: 94–5.

Dickson, P. and Sawyer, A. (1990) 'The price knowledge and search of supermarket shoppers'. *Journal of Marketing*, 54: 42–53.

Estelami, H. (2005) 'A cross-category examination of consumer price awareness in financial and non-financial services'. *Journal of Financial Services Marketing*, 10: 125–39.

Estelami, H. (2008) 'Consumer use of the price-quality cue in financial services'. *Journal of Product & Brand Management*, 17: 197–208.

Eugster, C.C., Kakkar, J.N. and Roegner, E.V. (2000) 'Bringing discipline to pricing'. *McKinsey Quarterly*, 14(1): 132–9.

Gourville, J. and Soman, D. (2002) 'Pricing and the psychology of consumption'. *Harvard Business Review*, 80(9): 91–6.

Grönroos, C. (2006) 'On defining marketing: finding a new roadmap for marketing'. *Marketing Theory*, 6: 395–417.

Hari, J. and Stros, M. (2007) The 30-second sale: Snap impressions of a retail sales person influence consumers decision making. EUKO conference proceedings, Salzburg.

Hari, J., Karathanasis, N. and Burri, S. (2008) 'Price sensitivity for green power in electricity markets: Results from a conjoint analysis and a representative survey in Switzerland', in S. Rothenberger and F. Siems (eds) *Pricing Perspectives*. Basingstoke: Palgrave Macmillan.

Herrmann, A., Huber, F., Sivakumar, K. and Wricke, M. (2004) 'An empirical analysis of the determinants of price tolerance'. *Psychology and Marketing*, 21: 533–51.

Kazaz, B., Dada, M. and Moskowitz, H. (2005) 'Global production planning under exchange-rate uncertainty'. *Management Science*, 51: 1101–19.

Laury, S.K. and McInnes, M.M. (2003) 'The impact of insurance prices on decision making biases: An experimental analysis'. *Journal of Risk and Insurance*, 70: 219–33.

Leigh, T.W., Pullins, E.B. and Comer, L.B. (2001) 'The top ten sales articles of the 20th century'. *Journal of Personal Selling and Sales Management*, 21: 217–27.

Lemmens, A., Croux, C. and Dekimps, M.G. (2007) 'Consumer confidence in Europe: United in diversity?' *International Journal of Research in Marketing*, 24: 113–27.

Müller, H. (2005) 'Statische und dynamische Messung des Preisempfindens'. *Marketing ZFP*, 27: 185–96.

Olsen, N.V. and Sallis, J. (2006) 'Market scanning for new service development'. *European Journal of Marketing*, 40: 466–84.

Perriello, B. (2008) 'Is the price right?' *Industrial Distribution*, 97: 31–5.

Plassmann, H., O'Doherty, J., Shiv, B. and Rangel, A. (2008) 'Marketing actions can modulate neural representations of experienced pleasantness'. *Proceedings of the National Academy of Sciences of the United States of America*, 105(3): 1050–4.

Rao, A.R. (2005) 'The quality of price as a quality cue'. *Journal of Marketing Research*, 42: 401–4.

Rao, A.R. and Monroe, K.B. (1988) 'The moderating effect of prior knowledge on cue utilization in product evaluations'. *Journal of Consumer Research*, 15: 252–64.

Rao, A.R. and Sieben, W.A. (1992) 'The effect of prior knowledge on price acceptability and the type of information examined'. *Journal of Consumer Research*, 26: 351–7.

Rothenberger, S., Grewal, D. and Iyer, G. (2008) Exploring the role of information and trust in price fairness judgments, in S. Rothenberger and F. Siems (eds) *Pricing Perspectives*. Basingstoke: Palgrave Macmillan.

Salvador, C., Rebolloso, E., Fernandez-Ramirez, B. and Canton, M. (2007) 'Service price components and their relationship with customer satisfaction'. *Journal of Revenue and Pricing Management*, 6: 40–50.

Shapira, Z. and Venezia, I. (2008) 'On the preference for full-coverage policies: Why do people buy too much insurance?' *Journal of Economic Policy*, 29: 747–61

Shin, J. (2007) 'How does free riding on customer service affect competition?' *Marketing Science*, 26: 488–505.

Shiv, B., Carmon, Z. and Ariely, D. (2005) 'Placebo effects of marketing actions: Consumers may get what they pay for'. *Journal of Marketing Research*, 42: 383–93.

Simon, H. and Butscher, S.A. (2001) 'Individualised pricing: Boosting profitability with the higher art of power pricing'. *European Management Journal*, 19: 109–14.

Simon, H., Butscher, S.A. and Sebastian, K.H. (2003) 'Better pricing processes for higher profits'. *Business Strategy Review*, 14: 63–8.

Van Dijk, M., Pomp, M., Douven, R. et al. (2008) 'Consumer price sensitivity in Dutch health insurance'. *International Journal of Health Care Finance and Economics*, 8: 224–44.

Van Kleef, E., Van Trijp, H.C. and Luning, P. (2005) 'Consumer research in the early stages of new product development: A critical review of methods and techniques'. *Food Quality and Preference*, 16: 181–201.

Völckner, F. (2008) 'The dual role of price: Decomposing consumers' reactions to price'. *Journal of Academy of Marketing Science*, 36: 359–77.

Völckner, F. and Hofmann, J. (2007) 'The price-perceived quality relationship: A meta-analytic review and assessment of its determinants'. *Marketing Letters*, 18: 181–96.

Weitz, B.A. (1978) 'Relationship between salesperson performance and understanding of customer decision making'. *Journal of Marketing Research,* 15: 501–16.

5

Managing brands with retailers: an international perspective

Mark S. Glynn

Learning outcomes

At the end of this chapter, readers should be able to:

1. Outline the sources of manufacturer brand value for retailers.

2. Specify the key long-term relationship outcomes important to retailers when considering manufacturer brands.

3. Explain how these sources of manufacturer brand value affect retailer relationship outcomes.

4. Evaluate how brand strength and the importance of the product category can affect retailer relationship outcomes.

Key points

- The value of manufacturer brands to retailers is not well understood as practitioners and academics have tended to use consumer brand perspectives to analyse retail brand buying.

- Manufacturers and retailers both use brands to target the end customer creating marketplace equity.

- An alternative brand perspective where brands are market-based assets of value to manufacturers in external relationships is more useful when considering the value of brands to retailers.

- A study in New Zealand identifies several sources of brand value for retailers including brand equity.

- These sources of brand value also affect aspects of long-term manufacturer–retailer relationships where the brand is the focus.

- Manufacturer–retailer relationships can also be influenced by brand strength and the importance of the product category.
- Retailers show the satisfaction, performance and commitment to the brand but attribute trust, cooperation and dependence to the manufacturer on matters concerning the brand.

Introduction

Little is known about how brands create value in manufacturer–retailer relationships. This chapter reports the findings of a New Zealand study investigating the role of brands in such relationships. The results show that manufacturer brands offer retailers several benefits, including the brand name, which affect retailer relationship outcomes.

This chapter discusses the role of brands in channel relationships. The sources of brand value are identified, followed by a discussion of the linkages between these sources and retailer relationships. The results show that manufacturers' brands have several sources of value that impact on relationship outcomes, such as satisfaction, performance, commitment, trust, dependence and cooperation as perceived by the retailer. To optimize the value of the manufacturer's brand from the business relationship, both manufacturers and retailers need to manage these sources of brand value. Although major brands offer value to retailers, minor brands can also be beneficial. In this chapter, a series of research propositions is presented that shows the impact of the sources of brand value within such relationships. The chapter begins by reviewing the theoretical background and existing literature, the research method and key findings are then discussed, and finally research propositions are developed.

Background

In the past decade, building strong manufacturer brands has become more difficult due to increased brand competition, the prevalence of retailer price promotions and changes in channel power in favour of the retailer. Thus the 'trade leverage' that strong brands give the manufacturer (Aaker, 1991) when dealing with retailers is being eroded (Shocker et al., 1994). However, countering this perception is an increased recognition by manufacturers of the strategic value of their brands. At the same time, manufacturers recognize the value of retailers to their overall business and through their key account managers build strong channel relationships that overcome conflict and lead to cooperation (Anderson and Narus, 1999).

The risk is that a poorly managed manufacturer–retailer relationship can undermine the value of the manufacturer's brand. As an example, a major US drinks brand 'Snapple' lost market share and sales because the company rationalized the distribution of that brand. This rationalization upset relationships with key Snapple distributors (Deighton, 2002). Part of the recovery plan for Snapple involved repairing these distributor relationships as well as addressing consumer concerns with the brand. Given the long-term strategic importance of branding and the necessity of having strong channel relationships, the question we need to ask is: What is the role of branding in creating and maintaining value for channel members?

Value creation provides direct benefits, which influence the performance of the relationship, and indirect benefits, which do not influence performance directly but may have importance at a later date (Walter et al., 2001). While brand theory examines the role of brands in building customer relationships (Keller, 1993), it is only recently that the value of brands for channel members has been considered (Webster, 2000). Furthermore, while brand theory explains how consumer brand equity is built, this consumer perspective is less useful in the retail buying context. In retail buying, brand purchase decisions are made by fewer buyers, who are often constrained by company policy and purchase directly from many manufacturers.

Anderson and Narus (1999) provide a useful starting point to conceptualize the role of brands in channels. They coined the following terms:

- *marketplace equity*, that is, the sum of brand equity from end customers, the customer–brand link
- *channel equity*, the business-to-business (B2B) link between manufacturer and retailer
- *reseller equity*, the link from the retailer to the end customer.

Thus a manufacturer's brand can be an important source of differentiation and an asset that provides the manufacturer with a competitive position within the channel (Porter, 1974). Brands are examples of market-based assets that firms can use to strengthen customer relationships (Srivastava et al., 1998). Research highlights the importance and complexities of consumer–brand relationships (Fournier, 1998). This complexity is also evident in B2B purchasing of brands where intense competition and price pressures are also increasing (Kotler et al., 2006). However, as noted by Brodie et al. (2002), a major limitation of these research traditions is the lack of explicit attention given to the role of brands in B2B relationships. Underlying these concepts about marketplace equity and market-based assets is the resource-based view (RBV) of the firm (Srivastava et al., 1998). The RBV provides a useful perspective for understanding how brands and other market-based assets create and maintain value within a channel.

The role of manufacturers' brands within channels of distribution has not been well articulated. Rao and McLaughlin (1989) examine product attributes such as uniqueness as it affects retailer buyer attitudes towards purchase decisions. While product uniqueness is important for brand differentiation, such a measure by itself does not reflect brand equity in total (Keller, 1993). However, some channel studies do include brand measures. For instance, Collins-Dodd and Louviere (1999) show that a manufacturer's brand equity does not influence retailer decisions on store advertising and promotions. In contrast, Verbeke et al. (2006) state that brand strength does influence retailer decisions such as shelf allocation and in-store promotional support. Baldauf et al. (2003) also found that brand measures such as awareness could influence retailers' perception of brand market performance and value for customers. For the most part, these research findings on the effects of manufacturer brands in channels are contradictory. Furthermore, these studies do not consider how brands should be managed over the longer term within manufacturer–retailer relationships.

Traditionally, relationships between retailers and manufacturers have been seen as adversarial (Gaski, 1984). Furthermore, manufacturers can use alternative channels to traditional retailers, and retailers themselves can develop private labels to compete alongside manufacturer brands. Taken together, both these strategies can negatively affect manufacturer–retail relationships (Frazier and Antia, 1995). Marketing channels research has moved away from examining power and conflict to focus on the relational constructs that hold channel relationships together (Weitz and Jap, 1995). This research stream has shown the value to channel partners in adopting a relational perspective (Boyle et al., 1992) but does not usually address manufacturer brands in the discussion. However, in the broader B2B marketing context, researchers have examined the role of brands and these studies are discussed next.

Hutton (1997) found that B2B brand buyers were more willing to pay a price premium. Firth (1993) showed that the users of professional accounting services were also willing to pay a price premium to use an accounting firm with a well-known name and reputation. Mudambi et al. (1997) highlighted the importance of intangible attributes in industrial purchasing where differentiation is difficult to maintain. Michell et al. (2001) showed that the key benefits of industrial brand equity were greater confidence in the purchase decision, an enhanced reputation of the purchasing company, a competitive advantage for the buying organization, and increased corporate credibility. Research into B2B branding initially examined the benefits of branding for sellers but now has a wider focus, which includes brands as relationship builders (de Chernatony and McDonald, 1998).

However, there are some important differences between industrial B2B buying and retail buying. In the B2B research stream, the focus has also been on a single brand in the purchase decision, whereas retail buyers purchase multiple brands across many categories and then resell these brands to customers (Nevin, 1995). Therefore, retail channel relationships can often be more complex.

Brands are viewed as a source of noncoercive power for manufacturers when dealing with retailers (Boyle et al., 1992). This view reflects a transactional exchange perspective, based on short-term, one-off purchase decisions rather than a more long-term view of business relationships. These views do not take into account the range of emerging perspectives of branding, including brands as:

- market-based assets
- business relationship builders
- important in developing customer brand knowledge.

In order to clarify the role of manufacturer brands within channel relationships, this chapter focuses on three broad research questions:

1. What are the sources of brand value within manufacturer–retailer relationships?
2. When considering manufacturer brands, what aspects of business relationships are important for retailers?
3. How do these sources of brand value influence key retailer relational outcomes?

Method

In-depth interviewing was used to understand the role of the brand within retailer relationships within the channel. This interviewing technique allows the importance of branding to be explored from the retail buyer perspective. Moreover, the relevant constructs and linkages between these constructs can be identified, leading to the development of research propositions. Semi-structured approach interviews were conducted using an interview protocol. This interview protocol consisted of predetermined open-ended questions, which allowed the interviewer to probe and clarify issues raised during the interview. Sixteen interviews were conducted, representing eight manufacturers and eight retailers. The selection criteria were that participants in this research had to be familiar with retail operations and could comment on brand equity at the retail level for a range of frequently purchased product categories.

The key participants in this research were manufacturers and retailers selected from the retail grocery and liquor industries in New Zealand. The manufacturer participants were marketing and sales managers, while the retailer participants consisted of head office buyers and retail store managers. By interviewing participants from both sides of the buyer–seller dyad, a better understanding of the relationship issues involved at different organizational levels was obtained. The interview questions focused on issues or activities where brands were relevant to retailers. The interviews were transcribed and the transcripts were returned to participants to check transcription accuracy.

Thematic analysis was used to code the data and generate meaning. This type of analysis allows researchers 'to identify the issues in the words of the participants that they use to conceptualize relational episodes' (Zorn and Ruccio, 1998). Major themes were then developed within each research question, including key phrases and quotes based on the words of the participants. A theme had to be recurrent (frequent), occur in a least 75% of interviews, and have relevance to the research questions.

Findings

To establish the sources of brand value within manufacturer–retailer relationships, participants were asked what benefits they thought manufacturer brands had for retailers and which benefits/aspects were most important. Three major themes emerged:

- the financial benefits that manufacturer brands offered retailers
- the nonfinancial benefits to retailers (usually in the product category)
- the benefits from satisfying the retailers' customers.

Financial benefits, the first theme, reflects the profit benefit of brands to the retailer's business (Zenor, 1994). Participants considered that the main financial considerations were having a good margin, the ability to charge a price premium, and that reducing the brand's selling price could stimulate sales. However, because of competition among retailers themselves, sometimes these brands were sold below cost to attract store traffic. The rationale was that although retailers could lose money on a particular brand, it was anticipated that customers would buy other products in the store which would compensate for this loss. For manufacturers, this situation was problematic because often retailers applied more pressure for a better deal in order to compensate the retailer for this loss.

Manufacturers and retailers reported that low pricing altered consumers' price expectations so that a return to 'normal' higher prices resulted in decreased sales for the brand. 'Loss leader' pricing for some brands was considered difficult to change by retailers even though selling at lower prices increased sales volumes. On the other hand, retailers were wary of charging too much of a price premium for a brand as sales volume could be reduced. For retailers to accept a minor brand in the store range, the manufacturer of that brand needed to offer a better gross margin compared to the major brand in the category.

The second theme was the nonfinancial benefits that brands brought to a retailer's business or product category. Retailers have to balance satisfying the demands of the customer with the need to optimize profit within the category (Broniarczyk et al., 1998). Manufacturer brands allow retailers to offer variety to their customers as retailers cannot provide this themselves. However, the shelf space allocated to a category was often limited and slow-selling lines were subject to deletion. Some retailers commented that it was difficult to get slow lines 'out of the system'. As a result, retailers were often supportive of manufacturers' initiatives to increase sales of slow-selling lines. This retailer support occurred because of the need to provide better variety for their customers.

Retailer participants mentioned that major brands required less effort to sell. Manufacturers' own advertising and support for a brand were seen as essential by retailers, who commented that a brand 'rarely sells by itself'. The brand's marketing mix also had benefits in stimulating the product category overall for the retailer through new products and manufacturer brand innovations. Manufacturers also provided product assistance in the form of brand merchandising, assisting retailers with displays, product demonstrations and shelf-filling services. Despite the availability of scanning data, retailers relied on the brand manufacturer to assist them by providing market information, allowing them to keep abreast of market trends.

The size of the category was an important consideration for retailers. For instance, wine was not only a high value category, offering the retailer an above-average margin, but was also a growth category in supermarket channels. Brands in this category are often frequently featured in price promotions. Leading brands were regarded as category 'captains' or leaders (Dupre and Gruen, 2004). However, some retailers were wary of a brand being too dominant within a category, preferring to have more interbrand competition. Brand manufacturers were expected to support the retailers' promotional programme with cooperative advertising. Retailers expected the level of brand support to match a brand's market share. So the manufacturer of a brand with the highest market share was expected to spend more on retailer promotions than a minor brand.

The third theme was that brands allow retailers to meet consumer demand overall for the store as well as demand for a particular brand. Participants regularly commented on the requirement to satisfy the needs of their customers and that major brands fulfilled this role for them. While major brands were useful in attracting retail customers, minor brands had a valuable role as they provided variety in the store. Retailers often supported the minor brand in order to offer this variety in their stores. These sources of brand value themes together with definitions and sample quotes are summarized in Table 5.1.

Table 5.1	Sources of brand value themes	

Theme	Definition	Sample quote
1. Financial benefits	From selling a brand less cost	It's usually in the *gross margin*. A brand will not be included in the store range if it's only going be at number three or four. If its profitability is not 5–10% more than the number one or two brand, we have no reason to sell this product when the number one or two brands can offer us the sales instead
	A price premium is charged for the brand	They give us the opportunity to perhaps charge a *little bit more for the brand*
	Retailer sells brand by price reduction	An example of that is product P's release ... The supermarkets sold it for ... I think they're making about 2% profit. And of course, we *weren't going to drop our price to that*
2. Nonfinancial benefits	Brand enhances retailer business	Frozen foods were in decline because there was no innovation. As soon as suppliers started *innovating* and *bringing new ideas* and a *lot more support, the categories started taking off*
	Importance of retail category	Some of our smaller categories, like salsa, tomato paste or condiments, they're not going to spend much time on
	Brand manufacturer assistance to retailer operations	As merchandising is an important function of the retailing business, we need to have products in store all the time and therefore we've got *manufacturers maintaining stock levels*
	Support including brand advertising and cooperative advertising	You've got to have that *marketing support and brand awareness*, before it actually sells. It's rare that you can just put something on a shelf and expect it to sell
3. Customer brand expectations	Retailers need to satisfy customer demand with brands	If a brand happens to be successful because there is a substantial *consumer demand* for it, then we have even greater reason to stock that particular product
	References to brands and brand equity	Product J is an example, it's a household *brand that everybody knows*, it's just extended from a standard bleach to in the bowl and in the cistern toilet cleaners, so they bring all that sort of equity

The second and third research questions examine the relational outcomes and the impact of the sources of brand value within the manufacturer–retailer relationship. To address these questions, respondents described their relationships with manufacturers on matters concerning the brand. For both questions, the analysis is from the retailer perspective.

The sources of brand value identified in the first research question affected retailer satisfaction with the brand. Retailers and manufacturers referred to how well brands were performing in the retail store. Many retailers had their own internal measures as to what a brand should achieve in terms of performance for their retail stores. These measures include sales volume, sales value, product category volume, product category growth, return per square foot of shelf space, hurdle rate and return on inventory. Retailers had regular reviews with manufacturers about how manufacturers' brands were performing within the category. These reviews focused on broader business issues, particularly what manufacturers could do with their brand to enhance the retailers' market offering and performance. Thus, satisfaction and performance are important brand attributes for retailers.

The third research question considered how manufacturer brand value influences other relationship outcomes, including commitment, trust, dependence and cooperation. Retailer commitment to a brand was evident as retailers needed to be competitive with other retailers. Brand benefits, such as brand advertising, product assistance and market information, allowed retailers to better achieve their business goals. Manufacturer brands were also an important part of the retail promotional programme and retailers had made a considerable commitment to the relationship with manufacturers. Some retailers recognized the importance of brands in the category and the need to support manufacturers to achieve the optimum return. Examples of retailers' comments on how brands can affect these relationship outcomes are shown in Table 5.2.

Trust in the brand was an important outcome in the manufacturer–retailer relationship. Retailer trust of brands is influenced by the reliability of brand supply, the credibility of marketing information shared, and the expertise of the leading brand manufacturer or the 'category captain'. Retailers expected manufacturer fairness and honesty in trading terms and discounts when dealing with competing retailers. A key retailer concern was that a manufacturer may give an additional discount to a competing retailer. As a result, retailers monitored the promotional programmes of competitors to ensure that retailer pricing of manufacturer brands was within expectations. Retailers needed this reassurance that manufacturers were being honest. Consistency of brand supply was important and 'brand out of stocks' were a concern to retailers, particularly with major brands, as the retailer would then be less competitive. Retailers thought that major brand manufacturers, because of their resources and systems, would be more reliable and trustworthy than brands supplied by smaller manufacturers. Trust on matters concerning the brand was attributed to the manufacturer of the brand rather than to the brand itself. This finding differs from consumer studies on brand trust where consumers simply trusted the brand itself (Chauduri and Holbrook, 2001).

Manufacturers and retailers are interdependent within channel relationships (Hogarth-Scott and Dapiran, 1997). Manufacturers realized that retailers provide access to the end customer, while retailers were dependent on manufacturers' brands to satisfy customer demand and provide variety. Retailers needed manufacturers' brands to provide innovation and brand support to help develop the product category. Category management helps retailers manage their dependence on brand manufacturers. Retailers sought to reduce this dependence on the manufacturers of major brands, by offering minor brands and private labels. To remain competitive with other retailers and satisfy consumer demand, retailers needed to cooperate with manufac-

| Table 5.2 | Brand relationship outcomes for retailers | |

Theme	Definition	Sample quote
1. Satisfaction	Brand meets the retailers' satisfaction expectation	And we've just got another range extension to the E range with a straight Merlot. So because they know the brand has a really good name and has done extremely well, the range was established, we got a listing straightway on the strength of that
2. Performance	Brand meets the retailers' performance expectation	Because, at the end of the day, *we really work on more sales, a profitability and customer count, return on shelf space* … so it's a lot more financial than it is subjective
3. Commitment	Desire for the retailer to continue with the brand	K (brand), an up-and-coming winemaker, is *doing exceptionally well and tripling his amount of wine every year,* for a place like us we *need to be able to keep up* with that, it's very important we're able to and *we can keep pushing it*
4. Trust	Belief that one party acts in the best interest of the other	The *consistency* of their (manufacturers') processes and systems. You can have a company with a very big brand that you could never imagine ever stepping outside the bounds of a deal or giving this retailer more than that retailer, but God help them if we found out that they did
5. Dependence	The potential for interorganizational influence	So we rely heavily on the manufacturer to supply the product, to give us money to do some special prices for the customer, and be able to contribute to our advertising
6. Cooperation	Coordinated actions taken by firms to achieve mutual outcomes	H beer is doing a reasonably large promotion with the Tennis Open (event). We extended that promotion, so guaranteeing H display space in the premium area

turers to access the potential benefits that brands offer. Areas of cooperation were pricing, promotional activities and category management, including store shelf layout and category growth.

Discussion

The major findings from this study are, first, that brands offer several benefits to retailers. The findings of the first research question show that a key area where brands create value is the potential financial benefits. Previous research used brand sales volume and profitability as the retail performance measures (Lassar, 1998). This study showed that other measures are important, including category profitability, category sales volume, category sales value, stock turnover and return on inventory. Another source of brand value is the nonfinancial benefits, which include manufacturer support and category management benefits. The last source of value is the brand name itself as the retailer's customers expect the retailer to offer the brand, which is different to demand for the brand. Second, to answer the second and third research questions, these sources of brand value enhance the manufacturer–retailer relationship through performance satisfaction with the manufacturer brand. The retailer's overall satisfaction with the brand and performance of the brand in turn influences several key relationship variables.

Based on this analysis, the following propositions illustrate the effects of the sources of brand value on the retailer's relationship with the manufacturer:

P1a: The relationship value of a manufacturer brand to a retailer will be positively influenced by whether the brand has an above-average level of financial benefit

P1b: The relationship value of a manufacturer brand to a retailer will be positively influenced by whether the brand has an above-average level of nonfinancial benefit in that category

P1c: The relationship value of a manufacturer brand to a retailer will be positively influenced by whether the brand has an above-average level of consumer brand equity

The key relationship variables that emerged from the data as being important in the manufacturer–retailer relationship were satisfaction, performance, commitment, dependence, trust and cooperation. As category management is a key process in retailer performance, this research confirms an earlier study (Gruen and Shah, 2000) on the importance of relational variables such as commitment in category performance. The second set of propositions reflects the impact of the brand on the manufacturer–retailer relationship:

P2a: Brands with high levels of financial benefits, nonfinancial benefits and customer brand equity will influence retailer satisfaction, performance and commitment towards the brand

P2b: Brands with high levels of financial benefits, nonfinancial benefits and customer brand equity will influence retailer trust, cooperation and dependence on the manufacturer on matters concerning the brand

This research has also identified that both major and minor brands are important to retailers and moderate a brand's influence within the manufacturer–retailer relationship. Ogbonna and Wilkinson (1998) found that the adversarial nature of manufacturer–retailer relationships often depended on whether or not a particular manufacturer dominated a particular product category. Major brands are valuable in generating store traffic, while minor brands allow retailers to satisfy customer demands for wider variety and counterbalance the power of the major brands. Furthermore, this research reveals that the product category is also an important moderating variable. In higher value categories such as wine, branding is important, whereas brands are less important in smaller categories such as tomato paste/puree.

The third set of propositions reflects the influence of two moderating variables, brand strength and the product category, on the manufacturer–retailer relationship:

P3a: Brand strength moderates the effects of the sources of brand value on retailer relationship outcomes

P3b: The importance of the product category to the retailer moderates the effects of the sources of brand value on retailer relationships outcomes

The findings indicate that the value of manufacturer brands to retailers is multidimensional and that brand equity is only one factor that is important in channels. For retailers, the multidimensional aspects include the financial benefits attributable to the brand, nonfinancial benefits such as the level of manufacturer support, as well as the consumer brand demand aspects. This multidimensional nature of branding is also evident in industrial buying studies (Bendixen et al., 2004) and means that retail buyers also consider other aspects related to the brand and provided by the manufacturer, and not just the brand name itself. These multidimensional brand benefits affect relationship outcomes such as commitment, satisfaction and performance. Moreover, retailers evaluate commitment, satisfaction and performance of the brand itself. In contrast, retailers attribute other relationship constructs such as trust, cooperation and dependence to the manufacturer.

Conclusion

Brands with strong consumer-based brand equity bring a number of benefits to retailers reselling the manufacturer's brand. However, traditional consumer brand equity perspectives are not fully relevant to the retail buying context. A market-based assets perspective of the brand, which focuses on the value of brands in external relationships, is more relevant to retail buyers. This perspective has allowed the development of a series of propositions that link the benefits of manufacturer brands to the brand outcomes of a retailer relationship. This study also shows that brand strength and the product category are important influences. Brands offer retailers financial benefits and are supported by manufacturers with other resources, such as advertising, participation in the retailer's promotional programme and market information. Brands also attract customers to the retail outlet as well providing pre-established demand for the brand. This chapter shows that it is not just the brand name itself that is important to retailers but also the other manufacturer resources such as brand support that are linked to the brand. Retailers need to take advantage of these manufacturer resources to optimize performance satisfaction, trust, commitment, dependence and cooperation.

Issues for further discussion

1. What do you think about the manufacturer brand benefits for retailers discussed in this chapter? Can you think of any other brand benefits that may be important for retailers in your country?
2. Do you think retailers would have better business relationships with manufacturers of major brands or manufacturers of minor brands? Give your reasons.

CASE STUDY

Managing brands with retailers: an international perspective

A wine company from the Marlborough wine region of New Zealand has launched a new range consisting of three varieties: Chardonnay and Sauvignon Blanc white wines and a Pinot Noir red wine. They are available in standard 750 ml wine bottles and the wine company designed new labels to appeal to supermarket shoppers. The new wine label has a prominent sub-brand 'Cardigan's Choice' (named after a famous local racehorse), together with the wine company's corporate brand (in a smaller typeface above the sub-brand).

The reason for introducing the new range was that the company had acquired a vineyard from a firm that had gone out of business. The wine company was unsure of the quality of grapes from this new vineyard and introducing a new range was viewed as the best way of using these grapes and tapping into consumer demand for more affordable wines. However, the new range was regarded by many retailers in the wine trade as potentially damaging to the existing premium range. The company has a reputation for producing premium quality red and white wines, regularly winning awards in wine competitions for its existing range. Many consumers use the results from these awards to help them decide which wines to buy. The existing range has also been advertised extensively in local wine and food-related magazines for many years.

This new range has a lower selling price than the existing premium range and no consumer brand advertising has been planned. The Cardigan's Choice range had not been entered into any wine competitions that are judged by prominent wine critics and was therefore largely unknown to consumers. Tastings of the new range conducted with local wine journalists and reported in daily newspaper wine columns showed that all three varieties were good quality and value for money. However, the lower selling price meant that there were insufficient marketing funds to advertise the new range to consumers. The wine company hoped that the low pricing and good publicity in the press would be sufficient to encourage consumer trial of the new range.

After harvesting and bottling the first vintage from the new vineyard, the company needed to find a retail outlet for the new range. One major supermarket chain, which accounts for 30% of the New Zealand retail wine trade, decided to accept the new range in its stores. Supermarket chains in New Zealand sell wine and beer but compete with other liquor retailers who sell wine, beer and spirits. Wine sales are a growth category for supermarkets and are increasing at the expense of other wine retailers. The wine category also offers supermarkets a greater dollar value return compared to traditional grocery categories. Research conducted by the supermarket chain showed that its customers would prefer low priced local wines rather than low priced imported wines from countries like Australia and Chile.

Initial sales of this new wine range are good and the supermarket chain is happy with how many of its customers are buying the new wine range. The supermarket chain ran some special promotions selling Cardigan's Choice at a reduced price of $10.00 per bottle for the first three months to encourage shoppers to try the new range. The wine company supported this promotion by providing the chain with an extra discount for large quantities purchased. This discount compensated the retailer for the potential loss in margin per bottle because of the reduced selling price.

The new wine range had sold well over the initial three-month period; however, since the end of the promotion, the range has been sold at the higher regular price of $15.00 per bottle and sales have slowed. The wine company only provided the discount to the supermarket chain for the duration of the promotion. The supermarket purchased a large quantity of the new wine range with the discount and has some stock left over following the promotion. This remaining stock is now being sold to customers at the higher price. In contrast, sales of the wine company's premium range are still very buoyant in both the supermarket chain and other liquor outlets. These buoyant sales may be due to some favourable publicity the wine company received. A well-known international critic recently named the wine company as an outstanding Marlborough wine producer. The wine critic's comments received much publicity, with press coverage in both the local and international media.

The supermarket chain is concerned about the decrease in sales of the new range and has informed the wine company's sales manager. However, the retail wine buyer does not want to delete the range and has invited the wine company to provide some solutions that will improve sales in the retail chain. The wine company is also processing next year's vintage and is anxious to retain the support of the supermarket chain for the new range.

Questions

1. Examine the sources of brand value themes in Table 5.1. What brand benefits did the new Cardigan's Choice range offer the retailer?
2. Examine the brand relationship outcomes in Table 5.2. What retailer relationship outcomes are evident in the case study?
3. How do these brand benefits of the new wine range affect the retailer relationship outcomes in the case study?

References

Aaker, D. (1991) *Managing Brand Equity: Capitalizing on the Value of a Brand Name.* New York: Free Press.

Anderson, J. and Narus, J. (1999) *Business Market Management: Understanding, Creating and Delivering Value.* Upper Saddle River, NJ: Prentice Hall.

Baldauf, A., Cravens, K.S. and Binder, G. (2003) 'Performance consequences of brand equity management: Evidence from organizations in the value chain'. *Journal of Product and Brand Management*, 12(4): 220–36.

Bendixen, M., Bukasa, K.A. and Abratt, R. (2004) 'Brand equity in the business-to-business market'. *Industrial Marketing Management*, 33(5): 371–80.

Boyle, B., Dwyer, F., Robicheaux, R. and Simpson J. (1992) 'Influence strategies in marketing channels: Measures and use in different relationship structures'. *Journal of Marketing Research*, 29(4): 462–73.

Brodie, R., Glynn, M. and Van Durme, J. (2002) 'Towards a theory of marketplace equity: Integrating branding and relationship thinking with financial thinking'. *Marketing Theory*, 2(1): 5–28.

Broniarczyk, S., Hoyer, W. and McAlister, L. (1998) 'Consumers' perceptions of the assortment offered in a grocery category: The impact of item reduction'. *Journal of Marketing Research*, 35(2): 166–76.

Chaudhuri, A. and Holbrook, M.B. (2001) 'The chain of effects from brand trust and brand affect to brand performance: The role of brand loyalty'. *Journal of Marketing*, 65(2): 81–93.

Collins-Dodd, C. and Louviere, J.J. (1999) 'Brand equity and retailer acceptance of brand extensions'. *Journal of Retailing and Consumer Services*, 6(1): 1–13.

De Chernatony, L. and McDonald, M. (1998) *Creating Powerful Brands in Consumer, Service and Industrial Markets* (2nd edn). Oxford: Butterworth-Heinemann.

Deighton, J. (2002) 'How Snapple got its juice back'. *Harvard Business Review*, 80(1): 47–53.

Dupre, K. and Gruen, T.W. (2004) 'The use of category management practices to obtain a sustainable competitive advantage in the fast-moving-consumer-goods industry'. *Journal of Business and Industrial Marketing*, 19(7): 444–59.

Firth, M. (1993) 'Price setting and the value of a strong brand name'. *International Journal of Research in Marketing*, 10(4): 381–6.

Fournier, S. (1998) 'Consumers and their brands: Developing relationship theory in consumer research'. *Journal of Consumer Research*, 24(3): 343–73.

Frazier, G. and Antia, K. (1995) 'Exchange relationships and interfirm power in channels of distribution'. *Journal of the Academy of Marketing Science*, 23(4): 321–6.

Gaski, J. (1984) 'The theory of power and conflict in channels of distribution'. *Journal of Marketing*, 48(3): 9–29.

Gruen, T. and Shah, R. (2000) 'Determinants and outcomes of plan objectivity and implementation in category management relationships'. *Journal of Retailing*, 76(4): 483–510.

Hogarth-Scott, S. and Dapiran, G.P. (1997) 'Shifting category management relationships in the food distribution channels in the UK and Australia'. *Management Decision*, 35(4): 310–18.

Hutton, J. (1997) 'A study of brand equity in an organisational buying context'. *Journal of Product and Brand Management*, 6(6): 428–39.

Kotler, P., Pfoertsch, W. and Michi, I. (2006) *B2B Brand Management*. New York: Springer.

Keller, K. (1993) 'Conceptualising, measuring, managing customer based brand equity'. *Journal of Marketing*, 57(1): 1–22.

Lassar, W. (1998) 'Control systems in supplier-retailer relationships and their impact on brand performance'. *Journal of Retailing and Consumer Services*, 5(2): 65–75.

Michell, P., King, J. and Reast, J. (2001) 'Brand values related to industrial products'. *Industrial Marketing Management*, 30(5): 415–25.

Mudambi, S., Doyle, P. and Wong, V. (1997) 'An exploration of branding in industrial markets'. *Industrial Marketing Management*, 26: 433–46.

Nevin, J. (1995) 'Relationship marketing and distribution channels: Exploring fundamental issues'. *Journal of the Academy of Marketing Science*, 23(4): 327–34.

Ogbonna, E. and Wilkinson, B. (1998) 'Power relations in the UK grocery supply chain'. *Journal of Retailing and Consumer Services*, 5(2): 77–86.

Porter, M. (1974) 'Consumer behavior, retailer power and market performance in consumer goods industries'. *Review of Economics and Statistics*, 56(4): 419–36.

Rao, V.R. and McLaughlin, E.W. (1989) 'Modeling the decision to add new products by channel intermediaries'. *Journal of Marketing*, 53(1): 80–8.

Shocker, A., Srivastava, R. and Ruekert, R. (1994) 'Challenges and opportunities facing brand management: An introduction to the special issue'. *Journal of Marketing Research*, 31(2): 149–58.

Srivastava, R., Shervani, T. and Fahey, L. (1998) 'Market-based assets and shareholder value: A framework for analysis'. *Journal of Marketing*, 62(1): 2–18.

Verbeke, W., Bagozzi, R.P. and Farris, P. (2006) 'The role of key account programs, trust, and brand strength on resource allocation in the channel of distribution'. *European Journal of Marketing*, 40(5/6): 502–32.

Walter, A., Ritter, T. and Gemunden, H. (2001) 'Value creation in buyer-seller relation-ships: Theoretical considerations and empirical results from a supplier's perspec-tive'. *Industrial Marketing Management*, 30(4): 365–77.

Webster, F. (2000) 'Understanding the relationships among brands, consumers, and resellers'. *Journal of the Academy of Marketing Science*, 28(1): 17–23.

Weitz, B. and Jap, S. (1995) 'Relationship marketing and distribution channels'. *Journal of the Academy of Marketing Science*, 23(4): 305–20.

Zenor, M. (1994) 'The profit benefits of category management'. *Journal of Marketing Research*, 31(2): 202–13.

Zorn, T. and Ruccio, S. (1998) 'The use of communication to motivate sales teams'. *Journal of Business Communication*, 35(4): 468–99.

6

The concept of place in international strategic marketing decisions

Eva Kipnis and Amanda J. Broderick

Learning outcomes

At the end of this chapter, readers should be able to:

1. Understand the fundamental role of place association affects in making coherent strategic and positioning decisions.

2. Identify key categories of place, or country-of-origin, stereotypes and comprehend their behavioural affects in the context of consumption.

3. Specify the dimensions of the country-of-origin concept and understand the effects of using each of these dimensions as a positioning cue.

4. Appreciate the required advancements in the use of single and multiple place cues in brand positioning caused by the increased complexity of businesses' multinational operations and by the dynamic and dense interpenetration of multiple cultures in consumers' lives in many societies.

5. Appreciate the way place association affects can be utilized by social policy makers to promote a sense of national pride, enhance community cohesion and migrant integration, and to advance a country's competitiveness in the international marketplace.

Key points

- An understanding of consumer place associations is a salient strategic brand-building instrument; products associated with negatively perceived places/countries/cultures may be boycotted by consumers irrespective of the products' quality and functionality, while attributing a product to places/countries/cultures positively perceived by consumers enhances the product's overall competitiveness.

- The globalization of the international marketplace has led to products being designed, manufactured and assembled in multiple places, which, in turn, complicates the communication of place associations to consumers. Several dimensions of the place association concept have evolved: country of manufacture, country of design and culture of brand origin.

- Brand image cues, such as brand name, colour, sound, design, images, packaging and language, are essential in communicating place associations. Brand-building strategies may adopt multiple place cues, to strengthen place association affects in consumer product evaluations by emphasizing a product's design or manufacturing association with a country/culture favourably perceived by consumers, while maintaining a product's association with a different cultural heritage context.

- The emergence of consumer groups that maintain affective associations with multiple places/cultures necessitates academics and practitioners developing brand-building approaches that reflect relevant elements and dimensions of consumers' culture/place associations in brands' image.

- Informed use of single and/or multiple place cues has valuable advantages for companies and social policy makers. The development of brand-positioning strategies that integrate favourable place cues relevant for the target population groups assists companies with enhancing their competitive status in international markets and enables advancement of countries' image to attract investors, tourists and a skilled workforce. The use of place association cues can contribute to the development of social marketing and branding strategies that enhance the integration of ethnic minorities with mainstream society, promote community cohesion, and develop a sense of national belonging and pride.

Introduction

A command of place associations, or image characteristics assigned to particular cultures and/or geographical locations, plays a critical role in the development of competitive market strategies and brand-building decisions. If used strategically, an analysis and understanding of the positive or negative influences that a particular place has on the perception of the company, its products and actions can provide managers with a marketing tool that can deliver a competitive edge to the company's performance in a particular marketplace. On the other hand, neglecting to assess place association affects may have devastating consequences for the success of a company's particular products, and at times affect businesses' functions to such an extent they may be forced to terminate operations in certain countries or regions and incur significant losses of invested capital.

Inadequate understanding of the international marketplace can lead to business failure, product positioning mistakes and consumer misunderstanding. Keller and Moorthi (2003) drew a number of conclusions about the uneven performance of multinational brands such as Kellogg's, Levi's and McDonald's in China, Brazil, Hungary,

Poland and India. While these brands were well established in Western markets, they failed to achieve a respectable market share in the newly developing marketplaces. Keller and Moorthi (2003) concluded this was due to:

1. ineffective communication leading to image dysfunctionality
2. a poor understanding of consumer wants and buying habits and poor evaluations of the market opportunities leading to products' value dysfunctionality.

Both these dysfuctionalities may be a consequence of poor understanding of the concept of place, which, in the context of international strategic marketing decisions, not only relates to the country in which the products or brands are distributed but also to the country the product or brand represents.

All places and/or countries have certain images in people's minds and often a country may have a different image in different parts of the world. Our understanding of a particular country is based on the specific historical, political, social and econom-ical connotations of this country relevant to our personal context. Simply put, consumers use their associations with countries and places as a source of information when evaluating the product, and how good or bad people feel about a country overall may define their perception of the products or brands associated with this country. This can influence the perceptions of particular products or brands (Strutton et al., 1995; Li et al., 1997; Kaynak and Kara, 2000; Papadopoulos and Heslop, 2002). For example, consumer perceptions of French wine may be higher than perceptions of Australian wine, due to France's historical premier wine-producing image, but the more favourably people perceive Australia as a country, the better their evaluations of Australian products, including wine. Likewise, if the majority of consumers in a given country negatively stereotype a product due to the overall negative perception of the country image this product is believed to originate from, other strategic factors such as price or attractive advertising may have little effect. A recent example of the signifi-cance of country-of-origin (COO) effects on product evaluations is the disastrous effect of public scares involving different products manufactured in China on consumer perceptions of Chinese-made products, which instigated the 'made in China' campaign aimed at improving China's image as a trustworthy producer (MacLeod, 2010).

Papadopoulos and Heslop (2002, p. 295) note the importance of place association affects for companies operating in international markets, because 'unlike brand and corporate images, those of nations and other places are not directly under the marketers' control'. That is, the marketing strategies of a particular brand cannot create and control the perceptions of a country's image: consumer understanding of country meanings in a marketplace leads to products that are associated by consumers with certain countries to be either preferred or boycotted. For example, some consumers in China, while acknowledging the high quality of Japanese products, avoid purchasing them due to their historic dislike of the Japanese; some consumers in Nigeria prefer foreign products over domestic ones, irrespective of value for money in terms of quality, for status-enhancing reasons (Klein et al., 1998; Okechuku and Onyemah, 1999). Thus, marketing intelligence on consumer place associations is crucial for businesses as it forms the basis for strategic brand-positioning decisions. The following sections consider the types and the role of place associations in consumer behaviour and how single and multiple place associations, as product attributes, can be expressed through brand communications.

Country-of-origin perceptions in consumer product evaluation

Country-of-origin (COO), also known as product-country image, studies date back over 45 years. The idea that knowledge of where a product originates from may be a significant factor in consumers' acceptance of the product was first proposed by Dichter in 1962. He suggested that information about a product being 'made in' a particular geographical location plays an important role in people's evaluations and preferences of a product from a range of products that are otherwise similar in terms of quality, design and taste. The phenomenon of consumers' perceptions of their own country and other countries' images affecting consumer product evaluations due to products 'made in' associations is termed *COO stereotyping*. Country stereotypes or beliefs held by consumers about countries can be factual or inferred – they can be based on the knowledge, or lack of it, that consumers have about a country. COO stereotyping generates associations about the functionality, acceptability and desirability of a product or brand based on the country it is perceived to be 'made in' or to come from. Our assumptions on products' functionality are based on evaluations of product attributes (quality, design, level of technological advancement, taste), and COO information is used as an indicator of these attributes. In other words, we use our beliefs about a country's image to infer products' functional attributes. For instance, good quality cars are associated with Germany, good wine is associated with France, good vodka from Russia and so on. Having formed the assumptions of products' functionality, we also evaluate whether it is acceptable and/or desirable to consume and be seen to consume these products.

Consumers constantly evolve behavioural norms through life experience, directly or indirectly acquiring knowledge about the standards of behaviour accepted within societies. Beliefs about right and wrong develop through socialization – one's family upbringing, interacting with other individuals through friendship, school or work – and through the observation of societal role models, for example celebrities, fictional characters and politicians. Consumption is a large part of the behavioural norms we learn, as it allows us to visually materialize our beliefs about which norms or traditions of society we accept and follow and what our position is in relation to that society. In the context of COO, product evaluations are influenced by socially accepted norms of personal and collective integrity associated with consuming products stereotyped to originate from a particular location. Finally, countries' images have a symbolic and affective value to people and product attribute evaluations are significantly shaped by the emotional significance of certain countries for consumers (Cohen and Areni, 1991; Askegaard and Ger, 1998; Laroche et al., 2005). For example, in some developing countries, Western countries are perceived as symbols of modernity, wealth and success and Western products are often bought to convey the owner's sophistication and status, despite a quality similar to that of local products, higher price, impracticality or even lack of appropriate knowledge and means (such as electricity) to use them (Ger and Belk, 1996; Philbert and Jourdan, 1998; Batra et al., 2000). Consumption generates appearance, and products act as symbols of people's accomplishments, righteousness, status and style. Through consumption of products stereotyped to originate from a particular location or country, people express either emotional attachment to and support of, or dislike of and opposition to, a certain country or countries.

COO stereotypes, or biases, can influence consumers to buy products that originate from their own country (local products) or from other countries (nonlocal products) (Okechuku and Onyemah, 1999; Batra et al., 2000). Whether negative or positive, COO biases held by consumers can be generic and/or country specific and product category specific (Shimp and Sharma, 1987; Klein et al., 1998; Batra et al., 2000). Table 6.1 presents a summary of the categories of the COO stereotypes (Verlegh and Steenkamp, 1999; Laroche et al., 2005) and provides examples of generic and specific COO effects on consumer behaviour.

COO research is not without its controversies. The significance and equivalence of COO stereotyping effects have been found to be dependent on age, education, personal background, level of consumer expertise and involvement (Shimp and Sharma, 1987; Cordell, 1992; Maheswaran, 1994; Ettenson and Klein, 2000). Consumers also tend to use COO stereotypes in different ways, with some consumers not using them at all (Heslop and Papadopoulos, 1993). Therefore, market intelligence on consumers' general and specific perceptions of country images and on the significance of place associations in the evaluation of local and nonlocal products is essential for strategic brand building in international markets. By attributing the brand with either a 'localized' or 'foreign' image, the brand can be positioned to minimize or neutralize the COO stereotyping conflict and be more appealing to consumers (Elliott and Cameron, 1994; Alden et al., 1999; Batra et al., 2000; Douglas et al.. 2001; Alashban et al., 2002; Beverland and Lindgreen, 2002; Broderick, 2007).

From country of origin to country of manufacture, country of design and country of brand origin

The globalization of the international marketplace has led to companies outsourcing their manufacturing and assembly processes, making it difficult for consumers to evaluate products and brands on the basis of the country they are made in. In the global marketplace, a single product can often be associated with a variety of countries through ownership, manufacturing and advertising. Many products are designed or developed in one country, have different elements produced in a number of different countries, are assembled in another country, and have headquarters located in yet another country. For example, in 2005, only around 50% of the total production of Sony, a brand widely associated with Japan, took place in Japan. Other Sony manufacturing bases include the USA, Canada, China and many others – in total Sony has subsidiaries and affiliates in over 35 countries (Euromonitor International, 2007). Brands from developing economies, such as Acer (Taiwan), Lenovo (China), Tata Motors (India) and GazProm (Russia), have expanded into the multinational arena and are now manufactured and marketed in many countries worldwide. The expansion of such hybrid multinational brands has prompted various perspectives on the COO concept. Generally speaking, it became difficult to maintain the definition of COO, as the country where the company that manufactures and markets the product or brand is located (Johansson et al., 1985), to describe various elements of countries' images

Table 6.1 Country of origin stereotypes and their effects

COO stereotype	Definition	Generic COO effects	Specific COO effects
Cognitive	Country of origin used as an indicator of a product's quality, taste, safety	Consumers believe that a particular country or region has high or low production and product safety standards and/or high or low levels of technological advancement and infer these characteristics to all or a group of products originating from this country or region (Bilkey and Nes 1982; Han 1989; Steenkamp 1990; Elliott and Cameron 1994)	Consumers have positive associations with a country and with a leading specialist within a product category and prefer products within this category that are associated with this country's expertise and style (Leclerc et al., 1994; Laroche et al., 2005)
Normative (or conative)	Consumer beliefs about the socially accepted norms of personal and collective integrity associated with engagement with certain countries and consumption of their products	*Consumers either:* believe in the importance of supporting their own country's economy and protecting local manufacturing and favour home country and local products, while avoiding nonlocal products (Shimp and Sharma, 1987; Han, 1988; Balabanis and Diamantopoulos, 2004) *or:* prefer nonlocal products over local ones because of hostility towards their own society's politics or values (Mueller et al., 2009)	*Consumers either:* have strong negative perceptions of a particular foreign country and boycott its products (Klein et al. 1998) *or:* belong to a group of individuals who are strongly connected with a certain country or region (ethnic groups and diasporas), guide their lives by the norms of that country's society, and base their product choices on beliefs in the rightfulness of preserving their heritage and lifestyle (Berry 1980; Georgas et al., 1996; Snauwaert et al., 2003; Vida et al., 2008; Bhatia and Ram, 2009)
Affective	The symbolic value of a country for a consumer and the emotional significance of this value	Consumers have affective associations with countries *and either:* favour local products because of national pride and believe in their own country's uniqueness, superior status and the importance of preserving their country's authentic images and ways of life (Han 1988; Frank 1999; Balabanis et al., 2001) *or:* aspire to foreign countries or groups of foreign countries because of their superiority and advancement and prefer the nonlocal products associated with these countries' image, values and accomplishments (Thompson and Tambyah, 1999; Cannon and Yaprak, 2002; Laroche et al., 2005; Mueller et al., 2009)	Consumers have an emotional attachment to a particular country or region and favour this country's products because they want to support it or be associated with its images, values and ways of life (Berry, 1980; Penaloza, 1994; Quester and Chong, 2001; Askegaard and Bengtsson, 2005; Oberecker et al., 2008; Vida et al., 2008)

associations in consumer product evaluations. These elements have been categorized into the following designations.

Country of manufacture

The country of manufacture (COM) is the country where the final assembly of the good takes place (Samiee, 1994; Hui and Zhou, 2003; Insch and McBride, 2004; Essoussi and Merunka, 2007; Toncar, 2008). COM information is a salient determinant of product quality evaluations. Unfavourable COM associations can have damaging effects on overall consumer perceptions and can present challenges even for well-established reputable brands such as Sony (Tse and Gorn, 1993). Favourable COM associations can have stronger effects on overall product evaluations than brand names (Han and Terpstra, 1988).

Country of design

The country of design (COD) is the country where the product is designed and developed (Nebenzahl et al., 1997; Chao, 1998; Jaffé and Nebenzahl, 2006). The association of a country's competence in product design and in establishing its overall image and production standards have a significant effect on consumer product judgements (Essoussi and Merunka, 2007).

Culture of brand origin

Culture of brand origin (COBO) relates to consumer associations with the cultural origin or heritage communicated by the brand (Hulland, 1999; Lim and O'Cass, 2001). Lim and O'Cass (2001) suggest that for consumers, it is easier to identify and extract COBO associations from brand communications rather than elaborating on the COM or COD. In the modern marketplace, ownership structures constantly change – companies often acquire or sell brands, divide and sell off parts of family brands. Multinational corporations maintain complex structures of worldwide operations, where the same brand is developed and marketed in a number of markets in a standardized manner, while being manufactured by subsidiaries all over the world. For example, Procter & Gamble's manufacturing operations for such globally known brands as Ariel, Head and Shoulders, Gillette and Pampers are based in eight different regions (the USA, Canada, Mexico, Latin America, Europe, China, Africa and Australia). These complex organizational structures are difficult to clearly communicate to consumers in marketing messages and complicate the identification of COO, COM or COD evaluations for consumers. Finally, the development of global trade and media facilitates the emergence of a homogeneous global culture, with people across the world sharing unified values, beliefs and ways of life (Levitt, 1983; Alden et al., 1999, 2006; Crane, 2002; Ritzer, 2003; Zhou and Belk, 2004; Askegaard and Bengtsson, 2005). Some consumers seek brands that symbolize their belonging to the global society rather than a particular place or country (Strizhakova et al., 2008). Therefore, COBO associations (with local, particular foreign or global culture) become more relevant in the international marketplace and contribute to creating brand value (Leclerc et al., 1994; Alden et al., 1999; Steenkamp et al., 2003; Schuiling and Kapferer, 2004).

Creating place associations: an overview of brand positioning tools

How can brands create place associations relevant to the context of a particular marketplace? The most powerful tool in creating place associations is brand communications. Consumers evaluate brands by interpreting the image messages sent by brands. These messages, termed *cues*, are used by marketers to generate the unique set of associations with brands' attributes (quality, taste, values and so on). In other words, brand cues act as signals that lead consumers to develop particular associations with, and assign a particular meaning to, the brand. A simple example would be a picture of fresh oranges on a box of orange juice – the picture provides a mental shortcut for consumers to associate the brand with fresh orange juice and identify the brand's position in consumers' mental frame of products (juices). Positioning strategies create or increase consumer brand awareness, that is, the amount of brand associations retained in consumer memory, and, most importantly, contribute to consumer perceptions of brand image, that is, the uniqueness, strength and favourability of these associations (Keller, 1993).

Brand image cues include brand name, colour, sound, design, images and characters, packaging, and the language of the textual information. In the context of place associations, all these elements of brand image can be placed within a particular cultural heritage context, as they provide consumers with signals that can be interpreted into an association with a particular country or culture. The interpretation of and associations with the meaning of these cues can be different across cultures. For example, language and linguistic systems act as culture-specific cognitive and heuristic associations held by individuals in a given culture and play a significant role in determining consumers' processing of brand communications and brand name evaluations (Luna and Peracchio, 2001; Zhang and Schmitt, 2001). Language, alphabetical and lexical-semantic (related to writing systems and styles) information communicated by the brand name and messages place a brand within a specific cultural context (for example an Italian looking and sounding brand name connects the brand with Italian culture). Colours are used to express feelings and the same colour can represent different meanings for different cultures (red means beautiful in Russia, symbolizes good luck in China but is the colour of mourning in South Africa; purple is the colour of royalty in the UK and of widow's mourning in Thailand). Certain images have symbolic meanings associated with countries and places (national flags are unique for each country; images of certain landmarks such as the pyramids for Egypt or Eiffel Tower for France). Textual information (such as 'traditional Italian recipe' or 'finest Swiss chocolate') creates place-specific design or manufacture associations.

Some brands incorporate multiple cultural cues in their image. Sometimes multiple cues can emphasize brands' associations with positively perceived COBO, COD and/or COM. For example, the main message in a recent UK Honda advert, a Japanese origin brand, 'Local', (manufactured in the UK), accentuates the brand's association with the UK for consumers and may appeal to normative (caring for the needs of local society, protecting local jobs and economy) and affective (UK as homeland) COO stereotypes of UK consumers.

Multiple place cues can also be used to appeal to consumers' associations with multiple places and cultures. Studies of the impact of globalization on consumers' cultural preferences discovered that people can develop and maintain positive attitudes to both local and nonlocal places and cultures, and are willing to integrate their preferences in lifestyle and consumption preferences. For example, people integrate and interpret global culture's norms and practices in the context relevant to their own local cultures (Ritzer, 2003; Turner, 2003; Kjelgaard and Askegaard, 2006; Kjelgaard and Ostberg, 2007). People in diasporas and migrant ethnic groups integrate the practices and norms of their nation state with the cultural and consumption norms associated with the place of their ethnic origin/ancestry (Penaloza, 1994; Oswald, 1999; Benet-Martinez et al., 2002; Askegaard et al., 2005; Vida et al., 2008; Wamwara-Mbugua et al., 2008). Also, people develop an affection for a particular foreign country/culture through travel, short and long-term migration (for study or work), interaction with people from this country/culture, which may result in them adopting this culture's customs and ways of life and consuming brands that provide symbolic associations with this culture. The proliferation of multicultural consumption requires that brands are aware of the realities of consumers' cultural and place associations and incorporate relevant elements of cultures or places favoured by consumers into their image (Zhang and Schmitt, 2001; Hsieh and Lindridge, 2005). In some cases, place cues can imply an association with a country/culture to enhance consumers' positive perception of its brand image. A study by Mueller et al. (2001) terms this phenomenon *captious cues* (note that captious cues can be single and multiple). Captious cues are deceptive or misleading COO associations, for example an advert of a pizza with its brand name Ristorante and the name of the producer, Dr. Oetker. The brand name and pizza image provide a cue to Italy, which may evoke both cognitive COO stereotypes of Italy as the premier origin of pizza and the emotional affection of consumers to Italy as a place, while the brand name Dr. Oetker either conjures up the Germanic tradition of quality or its status as a multinational company whose brands are known and available in many countries around the world.

Business and social implications of the use of place associations in brand positioning

Adopting different approaches to place associations for brand positioning has its benefits for businesses and social policy makers. For businesses, the use of single or multiple place/cultural cues allows the creation of brand images that appeal to different consumer target groups by segmenting consumers on the basis of favourable or unfavourable perceptions of places and cultures. Single place/culture associations utilize favourable perceptions of a place/culture as a leader in a particular product category and/or appeal to those consumers maintaining strong beliefs in the importance of supporting their local economy and preserving local traditions and ways of life, or aspiring to be associated with either a particular foreign or global community. Using multiple place cues enables the integration of favourable perceptions of a particular place as a trusted manufacturer with the overall 'global' image of the brand to enhance a company's multinational status in consumers' view, and to appeal to those consumers who have multicultural affective preferences. Differing place association strategies in brand positioning allow multinational companies to make their global or foreign brands' image more relevant to the local context of a particular marketplace. Similarly, local brands can appeal to progressive consumers who are concerned with their country's development and advancement by integrating sophisticated 'globally relevant' elements in their image to signal compliance with the high lifestyle norms set by leading multinational brands.

From a wider social perspective, place associations can also be used strategically by policy makers to enhance the integration of new ethnic migrants into their new societies and promote multiculturalism and community cohesion, to develop a sense of national belonging and to enhance countries' competitive positioning in the international marketplace. As countries' populations all over the world become more heterogeneous, multiculturalism can be promoted by encouraging the development of products and brands that are relevant to 'multi-local' lifestyles and traditions. Showcasing a country's technological and business accomplishments in manufacturing and new product development enhances a country's overall image, thus advancing the competitiveness of that country's products and brands on international markets and instilling a sense of national pride in its people.

Conclusion

In this chapter, we have considered the effect of place, or COO stereotypes on consumer behaviour and strategic brand building with a view to increasing multicultural interpenetration within societies and multinational market operations. Both factors exemplify the need for advancing an understanding of the nature and dimensions of place-based biases held by consumers to inform managerial decisions on adopting either a single or multiple place cue approach for brand building. We outlined three major categories of place stereotypes that may be held by consumers, cognitive, conative and affective, and considered scenarios where these stereotypes lead to different consumption behaviours. We have also demonstrated that by integrating multiple place cues in brand communications, product associations can be placed within a number of (factual or implied) manufacturing, design or cultural dimensions to enhance a product's cognitive and affective appeal for consumers. Nowadays, most countries actively engage in international trade and migration flows – both products and people travel around the world and mix with varying cultural groups. As a result, consumers may develop positive (or negative) associations with multiple places or cultures, which will affect their product evaluations. The reality of the contemporary marketplace dictates that to maintain market share and competitive advantage, marketers must perfect the art of creating brands that communicate relevant place or cultural appeals to those consumer groups favouring a single culture and those associating with and favouring several cultures. Therefore an informed and comprehensive approach to using single or multiple place cues is required when developing branding strategies.

Issues for further discussion

1. Given the increased interpenetration of many cultures in societies, can cultures maintain their authentic characteristics?
2. Can brands as symbols of places or cultures have a transforming influence on the overall place associations of consumers, or is a positive place association a prerequisite for positive product evaluation? Can a consumption experience be regarded as a cultural experience?
3. Can a sense of societal unity and national pride be promoted using brand-building strategies in multicultural societies with large numbers of distinct ethnic and/or cultural groups?
4. What branding strategy recommendations for producers can be introduced by policy makers to enhance the overall country image as an advanced and trustworthy manufacturing place?
5. Did the global economic crisis of 2007–08 have an impact on consumers' place associations and place-based product evaluations?

CASE STUDY

The use of place cues in packaging for brand positioning

Brand image cues, including origin cues, can be communicated to consumers through a number of channels such as advertising, the internet, social media and packaging/labelling. Here we consider how place cues can be created through brand packaging. Packaging is one of the most important communication vehicles and plays a significant role in consumers' brand image perceptions and buying decisions (Clement, 2007; Silayoi and Speece, 2007; Rundh, 2009). It ensures communication with a wide consumer audience – consumers are almost inevitably reachable via packaging, whether while shopping or consuming what was bought by others for them (gift-giving and socializing). Often packaging is the first point of communication between the brand and the consumer. Therefore, a coherent use of packaging in combination with other brand-positioning tools enhances the success of companies' marketing efforts.

Here, we illustrate how single and multiple place cues can be used in packaging design to reflect brands' associations with places and cultures. The key categories of cues used in packaging that affect consumer perceptions are brand name, visual representation (that is, colour, images and other design elements), language (including writing styles) and textual information clearly visible on the package or label (Mueller et al., 2001; Alashban et al., 2002; Branthwaite, 2002; Zhang et al., 2003; Mikhailitchenko et al., 2009). We analysed the packaging place cues and brand-positioning approaches of the market leaders of two food product categories (chocolate and juice) in Russia. With Western markets saturating, the attractiveness of emerging markets for international companies increases. Russia is one of the largest emerging markets, with a 5.53% forecast GDP growth rate for 2011 (Datamonitor, 2008). Russia's consumer base is diverse and multiculturally aware – at least 15 ethnic groups co-reside in this country (Curtis, 1996). Since the demise of the Soviet Union, Russia has opened its borders to international trade and joined the global market economy, providing scope for foreign and global cultures to interact with Russia's population through media, trade and travel.

We selected the 10 strongest brands in chocolate and juice categories from the portfolios of companies with the largest market shares in Russia (Business Analytica, 2005, 2008; Euromonitor International, 2009a, 2009b) and conducted a critical visual analysis (Schroeder, 2006) of their pack images. Our analysis included the following categories: images and design elements of brand packaging, and language, alphabetical and lexical-semantic (writing styles) features of the brand name. When analysing brand packaging design elements, we focused on packaging form and images and distinguished between 'traditional' and 'sophisticated' design categories. In the early stages of economic growth in the 1990s, Western brands were regarded by consumers as 'glamorous', symbolizing affluence and a desire to belong to the modern global world (Cunliffe, 1995; Batra et al., 2000; De Abreu-Filho et al., 2003). When Russia opened its markets to free trade, local manufacturers produced products in similar-looking standardized packaging, for example juice was first sold in large 3-litre glass jars and later in rectangular boxes, and traditional boxes of chocolate assortments were rectangular. Sophisticated design elements of packaging (such as a prism form of the box) and added extras (such as screw-top or 'Westernized' images) enabled brands to associate themselves with Western consumption practices.

When analysing brand names, we distinguished between those in English, those in another foreign language and those in Russian. Global culture is defined as being associated with the West: the US is seen as one of the countries that contributes most to the development of global culture, with the conventional use of English as the dominant communication in the global community (Kearney, 1995; Alden et al., 2006). Therefore, brand names in English, if no other association was given on the packaging to a specific country (such as a flag, or emphasis on the product's origin, for example 'finest Belgian chocolate'), were categorized as associated with global culture. In contrast, foreign non-English and Russian brand names were categorized as those providing a cue to a particular foreign culture or local culture respectively. Also, as a considerable proportion of Russian brand name features were represented in Russian handwriting styles, we identified these names as providing a lexical-semantic association with Russian culture (Zhang et al., 2003). To contextualize companies' strategic approach to brands' positioning, we also analysed positioning concepts of focal brands as reported by brand manufacturing companies and Russian marketing and advertising agencies. Summary results are presented in Tables 6.2 and 6.3.

The case study demonstrates the use of single or multiple cultural cues in brand packaging to create a brand image integrated in different cultural contexts. Some brands are associated with a single culture (for example Russia: Dobryi, Rossiya; German: Ritter Sport); some are associated with two cultures (for example Russian and Ukrainian: Sadochok; global and Japanese: Caprice); and some integrate multiple cultural cues in their image (for example global, French and Russian: Comilfo). While earlier research on COBO-based brand positioning notes that by communicating multiple cultural identities, negative brand attitudes are created, as 'too much breadth ... may confuse consumers' (Alden et al., 1999, p. 84), the analysed brands are successful players on the Russian market. Furthermore, 10 of the analysed brands (Babaevsky, Fruktovyi Sad, Ya, Tonus, J7, SladCo, Dobryi, Moya Semya, Rossiya – Shedraya Dusha, Lyubimyi Sad) have been named by analysts among the 50 top-rated brands and the 40 strongest brands in Russia (BusinessWeek Russia, 2005). Although a number of strategic factors contribute to the success of all analysed brands, the multiplicity of cultural cues may be an important factor that creates positive brand attitudes, since some consumers may be developing multicultural belonging and are seeking to proclaim it through brand consumption.

Table 6.2   Findings of brand packaging analysis of chocolate brands in Russia

Brand name/sub-brand name	Brand/sub-brand name meaning/translation	Brand/sub-brand writing	Visual cues	Cultures represented in visual brand image	Owner company (local and global brand owner)	Company share, 2008 % retail value
Alpen Gold/ Composition	Gold of Alps/ Composition	Alpen Gold/ Composition	1. German brand name and association with Alps mountains reflected in image of mountains incorporated in the brand logo 2. Sophisticated, original packaging design 3. 'Western' sub-brand name, no language/ visual association with a particular foreign culture	Integrated cues to global/Western and foreign (German-Austrian) culture	Kraft Foods	5.4
A.Korkunov/ Morelia	First letter of name and surname of Andrei Korkunov, Russian businessman and company founder/ name of a city in Mexico (sub-brand name)	А.Коркунов/ A.Korkunov/ Morelia	1. Russian brand name (both Cyrillic and Latin alphabet writings used) 2. Packaging designed to appear 'familiar and instilling pride for preservation of wholesome traditions … and the drive to produce chocolate that is competitive on the world market' (www.super-brands.ru) 3. Spanish sub-brand name in Latin writing	Integrated cues to local (Russian), global/Western and foreign (Spanish) cultures	Mars Inc.	14.6
Rossiya – Shedraya Dusha/ Collectsiya	Russia – generous soul/Collection	Россия – щедрая душа/ Коллекция	1. Russian brand name (country name used as element of brand name) 2. This is the brand from the very heart of Russia (www.rossiashokolad.ru). It is inspired by and communicates the warmth and generosity of the Russian soul (www.boxide-clients.ru) 3. Russian sub-brand name in traditional Russian handwriting style	Local (Russian) culture	Rossiya CO OAO, owned by Nestlé SA	12.4

Brand name/sub-brand name	Brand/sub-brand name meaning/translation	Brand/sub-brand name writing	Visual cues	Cultures represented in visual brand image	Owner company (local and global brand owner)	Company share, 2008 % retail value
SladCo/Vechernii Romans	Double meaning of brand name: Slad Company and Sweet/Evening romance	СлаДКо/Вечерний романс	1. Russian brand name in traditional Russian handwriting style 2. Modern packaging design with elements of aristocratic 'empire' style. Verses of famous Russian poets, such as Pushkin, Lermontov, Esenin, and others are quoted on the pack, emphasizing adherence with traditions (www.sostav.ru) 3. Russian sub-brand name	Local (Russian) culture	SladCo OAO, owned by Orkla Group, Norway	4.7
Roshen/Zolotoye assorti	No meaning (brand name)/Gold selection	Roshen/Золотое Ассорти	1. 'Western' brand name, no language/ visual association with a particular foreign culture 2. Russian sub-brand name in Cyrillic writing 3. Brand concept: Roshen is a true Ukranian chocolate brand expanding into the Western markets	Integrated cues to global/Western and local (Russian) cultures	Roshen Kondyterskaya Korporaciya, Ukraine	1.2
Babaevsky/Originalnyi	From Babayevo (an area)/Original	Бабаевский/Оригинальный	1. Russian brand name 2. 'Soviet'-style packaging design evoking nostalgic associations with high-quality Soviet chocolate 3. Russian sub-brand name incorporating traditional Russian handwriting style of the Cyrillic capital letter 'Б'	Local (Russian) culture	Ob'yedinennye Konditery, Russia	16.1

Brand name/sub-brand name	Brand/sub-brand name meaning/translation	Brand/sub-brand name writing	Visual cues	Cultures represented in visual brand image	Owner company (local and global brand owner)	Company share, 2008 % retail value
Comilfo	Comme il faut (French) – properly, as it should be Brand name is written in Cyrillic and is spelt as it sounds in Russian	Комильфо	1. French brand name written in Cyrillic and spelt in Russian 2. Sophisticated and modern packaging design, using Belgium postcard representing association with unique technologies of Belgian chocolatiers 3. Emphasis on 'Western-style' product: visuals of sophisticated premium chocolate selection different from chocolates in traditional selection boxes for Russian consumers	Integrated cues to foreign (French and Belgian), local (Russian) and global/Western cultures	Ruzanna OJSC, owned by Nestlé SA	12.9
Ritter Sport	No meaning	Ritter Sport	1. German brand name 2. Globally standardized packaging and design	Integrated cues to foreign (German) and global/Western cultures	Ritter GmbH and Co.	0.6
Nestlé Classic	Nestlé Classic	Nestlé Classic	1. Emphasis on globally recognized brand name element (large Nestlé) in brand name with 'Western' element incorporated (Classic), no language/ visual association with a particular foreign culture 2. Message in Russian 'Сама нежность' ('Tenderness itself') in Russian handwriting style 3. Sophisticated packaging design	Integrated cues to global/Western and local (Russian) culture	Nestlé Russia OOO, Nestlé SA	3.0
Rafaello	No meaning	Rafaello	1. Italian brand name 2. Globally standardized sophisticated packaging design	Integrated cues to foreign (Italian) and global/Western cultures	Ferrero Group, Italy	3.6

Table 6.3 Summary of brand packaging analysis of juice brands in Russia

Brand name	Brand name meaning/ translation	Brand name writing	Visual cues	Cultures represented in visual brand image	Owner company (local and global brand owner)	Company share, 2008 % off-trade value
Ya	Me	Я	1. Russian brand name and brand name writing communicating an individual-centred image 2. Sophisticated packaging and design	Integrated cues to global/Western and local (Russian) cultures	Lebedyansky JSC, owned by PepsiCo. Inc.	25.4
Dobryi	Kind, good	Добрый	1. Russian brand name in an old-fashioned print style of brand name writing 2. Brand communicates a 'caring, kind and friendly Russian product' message 3. Traditional packaging and design	Local (Russian) culture	Multon ZAO, owned by Coca-Cola Hellenic Bottling Co. SA	17.9
Fruktovyi Sad	Fruit Garden	Фруктовый Сад	1. Russian brand name and Russian handwriting style of the word 'Sad' ('Garden') 2. Elements of brand package design (image of fruit tree, brand logo) communicate 'garden of childhood' message and symbolize family values 3. Traditional packaging and design	Local (Russian) culture	Lebedyansky JSC, owned by PepsiCo. Inc.	25.4
Moya Semya	My Family	Моя Семья	1. Russian brand name with elements (word 'Semya', that is, 'Family') in Russian handwriting. The name 'speaks for itself' and communicates the value of the family 2. Traditional 'local' packaging and design	Local (Russian) culture	Nidan Holding Ltd, owned by Lion Capital LLP, UK	12.8
Nico Biotime		Nico Biotime	1. 'Western' brand name, no language/visual association with a particular foreign culture 2. Brand name and elements of packaging design emphasize health benefits of the brand, that is, name association with time for living and '5-a-day' message in the bottom right-hand corner 3. Sophisticated packaging and design	Global/Western culture	Multon ZAO, owned by Coca-Cola Hellenic Bottling Co. SA	17.9
Lyubimyi Sad	Favorite Garden	Любимый Сад	1. Russian brand name in Russian handwriting style 2. Brand communicates value of caring for loved ones and friends (www.boxside-brands.ru) 3. Traditional packaging and design	Local (Russian) culture	Wimm-Bill-Dann Produkty Pitaniya OAO	12.0

Brand name	Brand name meaning/ translation	Brand name writing	Visual cues	Cultures represented in visual brand image	Owner company (local and global brand owner)	Company share, 2008 % off-trade value
J7	No meaning	J7	1. 'Western' brand name, no language/visual association with a particular foreign culture 2. Brand communicates 'premium Russian product made to Western standards' 3. Sophisticated packaging and design	Global/Western culture	Wimm-Bill-Dann Produkty Pitaniya OAO	12.0
Tonus	Vitality	Тонус	1. Russian brand name 2. Brand communicates 'health benefit from juice' 3. Sophisticated packaging	Integrated cues to global and local (Russian) cultures	Lebedyansky JSC, owned by Pepsi Co. Inc.	25.4
Da!	Yes!	Да!	1. Russian brand name in traditional Russian handwriting style 2. Traditional packaging design	Local (Russian) culture	Nidan Holding Ltd, owned by Lion Capital LLP, UK	12.8
Rich	No translation required	Rich	1. 'Western' brand name symbolizing wealth, no language/visual association with a particular foreign culture 2. Sophisticated packaging and design	Global culture	Multon ZAO, owned by Coca-Cola Hellenic Bottling Co. SA	17.9
Caprice	No translation required	Caprice	1. 'Western' brand name 2. Visual cue to Japanese culture: brand name writing and packaging design associated with Japanese origami 3. Sophisticated packaging and design	Integrated cues to global and foreign (Japanese) cultures	Nidan Holding Ltd, owned by Lion Capital LLP, UK	12.8
Sadochok[1]	Little Garden in Ukrainian	Садочок	1. Ukrainian brand name communicating a language/ geographical association with Ukraine 2. Traditional packaging and design similar to those brands positioned as local (Russian)	Integrated cues to foreign (Ukrainian) and local (Russian) cultures	Sandora LLC, jointly owned by PepsiCo. Inc. and PepsiAmericas	N/A

1. Sadochok juice was included to illustrate the positioning of other 'non-Western' foreign brands

Questions

1. Consider the names and visual cues of the brands discussed in the case study. What place stereotypes, that is, cognitive, conative and affective, do each of these brands evoke?
2. Using the brands discussed in the case study as examples, discuss how language and writing style cues can be used to create multiple place cues.
3. Identify three multinational brands and consider how these brands use cultural cues in brand communications to create 'global' COBO-based brand image. Can multinational brands from emerging markets create a 'global' image using similar branding strategies?
4. Cayla and Arnould (2008, p. 87) note increasing cultural symbolism of brands and suggest that consumers use brands as 'a specific symbolic form of talking about and seeing the world'. What symbolic values could consumers derive from brands incorporating multiple cultural cues in their image?

References

Alashban, A.A., Hayes, L.A., Zinkhan, G.M. and Balazs, A.L. (2002) 'International brand-name standardization/adaptation: Antecedents and consequences'. *Journal of International Marketing,* 10: 22–48.

Alden, D.L., Steenkamp, J.-B. and Batra, R. (1999) 'Brand positioning through advertising in Asia, North America, and Europe: The role of global consumer culture'. *Journal of Marketing,* 63(1): 75–87.

Alden, D.L., Steenkamp, J.-B. and Batra, R. (2006) 'Consumer attitudes toward marketplace globalization: Structure, antecedents and consequences'. *International Journal of Research in Marketing,* 23(3): 227–39.

Askegaard, S. and Bengtsson, A. (2005) 'When Hershey met Betty: Love, lust and co-branding'. *Journal of Product and Brand Management,* 14(5): 322–9.

Askegaard, S. and Ger, G. (1998) 'Product-country images: Towards a contextualised approach'. *European Advances in Consumer Research,* 3: 50–8.

Balabanis, G. and Diamantopoulos, A. (2004) 'Domestic country bias, country-of-origin effects, and consumer ethnocentrism: A multidimensional unfolding approach'. *Journal of the Academy of Marketing Science,* 32(1): 80–95.

Balabanis, G., Diamantopoulos, A., Mueller, R.D. and Melewar, T.C. (2001) 'The impact of nationalism, patriotism and internationalism on consumer ethnocentric tendencies'. *Journal of International Business Studies,* 32(1): 157–75.

Batra, R., Ramaswamy, V., Alden, D.L. et al. (2000) 'Effects of brand local and nonlocal origin on consumer attitudes in developing countries'. *Journal of Consumer Psychology,* 9(2): 83–95.

Benet-Martinez, V., Leu, J., Lee, F. and Morris, M.W. (2002) 'Negotiating biculturalism: Cultural frame switching in biculturals with oppositional versus compatible cultural identities'. *Journal of Cross-Cultural Psychology,* 33(5): 492–516.

Berry, J.W. (1980) 'Acculturation as varieties of adaptation', in A.M. Padilla (ed.) *Acculturation: Theory Models and Some New Findings.* Boulder, CO: Westview.

Beverland, M. and Lindgreen, A. (2002) 'Using country of origin in strategy: The importance of context and strategic action'. *Journal of Brand Management,* 10(2): 147.

Bhatia, S. and Ram, A. (2009) 'Theorizing identity in transnational and diaspora cultures: A critical approach to acculturation'. *International Journal of Intercultural Relations*, 33(2): 140–9.

Bilkey, W.J. and Nes, E. (1982) 'Country-of-origin effects on product evaluations'. *Journal of International Business Studies*, 13(1): 89–99.

Branthwaite, A. (2002) 'Investigating the power of imagery in marketing communication: Evidence-based techniques'. *Qualitative Market Research: An International Journal*, 5(3): 164–71.

Broderick, A.J. (2007) 'A cross-national study of the individual and national-cultural nomological network of consumer involvement'. *Psychology and Marketing*, 24(4): 343–74.

Business Analytica (2005) 'The survey of Russian juice market'. *Russian Food and Drinks Market Magazine*, pp. 20–3.

Business Analytica (2008) 'Review of Russian market of packed chocolate sweets'. *Russian Food and Drinks Market Magazine*, pp. 8–11.

Cannon, H.M. and Yaprak, A. (2002) 'Will the real-world citizen please stand up! The many faces of cosmopolitan consumer behavior'. *Journal of International Marketing*, 10(4): 30–52.

Cayla, J. and Arnould, E.J. (2008) 'A cultural approach to branding in the global marketplace'. *Journal of International Marketing*, 16(4): 86–112.

Chao, P. (1998) 'Impact of country-of-origin dimensions on product quality and design quality perceptions'. *Journal of Business Research*, 42(1): 1–6.

Clement, J. (2007) 'Visual influence on in-store buying decisions: An eye-track experiment on the visual influence of packaging design'. *Journal of Marketing Management*, 23(9/10): 917–28.

Cohen, J.B. and Areni, C.S. (1991) 'Affect and consumer behavior', in T.S. Robertson and H.H. Kassarjian (eds) *Handbook of Consumer Behavior*. Englewood Cliffs, NJ: Prentice Hall.

Cordell, V.V. (1992) 'Effects of consumer preferences for foreign sourced products'. *Journal of International Business Studies*, 23(2): 251–69.

Crane, D. (2002) 'Culture and globalization', in D. Crane, N. Kawashima and K. Kawasaki (eds) *Global Culture: Media, Arts, Policy and Globalization*. New York: Routledge.

Cunliffe, A. (1995) 'CIS and eastern Europe: The threat or opportunity for the western company'. *British Food Journal*, 97(6).

Curtis, G.E. (1996) *Russia: A Country Study*. Washington, DC: GPO for the Library of Congress.

Datamonitor (2008) *Russia. Country Profile*.

De Abreu Filho, G.D., Calicchio, N. and Lunardini, F. (2003) 'Brand building in emerging markets'. *McKinsey Quarterly*, (2): 6–9.

Dichter, E. (1962) 'The world customer'. *Harvard Business Review*, 40(4): 113.

Douglas, S.P., Craig, C.S. and Nijssen, E.J. (2001) 'Executive insights: Integrating branding strategy across markets: Building international brand architecture'. *Journal of International Marketing*, 9(2): 97–114.

Elliott, G.R. and Cameron, R.C. (1994) 'Consumer perception of product quality and the country-of-origin effect'. *Journal of International Marketing*, 2(2): 49–62.

Essoussi, L.H. and Merunka, D. (2007) 'Consumers' product evaluations in emerging markets: Does country of design, country of manufacture, or brand image matter?' *International Marketing Review*, 24(4): 409–26.

Ettenson, R. and Klein, J. (2000) 'Branded by the past'. *Harvard Business Review,* 78(6): 28–28.

Euromonitor International (2007) *Sony Corp in Consumer Electronics*.

Euromonitor International (2009a) *Chocolate Confectionary – Russia*, October 2009.

Euromonitor International (2009b) *Fruit/vegetable Juice – Russia*, June 2009.

Frank, D. (1999) *Buy American: The Untold Story of Economic Nationalism*. Boston, MA: Beacon Press.

Georgas, J., Berry, J.W., Shaw, A. et al. (1996) 'Acculturation of Greek family values'. *Journal of Cross-Cultural Psychology*, 27(3): 329–38.

Ger, G. and Belk, R.W. (1996) 'Cross-cultural differences in materialism'. *Journal of Economic Psychology*, 17(1): 55.

Han, C.M. (1988) 'The role of consumer patriotism in the choice of domestic versus foreign products'. *Journal of Advertising Research*, 28(3): 25.

Han, C.M. (1989) 'Country image: Halo or summary construct?' *Journal of Marketing Research*, 26(2): 222–9.

Han, C.M. and Terpstra, V. (1988) 'Country-of-origin effects for uni-national and bi-national products'. *Journal of International Business Studies*, 19(2): 235–55.

Heslop, L.A. and Papadopoulos, N. (1993) 'But who knows where or when: Reflections on the images of countries and their products', in N. Papadopoulos and L.A. Heslop (eds) *Product-Country Images: Impact and Role in International Marketing*. London: Haworth Press.

Hsieh, M.-H. and Lindridge, A. (2005) 'Universal appeals with local specifications'. *Journal of Product and Brand Management*, 14(1): 14–28.

Hui, M.K. and Zhou, L. (2003) 'Country-of-manufacture effects for known brands'. *European Journal of Marketing*, 37(1/2): 133–53.

Hulland, J.S. (1999) 'The effects of country-of-brand and brand bame on product evaluation and consideration: A cross'. *Journal of International Consumer Marketing*, 11(1): 23.

Insch, G.S. and McBride, J.B. (2004) 'The impact of country-of-origin cues on consumer perceptions of product quality: A binational test of the decomposed country-of-origin construct'. *Journal of Business Research*, 57(3): 256–65.

Jaffe, E.D. and Nebenzahl, I.D. (2006) *National Image and Competitive Advantage: The Theory and Practice of Place Branding* (2nd edn). Copenhagen: Copenhagen Business School Press.

Johansson, J.K., Douglas, S.P. and Nonaka, I. (1985) 'Assessing the impact of country of origin on product evaluations: A new methodological perspective'. *Journal of Marketing Research*, 22(4): 388–96.

Kaynak, E. and Kara, A. (2000) 'Consumer perceptions of foreign products. An analysis of product-country images and ethnocentrism'. *European Journal of Marketing*, 36(7/8): 928–49.

Kearney, M. (1995) 'The local and the global: The anthropology of globalization and transnationalism'. *Annual Review of Anthropology*, 24(1): 547–65.

Keller, K.L. (1993) 'Conceptualizing, measuring, managing customer-based brand equity'. *Journal of Marketing*, 57(1): 1–22.

Keller, K.L. and Moorthi, Y.L. (2003) 'Branding in developing markets'. *Business Horizons*, 46(3): 49–59.

Kjeldgaard, D. and Askegaard, S.R. (2006) 'The glocalization of youth culture: The global youth segment as structures of common difference'. *Journal of Consumer Research*, 33(2): 231–47.

Kjeldgaard, D. and Ostberg, J. (2007) 'Coffee grounds and the global cup: Glocal consumer culture in Scandinavia'. *Consumption, Markets and Culture*, 10(2): 175–87.

Klein, J.G., Ettenson, R. and Morris, M.D. (1998) 'The animosity model of foreign product purchase: An empirical test in the People's Republic of China'. *Journal of Marketing*, 62(1): 89–100.

Laroche, M., Papadopoulos, N., Heslop, L.A. and Mourali, M. (2005) 'The influence of country image structure on consumer evaluations of foreign products'. *International Marketing Review*, 22(1): 96–115.

Leclerc, F., Schmitt, B.H. and Dube, L. (1994) 'Foreign branding and its effects on product perceptions and attitudes'. *Journal of Marketing Research*, 31(2): 263–70.

Levitt, T. (1983) 'The globalization of markets'. *Harvard Business Review*, 61(3): 92.

Li, Z.G., Shenzhao, F. and Murray, L.W. (1997) 'Country and product images: The perceptions of consumers in the People's Republic of China. *Journal of International Consumer Marketing*, 10(1/2): 115.

Lim, K. and O'Cass, A. (2001) 'Consumer brand classifications: An assessment of culture-of-origin versus country-of-origin'. *Journal of Product and Brand Management*, 10(2): 120.

Luna, D. and Peracchio, L.A. (2001) 'Moderators of language effects in advertising to bilinguals: A psycholinguistic approach'. *Journal of Consumer Research*, 28(2): 284–95.

MacLeod, C. (2010) 'New ad campaign touts "made in China"'. *USA Today*: usatoday.com.

Maheswaran, D. (1994) 'Country of origin as a stereotype: Effects of consumer expertise and attribute strength on product evaluations'. *Journal of Consumer Research*, 21(2): 354–65.

Mikhailitchenko, A., Javalgi, R.G., Mikhailitchenko, G. and Laroche, M. (2009) 'Cross-cultural advertising communication: Visual imagery, brand familiarity, and brand recall'. *Journal of Business Research*, 62(10): 931–8.

Mueller, R.D., Broderick, A.J. and Kipnis, E. (2009) *Consumer Xenocentrism: An Alternative Explanation for Foreign Product Bias*. Charleston, SC: College and University of Charleston.

Mueller, R.D., Broderick, A.J. and Mack, R. (2001) Captious Cues: The Use of Misleading, Deceptive or Ambiguous Country-of-Origin Cues. Paper presented at the European Marketing Academy, Bergen, 8–11 May.

Nebenzahl, I.D., Jaffe, E.D. and Lampert, S.I. (1997) 'Towards a theory of country image effect on product evaluation'. *Management International Review*, 37(1): 27–49.

Oberecker, E.M., Riefler, P. and Diamantopoulos, A. (2008) 'The consumer affinity construct: Conceptualization, qualitative investigation, and research agenda'. *Journal of International Marketing*, 16(3): 23–56.

Okechuku, C. and Onyemah, V. (1999) 'Nigerian consumer attitudes toward foreign and domestic products'. *Journal of International Business Studies*, 30(3): 611–22.

Oswald, L.R. (1999) 'Culture swapping: Consumption and the ethnogenesis of middle-class Haitian immigrants'. *Journal of Consumer Research*, 25(4): 303–18.

Papadopoulos, N. and Heslop, L. (2002) 'Country equity and country branding: Problems and prospects'. *Journal of Brand Management*, 9(4/5): 294.

Penaloza, L.N. (1994) 'Atravesando fronteras/border crossings: A critical ethnographic exploration of the consumer acculturation of Mexican immigrants'. *Journal of Consumer Research*, 21(1): 32–54.

Philbert, J.-M. and Jourdan, C. (1998) 'Perishable goods: Modes of consumption in the Pacific Islands', in D. Howes (ed.) *Cross Cultural Consumption: Global Markets Local Realities*. London: Routledge.

Quester, P.G. and Chong, I. (2001) 'Validating acculturation models: The case of the Australian-Chinese consumers'. *Journal of Consumer Marketing*, 18(3): 203–18.

Ritzer, G. (2003) 'Rethinking globalization: Glocalization/grobalization and something/nothing'. *Sociological Theory*, 21(3): 193–209.

Rundh, B. (2009) 'Packaging design: Creating competitive advantage with product packaging'. *British Food Journal*, 111(9): 988–1002.

Samiee, S. (1994) 'Customer evaluation of products in a global market'. *Journal of International Business Studies*, 25(3): 579–604.

Schroeder, J.C. (2006) 'Critical visual analysis', in R.W. Belk (ed.) *Handbook of Research Methods in Qualitative Marketing Research*. Cheltenham: Edward Elgar.

Schuiling, I. and Kapferer, J.-N. (2004) 'Executive insights: Real differences between local and international brands: Strategic implications for international marketers'. *Journal of International Marketing*, 12(4): 97–112.

Shimp, T.A. and Sharma, S. (1987) 'Consumer ethnocentrism: Construction and validation of the CETSCALE'. *Journal of Marketing Research*, 24(3): 280–9.

Silayoi, P. and Speece, M. (2007) 'The importance of packaging attributes: A conjoint analysis approach'. *European Journal of Marketing*, 41(11/12): 1495–517.

Snauwaert, B., Soenens, B., Vanbeselaere, N. and Boen, F. (2003) 'When integration does not necessarily imply integration: Different conceptualizations of acculturation orientations lead to different classifications'. *Journal of Cross-Cultural Psychology*, 34(2): 231–9.

Steenkamp, J.-B. (1990) 'Conceptual model of the quality perception process'. *Journal of Business Research*, 21(4): 309–33.

Steenkamp, J.-B., Batra, R. and Alden, D.L. (2003) 'How perceived brand globalness creates brand value'. *Journal of International Business Studies*, 34(1): 53–65.

Strizhakova, Y., Coulter, R.A. and Price, L.L. (2008) 'Branded products as a passport to global citizenship: Perspectives from developed and developing countries'. *Journal of International Marketing*, 16(4): 57–85.

Strutton, D., True, S.L. and Rody, R.C. (1995) 'Russian consumer perceptions of foreign and domestic consumer goods: An analysis of country-of-origin stereotypes with implications for promotions and positioning'. *Journal of Marketing Theory and Practice*, 3(3): 76.

Thompson, C.J. and Tambyah, S.K. (1999) 'Trying to be cosmopolitan'. *Journal of Consumer Research*, 26(3): 214–41.

Toncar, M.F. (2008) 'The US consumer perceptions of imported automobiles: The challenges for emerging market country manufacturer'. *International Journal of Chinese Culture and Management*, 1(4): 439–50.

Tse, D.K. and Gorn, G.J. (1993) 'An experiment on the salience of country-or-origin in the era of global brands'. *Journal of International Marketing*, 1(1): 57–76.

Turner, B.S. (2003) 'McDonaldization: Linearity and liquidity in consumer cultures'. *The American Behavioral Scientist*, 47(2): 137–53.

Verlegh, P.W. and Steenkamp, J.-B. (1999) 'A review and meta-analysis of country-of-origin research'. *Journal of Economic Psychology*, 20(5): 521–46.

Vida, I., Dmitrovic, T. and Obadia, C. (2008) 'The role of ethnic affiliation in consumer ethnocentrism'. *European Journal of Marketing*, 42(3/4): 327–43.

Wamwara-Mbugua, L.W., Cornwell, T.B. and Boller, G. (2008) 'Triple acculturation: The role of African Americans in the consumer acculturation of Kenyan immigrants'. *Journal of Business Research*, 61(2): 83–90.

Zhang, S. and Schmitt, B.H. (2001) 'Creating local brands in multilingual international markets'. *Journal of Marketing Research*, 38(3): 313–25.

Zhang, S., Schmitt, B.H. and Haley, H. (2003) 'Language and culture: Linguistic effects on consumer behavior in international marketing research', in S.C. Jain (ed.) *Handbook of Research in International Marketing*. Cheltenham: Edward Elgar.

Zhou, N. and Belk, R.W. (2004) 'Chinese consumer readings of global and local advertising appeals'. *Journal of Advertising*, 33(3): 63–76.

7

International marketing communication as the global marketing change agent

Don E. Schultz

Learning outcomes

At the end of this chapter, readers should be able to:

1. Understand how marketing communication should and can become a primary change agent in any type of global marketing organization.

2. Recognize how the transition of information technology has given customers control of the marketplace.

3. Identify how 'push-pull' communication systems operate in a networked system and how they should be managed.

4. Develop preliminary horizontal communication structures.

Key points

- The 4Ps have now evolved to the 7Ps – including people, processes and physical evidence.
- The traditional hierarchy of effects communication model is no longer relevant in an interactive marketplace.
- Push and pull communication systems are critical for all marketers in all market-places.
- Organizations must shift from a vertical to a horizontal communication planning and execution model.

- Marketing, marketing communication and finance must be aligned and customer focused.
- Internal marketing and marketing communication must become central in the overall communication process.

Marketing communication and the 7Ps

Present-day marketing evolved from an advertising function, developed in the US in the early 20th century (Russell and Lane, 1996). As firms began to practise mass production, selling and communication, marketing was developed to sell the products they had made. Thus, the basic marketing methodology for most consumer goods companies developed along the same lines: design a product, produce it in large quantities, achieve economies of scale, offer it through a set of distribution channels and then communicate information about the product to end users via various media systems. In that sense, most marketing has not really moved far from its century-old roots.

From the 4Ps to the 7Ps

The 4Ps concept, as codified by McCarthy (1960) and proselytized by Kotler and Armstrong (1980) and others, has become the basic mantra of the modern marketing organization. As has been demonstrated in other chapters in this book, marketplace changes have required change. That change has been met through the addition of the other 3Ps … people, processes and physical evidence.

The 7Ps framework reflects the shifting focus of marketing thought, as academicians and practitioners move theory from its original manufacturing base to one in which services, people and processes or systems become key (Grönroos, 2000). This increasing emphasis on the service components of the marketing mix allows the firm to manage brands and other intangible assets, an increasingly important part of the firm's financial value.

From support to leadership: increasing the role of marketing communication

Marketing and marketing communication, as support functions to sales and operations, have not commonly been considered critical to the firm's success, or highly rated on senior management's list of priorities. Make a good product and customers will buy and continue to buy seems to be the premise. Clear evidence of the lack of importance given to marketing communication is demonstrated by senior management's common reaction to a downturn in sales or an economic problem, that is, to cut, cap or rescind brand and communication budgets and spending. This is probably the greatest challenge to marketing communication management, simply convincing senior management of the value of communication programmes.

The new global scope of networked economies and the diffusion of information technology are making a new view critical. Consumers and customers have more marketplace, product and competitive knowledge and information than ever before. Therefore, communications must move from a support to a leadership role in the organization for the firm to be competitively viable. Additionally, the emerging new economies, such as China, India, Brazil and Russia, are often leapfrogging traditional established market development models. All this is forcing management to re-evaluate the importance of marketing, promotion and particularly marketing communication in the firm. Increasingly, they are being recognized as the key drivers for the future. It is for these reasons, we argue, that marketing communication must lead organizational change and not continue to be viewed simply as a support function.

Central to this theme is that organizations operate in a dynamic and ever-changing marketplace, not the static, linear, sequential models that have been developed in the past. Promotion and marketing communication must, therefore, continuously change, adapt and evolve. Speed will be a major factor, often determining marketplace winners and losers. Unfortunately, most marketing communication models are oriented towards 'talking' and not 'responding', an issue we discuss later.

All these changes create challenges for both communications and senior firm managers who are accustomed to controlling the system by determining what messages are sent, when, through what media forms, in what volume and so on. Formerly, they managed all these resources independently, but they must now be shared with customers, channels and even the media. It is from these historical roots of total marketer control of the system to an interactive, dialogue-based marketplace of today and tomorrow that is challenging all managers, particularly those in communications.

To understand what must be done, a brief review of how the present system developed will provide a platform to move forward.

Development of outbound marketing communication

Traditionally, marketing communication has been an outbound, marketer-to-buyer system in which the marketing organization controlled most of the elements. As the marketplace has changed, so must marketing communication management.

Mass media drives the initial system

Most marketing communication concepts can be traced back to mass communication theory, which was developed in the 1930s (Schramm and Roberts, 1971). The basic concept has been one of an outbound, sender → media form → receiver model. The receiver has been assumed to be a passive recipient of the sender's information (Ray, 1982). The concept, 75 years later, is not much different, although TV has replaced radio as the dominant mass medium in most developed markets.

Building an advertising model

As mass media became the distribution system of choice in Western markets, new models were needed. Since all advertised products and services did not lend themselves to immediate consumer purchase, researchers began to develop models of how they believed 'advertising worked' in both the short and long term. Borrowing heavily from psychological models, particularly behaviourist psychology, scholars hypothesized that advertising 'worked' based on a stimulus–response approach. That is, the advertiser sent a message (stimulus) through a medium to which consumers were supposed to respond (response). This approach was modelled on the earlier psychological studies of 'conditioned response', as described by Pavlov (1927) and Skinner (1965), and based loosely on Maslow's (1943) hierarchy of human needs. Called the hierarchy of effects model, as illustrated in Figure 7.1, researchers posited that exposure to marketing communication messages moved consumers through a series of measurable 'attitudinal steps' on the way to a purchase decision.

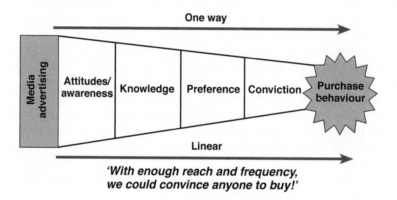

| **Figure 7.1** | Hierarchy of effects model

The model's measurement 'yardstick' was a series of attitudinal steps – awareness, knowledge, preference, conviction and, ultimately, purchase behaviour. Lavidge and Steiner (1961) and Colley (1961) developed similar advertising models in the early 1960s. Both were outbound and linear, driven by the amount of money the marketer spent in pushing out messages.

The acceptance of these hierarchy of effects models, focused on attitudinal change, has proved to be both a blessing and a curse for marketing communicators. The models have provided various media planning concepts such as 'reach', 'frequency' and even 'share of voice', which haven't changed in more than 50 years. Inherent in the models were:

- the marketer controlled the system through media investments
- messages were outbound only
- all assumed an audience willing to attend to the messages, albeit passively.

This was the 'exchange' between the seller and the buyer, that is, attention to the information and entertainment provided, which was free of charge.

Communication system drivers

With marketer message distribution to the media-assembled audiences, the system is easy to understand. The media forms, that is, TV and radio stations, newspapers, magazines and even skywriting, were all judged on the size of audience they could develop. The larger the audience, the higher the rent the medium could charge the marketer for access. Inherent in this is the belief that more eyes and ears attending to the messages are always better. Thus, relatively easy to acquire audience statistics such as demographics, geographic locations and so on have been used to differentiate between the various audiences and media forms. A focus on intramedia comparison developed, but not on the much more relevant issue of intermedia synergy. This led to efficiency of message delivery becoming the primary media evaluation tool, that is, the greatest number of eyes or ears exposed to the media form at the lowest cost is the basis of almost all media optimization models today.

What about measurement?

As alluded to earlier, most marketing communication measures have focused on measuring 'communication effects', that is, changes in consumer awareness or attitudes. While acceptable in less rigorous financial times, the marketer's inability to connect communication investments to sales returns continues to plague the field. Simply measuring the efficiency of marketing communication message distribution, or the limited ability to measure awareness or attitudinal change, continues to challenge the field. When these measures are attempted with the increasingly fragmented media audiences, it becomes clear why new marketing communication approaches and methodologies are needed.

Transitioning to consumer control

While marketing communication managers have increasingly tried to improve their traditional outbound, offline programmes, consumers seem to be rushing headlong in the other direction, to the new technologies and media forms. Thus, there is a dichotomy: consumers are embracing and expanding their use of online and digital communication systems, while advertisers seem intent on trying to protect their existing tools and techniques, such as over-the-air TV and radio, print and so on. This seems to be a missed marketplace connection. This online or offline battle is clearly one consumers will win. The communication forms they choose will ultimately prevail, not the ones marketers prefer, no matter how much money they pour into them.

The push-pull marketing communication system

The challenge is simple. Marketing communication managers must learn to use both traditional outbound, marketer-controlled 'push' systems in combination with the new, consumer-controlled 'pull' systems such as digital, search, mobile, social networks and so on. Figure 7.2 illustrates the challenges. Marketers will continue to 'push' marketing communication out (note the outbound arrow). That's their experience base and background. Elaborate internal and external systems to maintain these outbound programmes have been established, such as research firms, media planning organizations and agencies, to assist them.

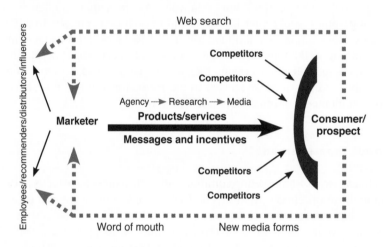

| Figure 7.2 | Push-pull marketplace |

Acting as a buffer between the marketer's outbound messages and consumers' acceptance are the screens or shields that consumers have either constructed themselves or that have been made available to them. These screens help consumers control, avoid or restrict the onslaught of marketer-initiated messages. These range from TV remote controls to 'do not call' or 'do not mail' lists to electronic systems such as TiVo.

Alternatively, from the consumer's viewpoint, new forms of inbound, online or access facilities are now available. Consumers can increasingly 'pull in' information, content, news and entertainment through various devices such as the Web, mobile devices, social networks and so on.

The external portions of the push-pull model above illustrate the three key 'pull' elements:

1. the World Wide Web and all the permutations of the internet, driven by search engines such as Google, Yahoo! and Baidu

2. quickly emerging new mobile communication forms based on various telecommunication backbones and systems
3. word of mouth, which has now become global and electronic in the form of social networks such as Facebook, MySpace and YouTube.

All give consumers more access to content and information than ever before. Most importantly, these new 'pull' communication systems enable consumers to talk among themselves, thus expanding consumer communication networks far beyond what is commercially available today.

The push-pull model shows why it's easy to argue that consumers now control the marketing communication systems. True, marketers can still dominate traditional media with messages and incentives by purchasing time or space. But with the increasing availability of communication alternatives, the impact of those outbound messages is clearly on the decline. Thus the marketer must accept the consumer's choice, not the marketer's preferences in marketing communication systems.

The future will, additionally, be driven by information diffusion and network theory.

Information diffusion and networks

A key element in how consumers have gained control of the information marketplace rests on the increasing number of available resources at continuously declining costs, in terms of both time and money. Historically, marketplace information was controlled and parcelled out by authorities such as governments, religious groups and even marketing organizations. Today, however, information is available free or almost free to anyone with an online connection. The internet and the World Wide Web are obviously key elements. There are few limits for prospective buyers to information availability on products, services, the marketing organization, retail channels and so on. Consumers have as much, or perhaps more information about the products and services they are seeking than the maker or seller. Plus, they have a major advantage – they know their own needs and requirements. This diffusion of marketplace information and thus, power, clearly favours the buyer.

Another major factor is the increased understanding and development of network theory, as posited by Watts and Strogatz (1998) and Barabasi (2002).

Historically, marketing communication has been point-to-point. Witness the great publishing houses of the print era – reporters and writers developing content with editors polishing it, gigantic presses printing the newspapers and magazines and logistical systems to get the print product to readers. Radio and TV operated the same way – from a studio, over the air to the receiving consumer. All outbound, all one way and all under the control of the media owner and the marketing organization.

The internet and the World Wide Web created new networked communication systems. Information and content don't necessarily travel from point-to-point. Systems can be connected and networked to travel to multiple points where the content can be enhanced or expanded and then sent on. What we now call *interactive communication* depends on the receiver, not just the sender. Thus networks occur among willing partners or associates. This encourages interaction and dialogue. It's this ability of the communication receiver to create various dialogues among themselves and with others that has really changed the balance of power in the communication market-place. That's the second key element in the shift of marketplace control.

Organizational challenges in push-pull communication models

As the truly integrated, push-pull communication system develops, it creates many needed changes. One of the primary ones must be organizational structure. Today, most organizations are structured in vertical functional silos, such as sales, marketing, human resources, finance and so on. All report upwards to senior management. Customers are often set off to the side to be dealt with when time and resources permit.

In a push-pull system, some type of horizontal structure is required. Customer acquisition, retention and growth thus become the primary goals of the firm, with the focus of the organization on meeting customer needs in a timely and relevant fashion. Customer focus is almost impossible for siloed organizations, since the goal of the function is always to carry out its activities in the most efficient manner possible. Thus, customers 'get in the way' of functional groups in achieving their goals.

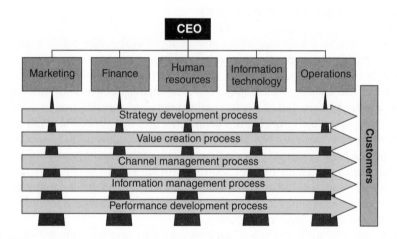

Figure 7.3   Silos with horizontal structures

As Figure 7.3 shows, customers are often outside the view of the functional silos. To resolve this issue, horizontal systems are needed. One solution is overlaying a series of customer-focused processes on the vertical silos. This emphasizes that all functional groups or silos have something to do with creating customer-focused and customer-satisfying organizations. Further, it demonstrates that marketing communication should be carried out by the entire organization, not simply a functional group.

The role of marketing and marketing communication in this structure is to bring the customer view into the firm and help the functional silos identify the role or roles they can play in finding ways to attract, encourage and maintain customers in the short and long term. This approach has proved to be effective in a number of organizations and is transformational in nature. This is illustrated in the CEMEX case at the end of the chapter.

Marketing communication as the integrating force

If, as outlined, marketing communication is to become the organization's integrating force in the push-pull marketplace, several additional changes must occur. These go far beyond the traditional role marketing communication has had in the historic outbound, push-driven communication systems.

Leading organizational change

As before, our view is that marketing communication must become the organization's 'change agent' in the push-pull marketplace. In functional structures, customers are commonly shunted to the side to free the silos to implement their programmes. To become truly customer focused, being able to communicate with and respond to customer needs, the organization must develop new skills. These range from understanding customers' needs, wants and desires, solving customer product or service problems to identifying the next level of products or services that the firm should develop to ensure ongoing customer loyalty.

A key element is the development of a customer-oriented structure in which the firm is organized around customers and customer groups, not products. This replaces the traditional, internally focused product management system and becomes the organizational lynchpin. Communications becomes the glue that holds the organization together and cements its relationships with customers and prospects. The horizontal process, shown in Figure 7.3, illustrates how the marketing communication group brings customer information into the firm and distributes it across the functional silos, while gathering customer information from the functional silos and redistributing it across the organization.

Needed: a responsive organization

The push-pull marketplace clearly requires a system that can drive messages and incentives out, but it must also be responsive to customer needs and wants. Here, responsiveness is defined broadly, ranging from answering current customers' questions and comments that arrive through the various interactive systems by continuously monitoring company website, blogs and social networks to identify and diffuse perceived customer concerns to dealing with internal and employee issues.

A key element in the future will be building internal 'customer listening' resources. Those could include formal research, inquiries to customer service or technical support, customer satisfaction studies, monitoring social networks and blogs and so on. Typically, the challenge is not a lack of resources or access but simply that the organization has no formalized way to gather, maintain and analyse the data it has.

Some of the suggestions above will require organizational management and structural changes. The problem is that, historically, marketing communication has been viewed as a support, not a leadership function. This come about because, in an outbound, push organization, the firm controlled most, if not all the communication systems. In the push-pull marketplace, this must change and new management approaches and methods are required. Marketing communication must lead, not follow.

Building financial models

The new marketing communication structures required in a push-pull marketplace also demand a new financial view of activities. Treating customers as the assets of the organization, rather than the normal view of plant, inventory, rolling stock and cash being what the firm manages, clearly changes the role of the firm's marketing communication. Only the customer creates income for the firm. All the other assets, whether tangible or intangible, are there primarily to gain, serve and maintain customers and that is the focus of the new communications group.

A new way of thinking about the role of marketing communication is that of being asset managers, that is, generating and managing the continuing flow of customer income. The role of marketing communication thus becomes one of identifying groups of customers to serve, determining their needs, assisting in aligning the organization to meet those needs, and then making sure the goods and services those customers will require are available for purchase at a profit to the organization. This moves marketing communication from being an organizational expense to managing income flows and organizational profits. In this new role, the marketing communication group becomes the conduit between the customer and the marketing firm. This new financial role for marketing communication will be one of the most difficult for existing organizations to accept and adopt because it requires a totally integrated system that combines marketing, marketing communication and finance.

The intersection of marketing communication and finance

Marketing communication and finance have traditionally been separated and often at odds with each other. Finance has viewed marketing communication as soft, often fuzzy activities because of a perceived lack of accountability, while marketing communication has viewed finance as 'bean counters', demanding measures of returns on all expenditures, whether relevant or not. Thus, a dichotomy has developed as to whether marketing communication is an 'art' or a 'science'.

In some enlightened organizations today, marketing communication and finance are being merged into one organizational group, whose primary duties are to develop and implement cost-effective, measurable marketing and communications programmes for specified customers on behalf of the entire firm. It is this merging of the 'black-and-white' or 'science' views of the financial people with the 'grey' or more 'artistic' areas of marketing communication that is critical to the future success of the organization in the push-pull marketplace. In some organizations, the chief financial officer may well become the chief marketing communication officer as well. If not, the chief financial officer should at least work hand in glove with the chief marketing officer to make sure that both soft and hard measures are identified and managed.

This radical view of marketing communication, its responsibilities, structures and activities, leads us to the final section – the next steps in this transition of marketing communication that are needed to meet the rise of the push-pull marketplace.

Next steps in the transition

If marketing communication is to truly provide the firm's future organizational focus, three traditional approaches must change.

Generalists, not more specialists

In an increasingly complex world, more generalists and not more specialists will be needed, that is, a macro- not a micro-view of the market and customers. This means being able to step back, use a customer view to identify potential alternatives and then develop and implement customer-beneficial programmes. These can't come from a limited, functional specialist view of the marketplace.

The problem is that a 'generalist' appreciation comes primarily from experience. Having tried and failed, or trying and succeeding and then replicating that success are the key elements here. This challenge exists for both academics and practitioners.

The crux of the issue is how to develop marketing theory and then implement it. Some efforts are being made in educational units to review, revise and renew their curricula. Whether these will be the right ones or not, only time will tell.

Internal training programmes must change as well. It's not enough to simply improve the manager's skill levels, that is, improve present practices. Senior management must rethink organizational training and development, which should include a much broader view of marketing communication as an organizational priority.

Global markets and global views

In an interconnected world, what happens in Seoul has an impact the next day in Munich, whether that's in new product development, the financial markets, marketing communication or even social systems. This requires marketing communication managers looking beyond their local markets and understanding the global impact and effect of their programmes. Marketing communication programmes of today and tomorrow have no localization or limits. Once launched, they soar – far beyond the local market. The local pizza maker becomes a global marketer whether they want to be or not. It's this new global, instantaneous nature of marketing communication that makes it such a critical issue for all organizations. Thus the firm must be populated with communicators who know, understand and can relate to the world as a whole, while keeping an eye on what to do locally.

Today, cultures are critical to success. What works in Dublin may be totally irrelevant, or perhaps even harmful, in Dubai. Yet communication without borders exists. This requires a different type of communicator. Culture and cultural understanding become increasingly important in all organizations. This necessitates a cadre of managers who are 'global citizens', people who quickly grasp the ramifications of the firm's actions and relate them to those groups, countries or regions where they may play well or where they may seriously harm the firm's future. The future marketing communication manager must be part sociologist, part communicator, part politician, part marketer, in short, a polymath who can lead, develop global associates and affiliates and build a group of followers who can implement the needed communications programmes.

Internal marketing grows in importance

Most of this chapter has focused on external marketing communication. Equally important are the people inside and those attached to the marketing firm, the internal audiences. The largest group is generally the firm's own employees, those people who actually deliver the organization's promises, whether through products, services, support or social programmes.

These groups are multiplying rapidly, however, as the firm outsources, takes on part-time workers, builds strategic alliances, engages external consultants and so on. These expanded groups are termed 'stakeholders' – they are part-time marketing communicators, delivering the company's brand experiences, often without formal training or development. While these stakeholders are critical to success, they're often overlooked or neglected in marketing communication plans. Since they generally aren't direct reports to the marketing group, it's often assumed they're being 'kept in the loop' by their managers. Sadly, that's not always the case. Thus there is a important role for marketing communicators through building, implementing and maintaining ongoing, relevant communication programmes with all the firm's stakeholders. This again leads to our premise: marketing communication must become the organization's change agent in the push-pull marketplace.

A technologically divided world

The place-based and mobile dichotomy that is emerging in the new markets of China, India, Korea, Finland and others raises a final question on which to end this chapter.

In our view, place-based or laptop- or desktop-delivered communications will dominate some markets. Others will develop around mobile or hand-held communication devices. Will a new communication theory be required to accommodate these new technologies, that is, is place-based communications different from mobile communications and if so, how and in what way? We started this chapter with mass communication, how it developed and has driven marketing communication for the past 90 years or so – mass circulation newspapers, then magazines, then radio, then TV and now the internet and the World Wide Web. These are all systems that assumed an interested population, willing to trade time and commercial interruption for free or almost free information and entertainment. That's really what today's push-pull marketplace is all about. The transition from push to the inclusion of pull.

Should consideration be given to a new model of customer-created content, where the audiences create not just the materials but determine how they will be distributed? That will require major changes in the way marketing communication is developed, implemented and measured. Will marketers develop these systems? Will it be the traditional middlemen such as the current media organizations? Or will it be the consumers or buyers or their agents creating the systems that bring buyers and sellers together? These questions are yet to be resolved.

Is it enough, at this point, for current marketing communication managers to simply understand the push-pull marketplace and its impact or should we be thinking beyond that?

The push-pull marketplace promises to be an interesting experience for marketing communication managers. Hopefully, this chapter has helped place the field in the proper perspective as we evolve from the 4Ps to the 7Ps and from the traditional outbound push to the new, inbound pull marketplace. The key element is, of course, change. That's why we propose that the marketing communication manager must become the agent for change in the marketing firm. If the marketing communication manager can accept and fulfil that role, the entire organization will be better served in the future.

Issues for further discussion

1. In this chapter, the argument has been made that marketing must take a more 'service-based' approach, rather than the 'manufacturing' focus that has traditionally been used. What are the planning and implementation issues that marketing and marketing communication managers face in adopting this suggestion?
2. If marketing and marketing communication are to take on more of a financial view and role in the organization, what should be the relationship between marketing/ marketing communication and finance? Should they be joined together?
3. What new skills will marketing communication managers need to successfully manage the broad spectrum of the 'push and pull' marketing communication system?
4. Historically, there have been few marketing processes. Outside a traditional marketing plan, most marketing activities appear to be 'ad hoc'. What 'processes' do marketing communication managers need to develop in the future?

CASE STUDY

Building a global communications programme

CEMEX is the third largest cement producer and distributor in the world. From humble beginnings in its home market of Monterrey, Mexico, CEMEX has grown to a global firm that now operates in 50 countries, with 57,000 employees and a turnover in 2008 of £13.5bn. The company sells bulk and bagged cement, ready-mix and aggregates to both end users and other business organizations.

CEMEX, like many present-day manufacturing organizations, grew primarily by acquisition, purchasing other cement producers and marketers in strategic locations. And, like many organizations that grew through acquisition, CEMEX acquired existing companies, kept some local management in place, added its own logistical and operating systems and then let each acquisition operate independently in their local markets. The CEMEX premise was that corporate management would install operating systems to drive down costs, but the acquired firm would continue to manage its own sales, marketing and communications activities.

The plan worked. CEMEX grew exponentially in the late 1990s and into the 21st century. In 2002–03, given the firm's rapid growth, CEMEX's decentralized marketing and communications approach began to show signs of being stretched too thin. In a series of communication-based incidents, where local managers misjudged or did not understand the implications of local market initiatives on the overall CEMEX global brand, it became clear that some type of corporate oversight was needed to protect the increasing value of the global CEMEX brand.

CEMEX's CEO Lorenzo Zambrano and his senior management team initiated a programme to centralize control of the CEMEX brand in Monterrey. The goal was to provide more structure and guidance for local managers in their communication activities. Under the guidance of Javier Trevino, vice president of communications, and Jose Alvarado, global brand manager, a coordinated plan to build a world-class corporate branding and communication organization was developed.

The group started by first reviewing the present structure of the organization and the investment levels being made in corporate marketing communication. The initial study, conducted by an external consulting company and a global brand valuation organization, identified the corporate audiences with which CEMEX communicated, the annual investment levels and the estimated returns. This provided the baseline for future activities.

Once CEMEX management knew their overall communication investment levels, along with the historical trends, the next step was to develop a valuation process for the CEMEX brand. Trevino and Alvarado, knowing how operationally and financially focused the organization was, recognized that having some type of financial brand valuation was the only way to gain upper and middle management's attention. With the consultants, they developed a brand scorecard. This enabled managers to determine the impact of their communication investments, that is, whether their activities were building or destroying brand value. The brand valuation and scorecard approach worked. Corporate managers at CEMEX Central began to realize that often the brand had as much financial value as some of their operating units.

With corporate spending levels, brand valuation and scorecard in hand, Trevino and Alvarado began the task of shifting the corporate culture from its tightly focused, operations-oriented focus to one that recognized and valued the communication potential for CEMEX in the future. In a series of two-day seminars, first with the CEMEX Central management team, and then with a group of country managers, two major initiatives were developed:

1. To define the CEMEX brand and build a CEMEX brand vision that all managers and employees around the world could agree upon and support.
2. To install a brand communication approach that moved the firm from being totally operations driven to one that understood and valued audiences and customers.

The brand vision and mission statement came together fairly quickly as there was considerable internal consensus on what CEMEX stood for, what it meant and what it was trying to do. The shift from an operations to a customer view was a bit more difficult.

The basic approach Trevino, Alvarado and the consultants used was the 'key audience leader' (KAL) approach. This meant that the organization began to look at its key audiences, that is, those people, firms and groups that were important to the ongoing success of the firm and the brand. It turned out that these were the same groups that had been identified in the initial investment study. Eight major audiences were identified: four that had direct financial impact on the organization, that is, customers/end users, suppliers, the financial community and employees. The four peripheral groups were:

- academic institutions, where CEMEX recruited engineers and management people
- the press/media organizations
- industry groups
- permission-givers – regulatory bodies, local communities and environmental groups that gave CEMEX permission to operate in the various markets.

Because of its operating philosophy, CEMEX was organized around functional groups, such as logistics, human resources, finance and operations. These functional silos had specific tasks to accomplish, and so went about their activities with limited contact with the other functional groups. At the corporate level, customers were almost unknown. They were the responsibility of the operating units in the local markets.

The first task was to get corporate managers to recognize that their communication activities influenced groups that had an impact on CEMEX success, and not just on their groups but on the overall success of the firm. This was done by organizationally overlaying the eight communication audiences horizontally across the vertical functional groups (see Figure 7.3). Managers could then begin to see that what they did influenced the other functional groups and that what they all did together had a major impact on the overall results of the organization.

The KAL idea was the key to the horizontal overlay system. The functional group with the most knowledge about each of the eight identified audiences became the KAL for that group. They provided information and direction to the other functional groups in terms of their value, importance and communication needs.

The end result of the organizational structuring was that all CEMEX Central managers began thinking of audiences and, ultimately, customers, not just operating units and systems. This same approach was transferred to the operating units in the various countries. They now assist CEMEX Central in creating a coordinated and aligned communication programme for the entire organization. Today, CEMEX is rolling out its KAL system around the world.

Used with permission of CEMEX, S.A., 2009

Questions

1. CEMEX had been able to ignore the need for a global communication strategy during the time of its rapid growth. What factors forced CEMEX management to start to think of a 'global solution'?
2. Historically, CEMEX had not valued corporate communication highly or as important to the success of the firm. What approaches and methodologies did the corporate communication leaders use to raise the level of the function in the overall value of the organization?
3. What was the key element in getting management 'buy-in' for the global corporate communication plan?
4. How did the 'key audience leader' structural approach for managing the CEMEX corporate brand resolve many of the organizational issues the firm faced?

References

Barabasi, A.L. (2002) *Linked: The New Science of Networks*. Cambridge: Perseus Publishing.

Colley, R.H. (1961) *Defining Advertising Goals for Measured Advertising Results*. New York: Association of National Advertisers.

Grönroos, C. (2000) *Service Management and Marketing: A Customer Relationship Management Approach*. Hoboken, NJ: Wiley.

Kotler, P. and Armstrong, G. (1980) *Principles of Marketing*. Upper Saddle River, NJ: Prentice Hall.

Lavidge, R.J. and Steiner, G.A. (1961) 'A model of predictive measurements of advertising effectiveness'. *Journal of Marketing*, 25: 59–62.

Maslow, A.H. (1943) 'A theory of human motivation'. *Psychological Review*, 50: 370–96.

McCarthy, E.J. (1960) *Basic Marketing: A Managerial Approach*. Homewood, IL: Irwin.

Pavlov, I.P. (1927) *Conditioned Reflexes An Investigation of the Physiological Activity of the Cerebral Cortex*. Oxford: Oxford University Press.

Ray, M.L. (1982) *Advertising and Communication Management*. Englewood Cliffs, NJ: Prentice Hall.

Russell, J.T. and Lane, W.R. (1996) *Klepner's Advertising Procedure* (13th edn). Englewood Cliffs, NJ: Prentice Hall.

Schramm, W. and Roberts, D. (eds) (1971) *The Process and Effects of Mass Communication*. Urbana, IL: University of Illinois Press.

Skinner, B.F. (1965) *Science and Human Behavior*. New York: Free Press.

Watts. D.J. and Strogatz, S.H. (1998) 'Collective dynamics of "small-world" networks'. *Nature*, 393: 409–10.

8

The adoption of interactive digital television by advertising professionals: exploring an international marketing communication medium

Verolien Cauberghe and Patrick de Pelsmacker

Learning outcomes

At the end of this chapter, readers should be able to:

1. Understand why interactive digital television (IDTV) advertising could be an added value to marketing communication professionals.

2. Assess what drives advertising professionals to use IDTV advertising and what stops them from doing so.

3. Understand the logic behind the technology acceptance model and the theory of planned behaviour and why these models are relevant to understand IDTV advertising adoption behaviour.

4. Have an insight into the drivers of IDTV advertising adoption and how this adoption can be improved.

Key points

- IDTV advertising is an emerging medium that is becoming increasingly important in international marketing communications.
- The perceived ease of use of IDTV advertising has substantially more impact on the intention to adopt IDTV as an advertising medium than perceived usefulness.
- Internal and external reference groups have an equal impact on the intention to adopt IDTV advertising.
- In the initial stages of the IDTV adoption process, reference groups have a substantial impact on all intermediate factors that influence IDTV adoption, such as perceived ease of use and perceived behavioural control.
- The attitude towards IDTV advertising has a significant impact on the intention to adopt it, but less than reference group influence. In the early stages of the process, the internalization of the adoption decision is not very well developed.

IDTV as an emerging marketing communication medium

Digitalization is changing the media landscape worldwide by blurring the lines between existing media (Calder and Malthouse, 2005; Edelman, 2007). Interactive digital television (IDTV) is an outcome of this convergence by merging traditional broadcasting and digital (telecommunication) technology. Although IDTV imposes threats for advertising professionals in terms of advert skipping (Fortunato and Windels, 2005), it also offers many new advertising opportunities and formats, such as interactive ads, banners, product placement and 'walled garden' applications (Tauder, 2005; Cauberghe and de Pelsmacker, 2006). While IDTV is being adopted in many countries worldwide, advertising professionals are sceptical of investing in IDTV because of its slow adoption rate by end users (Tauder, 2005). The diffusion process of interactive telecommunication technologies (such as IDTV) is characterized by a long takeoff, followed by a steep increase when a critical mass is achieved, until saturation (Rogers, 1995; Shapiro and Varian, 1999; Kim and Kim, 2007). Advertising investments in IDTV can decrease the cost for broadcasters and telecommunication operators to develop interactive IDTV services in general, for example interactive TV programmes, games, electronic programme guide. Indirectly, the threshold for the end user to adopt IDTV will then be lowered due to lower prices, for example to view movies on demand. Given the interdependence of broadcasters, advertisers and end users, the adoption of this new medium by advertisers is crucial for its success (Leckenby, 2003). Hence, understanding the decision-making process to adopt IDTV as a potential marketing communication medium is vital.

The purpose of this study is to gain insight into what drives advertising professionals in Belgium to adopt IDTV advertising by building and empirically validating a predictive model of IDTV advertising adoption intention. The unit of analysis of the study is the individual in an organization who is in charge of buying, budgeting, employing or outsourcing the advertising budget. The technology acceptance model

(TAM) (Davis, 1989) and the (decomposed) theory of planned behaviour (TPB) (Ajzen, 1991; Taylor and Todd, 1995), both extensions of the theory of reasoned action (Ajzen and Fishbein, 1980), are used to examine the initial adoption intention by advertising professionals of IDTV. The TAM focuses on the cognitive beliefs based on the characteristics of the innovation that influence the attitude towards using the innovation, whereas the TPB explains the underlying mechanism of the adoption process of innovations based on the attitude towards the innovation, the social influence to use the innovation, and the perceived control of the user to use it.

Conceptual framework

An innovation in an organization can be defined as 'the adoption of a new product, service, process, technology, policy, structure or administrative system' (Damanpour and Schneider, 2006, p. 216). Frambach and Schillewaert (2002) identify two types of organizational adoption decisions: the decision made by the organization (Leonard-Barton and Deschamps, 1988; Fishman and Kemerer, 1997; Dewan et al., 1998) and the decision made by the individual within the organization, referred to as intraorganizational adoption. The latter type refers to the adoption process of employees at the implementation phase. In general, two stages can be discerned: the initiation and the implementation stage (Zaltman et al., 1973; Damanpour, 1991):

- In the *initiation stage*, the management in an organization becomes aware of the innovation, evaluates it and forms an attitude towards it.
- In the *implementation stage*, the purchase decision is made and the innovation is used within the organization. In this stage, widespread acceptance of the innovation by all employees in the organization becomes crucial.

The initiation stage and the implementation stage are separated by the adoption decision (Zmud, 1982; Damanpour and Schneider, 2006). In this study, the focus is on the individual adoption decision process to use IDTV as an advertising tool within an organization (advertising professional) at the initiation stage (before implementation), and will focus on the determinants that influence the individual's adoption intention. This is a valid approach, since decisions on how to spend advertising budgets are generally not organizational adoption decisions, but are choices made by marketing or brand managers in a company.

One of the most widely used models to explain and predict the motivational factors underlying user acceptance of technology within a work environment is Davis's (1989) technology acceptance model (TAM). The TAM assumes that a person's attitude and behavioural intention towards using a new technology are influenced by the perceived usefulness (PU) and the perceived ease of use (PEOU) of the innovation:

- *perceived usefulness* can be described as 'the degree to which a person believes that using a particular technology will enhance his/her job performance'.
- *perceived ease of use* is 'the degree to which a person believes that using the system will be effortless' (Davis, 1989, p. 320).

Although the TAM model has proved its robustness (for meta-analyses, see King and He, 2006; Schepers and Wetzels, 2007), it does not incorporate the influence of the social system surrounding an individual, as proposed by innovation diffusion theory (Rogers, 1995). Therefore, Venkatesh and Davis (2000) incorporated the influence of the subjective norm, that is, the influence of significant others, in TAM2. They found that the subjective norm had a direct effect on the behavioural intention of individuals. This 'compliance effect' occurs because people choose to perform an action when one or more important people in their environment say they should, independent of whether they like it or believe in it. In TAM2, the subjective norm also has an indirect effect on the behavioural intention through PU and PEOU. This 'internalization process' represents the tendency of people to believe the information of others as reality.

The theory of planned behaviour (TPB, Ajzen, 1991) has also been widely used to predict individual acceptance of information technology (Taylor and Todd, 1995; Chau and Hu, 2001; Hsu and Chiu, 2004; Hung and Chang, 2005; Wu and Chen, 2005; Hsu et al., 2006). According to the TPB, behavioural intention is an adequate predictor of actual behaviour (Ajzen and Fishbein, 1980; Sheppard et al., 1988; Ajzen, 1991). The TPB states that behavioural intentions are influenced by three dimensions; the individual's attitude, the subjective norm and perceived behavioural control. According to Pavlou and Fygenson (2006, pp. 117–19):

- *attitude* is 'a person's overall evaluation of performing a behaviour'
- *subjective norm* is 'the person's perception of the expectations of important others about a specific behaviour'
- *perceived behavioural control* is 'a person's perception of how easy or difficult it would be to carry out a behaviour'. Perceived behavioural control not only influences the intention to perform certain behaviours, but also has a direct effect on actual behaviour.

All three factors are influenced by a set of cognitive beliefs about the innovation.

Although the TPB has proved its explanatory power to predict and understand future behaviour, it has some practical and theoretical disadvantages. Therefore, Taylor and Todd (1995) introduced the decomposed TPB, which decomposes the three main dimensions of behavioural intention (attitude, subjective norm and behavioural control) into a set of salient beliefs based on innovation diffusion theory and the TAM:

1. Decomposing the attitude construct integrates the three most stable innovation characteristics defined by innovation diffusion theory (Torznatzky and Fleischer, 1990; Moore and Benbasat, 1991): complexity, relative advantage and compatibility (Taylor and Todd, 1995). *Complexity* is similar to the PEOU construct of the TAM, *relative advantage* is comparable with PU (Davis et al., 1989; Moore and Benbasat, 1991; Plouffe et al., 2001) and *compatibility* is 'the degree to which the innovation fits with the potential adopter's existing values, previous experiences and current needs' (Rogers, 1995, pp. 132).
2. The subjective norm is decomposed into different reference groups. A *reference group* can be defined as a group that serves as comparison point, and whose meaning is perceived as important for the individual (Shibutani, 1955). Taylor and

Todd (1995) argue that in an organizational setting, peers, superiors and subordinates may be important reference groups.

3. For perceived behavioural control, Taylor and Todd (1995) follow Ajzen's (1991) conceptualization. He refers to the internal notion of individual *self-efficacy* (Bandura, 1986), which is related to perceived ability and external resource constraints, which is similar to Triandis's (1977) *facilitating conditions*. In an organizational setting, these facilitating conditions consist of two dimensions; resources (such as time and money) and technological compatibility.

The conceptual model developed in this study (see Figure 8.1) integrates the technology acceptance model and the decomposed theory of planned behaviour. In general, the attitude towards adopting IDTV, the subjective norm and perceived behavioural control are expected to have a positive direct effect on the adoption intention. PU and PEOU are expected to partly mediate the impact of the subjective norm on attitude. PEOU is also expected to partly mediate the impact of the subjective norm on perceived behavioural control.

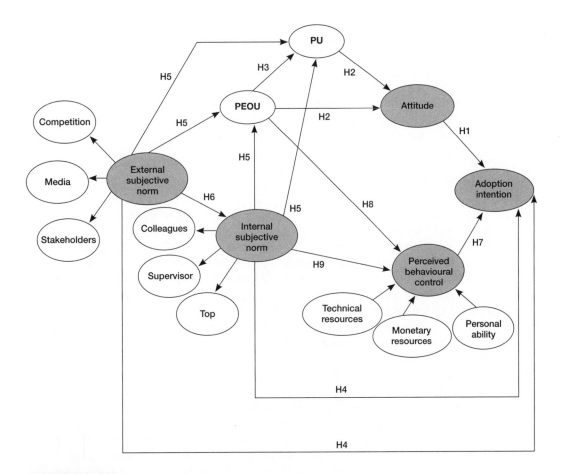

Figure 8.1 Conceptual model of technology adoption

Hypotheses

We now draw up some hypotheses under the three main headings of behavioural intention – attitude, subjective norm and perceived behavioural control.

Attitude

The effect of attitude on behavioural intentions is found in most user acceptance studies (for an overview, see Venkatesh et al., 2003). According to the decomposed TPB and the TAM, the two most salient cognitive beliefs that influence the attitude towards the innovation are PU (perceived usefulness) and PEOU (perceived ease of use). Compatibility is not incorporated into the model, given the conceptual and empirical overlap with PU found in most previous studies (Moore and Benbasat, 1991; Karahanna et al., 2006). In their meta-analysis, Sun and Zhang (2006) concluded that PU had a significant effect on attitude in 71 of 72 adoption studies. Most studies also confirm the positive effect of PEOU on attitude. Schepers and Wetzels' (2007) meta-analysis, which included 63 studies about the TAM, found that the effect of PU is much stronger than that of PEOU. PEOU has been found to have a positively significant effect on PU by the majority of studies (Davis, 1989; Taylor and Todd, 1995; Venkatesh and Davis, 2000; Avlonitis and Panagopoulos, 2005). This leads to the following hypotheses:

H1:   The attitude towards using IDTV has a positive effect on behavioural intention
H2:   PU and PEOU have a positive effect on attitude
H3:   PEOU has a positive effect on PU

Subjective norm

In mandatory contexts, in which individuals are obliged or feel they are obliged to adopt and use an innovation, such as in organizational settings, the effect of the subjective norm for predicting behavioural intentions is expected to be more substantial than in voluntary contexts, where the adoption decision is a free choice for the individual (Davis et al., 1992; Moore and Benbasat, 1993; Armstrong and Sambamurthy, 1999; Hartwick and Barki, 1994; Workman, 2005). Because of the organizational context of the advertising professionals in this study, the subjective norm can be expected to have a significant impact on their behavioural intention. However, the impact of the perceived opinion of different reference groups may differ (Tan and Teo, 2000; Hung and Chang, 2005). The subjective normative influence for advertising professionals within an organization can be divided into two dimensions: the external, environmental subjective norm and the internal, organizational subjective norm. Since their potential influence on the adoption decision model is different, their influence on usage intention is explored as separate factors.

The external subjective norm is determined by three reference groups: stakeholders (Riemenschneider et al., 2003), competition (Frambach and Schillewaert, 2002; Papastathopoulou et al., 2007) and media (Rogers, 1995). A stakeholder can be defined as a group or a person who can influence or is influenced by an organization (Freeman, 1984). In the IDTV business network, broadcasters and telecommunication providers are important stakeholders. For instance, Damanpour and Schneider (2006) found that external communication, measured through involvement in professional associations (stakeholders), positively affected the adoption process. Previous research has found that more intense competitive markets generate a higher adoption rate (Frambach, 1993; Chan and Ngai, 2007; Papastathopoulou et al., 2007). Weber and Evans (2002) investigated the importance of mass media in the diffusion of digital TV in Britain, Australia and the US. Their results show that media coverage is positively linked to the degree and success of the diffusion of digital TV.

In this study, the internal subjective norm is defined by the following reference groups: the advertising professional's top management (Taylor and Todd, 1995; Tarafdat and Vaidya, 2006), their direct supervisor (Avlonitis and Panagopoulos, 2005) and colleagues (Taylor and Todd, 1995). Tarafdar and Vaidya (2006) found that top managers who were well informed about new technologies could influence and induce other managers to consider their use. Organizational and strategic leadership research posits that top management establishes an organizational culture, in which they can motivate and enable managers to adopt innovations and build the capacity for change and innovation (Daft, 2001; Elenkov et al., 2005). Top managers and direct supervisors scan the environment to develop a strategy to respond to the changing context. They can be considered gatekeepers, in that they control the resources and are involved in major decisions. Finally, advertising professionals often work in teams. Therefore, when colleagues or peers use IDTV, their use will impact the perception and adoption intention of advertising professionals (Jones et al., 2002). Based on the TAM and the decomposed TPB models and past studies, the compliance effect suggests a direct impact of both the internal and external subjective norm on the behavioural intention to adopt IDTV advertising.

The internalization effect leads to the expectation that the opinion of important reference groups also has an influence on the individual's PU and PEOU of the innovation. Subjective norm has been identified as one of the most influential antecedents of PU and PEOU (Sun and Zhang, 2006; Schepers and Wetzels, 2007).

Rogers (1995) claims that in the pre-adoption period, mass media and external communication have an important role in diffusing information about the innovation and in increasing its awareness among the social network. In this study, the external subjective norm of mass media was supplemented with stakeholders and competition. The organization's top management, middle management and employees will learn about IDTV through the mass media, but also through their interaction with professional associations, competition and stakeholders of IDTV (Tarafdar and Vaidya, 2006). We expect that external reference groups will have a significant effect on the attitude of internal reference groups. This leads to our next set of hypotheses:

H4:   The external subjective norm (media, competition, stakeholders) and the internal subjective norm (top management, direct supervisors and colleagues) have a positive effect on behavioural intention

H5:   The external subjective norm (media, competition, stakeholders) and the internal subjective norm (top management, direct supervisor, and colleagues) have a positive effect on PU and PEOU

H6: The external subjective norm (media, competition, stakeholders) has a positive effect on the internal subjective norm (top management, direct supervisors, colleagues)

Perceived behavioural control

Perceived behavioural control is the perception of the ease or difficulty for advertising professionals to adopt and invest in IDTV. The decomposed TPB proposes two factors that constitute perceived behavioural control – self-efficacy (personal ability) and facilitating factors (time and money resources and technological ability) (Taylor and Todd, 1995). Pavlou and Fygenson (2006) found that monetary resources had a positive effect on behavioural control to achieve an online purchase. Riemenschneider et al. (2003) also reported technically related cognitive beliefs to influence perceived behavioural control in their study on the adoption of the use of a corporate website among small businesses. In general, most studies find a positive effect of perceived behavioural control on behavioural intention.

Pavlou and Fygenson (2006) found that the PEOU to search for online information and to make an online purchase were highly correlated with the perceived behavioural control of both behaviours. Other researchers have confirmed the strong correlation between PEOU and behavioural control (Riemenschneider et al., 2003; Yi et al., 2006). Therefore, we expect a positive effect of PEOU on perceived behavioural control.

One of the roles of top and middle management is to provide the resources to adopt innovations. For information technologies, management also plays a role in providing the adequate technological infrastructure. In their meta-analysis, Sabherwal et al. (2006) found that management support is positively associated with facilitating conditions, such as resources and technological ability. Given that personal ability is another dimension of perceived behavioural control, we can also expect that peers/colleagues might have an influence on perceived behavioural control. We expect that the internal subjective norm will have a positive effect on perceived behavioural control. So we arrive at our last set of hypotheses:

H7: Perceived behavioural control has a positive effect on behavioural intention
H8: PEOU has a positive effect on perceived behavioural control
H9: The internal subjective norm (top management, direct supervisors, colleagues) has a positive effect on perceived behavioural control

Method

Data collection

An online survey was used to collect the data. The survey instrument was developed based on established scales retrieved from marketing, management and information systems literature. The sampling frame consisted of three databases of different marketing institutions:

- the largest commercial broadcaster in Belgium (VMMa)
- a specialized advertising magazine (*Pub Magazine*)
- a market research company (InSites).

In May 2007, a total of 2,680 advertising professionals received an email containing the link to the questionnaire and an introduction about IDTV and its advertising possibilities. At that time, the adoption rate of IDTV by end users was approximately 10%. This introduction was important to make sure that all respondents perceived IDTV in the same way. In total, 437 advertising professionals (response rate = 16.3%) completed the questionnaire (see Table 8.1 for sample description). To check the non-response bias, the characteristics of the total sample frame were compared with those of the sample. The results showed that there were no significant differences between the groups.

Table 8.1   Sample characteristics

	Percentage share	
Type of company		
Advertising agency	11.2	
Media planning	5.0	
Advertiser	83.3	
Fast moving consumer goods		10.5
Durables		9.2
Services		53.3
Non-profit		10.8
Function		
Sales	44.9	
Marketing	20.4	
Research	14.6	
Communication	20.1	
Level		
Junior management	18.8	
Middle management	43.0	
Top management	38.2	
Gender		
Male	73.9	
Female	26.1	
Years of marketing experience		
0–3 years	27.1	
3–10 years	21.2	
> 10 years	41.7	

Measurements

All constructs were measured using 5-point Likert scales (ranging from 'strongly disagree' to 'strongly agree') or semantic differential scales. PU and PEOU were measured using Davis's scale (1989) adjusted by Moore and Benbasat (1991). The attitude construct, perceived behavioural control and its antecedents, personal ability and technological facilitating conditions, and the behavioural intention were measured by Taylor and Todd's scale (1995). The external social influence was defined by three constructs. The influence of media was measured by Taylor and Todd's scale, also used by Hung and Chang (2005). The external subjective influence of competition was measured by the scale developed by Avlonitis and Panagopoulos (2005), based on Schillewaert et al.'s scale (2000). The influence of stakeholders was measured by a self-developed scale including the most important stakeholders for the IDTV business model in Belgium. The internal social influence was also defined by three constructs. The influence of top management and colleagues was measured by Leonard-Barton and Deschamps' scale (1988). The normative influence imposed by the direct supervisor was assessed by Avlonitis and Panagopoulos's scale (2005), based on Schillewaert et al.'s scale (2000).

A pilot study was conducted to validate and clarify the measurement instruments. The questionnaire was send to 72 Belgian advertising professionals, 44 of whom completed the questionnaire (response rate = 61.1%). Based on this pre-test, some items were removed, reformulated or clarified more precisely.

Results

Measurement model

Exploratory factor analysis (EFA, principal components) with Varimax rotation was used to examine if the theorized underlying factors of the model were represented in the data. For the components or antecedents of each main dimension (attitude, internal subjective norm, external subjective norm and perceived behavioural control – four EFAs in total), factors were extracted based on the Eigenvalue >1.0 rule. As expected, the items of PU and PEOU, as the cognitive beliefs of attitude, represent two separate factors. All items of the theorized internal subjective norm antecedents loaded on one factor. The items of the perceived behavioural control antecedents also loaded on one factor. Therefore, in subsequent analyses, we only use one factor to define internal subjective norm and perceived behavioural control. Media, competition and stakeholders items load on three separate factors. A supplementary confirmatory factor analysis was carried out in which 'external subjective norm' was defined as a second-order latent construct by the three first-order constructs. This analysis showed good reliability and validity. Therefore, the second-order construct external subjective norm, for which the different reference groups (media, competition, stakeholders) are the indicators, was included in the model. Across the four EFAs, seven items did not possess satisfactory convergent validity and discriminating power and were left out of the model.

With the SEM module of SPSS, AMOS 6.0, the measurement model was tested using the maximum likelihood estimation method. Based on loadings, information on standardized residual covariances and modification indices (Steenkamp and van Trijp, 1991), disturbing items were screened and removed. To deal with the non-normal distributed data, the bootstrapping method (Bollen and Stine, 1992) was applied. The final (general) model met all the fit indices using the common cutoff values (Bollen and Stine, 1992) (chi^2 = 728.596, df = 307, chi^2/df = 2.373, TLI = 0.942, CFI = 0.956, RMSEA = 0.055).

In addition to a satisfactory model fit, the measurement model should possess convergent validity, reliability and discriminant validity. All item-construct correlations were higher than the recommended cutoff value of 0.60. In addition, the average variance extracted (AVE) of all latent constructs was larger than the recommended cutoff value of 0.50, which provides additional proof of convergent validity. All Cronbach's alphas exceed the threshold of 0.70, implying a satisfactory level of reliability (Bagozzi and Yi, 1988). Also the composite reliabilities, with values of over 0.700, indicate reliability and unidimensionality of the scales (Steenkamp and van Trijp, 1991). Finally, all the correlations between the constructs are significantly different from one, indicating discriminant validity (Singh and Rhoads, 1991). For all constructs, except for a mild violation for PEOU, the AVE value of the factor is also greater than the squared correlation between the factor and another factor, which gives an additional indication for discriminant validity. Based on these results, it can be concluded that the measurement model adequately fits the data.

Structural model

- As expected, attitude has a positive effect on the adoption intention (ß = 0.264, p<0.001). *H1 is supported.*
- Contrary to our expectations, PU did not have a significant positive effect on attitude (ß =0.081, p = 0.304). However, PEOU has a strong positive effect on attitude (ß = 0.679, p<0.001). *H2 is partly supported.*
- The effect of PEOU on PU is positive, as we expected (ß = 0.545, p<0.001). *H3 is supported.*
- The external subjective norm has a positive direct effect on adoption intention (ß = 0.215, p<0.001). The effect of the internal subjective norm is also positive (ß = 0.240, p<0.001). *H4 is supported.*

These results are in line with the compliance mechanism of subjective norm on adoption intention.

- The internalization effect of the external subjective norm is also apparent. The external subjective norm has a significant effect on both PU (ß = 0.233, p = 0.002) and PEOU (ß = 0.420, p<0.001). For the internal subjective norm, the effect on PU is not significant (ß = 0.009, p = 0.883). The effect of the internal subjective norm on PEOU is, however, significantly positive (ß = 0.213, p = 0.005). *H5 is partly supported.*
- The external subjective norm does have a strong positive effect on the internal subjective norm (ß = 0.685, p<0.001). *H6 is supported.*
- Perceived behavioural control has a positive effect on the adoption intention (ß = .294, p<.001), *supporting H7.*

- PEOU has a positive influence on perceived behavioural control (ß = 0.597, p<0.001). *H8 is supported*.
- The effect of the internal subjective norm on perceived behavioural control is also positive (ß = 0.320, p<0.001), *supporting H9*.

Finally, the reflective dimensions of the second-order construct, external subjective norm, all loaded highly on the latent construct (competition: ß = −0.779, p<0.001; media: ß = 0.789, p<0.001; stakeholders: ß = 0.850, p<0.001).

Table 8.2   Standardized regression weights and significance in structural model

Parameter			Standardized regression weight	Sign. level
Intention	←	Attitude	0.264	<0.001
Intention	←	Perceived behavioural control	0.294	<0.001
Intention	←	External subjective norm	0.215	<0.001
Intention	←	Internal subjective norm	0.240	<0.001
Attitude	←	Perceived usefulness	−0.081	0.304
Attitude	←	Perceived ease of use	0.679	<0.001
Perceived usefulness	←	Perceived ease of use	0.545	<0.001
Perceived usefulness	←	External subjective norm	0.233	0.002
Perceived ease of use	←	External subjective norm	0.420	<0.001
Perceived usefulness	←	Internal subjective norm	0.009	0.883
Perceived ease of use	←	Internal subjective norm	0.213	0.005
Internal subjective norm	←	External subjective norm	0.685	<0.001
Perceived behaviour control	←	Perceived ease of use	0.597	<0.001
Perceived behaviour control	←	Internal subjective norm	0.320	<0.001

Conclusions

The three main dimensions of the (decomposed) TPB (attitude, subjective normative influence and perceived behavioural control) in combination with cognitive beliefs about the innovation based on the TAM (PU and PEOU) explain 69.2% of the variance of the behavioural intention to use IDTV as an advertising tool. This explanatory power is high compared to the findings of Sun and Zhang (2006). Based on their overview of innovation research, they conclude that the average explanatory power of the innovation adoption models is less than 40%. Therefore, our model is satisfactory in explaining the adoption intention.

The results show that the direct effects of the attitude towards the innovation, perceived behavioural control and the external and internal subjective norm on the adoption intention are about equally strong. PEOU has a positive influence on attitude, as expected. However, the influence of PU on the attitude towards adopting IDTV is insignificant. This contradicts our expectation and past results, which found that the role of PU was the most important predictor of attitude (Schepers and Wetzels,

2007). When individuals consider adopting a new technology, the perceived utility of the technology normally has a stronger influence than its complexity (PEOU). Apparently, advertising professionals find it more important to know if IDTV is easy to use in their job than what the effectiveness of using it would be. A possible explanation could be the early negative results of pioneers who launched interactive campaigns on IDTV in Belgium. The past technological hurdles with the IDTV infrastructure in Belgium may explain why advertising professionals emphasize the ease of using IDTV advertising properly.

Perceived ease of use plays a central role in the model. It strongly influences perceived usefulness, attitude and perceived behavioural control. Besides the significant and relatively strong compliance mechanism of the external and internal subjective norm on the adoption intention, both types of subjective norm also influence cognitive beliefs about IDTV as an advertising tool. For the external subjective norm, this internalization effect is apparent for both PU and PEOU. The internal subjective norm only influences the perceptions of the PEOU of using IDTV advertising, but not the perceptions about its usefulness. A possible explanation could be that the internal reference groups themselves are not convinced about the usefulness of IDTV as an advertising tool.

The internal subjective norm, based on the influence of top management and the direct supervisor, had no influence at all on the PU of IDTV as an advertising tool. The internalization effect is mainly induced by the influence of the external subjective norm, instead of the internal subjective norm. However, top management and supervisors have a more substantial effect on the perceived behavioural control to adopt IDTV than the external reference groups. In line with previous studies, we can conclude that top management and direct supervisors scan the environment (strong influence of external subjective norm on internal subjective norm), and next investigate what the possibilities (in terms of resources) are within the company to respond to the environmental needs, thereby influencing the perceived behavioural control of the advertising professional. Besides the influence of the internal subjective norm, PEOU also has a strong impact on perceived behavioural control. In sum, the results show that the impact of perceived usefulness on the adoption decision process is low, especially compared to the impact of perceived ease of use and the subjective norm.

Managerial implications

The results of this study have implications for advertising professionals and stakeholders interested in the diffusion of IDTV. It provides insights for stakeholders within the IDTV business model on how best to approach advertising professionals, to motivate their adoption behaviour positively. The results show that perceived ease of use and also the external subjective norm are important driving forces. Positive media attention and the influence of stakeholders, through seminars, conferences, presentations at early stages in the process, are the best tools to convince advertisers of the potential of IDTV. Because of the strong effect of the external subjective norm on the internal subjective norm, top management and middle management should be targeted for these events. Given the lack of the internalization effect of the internal reference groups on the perceived usefulness, they have to be persuaded about the positive benefits and usefulness of IDTV advertising, a factor that until now has had only a limited impact on advertising professionals' adoption intention.

As perceived ease of use has an important influence, (mass) communication should also focus on the user-friendliness of advertising on IDTV. The insignificance of the perceived usefulness on attitude is rather troublesome. IDTV needs success stories of pioneers willing to try out interactive campaigns on IDTV. This might increase the perception of the usefulness of IDTV as an advertising tool. The offering of free trials or cheap development costs by telecommunication providers and broadcasters to persuade these pioneers might increase the takeoff of IDTV by advertisers. Conversely, increasing the adoption of IDTV by end users may force advertisers to eventually use the medium in their marketing mix. Allen (1988) argued that promotion strategies such as subsidized pricing and free trials were critical for the success of Minitel. Nowadays, in the UK, the delivery of free set top boxes or subsidies when hiring a digital decoder, promotions, and so on are used to boost the adoption of IDTV by end users.

Further research

This study has some limitations that can provide guidance for further research. First, there are generally known biases in the adoption research literature (Jeyaraj et al., 2006) that might also be present in this study, such as the rationality bias (adopters make rational decisions) (Rogers, 1995; Fishman, 2004). Kim et al. (2007) integrated pleasure and arousal in the TAM model. They found that both affective dimensions in combination with the cognitive component PU shaped the attitude towards the overall evaluation of the use of mobile internet services, which in turn had a positive effect on the intention to continue to use the innovation. The role of affect on the decision-making process of professionals within an organization has rarely been investigated, and would be an ally for further research.

Another method bias that has been a recurring problem within the technology acceptance modelling research, and which is also present in this study, is the common method bias (Woszczynski and Whitman, 2004). Further, using cross-sectional data, the direction of the causality cannot be unambiguously ascertained. Further research should measure the different constructs at various moments in time.

Further research could measure advertising professionals' perceptions and behavioural intentions at different moments in time to study the change in relative importance of the different variables in the model. Linking these longitudinal data individually would also make it possible to incorporate the feedback mechanisms, which might have an influence on the re-evaluation of the innovation (Kim and Malhotra, 2005). In general, further research on IDTV advertising adoption should further investigate the longitudinal character of the process, expanding beyond the pre-adoption stage into the adoption decision and post-adoption behaviour.

Finally, potentially moderating variables that might have an influence on how the adoption process proceeds should be examined, such as personality traits, for example innovativeness (Agarwal and Prasad, 1998), and organizational factors (structure).

Issues for further discussion

1. Speculate on how the structural equation model could be used to design campaigns to improve the adoption of IDTV advertising.
2. Suppose we did the same study in a couple of years' time, how would the importance of the determining factors of IDTV advertising adoption change? Why?
3. Which organizational factors (size of the company, type of company, industry) could have an impact on the adoption of IDTV advertising? Why?

CASE STUDY

The effectiveness of an interactive TV advert

One of the new interactive TV advertising formats is the telescopic advert. This format consists of a '30-second TV ad with a call-to-action button with clickable content or microsites featuring individual still screens providing additional product information' (Bellman and Varan, 2004, p. 2). When the viewer clicks on the call-to-action button, they leave the linear broadcast stream to enter a dedicated advertising location (DAL). There, they can navigate through the additional information, which can be structured in different layers. This new format is promising, given that earlier empirical studies show that the synergy of a TV advert and exposure to a website results in better advertising effects than the mere repetition of a traditional TV advert (Chang and Thorson, 2004). For instance, Maddox and Mehta (2007) found that the inclusion of web addresses in traditional mass media commercials (TV, magazines) leads to a positive influence on the brand's perception in terms of customer orientation, reliability, responsiveness and informativeness.

Bellman and Varan's study (2004) also demonstrates that the impact of one exposure to an interactive advert with additional information equals that of three repetitive exposures to a traditional 30-second TV commercial in terms of brand recall, attitude and behavioural intentions. In addition, Reading et al. (2006) provide evidence of the positive impact of a telescopic advert on advertisement and brand attitudes, compared to a traditional 30-second commercial and a long (30 minutes) infomercial. Compared to a traditional advert, a telescopic advert is usually more complex, as a result of the additional information and embedded interactivity. Internet research demonstrated that the level of complexity and the resulting information (cognitive) load of a website may have a negative impact on advertising effectiveness (Wang et al., 2007). Similar to an internet context, IDTV advertising designers are facing the challenge of defining the optimal level of complexity of the DAL on IDTV for maximum advertising effectiveness.

A recent experimental study illustrates that a possible negative impact of information overload induced by a complex advertising stimulus (manipulated by the amount of information and the level of interactivity) on brand responses is not likely to occur in a context in which individuals can interact with the DAL without any time constraint. The interactivity embedded in the DAL allows individuals to take control over the information processing. The user can decide the sequence and how much time they spend processing the information, and so manages the information load themselves. The results show that both the amount of information and the level of interactivity increase the time consumers spend in the DAL. Therefore, the amount of information did not lead to a negative overload effect on the advertising outcomes, since consumers had more time to process the stimulus. In line with previous studies (Bellman and Varan, 2004; Reading, et al., 2006), the study showed that the telescopic advert, which offers more information to consumers and makes interactivity possible, thereby increasing the time spent with the persuasive content, performed notably better in terms of brand recall and attitude than a traditional 30-second commercial.

Besides the increased advertising impact of the telescopic advert, this new advertising format has other advantages. A telescopic advert fits into the three new advertising models that Rappaport (2007) describes:

1. The telescopic advert can be used *on demand*, because of the technical possibility of storing the DAL on the TV using the personal video recorder (PVR). This allows the viewer to demand product information whenever convenient for them.
2. The telescopic advert can also be the starting point to increase the *engagement* with the brand. All consumer data (clicking behaviour, time spent, email) can be stored on the TV (on the PVR) and can be used to develop long-lasting, engaging relationships.
3. A telescopic advert can be used as an extra *service* for consumers. This is particularly relevant for product categories, such as travel agencies, as well as other types of products that are at least moderately involving, such as banking, insurances and durables.

Questions

1. Why does an interactive advert lead to more positive advertising effects compared to a traditional 30-second advert?
2. Interactive adverts also offer the possibility of broadcasting the linear video stream in the upper right-hand corner of the screen using the picture-in-picture technology, so the viewer does not miss part of their programme while navigating through the interactive information. Would this split-screen technology enhance the advertising effectiveness of the interactive advert or not?
3. Would there be an effect of the call-to-action type on the effectiveness of the interactive advert? For example, *'press the red button and have a chance to win a bicycle'* or *'press the red button for more information'*.
4. IDTV advertising using sophisticated formats such as the dedicated advertising location (DAL) is not often used by advertisers. What could be the reason for that? How would a DAL have to be made to be effective?

References

Agarwal, R. and Prasad, P. (1998) 'A conceptual and operational definition of personal innovativeness in the domain of information technology'. *Information Systems Research*, 9: 204–15.

Ajzen, I. (1991) 'The theory of planned behaviour'. *Organizational Behaviour and Human Decision Processes*, 50: 179–211.

Ajzen, I. and Fishbein, M. (1980) *Understanding Attitudes and Predicting Social Behaviour*. Englewood Cliffs, NJ: Prentice Hall.

Allen, D. (1988) 'New communications services: Network externalities and critical mass'. *Telecommunications Policy*, 12: 257–71.

Armstrong, C.P. and Sambamurthy, V. (1999) 'Information technology assimilation in firms: The influence of senior leadership and IT infrastructure'. *Information Systems Research*, 10(4): 304–27.

Avlonitis, G.J. and Panagopoulos, N.G. (2005) 'Antecedents and consequences of CRM technology acceptance in the sales forces'. *Industrial Marketing Management*, 34(4): 355–68.

Bagozzi, R.P. and Yi, Y. (1988) 'On the evaluation of structural equation models'. *Journal of the Academy of Marketing Science*, 16: 74–94.

Bandura, A. (1986) *Social Foundations of Thought and Action*. Englewood Cliffs, NJ: Prentice Hall.

Bellman, S. and Varan, D. (2004) The Impact of Adding Additional Information to Television Advertising on Elaboration, Recall, Persuasion. Paper presented at the ANZMAC Conference, Wellington.

Bollen, K.A. and Stine, R.A. (1992) 'Bootstrapping goodness-of-fit measures in structural equation models'. *Sociological Methods and Research*, 21: 205–29.

Calder, B.J. and Malthouse, E.C. (2005) 'Managing media and advertising change with integrated marketing'. *Journal of Advertising Research*, 45(4): 356–61.

Cauberghe, V. and de Pelsmacker, P. (2006) 'Opportunities and thresholds for advertising on interactive, digital TV: A view from advertising professionals'. *Journal of Interactive Advertising*, 7(3): 49–58.

Chan, S.C. and Ngai, E.W. (2007) 'A qualitative study of information technology adoption: How ten organizations adopted web-based training'. *Information Systems Journal*, 17(4): 289–315.

Chang, Y. and Thorson, E. (2004) 'Television and web advertising synergies'. *Journal of Advertising*, 33(2): 75–84.

Chau, P.Y. and Hu, P.J. (2001) 'Information technology acceptance by individual professionals: A model comparison approach'. *Decision Sciences*, 32(4): 699–719.

Daft, R.L. (2001) *Organization Theory and Design*. Cincinnati, OH: South-Western.

Damanpour, F. (1991) 'Organisational innovation: a meta-analysis of effect of determinants and moderators'. *Academy of Management Journal*, 34: 555–90.

Damanpour, F. and Schneider, M. (2006) 'Phases of the adoption of innovation in organizations: Effects of environment, organization and top managers'. *British Journal of Management*, 17(3): 215–36.

Davis, F.D. (1989) 'Perceived usefulness, perceived ease of use, and user acceptance of information technology'. *MIS Quarterly*, 13(3): 319–39.

Davis, F.D., Bagozzi, R.P. and Warshaw, P.R. (1989) 'User acceptance of computer technology: A comparison of two theoretical models'. *Management Science*, 35(8): 982–1002.

Davis, F.D., Bagozzi, R.P. and Warshaw, P.R. (1992) 'Extrinsic and intrinsic motivation to use computers in the workplace'. *Journal of Applied Social Psychology*, 22: 1111–32.

Deutsch, M. and Gerard, H.B. (1955) 'A study of informational and normative social influence upon individual judgement'. *Journal of Abnormal and Social Psychology*, 51: 629–36.

Dewan, S., Michael, S.C. and Min, C.K. (1998) 'Firm characteristics and investments in information technology: Scale and scope effects'. *Information Systems Research*, 9(3): 219–32.

Edelman, D.C. (2007) 'From the periphery to the core: As online strategy becomes overall strategy, marketing organizations and agencies will never be the same'. *Journal of Advertising Research*, 47(2): 130–4.

Elenkov, D.S., Judge, W. and Wright, P. (2005) 'Strategic leadership and executive innovation influence: An international multi-cluster comparative study'. *Strategic Management Journal*, 26: 665–82.

Fishman, F.F. and Kemerer, C.F. (1997) 'The assimilation of software process innovations: An organizational learning perspective'. *Management Science*, 43(10): 1345–63.

Fishman, R.G. (2004) 'Going beyond the dominant paradigm for information technology innovation research: Emerging concepts and methods'. *Journal of the AIS*, 5: 314–55.

Fortunato, J.A. and Windels, D.M. (2005) 'Adoption of digital video recorders and advertising: Threats or opportunities?' *Journal of Interactive Advertising*, 6(1): 137–88.

Frambach, R.T. (1993) 'An integrated model of organizational adoption and diffusion of innovations'. *European Journal of Marketing*, 27(5): 22–41.

Frambach, R.T. and Schillewaert, N. (2002) 'Organizational innovation adoption. A multi-level framework of determinants and opportunities for future research'. *Journal of Business Research*, 55(2): 163–76.

Freeman, R.E. (1984) *Strategic Management: A Stakeholder Approach*. Boston: Pitman.

Hartwick, J. and Barki, H. (1994) 'Explaining the role of user participation in information system use'. *Management Science*, 40(4) : 440–65.

Hsu, M.H. and Chiu, C.M. (2004) 'Internet self-efficacy and electronic service acceptance'. *Decision Support Systems*, 38(3): 369–91.

Hsu, M.H., Yen, C.H., Chiu, C.M. and Chang, C.M. (2006) 'A longitudinal investigation of continued online shopping behaviour: An extension of the theory of planned behaviour'. *International Journal of Human-Computer Studies*, 64: 889–904.

Hung, S.Y. and Chang, C.M. (2005) 'User acceptance of WAP services: Test of competing theories'. *Computer Standards and Interfaces*, 27(4): 359–70.

Jeyaraj, A., Rottman, J.W. and Lacity, M.C. (2006) 'A review of the predictors, linkages and biases in IT innovation adoption research'. *Journal of Information Technology*, 21(1): 1–23.

Jones, E., Sundaram, S. and Chin, W. (2002) 'Factors leading to sales force automation use: A longitudinal analysis'. *Journal of Personal Selling and Sales Management*, 22(3): 145–56.

Karahanna, E., Argarwal, R. and Angst, C.M. (2006) 'Reconceptualizing compatibility beliefs in technology acceptance research'. *MIS Quarterly*, 30(4): 781–804.

Kim, H.-W., Chan, H.C. and Chan, Y.P. (2007) 'A balanced thinking-feelings model of information systems continuance'. *International Journal of Human-Computer Studies*, 65(6): 511–25.

Kim, M.-S. and Kim, H. (2007) 'Is there early take-off phenomenon in diffusion of IP-based telecommunications services?' *Omega*, 35(6): 727–39.

Kim, S.S. and Malhotra, N.K. (2005) 'A longitudinal model of continued IS use: An integrative view of four mechanisms underlying postadoption phenomena'. *Management Science*, 51(5): 741–55.

King, W.R. and He, J. (2006) 'A meta-analysis of technology acceptance model'. *Information and Management*, 43(6) : 740–55.

Leckenby, J.D. (2003) The Interaction of Traditional and New Media. Working Paper, US, University of Texas at Austin, Communication College.

Leonard-Barton, D. and Deschamps, I. (1988) 'Managerial influence in the implementation of new technology'. *Management Science*, 34(10): 1252–65.

Maddox, L.W. and Mehta, D. (1997) 'The role and effect of web addresses in advertising'. *Journal of Advertising Research*, 37(2): 47–60.

Moore, G.C. and Benbasat, I. (1991) 'Development of an instrument to measure the perceptions of adopting an information technology innovation'. *Information Systems Research*, 2(3): 192–222.

Papastathopoulou, P., Avlonitis, G.J. and Panagopoulos, N.G. (2007) 'Intraorganizational information and communication technology diffusion: Implications for industrial sellers and buyers'. *Industrial Marketing Management*, 36: 322–36.

Pavlou, P.A. and Fygenson, M. (2006) 'Understanding and predicting electronic commerce adoption: An extension of the theory of planned behaviour'. *MIS Quarterly*, 30(1): 115–43.

Plouffe, C.R., Hulland, J.S. and Vandenbosch, M. (2001) 'Research report: Richness versus parsimony in modelling technology adoption decisions – understanding merchant adoption of a smart card-based payment system'. *Information Systems Research*, 12(2): 208–22.

Rappaport, S.D. (2007) 'Lessons from online practice: New advertising models'. *Journal of Advertising Research*, 47: 135–41.

Reading, N., Bellman, S., Varan, D. and Winzar, H. (2006) 'Effectiveness of telescopic advertisements delivered by personal video recorders'. *Journal of Advertising Research*, 46(2), 217–27.

Riemenschneider, C.K., Harrison, D.A. and Mykytyn, P.P. (2003) 'Understanding IT adoption decisions in small business: Integrating current theories'. *Information and Management*, 40(4): 269–85.

Rogers, E.M. (1995) *Diffusion of Innovation*. New York: Free Press.

Sabherwal, R., Jeyaraj, A. and Chowa, C. (2006) 'Information system success: individual and organizational determinants'. *Management Science*, 52(12): 1849–64.

Schepers, J. and Wetzels, M. (2007) 'A meta-analysis of the technology acceptance model: Investigating subjective norm and moderation effects'. *Information and Management*, 44: 90–103.

Schillewaert, N., Ahearne, M.J., Frambach, R.T. and Moenaert, R. (2000) *The Acceptance of Information Technology in the Sales Force*, ISBM Report No.15-2000. Institute for the Study of Business Markets, Pennsylvania State University.

Shapiro, C. and Varian, H.R. (1999) *Information Rules*. Boston: Harvard Business School Press.

Sheppard, B.H., Hartwick, J. and Warshaw P. (1988) 'The theory of reasoned action: A meta-analysis of past research with recommendations for modifications and future research'. *Journal of Consumer Research*, 15(3): 325–43.

Shibutani, T. (1955) 'Reference groups as perspective'. *American Journal of Sociology*, 60: 562–9.

Singh, J. and Rhoads, R. (1991) 'Boundary role ambiguity in marketing-oriented positions: a multidimensional, multifaceted operationalization'. *Journal of Marketing Research*, 28: 328–38.

Steenkamp, J.-B. and Van Trijp, H. (1991) 'The use of Lisrel in validating marketing constructs'. *International Journal of Research in Marketing*, 8(4): 283–99.

Sun, H. and Zhang, P. (2006) 'The role of moderating factors in user technology acceptance'. *International Journal of Human-Computer Studies*, 64: 53–78.

Tan, M. and Teo, T. (2000) 'Factors influencing the adoption of Internet banking'. *Journal of the Association for Information Systems*, 1(5): 1–42.

Tarafdar, M. and Vaidya, S.D. (2006) 'Challenges in the adoption of e-commerce technologies in India: The role of organizational factors'. *International Journal of Information Management*, 26: 428–41.

Tauder, A.R. (2005) 'Getting ready for the next generation of marketing communications'. *Journal of Advertising Research*, 45(1): 5–8.

Taylor, S. and Todd, P. (1995) 'Understanding information technology usage: A test of competing models'. *Information Systems Research*, 6(2): 144–76.

Tornatzky, L.G. and Fleischer, M. (1990) *The Process of Technological Innovation*. Lextington, MA: Lexington Books.

Triandis, H.C. (1977) *Interpersonal Behavior.* Monterey, CA: Brooks Cole.

Venkatesh, V. and Davis, F.D. (2000) 'A theoretical extension of the technology acceptance model: Four longitudinal studies'. *Management Science*, 46(2): 186–204.

Venkatesh, V., Morris, M.G., Davis, G.B. and Davis, F.D. (2003) 'User acceptance of information technology: Toward a unified view'. *MIS Quarterly*, 27(3): 425–78.

Wang, K.C., Chou, S.H., Su, S.J. and Tsai, H.Y. (2007) 'More information, stronger effectiveness? Different group package tour advertising component on web page'. *Journal of Business Research*, 60: 382–7.

Weber, I. and Evans, V. (2002) 'Constructing the meaning of digital television in Britain, the United States and Australia'. *New Media and Society*, 4(4): 435–56.

Workman, M. (2005) 'Expert decision support system use, disuse, and misuse: A study using theory of planned behaviour'. *Computers in Human Behavior*, 21: 211–31.

Woszczynski, A.B. and Whitman, M.E. (2004) 'The problem of common method variance in IS research', in M.E. Whitma and A.B. Woszczynski (eds) *The Handbook of Information Systems Research*. Hershey, PA: Idea Group Publishing.

Wu, I.L. and Chen, J.L. (2005) 'An extension of Trust and TAM model with TPB in the initial adoption of online-tax: An empirical study'. *International Journal of Human-Computer Studies*, 62(6): 784–808.

Yi, M.Y., Jackson, J.D., Park, J.S. and Probst, J.C. (2006) 'Understanding information technology acceptance by individual professionals: Toward an integrative view'. *Information and Management*, 43(3): 350–63.

Zaltman, G., Duncan, R. and Holbek, J. (1973) *Innovations and Organizations*. New York: Wiley.

Zmud, R.W. (1982) 'Diffusion of modern software practices: Influences of centralization and formalization'. *Management Science*, 28(12): 1421–31.

9

Employee development in the international arena: internal marketing and human resource management perspectives

Klement Podnar, Andrej Kohont and Zlatko Jančič

Learning outcomes

At the end of this chapter, readers should be able to:

1. Understand the importance of internal marketing.
2. Understand what is meant by international human resource management (IHRM) and the importance of human resources (HR) in achieving competitiveness in the international business context.
3. Specify the key HR challenges for international marketing managers.
4. Gain an insight into the career development practices of international firms.

Key points

- Organizational culture and human resources are important for organizational success.
- Employees should no longer be seen as mere costs to the organization but as an important organizational resource in the international arena.
- IHRM refers to themes and problems in the frame of HRM that appear with the internationalization of business.
- There are different practices that firms can use for employee career development, such as networking, formal career plans, participation in project teamwork, special tasks/projects to stimulate learning, involvement in cross-organizational discipli-

nary/functional tasks, assessment centres, planned job rotation, succession plans, experience schemes, 'high-flyer' schemes, and secondments to other organizations.

- The most widely used methods in EU-based organizations are participation in project teamwork and involvement in cross-organizational tasks. The biggest difference between EU and US organizations seems to be in formal career plans, since more than a quarter of US companies use this method extensively compared to only a few of the EU-based organizations.

Introduction

The aim of this chapter is to contribute to the body of literature in the domain of 'human resources' and its development in international organizations, an area in which there is a paucity of research. It combines knowledge from internal marketing and human resource management (HRM) literature to develop the framework for research on management career development in international firms. Employee development initiatives have become increasingly popular in theory, but little is known about their appeal in international firms. The chapter concludes with a comparative analysis of the use of manager development practices in international companies based in the EU and North America.

The power of employees became evident in the early 1980s due to the rapid influx of Japanese brands into Western markets. In order to explain this phenomenon, an enormous amount of research has been carried out in the fields of strategic management, total quality management, organizational theory, and marketing (Peters and Waterman, 1982; Kotler et al., 1985; Porter, 1985; Pascale and Athos, 1986; Veltrop and Harrington, 1986). One of the main findings was the renewed importance of the social organizational culture (Ouchi, 1981; Deal and Kennedy, 1982), which promotes the commitment of employees to organizational success. This phenomenon was studied extensively by Hofstede (1985) in international surroundings. Since then, national and organizational culture has become an analytical basis for international marketing research (Steenkamp, 2001). It became evident that people should no longer be seen as mere costs to the organization but as an important organizational resource, in some cases even as key members who constitute the vibrant and creative corporate community.

An important breakthrough also happened in the marketing discipline, where research turned inwards to focus on the internal stakeholders, namely employees and managers. The concept of internal marketing (Sasser and Arbeit, 1976; Grönroos, 1978; Berry, 1981; Flipo, 1986; Jančič, 1990; Thomson, 1990; Percy and Morgan, 1991) was born, with the idea that companies should treat their employees as internal customers who give their efforts, energies and competences in exchange for a job and a set of rewards from the organization. The notion of internal marketing is a big step forward from the predominant one-way internal communication preferred by managers and their specialists in employee communication, who were, according to Grunig (1992), known as industrial editors and business journalists. Despite the fact that the development of the marketing paradigm has brought about the development of the concept of internal marketing from the transactional-oriented to the relationship-oriented approach (see Rafiq and Ahmed, 2000), its basic idea remains unchanged: an organization will not be successful in the external market if it has not first established reciprocal relationships in its internal market. In view of the diversity of definitions, internal marketing is defined as:

> a planned effort using a marketing-like approach to overcome organizational resistance to change and to align, motivate and interfunctionally co-ordinate and integrate employees towards the effective implementation of corporate and functional strategies in order to deliver customer satisfaction through a process of creating motivated and customer orientated employees. (Rafiq and Ahmed, 2000, p. 454)

Although established as an important research field, most practical internal marketing activities remained organization centred and merely communications oriented. Through a lack of understanding of the complex exchange loops that take place within the internal marketing environment, substantial changes on the side of organization were, in many cases, not made. Internal marketing projects were concocted in 'ivory towers' or through the use of outside consultants and thus did not represent a genuine approach and had few successful results, and sometimes even the opposite effect of a lowering of trust in the real intentions of the organization. The psychological contract between employees and organization (Handy, 1985) mostly remained calculative and non-cooperative.

International marketing textbooks recognize people as a vital resource to an international or global firm, but studies researching employees in an international marketing context are still rather scarce. The people factor is usually mentioned together with the problems of organization, organizational structure and managerial style. Authors who combine international and internal marketing knowledge are rare. A literature review shows us that the concept of internal marketing is elaborated in 'vacuum' conditions, regardless of where the organization markets its products or services. Less is known, however, about the diversities that are present in international or global settings.

The reluctance of the marketing discipline to address the problems of internal marketing opened the field to other disciplines, especially HRM. The complexity of the people factor led Varey (2002, p. 217) to make the following claim: 'internal marketing is the overlap between marketing management and human resources management'. To fill this gap, we will try to seek further answers in the field of HRM.

HR in international business has received the attention of both scholars and practising managers, although it is questioned whether international companies based in the EU and North America are equally enthusiastic about the different methods of employee development. The purpose of this chapter is therefore to examine some contemporary issues regarding HR in the international business context. First we present a brief discussion on the concept of international HRM and the identification of HR challenges for international managers, as well an introduction to the problem of manager development in the international arena. This is followed by an introduction to the research methodology and analysis. Results for the EU are compared, wherever possible, with those for North America to demonstrate the differences in manager development practices. The chapter concludes with a discussion.

International human resource management

Recently, it has become widely accepted that HRM is more and more important for achieving success and retaining or strengthening domestic as well as international competitiveness (Pfeffer, 1994). The distinction between domestic HRM and international HRM (IHRM) comes from the novel approaches, adjustments and adaptations necessitated by cultural diversity, the legal environment, and increased geographical distances. It is certain that if a company operating in the domestic market enters the international arena, the different institutional and cultural environments will force it to deal with 'several new aspects of HRM not relevant to domestic environments, in order to ensure successful operation' (Dowling and Welch, 2004, p. 8).

More than 40 years ago, Fayerweather (1960) and some years later Bormann (1968) wrote about the difficulties faced by expatriates in different cultures. But it is important to emphasize that for a long time in publications, only foreign trade, investment and marketing aspects had a role in relation to the globalization of companies. Until now, the most influential theory of IHRM was published by Perlmutter in 1969 (quoted in Scullion et al., 2007), who emphasized that the IHRM practices of various multinational companies (MNCs) largely depend on how their local (ethnocentric) HRM practice is followed abroad or how they adapt to the local (polycentric), regional (regiocentric), and global (geocentric) conditions.

As a result of internationalization and globalization, the discipline of IHRM appeared. IRHM is defined as HRM issues, functions, policies and practices that result from the strategic activities of MNCs and impact the international concerns and goals of these companies (Schuler et al., 1993, quoted in Briscoe and Schuller, 2004). In other words, IHRM refers to themes and problems in the frame of HRM that appear with the internationalization of business and all the HRM strategies, activities and orientations that a company uses because of its internationalization (De Cieri and Dowling et al., 2006). The main reasons for the growth of interest in IHRM have been outlined by Scullion and Paauwe (2004), following their extensive literature review:

1. The rapid growth of internationalization and global competition has increased the number and significance of MNCs in recent years and has resulted in increased mobility of HR.
2. The effective management of HR is increasingly recognized as a major determinant of success or failure in international business (Black et al., 1999), and it has been argued that the success of a global business depends, importantly, on the quality of management in the MNC (Stroh and Caliguiri, 1998).
3. Underperformance or failure in international assignments continues to be costly, both in financial and human terms, and research suggests that the indirect costs of poor performance in international assignments, such as damage to foreign customer relations, may be particularly costly (Dowling et al., 1999).
4. The implementation of global strategies is frequently constrained by shortages of international management talent (Caliguri and Cascio, 1998), which constrain corporate efforts to expand abroad (Scullion and Starkey, 2000).
5. IHRM issues are increasingly important in a wider range of organizations, partly due to the rapid growth of internationalization in small and medium-sized enterprises in

recent years, and the internationalization theories that have been developed for larger MNCs do not adequately explain the approaches used in smaller firms.

6. The movement away from traditional hierarchical organizational structures towards the network MNC organization has been facilitated by the development of networks of personal relationships and horizontal communication channels (Forsgren, 1989; Barlett and Ghoshal, 1989), and it has been argued that HR play a more significant role in network organizations (Marschan et al., 1997).

7. Finally, there is growing evidence that HR strategy plays a more significant role in implementation and control in the international firm (Scullion and Starkey, 2000). It has been suggested that in a rapidly globalizing environment, many MNCs have less difficulty determining which strategies to pursue than determining how to implement them, and it has been argued that the success of any global or transnational strategy has less to do with structural innovations than with developing often radically different organizational cultures (Barlett and Ghoshal, 1989).

According to Sparrow et al. (2004), the key debates in the IHRM literature relate to the following four issues:

1. the strategy–structure configurations of international organizations
2. the differences between domestic and international HRM
3. the question of how MNCs approach the staffing and measurement of their subsidiaries
4. the role of organizational factors in determining the extent of international consistency or local isomorphism.

It is clear from references in the studies that the situation has now changed significantly, and researchers have widened the scope of their surveys, although in different ways in terms of detail and attention, to cover the following new topics:

• global values, organizational culture and intercultural communication (Harzing and Ruysseveldt, 2004; Paauwe and Farndale, 2006)
• the avoidance of cultural shocks (Husted, 2003)
• the roles of HRM departments in multinational companies (Tung, 2001; Dowling and Welch, 2004; Stiles and Trevor, 2006)
• the standardization and transfers of HRM practices (Taylor, 1996, quoted in Harzing and Ruysseveldt, 2004)
• intercultural development and the efficient preparation of employees and their families prior to work assignments (Briscoe and Schuller, 2004; Tarique and Caligiuri, 2004; Parkinson and Morley, 2006)
• the reintegration process and future career opportunities (Lazarova and Caligiuri, 2004)
• knowledge sharing (Sparrow et al., 2004; Osland et al., 2006)
• HRM issues related to local human resources (Evans et al., 2002; Dowling and Welch, 2004).

There are also efforts to develop an integrative frame for the purpose of analysing strategic IHRM that would involve internal and external factors (Schuller and Jackson,

1999; Brewster et al., 2000; Paauwe and Farnadale, 2005). Internal factors represent the characteristics of different sectors, technologies, competitors, scope and speed of changes, and national and regional characteristics (political, economic and sociocultural characteristics, legal regulations and so on). Approaches to internal factors by authors consider MNCs' market entrance strategies, orientation of the headquarters, policies, customs (for example Tylor's flexible export and integrative strategies) and the scope of internationalization experiences. Approaches to IHRM differ and we can distinguish between the comparative perspective, the perspective of cultural and national differences, and discussions about convergence, divergence and combinations of HRM practices and tools.

Sparrow and Hiltrop (1997, quoted in Sparrow et al., 2004) suggest that IHRM analyses should always consider three factors:

1. The scope and diversity of factors that influence national and local HRM practices
2. Strategies and pressures that require national HRM models to be adapted to changes and further developed
3. Processes at the company level that will (or will not) make the HRM changes and developmental shifts possible.

A key question for MNCs is not the determination of the best HRM policy but how to ensure the best fit between the company's strategy, structure and HRM approach. International business strategy is an important determinant of HRM policies and practices and at the same time international human resources are strategic resources that have an influence on strategy design and implementation (Harvey, 1997, quoted in Paauwe, 2004). The HRM contribution in an MNC is reflected in its competence to manage the fragile equilibrium between the coordination of the HRM system at the MNC level as a whole and in its response to local needs, which involve cultural and institutional differences on one side and business orientation and company culture and philosophy on the other (Sparrow et al., 2004).

Key HR challenges for international managers

The first challenge that companies face when focusing on international HR is the question of whether they will send employees on an assignment abroad or meet their staff needs in cooperation with people from local areas (host or third country nationals). This is an important issue, especially since research shows that the reasons for posting abroad affect expatriates' performance and adjustment in the new cultural environment (Shay and Baack, 2004, quoted in Collings and Scullion, 2006). Edström and Galbraith (1977, quoted in Collings and Scullion, 2006), indicate the three main motives that lead companies to use expatriates: to fill vacancies, to use international assignments for managers' development purposes, or to use them for company development.

International assignments depend on people's characteristics, competences and experiences. With appropriate selection prior to an international assignment, the company can be more aware of the employee's characteristics and can minimize the threat of posting employees who do not possess the required characteristics. In the first major study of the selection criteria for international business, Tung (1981, quoted in Harzing and Ruysseveldt, 2004) identified four factors that affect the performance of expatriates and should therefore be taken into account when selecting employees in international companies:

1. professional or job-specific competence
2. personal characteristics and the ability to make new contacts
3. the ability to deal with new environmental factors
4. family situation.

Despite these criteria, a number of international companies still emphasize the professional competences in their selection.

Another internationalization decision is linked with investments in equipment and facilities, and the company's success is largely dependent on the people who are responsible for the management of the subsidiary. Therefore, one of the key decisions in relation to the selection is who will manage the subsidiary.

The next important issue is the preparation of employees to work abroad. International assignments contribute to the development of employees and the company, since they are the source of new knowledge, but they can also be a source of problems, especially if employees do not know enough about the new cultural environment. Employees will be more effective in foreign environments and will overcome cultural shocks sooner if they are familiar with the norms and values of the host country. Many international firms offer intercultural training, which can be any form of training that enables personnel to acquire the knowledge and skills needed to successfully live and work abroad and contribute to the achievement of life satisfaction in an unknown foreign culture (Kealey and Protheroe, 1996, quoted in Tarique and Caligiuri, 2004).

Another challenge is employee adaptation. Black et al. (1991, quoted in Harzing and Ruysseveldt, 2004) consider that the adaptation of employees posted abroad includes pre-adjustment and adaptation in the host country. Preliminary alignment, cross-cultural training and positive prior international experience contribute to faster adaptation in the host country. Both types of adjustment contribute to the creation of realistic expectations. The more realistic the expectations of the employee sent abroad, the lower the level of uncertainty and the fewer the surprises and cultural shocks. Adjustment in the host country has been studied by Shaffer et al. (1999, quoted in Harzing and Ruysseveldt, 2004). They found that adjustment is most dependent on the tasks performed by the worker abroad and their language skills, especially how fluent they are in the language of the host country. They further observed that the clarity of tasks and the level of autonomy in performing them have a positive impact on the adjustment to the work, while co-workers' support and logistical support contribute to better interactions with the host country nationals. The adaptation of the spouse or partner contributes most to the general adaptation to life conditions in the host country.

It is also worth mentioning the factors that affect the performance of expatriates. Dowling et al. (2008) identified the reward package and career development opportunities, employee job or role, support from headquarters, the business environment in the host country, and the cultural adaptation of the employee and their family.

According to Gomez-Meija et al. (2004), expatriate failure or low performance abroad can be a consequence of career block, cultural shock, lack of intercultural training before departure abroad, emphasis on technical competence, the company tendency to send problematic colleagues on international assignments, and family problems.

International assignments also have a huge impact on the professional and career development of individuals, allowing them to acquire knowledge and experience that can improve their performance and are useful for business. The retention of returnees and their reintegration after returning from abroad also represent challenges to HRM in an international company. Returnees provide the company with a stock of knowledge about the international environment; they have knowledge of the local market, business climate, cultural patterns, habits of consumers and local suppliers, and they have established a broad social network in the environment in which they were working. If it is overlooked or not properly planned, the reintegration of returnees may also be a source of personal and professional problems and concerns. The majority of employees sent abroad face reverse culture shock (Gullahorm and Gullahorn, 1963, quoted in Lazarova and Caligiuri, 2004) when they come back, so the return to the home country can sometimes be quite stressful. The consequences of the return to the home country can be reflected in a loss of the status, power, prestige, independence and authority that were characteristic of the work abroad. The problems may also include the returnee's inability to use the gained knowledge, a lack of respect, or the rapid decline of co-workers', friends' and acquaintances' interest in the lessons and experiences that were acquired abroad. Return to the home country can bring further disappointment in the professional field if the company planned the returnee's role and place of work after the return poorly. This is why a special area in IHRM is the development of international managers and their careers.

International employee development

In an international and global context, a great challenge is to educate international managers, who must have a wide range of international experience, competences and skills that are also consistent with the global business strategy. From the internal marketing perspective, employee development can be seen as an important exchange component in the firm's relationships with its employees. As noted by Maurer and Lippstreu (2008), employees are favourably disposed towards an organization that provides something valuable to employees: 'Following this logic, when an organization provides something valuable such as support for employee development, this should create a mindset in employees that is positive toward the organization' (Maurer and Lippstreu, 2008, p. 329). There is a great deal of literature and evidence confirming the beneficial effects of employee development practices, where authors focus on different approaches to employee training and development that support the employing organization's business goals and strategy. Surveys suggest that when organizations make efforts to develop their managers, the managers become more committed to the organization and are also more likely to develop their employees (Tansky and Cohen, 2002).

The literature suggests several different practices that firms can use for employee career development: networking, formal career plans, participation in project teamwork, special tasks/projects to stimulate learning, involvement in cross-organizational disciplinary/functional tasks, assessment centres, planned job rotation, succession plans, experience schemes, 'high-flyer' schemes, and secondments to other organizations.

Although it is important, the training of managers in an international context is not easy, because it requires additional resources and brings more complexity to established policies and programmes of training and development in the company. In addition, there are also cultural factors that are responsible for relative deficiencies in learning and skill acquisition that are characteristic for some companies. In this context, we now examine the forms of employee development practices prevailing in selected companies based in the EU and North America. Comparative analyses will show whether there are any differences between international companies based in the EU and North America regarding the use of manager development practices. A study of this nature will add to the body of literature on cross-cultural management practices. It will also provide insights into the management practices of international firms from the two most developed markets.

Methodology and data

The data are drawn from the Cranet (Cranfield Network on International Human Resource Management) international survey, which is the largest and most representative independent longitudinal survey in HRM (Stavrou, 2005). The Cranet survey meets all the requirements in terms of validity concerning the size of organizations in the sample (on average they have 1,546 employees), the expertise of the source responding (members of the corporate HR team), and the clarity of items in the survey achieved by the international Cranet team of experts (Brewster et al., 1996).

These data are based on the latest survey, which contained responses from 8,000 organizations across 32 countries. The questionnaire was distributed by post among senior HR directors. Our sample consists of 2,095 private sector organizations from 31 countries, with around 80% of them having headquarters in the EU and the rest coming from the US and Canada. The organizations in our sample are all international organizations selling their goods to regional markets (13.4%), EU markets (22.6%), or worldwide (64%).

The variable studied in this section is part of the question on employee development. Respondents were asked to evaluate the extent to which they use different methods for managerial career development on a scale ranging from 'not at all', 'to a small extent', 'to a large extent', or 'entirely'.

Results

Interestingly, although the development of global managers seems to be an important topic and an emerging research agenda (Dowling and Welch, 2004), the data from the analysed survey show that organizations serving international markets tend to use methods of managerial development to a lesser extent, on average (see Table 9.1).

Table 9.1		Percentages, means and medians of career development methods used in international organizations				

Method	Not at all	To a small extent	To a large extent	Entirely	Mean	Median
Special tasks/projects to stimulate learning	18.6	49.0	30.0	2.3	2.16	2.00
Involvement in cross-organizational/disciplinary/functional tasks	15.0	45.2	36.8	3.0	2.28	2.00
Participation in project teamwork	8.5	37.0	48.8	5.7	2.52	3.00
Networking	27.3	46.2	24.2	2.4	2.02	2.00
Formal career plans	38.0	42.5	17.1	2.4	1.84	2.00
Assessment centres	66.3	23.6	8.6	1.6	1.45	1.00
Succession plans	31.9	43.2	22.3	2.6	1.96	2.00
Planned job rotation	47.6	40.7	10.9	0.8	1.65	2.00
High-flyer schemes	50.6	31.0	15.9	2.5	1.70	1.00
Secondments to other organizations	59.0	34.8	5.7	0.5	1.48	1.00

Only the method of participation in project teamwork is used to a large extent by almost 50% of the surveyed organizations. Assessments centres, high-flyer schemes and secondments to other organizations are, on average, not used at all in the surveyed organizations (median = 1).

Comparing the organizations based in the EU and North America using ANOVA, statistically significant differences were found to exist in the implementation of methods of career development in the cases of special tasks to stimulate learning (F = 7.534, p = 0.006), participation in project teamwork (F = 6.835, p = 0.009), networking (F = 11.830, p = 0.001), formal career plans (F = 49.147, p = 0.000), and succession plans (F = 26.892, p < 0.000). As can be seen from Table 9.2, all the methods where statistically significant differences exist are more extensively used in the organizations with headquarters in North America. However, we must note that the differences are very small.

A closer examination of the percentages (see Table 9.3) representing the usage of a particular method for managerial career development in the organizations with headquarters in the EU shows that these organizations did not fully use of the methods of assessment centres, planned job rotation, high-flyer schemes and secondments to other organizations in improving managerial careers. These methods are not used in more than half of EU-based organizations. A similar picture can be seen in the case of North American organizations. However, the percentage of those using high-flyer schemes is significantly lower – 45.9% in North American organizations compared to 52% in the EU-based organizations. It also seems that many EU organizations (41%)

Table 9.2	Results of the ANOVA analysis in the EU and North America (NA)

Method	Mean		F value	Sig.
	EU	NA		
Special tasks/projects to stimulate learning	2.14	2.28	7.534	0.006*
Involvement in cross-organizational/ disciplinary/functional tasks	2.27	2.31	0.717	0.397
Participation in project teamwork	2.49	2.60	6.835	0.009*
Networking	1.98	2.14	11.830	0.001*
Formal career plans	1.78	2.10	49.147	0.000*
Assessment centres	1.45	1.44	0.123	0.726
Succession plans	1.91	2.14	26.892	0.000*
Planned job rotation	1.64	1.67	0.648	0.421
High-flyer schemes	1.69	1.77	3.409	0.065
Secondments to other organizations	1.48	1.48	0.070	0.791

Note: * Significant at the 0.05 level

Table 9.3	Comparison of career development methods used in companies based in the EU and North America (NA)

Method	Not at all		To a small extent		To a large extent		Entirely	
	EU	NA	EU	NA	EU	NA	EU	NA
Special tasks/projects to stimulate learning	19.7	14.5	49.3	47.9	28.6	35.6	2.4	2.0
Involvement in cross-organizational/ disciplinary/functional tasks	15.6	12.6	44.8	46.9	36.6	37.8	3.0	2.7
Participation in project teamwork	9.6	4.5	36.9	37.1	47.9	52.2	5.6	6.2
Networking	29.0	20.5	45.2	50.1	24.1	24.6	1.8	4.8
Formal career plans	41.0	26.1	42.2	43.9	15.0	25.4	1.8	4.6
Assessment centres	66.3	66.1	23.5	23.8	8.2	9.9	1.9	0.3
Succession plans	33.9	24.1	43.3	42.5	20.7	28.6	2.0	4.8
Planned job rotation	48.4	44.3	39.7	45.0	11.3	9.7	0.7	1.0
High-flyer schemes	51.8	45.9	30.2	34.4	15.7	16.4	2.3	3.3
Secondments to other organizations	58.5	61.3	35.7	30.8	5.2	7.7	0.6	0.3

Note: The numbers are the percentages of firms using or not using a particular method

do not use formal career plans as a career development tool compared to only 26% of North American organizations who do not use them.

The most widely used methods in the EU-based organizations are participation in project teamwork (used by 48% of organizations) and involvement in cross-organizational tasks (almost 37% of organizations use it to a larger extent). The situation is quite similar in the organizations based in North America: more than half of them use participation in project teamwork as a method of career development. The biggest difference between organizations seems to be in formal career plans: more than a quarter of North American companies use this method extensively compared to only 15% of the EU-based organizations, where formal career plans are obviously not seen as an attractive method of fostering managerial careers.

Conclusion

Internal marketing seen through the social exchange perspective offers the necessary theoretical foundation for the study of HR. It is based on the notion of the importance of productive reciprocal relationships within organizations. However, practice shows us that these relationships are often underdeveloped and in many cases only lip service is paid to them. Due to the reluctance of marketing academia to accept the universality of marketing manifested in its broadened conception, the concept of internal marketing has never reached its full potential. Many marketing academics believe that the internal exchange should be regarded as an organizational behaviour discipline, specially part of the study of HRM. The long history of the discipline of HRM and its vast body of knowledge should produce the required answers to this special topic.

This chapter offers an overview of some of the important topics and challenges that IHRM brings to the international marketing agenda, such as international assignments, the selection process prior to an international assignment, the preparation of employees to work abroad, employee adaptation, and the management of factors that affect the performance of expatriates. Among the special topics that relate directly to internal marketing are career and employee development, especially at the management level, which allow employees to acquire knowledge and experience that can improve their performance and contribute to the success of the international business.

Although the literature suggests different practices that firms can use for employee career development, our comparative analysis shows that the majority of companies based in the EU and North America rarely use them in practice. Among the most widely used methods are participation in project teamwork and involvement in cross-organizational tasks, while the methods of assessment centres, planned job rotation, high-flyer schemes and secondments to other organizations in order to stimulate managerial careers are not used by more than half the international organizations included in the Cranet sample. Interesting questions are why the methods of management career development are used relatively rarely in practice and how to stimulate international organizations to use them to a larger extent.

Without denying the importance of HRM, we still believe that the concept of internal marketing is strongly needed, since it emphasizes the importance of reciprocity between organizations and their members. Internal marketing can be regarded as an overlap between marketing and HRM, and thus further cooperation between both disciplines is strongly needed, especially in the context of international marketing.

Issues for further discussion

1. The data presented show that organizations serving international markets tend to use methods for managerial development to a lesser extent. What could be the reasons for this situation?
2. If you were a member of an international team selecting candidates for the position of marketing manager, which selection criteria would you recommend?
3. What could be the consequences for the organization of not using methods to stimulate learning? Think about its internal and external environment.
4. What, in your opinion, are the obstacles that prevent the internal marketing concept from reaching its full potential?
5. What is the relationship between internal and external marketing in the international business context?
6. What is your opinion on the importance of internal marketing and its relation to marketing and HRM?

CASE STUDY

The development of HR in an international retail chain

The Mercator Group is one of the largest and most successful commercial chains in southeastern Europe; it is the leading commercial chain in Slovenia and is rapidly becoming an established chain in the markets of Serbia, Croatia, and Bosnia and Herzegovina. In 2005, it entered the Macedonian market. These are all fast-growing markets, where it builds shopping malls in capitals and regional centres with the largest potential in terms of the number of residents and purchasing power. Mercator hopes to attain a considerable market share in a short period of time, becoming the first or second largest fast-moving consumer goods retailer in each market. The company is known for its excellent business results and persistent targeting of markets across domestic borders. With professional service and a warm smile, it seeks to establish a personalized relationship with customers who confide in it and are happy to return to its stores.

The Mercator Group has over 21,000 employees. Care for employees is the most important task of the HR division, as the successful pursuit of the company's business strategy depends predominantly on its employees. To effectively deliver what is defined in its mission, the HR division has formulated an HR strategy to ensure the flexibility of HR and the organization as a whole. The HR priorities are as follows:

- *Career planning of key and promising personnel:* A programme has been introduced to develop the careers of key and promising personnel, which will, in the long term, ensure optimal staffing for the most important positions at Mercator Group.
- *Dialogue with employees at all levels:* Mercator wishes to improve internal communication through dialogue with employees. For the HR manager, both formal and informal communication channels are important; it uses an internal newspaper, messages for employees, systematic meetings, announcements on bulletin boards, celebration of achievements, annual interviews and so on.

- *The transfer of knowledge and experience:* The exchange of knowledge and experience between employees creates new knowledge quality. Education is the responsibility of employees, especially management, who want to encourage the transfer of know-how from older employees to the young, from experienced to less experienced, from those previously employed to those who are new to the business.
- *Internal and external staffing policy:* The CEO and HR department have formulated rules of internal staffing, which enable quickness, simplicity and clarity in calls for application and in the corresponding procedures. They wish to encourage promising employees to experience various fields of the business and thereby develop their professional career. The primary principle of internal staffing is that the desire to change workplaces is a legitimate and normal need of an individual. External staffing is also vital to Mercator, as this ensures freshness of ideas and the direct use of managerial, professional and international experience.
- *Rewards and motivation:* Realistic expectations with regard to rewards are defined in the psychological contract, and it is made clear that success is measured by the achievement of goals. In rewards and motivation, a system of both material and nonmaterial stimulation must be considered.
- *Intercultural organizational development:* Mercator employees work in an international company. Especially Slovenians employed at Mercator require a stronger awareness of the international dimension of the company. It is important to transfer Mercator's organizational culture to foreign markets, while taking into consideration the national cultures of countries where its companies are located.
- *Management of changes – innovation activity:* The strategic task of HR is also to continuously obtain suggestions for improvement from employees. A culture must be created that will encourage creativity and innovation among employees at all levels of the organization.
- *Safety and health of employees:* Mercator wishes to introduce a programme of ergonomic planning of the work environment and preventive health for employees, such as anti-stress programmes, promotion of a healthy lifestyle and so on, through which employees will retain their work capabilities in the long term.

There is more information at http://www.mercator.si/.

Questions

1. What communication tools would you recommend to the group to stimulate the transfer of knowledge and experience and to improve internal communication?
2. Based on the results of Cranet survey above regarding manager development practices, what would you include in a three-year HR development action plan to ensure the career planning and development of key and promising personnel for further internationalization of the Mercator Group.

References

Bartlett, C.A. and Ghoshal, S. (1989) *Managing Across Borders: The Transnational Solution*. London: Hutchinson.

Berry, L.L. (1981) 'The employee as customer'. *Journal of Retail Banking*, 3: 33–40.

Black, J.S., Gregersen, H.B., Mendenhall, M. and Stroh, L. (1999) *Globalizing People Through International Assignments*. Boston: Addison-Wesley.

Bormann, W.A. (1968) *Personalwirtschaftliche Sonderprobleme internationalen Unternehmungen*. München: Diss.

Brewster, C., Mayrhofer, W. and Morley, M. (eds) (2000) *New Challenges for European Human Resource Management*. Basingstoke: Macmillan – now Palgrave Macmillan.

Brewster, C., Tregaskis, O., Hegewisch, A. and Mayne, L. (1996) 'Comparative research in human resource management: A review and an example'. *International Journal of Human Resource Management*, 7(3): 585–604.

Briscoe, D.R. and Schuler, R.S. (2004) *International Human Resource Management: Policy and Practice for the Global Enterprise*. London: Routledge.

Caligiuri, P.M. and Cascio, W . (1998) 'Can we send her there? Maximizing the success of Western women on global assignments'. *Journal of World Business*, 33: 394–416.

Collings, D. and Scullion, H. (2006) 'Global staffing', in G.K. Stahl and I. Bjorkman (eds) *Handbook of Research in International Human Resource Management*. Cheltenham: Edward Elgar.

De Cieri, H. and Dowling, P.J. (2006) 'Strategic international human resource management in multinational enterprises: Developments and directions', in G.K. Stahl and I. Bjorkman (eds) *Handbook of Research in International Human Resource Management*. Cheltenham: Edward Elgar.

Deal, T.E. and Kennedy, A.A. (1982) *Corporate Cultures: The Rites and Rituals of Corporate Life*. Reading: Addison-Wesley.

Dowling, P.J. and Welch, D.E. (2004) *International Human Resource Management*. London: Thomson.

Dowling, P.J., Festing, M. and Engle, A.D. (2008) *International Human Resource Management: Managing People in a Multinational Context* (5th edn). London: Cengage Learning EMEA.

Dowling, P.J., Welch, D.E. and Schuler, R.S. (1999) *International Human Resource Management: Managing People in an International Context* (3rd edn). Cincinnati, OH: South-Western.

Evans, P., Pucik, V. and Barsoux, J. (2002) *The Global Challenge: Frameworks for International Human Resource Management*. Homewood, IL: McGraw-Hill/Irwin.

Fayerweather, J. (1960) *International Business Management: A Conceptual Framework*. New York: Greenwood Press.

Flipo, J.P. (1986) 'Service firms: Interdependence of external and internal marketing strategies'. *European Journal of Marketing*, 20(8): 5–14.

Forsgren, M. (1989) *Managing the Internationalisation Process: A Swedish Case*. London: Routledge.

Gomez-Meija, L.R., Balkin, D.B. and Cardy, R.L. (2004) *Managing Human Resources*. Upper Saddle River, NJ: Pearson/Prentice Hall.

Grönroos, C. (1978) 'A service-oriented approach to the marketing of services'. *European Journal of Marketing*, 12(8): 588–601.

Grunig, J.E. (1992) 'Symmetrical systems of internal communication', in J.E. Grunig (ed.) *Excellence in Public Relations and Communication Management*. Hillsdale, NJ: Lawrence Erlbaum.

Gummesson, E. (1999) *Total Relationship Marketing. Rethinking Marketing Management: From 4 Ps to 30Rs*. Oxford: Butterworth Heinemann.

Handy, C. (1985) *Understanding Organizations*. New York: Penguin Business.

Harzing, A.-W. and Ruysseveldt, J.V. (eds) (2004) *International Human Resource Management* (2nd edn). London: Sage.

Hofstede, G. (1985) 'The cultural perspective', in A. Brakel (ed.) *People and Organizations Interacting*. New York: John Wiley & Sons.

Husted, B. (2003) *Globalization and Cultural Change in International Business Research*. Copenhagen: Copenhagen Business School Press.

Jančič, Z. (1990) *Marketing: Studio Marketing (Strategija Menjave: Gospodarski Vestnik)*. Ljubljana: Economic Gazette.

Kotler, P., Fahey, L. and Jatusripitak, S. (1985) *The New Competition*. Englewood Cliffs, NJ: Prentice Hall.

Lazarova, M. and Caligiuri, P. (2004) 'Repatriation and knowledge management', in A.-W. Harzing, and J.V. Ruysseveldt (eds) *International Human Resource Management*. London: Sage.

Marschan, R., Welch, D. and Welch, L. (1997) 'Control in less hierarchical multinationals: The role of personal networks and informal communication'. *International Business Review*, 5(2): 137–50.

Maurer, T.J. and Lippstreu, M. (2008) 'Who will be committed to an organization that provides support for employee development?' *Journal of Management Development*, 27(3): 328–47.

Osland, J.S., Bird, A., Mendenhall, M. and Osland, A. (2006) 'Developing global leadership capabilities and global mindset: A review', in G.K. Stahl and I. Bjorkman (eds) *Handbook of Research in International Human Resource Management*. Cheltenham: Edward Elgar.

Ouchi, W.G. (1981) *Theory Z: How American Business Can Meet the Japanese Challenge*. Reading: Adison-Wesley.

Paauwe, J. (2004) *HRM and Performance: Unique Approaches for Achieving Long-term Viability*. Oxford: Oxford University Press.

Paauwe, J. and Farndale, E. (2006) 'International human resource management and firm performance', in G.K. Stahl and I. Bjorkman (eds) *Handbook of Research in International Human Resource Management*. Cheltenham: Edward Elgar.

Parkinson, E. and Morley, M.J. (2006) 'Cross-cultural training', in H. Scullion and G.D. Collings (eds) *Global Staffing*. London: Routledge.

Pascale, A.T. and Athos, A.G. (1986) *The Art of Japanese Management*. New York: Penguin Books.

Percy, N. and Morgan, N. (1991) 'Internal marketing: The missing half of the marketing programme'. *Long Range Planning*, 24(2): 82–93.

Peters, T.J. and Waterman, R.H. (1982) *In Search of Excellence*. New York: Harper & Row.

Pfeffer, J. (1994) *Competitive Advantage Through People*. Boston: Harvard Business School Press.

Porter, M. (1985) *Competitive Advantage*. New York: The Free Press.

Rafiq, M. and Ahmed, P. (2000) 'Advances in internal marketing concept: Definition, synthesis and extension'. *Journal of Services Marketing*, 14(6): 449–62.

Sasser, W.E. and Arbeit, S.F. (1976) 'Selling jobs in the service sector'. *Business Horizons*, June, 61–2.

Schuler, R.S. and Jackson, S.E. (eds) (1999) *Strategic International Human Resource Management: A Reader*. London: Blackwell.

Scullion, H. and Paauwe, J. (2004) 'International human resource management: Recent developments in theory and empirical research', in A.-W. Harzing and J.V. Ruyssevelt (eds) *International Human Resource Management*. London: Sage.

Scullion, H. and Starkey, K. (2000) 'The changing role of the corporate human resource function in the international firm'. *International Journal of Human Resource Management*, 11(6): 1061–81.

Scullion, H., Collings, D.G. and Gunnigle, P. (2007) 'International human resource management in the 21st century: Emerging themes and contemporary debates'. *Human Resource Management Journal*, 17(4): 309–19.

Sparrow, P., Brewster, C. and Harris, H. (2004) 'Knowledge management and global expertise networks', in P. Sparrow, C. Brewster and H. Harris (eds) *Globalizing Human Resource Management*. London: Routledge.

Stavrou, E.T. (2005) 'Flexible work bundles and organizational competitiveness: A cross-national study of the European work context'. *Journal of Organizational Behavior*, 26(8): 923–47.

Steenkamp, J.-B. (2001) 'The role of national culture in international marketing research'. *International Marketing Review*, 18(1): 30–44.

Stiles, P. and Trevor, J. (2006) 'The human resource department: Roles, coordination and influence', in G.K. Stahl and I. Bjorkman (eds) *Handbook of Research in International Human Resource Management*. Cheltenham: Edward Elgar.

Stroh, L.K. and Caligiuri, P.M. (1998) 'Increasing global effectiveness through effective people management'. *Journal of World Business*, 33(1): 1–17.

Tansky, J.W. and Cohen, D.J. (2002) 'The relationship between organizational support, employee development, and organizational commitment: An empirical study'. *Human Resource Development Quarterly*, 12(3): 285–300.

Tarique, I. and Caligiuri, P. (2004) 'Training and development of international staff', in A.-W. Harzing and J.V. Ruyssevelt (eds) *International Human Resource Management*. London: Sage.

Thomson, K. (1990) *The Employee Revolution: The Rise of Corporate Internal Marketing*. London: Pitman.

Tung, R.L. (2001) 'International human resource management', in M. Poole and M. Warner (eds) *The IEBM Handbook of Human Resource Management*. London: Thompson Learning.

Varey, R.J. (2002) *Marketing Communication: Principles and Practice*. London: Routledge.

Veltrop, B. and Harrington, K. (1988) 'Roadmap to new organizational territory'. *Training & Development Journal*, 42(6): 23–34.

10

An analysis of the people dimension in international marketing[1]

Michael R. Czinkota and A. Coskun Samli

Learning outcomes

At the end of this chapter, readers should be able to:

1. Understand the changing dynamics of international marketing.
2. Grasp how the role of marketing people in organizations has changed.
3. Understand why more emphasis must be put on marketing people's activities.
4. Discuss how marketing people cope with the changes in international markets.

Key points

- The role of marketing professionals can be characterized as changing through four distinct eras – coincidence, confluence, commingling, and creative conflicted collaboration.

- The roles, skills and performances of marketing professionals changed from salesman, to knowledge workers, then information workers and finally to being members of the decision-making team.

- Today's marketing people need many new skills to face the global challenges of global branding, strategizing, overcoming cultural complexities and developing a global vision.

---

1. This chapter has been developed based on Czinkota, M.R. and Samli, A.C. (2010) 'The people dimension in modern international marketing: Neglected but crucial'. *Thunderbird International Business Review*, 52(5): 391–401.

Introduction

This chapter deals with a critical but neglected aspect of international marketing. Although typically the 4Ps are considered to be the key elements of a marketing strategy, this has been extended to the 7Ps to include people, process and physical evidence. Our focus in this chapter is on the people dimension.

In differentiating the time since the Second World War into four time periods, Czinkota and Samli (2007) pointed out that international marketing has performed remarkably well during the second half of the twentieth century. In spite the substantial turmoil of 2008, the rise of international marketing's empowerment continues in the twenty-first century.

The fastest globalizing nations have enjoyed rates of economic growth up to 50% higher than those that have integrated into the world economy more slowly. Faster globalizing countries have also achieved relatively more gains in political freedom, and greater increases in life expectancy, literacy rates and overall standard of living (Global Business Policy Council, 2000).

The powerful political, social and economic forces of globalization have caused and been influenced by tremendous growth in international marketing. If engaged in international marketing, firms of all sizes and in all industries typically outperform their strictly domestic counterparts (Lewis and Richardson, 2001). Much research has taken place to analyse the problems and successes of international marketing. However, only rarely has there been a concurrent analysis of international marketing's people dimension. It is important to remedy this shortcoming, since marketing people play a key role in the internationalization process of the firm. Research has shown that a firm's international effort is typically initiated by the CEO or the vice president of marketing. When it comes to the execution of the international effort, the key person tends to be mostly the vice president of marketing (Czinkota et al., 2011).

In this chapter, we develop an overview of the status of the people internal to marketing in terms of their relative importance, their responsibilities with regard to their changing job descriptions, their specifications as to how they perform their responsibilities and their skills in terms of their personal characteristics.

The advent of change

Czinkota and Samli (2007) differentiated the time from the 1940s to today into four generational periods. In these eras, marketing has changed dramatically, as has the role of marketing people. Table 10.1 illustrates these four periods, together with the changing phases of international marketing and the resulting effect on the persons within the marketing field.

The *coincidence period* (1945–64) was largely characterized by shortage conditions, where for many products there was no surplus available for distribution. Demand for goods and services was very strong, due to its catch-up conditions. In consequence, both domestically and internationally, marketing people played their internal role with rather low visibility and influence. The key desire for stretching one's limited funds led to low competition, and even a climate of friendly collaboration. The heavy utilization of mass communication did not require much knowledge

| Table 10.1 | A chronological construct of international marketing | | |

Period	The world	International marketing phases	Marketing people's role
1945–64	A state of economic recuperation Unsatiated demand	*Coincidence:* Little effort needed to sell products everywhere. Shortage economy; trade precedes individual marketing strategies. Preliminary attempts to connect marketing functions to the economy. Growth facilitated the expansion of international marketing	Very little knowledge base. Heavy utilization of mass communication. Personal selling depended heavily on salesmanship
1965–84	Emergence of international organizations	*Confluence:* Four Asian tigers become a major international force mainly emphasizing Japanese-style marketing. Multinational corporations begin to use a marketing focus in their international outreach	Heavy reliance on home-trained expat marketing people who have been more heavily versed in industrial products
1985–2004	World markets become much larger, blurring borders Globalization's power results in benefits and dislocations	*Commingling:* Asian firms, first Japan then the four tigers and particularly China, became a major force, emphasizing economies of scale, low prices and delivery efficiency	From heavy reliance on exports to even heavier reliance on domestic sales forces. Emergence of information workers accelerated highly technical product marketing
2005 onwards	The need for understanding conflict and collaboration Combining them in the form of creative conflict	*Creative conflicted collaboration:* More and better communication. Reaching out to poorer markets. Develop better products and services. Taking advantage of the flattening world. Improving overall quality of life. Full synergistic collaboration of international marketing and globalization	Emergence of multiculturally trained and multiculturally sensitive marketing people who may become entrepreneurs and cater to poorer markets

and activity in either production or selling. Marketing people's engagement outside the firm took place primarily on the salesman and the transportation level. Driven in large measure by postwar experience, the international marketing concept was actively and prospectively developed in academia. The highly motivating but elusive golden fleece was to make marketing the pacifying impetus for the world. As observed by Richard Farmer (1987, p. 114):

Bright young people figure our how to tool the machines, not how the fire the latest missile. For some reason, they not only get rich fast, but also lose interest in military adventures … In short, if you trade a lot with someone, why fight? The logical answer – you don't – is perhaps the best news mankind has had in millennia.

During the *confluence era* (1965–84), international organizations gained much power and stature. Multinational corporations began to use a marketing focus in their international outreach. In support of global development, more sales were based on industrial products. During this period, an intense reliance emerged on home-trained expatriates calling on overseas prospective clients to sell heavy industrial equipment. It was during this era that marketing efforts were associated with persuasion, and persuasion was considered more a matter of strategy than of manipulation (Hauk, 1965).

During the *commingling era* (1985–2004), first Japan then the four Asian tigers (South Korea, Taiwan, Hong Kong and Singapore) became major international marketing forces by emphasizing economies of scale, high quality, low prices and delivery efficiency. In marketing, a change took place from reliance on expatriates to a heavy reliance on domestic nationals. During that period, products became more sophisticated and technologies advanced to a point where marketing people were forced to cope with highly technical problems.

Finally, the *creative conflicted collaboration era* (2005–) emphasizes the need for more and better communication as the global system attempts to reach the poorer markets of the world representing strong and traditional ethnic values with varying needs. Marketing people in this era are expected to be multiculturally trained and sensitive to cultural idiosyncrasies, and possess product knowledge of an ever-increasing number of alternative products with constantly increasing complexity. Marketing people are the key intermediaries who make complex products user friendly, by helping the consumer. In addition, international marketers are expected to reach out around the globe, where they need to provide insights, encouragement and a feeling of specialness to multiple (sub)cultures with very different needs and values. Not only will marketing staff need to do all this to address and satisfy international demand and augment marginal revenues, but its activity will also be crucial in order for the firm to remain competitive and stay in business in its home market.

The changing status

A half-century of marketing people's progress can be summarized as increased respect for marketers and for what they do (Drucker, 1999). In the coincidence phase of our chronological classification, marketing people were considered as subordinates and were assumed to have little or no skills. Marketing jobs were simplistic and relied much more on personal charisma. This era may be associated with the 'selling concept', where marketing's role was described as selling more stuff to more people (Kotler and Keller, 2006). Figure 10.1 depicts this era under the title of *salesman*.

As the confluence era emerged, international marketing of primarily industrial products necessitated the development of and reliance on home-trained expatriates calling on big and powerful prospective customers. Advancing economies began to understand that massive technology transfer was necessary to attain further progress (Kosenko and Samli, 1985). In this process of massive technology transfer, marketing people played the *field representative* role – providing information about the most

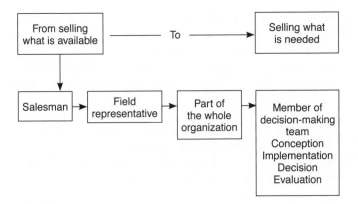

Figure 10.1   Progress in the status of marketing people

up-to-date technology and teaching others how to use and care for that technology. Over time, marketing people moved away from being subordinates to becoming a part of the whole organization, in the form of what Drucker (1999) coined *knowledge workers* or at least knowledgeable workers. In Drucker's way of thinking, knowledge workers 'must know more about their job than their boss does' (1999, p. 18).

By the commingling era, the emergence of *information workers* was accelerated. However, expatriates started working with and training the domestic marketers in supporting highly technical products. Increasingly, successful local marketers were also integrated into the global operations of their firm. As such, expatriates became part of the entire organization. Information worker units became a part of the organization at home, communicating with and solving problems for the firm and its customers worldwide.

As the creative conflicted collaboration era became a reality, information technologies and sophisticated high-tech products forced marketing people to know more and try to reach out and devise individual solutions to customer's unique problems. Here, in addition to being knowledgeable about technology, marketing people also became more sensitive to the increasing multicultural characteristics of their jobs. Whether at the office or on the firing line, they started becoming a key member of the decision-making teams dealing with, and often directing, strategic planning, and the evaluation and implementation of decisions.

The key aspect of Figure 10.1 is expressed by the movement from selling what is available to selling what is needed. This is the most critical progress in marketing, which would make a major contribution to the quality of life all over the globe.

Changing characteristics

As the nature of marketing changed when goods and services became more complex and more responsive, consumers' sophistication also increased. As a result, marketing people's status changed. More critically, their characteristics changed even more dramatically. Marketing had to deal with new tools and approaches, such as the internet, new moneys, such as Chinese and Indian currencies, and new problems, such as terrorism and currency and interest rate variations.

Table 10.2 illustrates some of the highlights of these dramatic developments that took place in the past 60 years or more in shifting the characteristics of marketing people, differentiated by skills, responsibilities and functions:

- *Skills* indicate the personal traits that marketing people have and display
- *Responsibilities* delineate what marketers are expected to do
- *Functions* indicate how the skills and responsibilities are combined to form new approaches to the execution of international marketing.

Table 10.2   Changing characteristics

Marketing people's characteristics	Eras			
	Coincidence	**Confluence**	**Commingling**	**Creative conflicted collaboration**
Skills	Outgoing Interactive Persuasive	Technical background Understands products	Understands other cultures Heavy technological background	Multicultural orientation High level of technological communication
Responsibilities	Tries to sell as much as possible Keeps customers and boss happy	Able to carry on highly technical conversations Travels Flexible in unexpected situations	Communicates with nationals Provides guidance and information for locals	Interacts with multiple cultural counterparts
Functions	Talks Communicates Understands	Communicates highly technical areas based on extensive knowledge	Expresses interest and understanding Displays knowledge	Displays sensitivity in different cultures Understands customer needs clearly

In the coincidence era, marketing people displayed outgoingness and persuasiveness to sell their products or services. They were primarily interactive with their prospective customers to fulfil their responsibilities. To achieve their goals, international marketers communicated effectively and showed a substantial level of sensitivity in understanding their customers' needs.

In the confluence era, marketing people cultivated ever-growing global marketing-related activities. They played a critical role in the globalization process and responded to increasingly voluminous and complicated customer requests (Kosenko and Samli,

1985). As field sales representatives, they carried greater responsibility in generating and closing sales. Their technical knowledge base grew substantially, necessitated by the increased professionalism of their prospective buyers. Technology transfer preceded the knowledge base of the field sales representatives. Thus, not only did they have to learn the technical aspects of industrial products but they also needed to learn to negotiate at higher levels for more sophisticated outcomes.

As the commingling era emerged, marketing people became substantially more multicultural than before and learned to deal with different people who belonged and were motivated by different cultural backgrounds. At the firing lines, marketing people were making decisions that influenced the whole wellbeing of their respective companies. They were under pressure to display interest in and understanding of highly complex customer problems relating to equally or even more complex products and services. This was a particularly progressive era for consumers in global markets. Constantly developing information and communication technologies increased consumer sophistication everywhere. Once again, marketing people needed to cope with this tremendous progress by displaying product knowledge, cultural sensitivity and communication skills.

Finally, in the present ongoing creative conflicted collaboration era, marketing people have greater responsibilities of carrying the benefits of globalization to remote corners of the world. As the world is flattened, globalization and international marketing will be even more important, striving to 'minimize alienation, celebrate interdependence, and emphasize inclusion' (Friedman, 2006, p. 443). Marketing people play an increasingly critical role. For globalization to work, developing countries must be enabled to absorb and make use of available technologies for economic development (Stiglitz, 2006). Marketing people will be more involved in making plans to reach out to remote markets of the developing world. This means they will display forceful sensitivity to understand the needs and idiosyncrasies of consumers in these parts of the world (Samli, 2004). More than ever before, they will require product and service knowledge and be able to advise consumers or prospective buyers in great detail. As these parts of the world become economically better off, marketing people will have to cope with Weber's law, which maintains that customers are more attuned to relative than absolute differences (Kotler and Keller, 2006). In increasingly volatile times, international marketers will need to explain and defend the underlying principles to their activities. The foundations of marketing, such as the benefits of competition, the issue of risk, the concept of profit and the importance of ownership, will need to be newly understood and justified. Juxtapositions and conflicts will have to be defined. For example, 'market forces' and 'government regulation' are not necessarily mutually exclusive, just as we have learned in food preparation that 'fresh' and 'frozen' are not opposites.

The challenge for marketing people in this creative conflicted collaboration era will be greater than ever before as they contribute to the quality of life of their customers.

The global people challenge for international marketers

Marketing people are increasingly required to explain important goods and service differences in a number of cultures. Their work will help define the market offerings that people receive and value. Figure 10.2 illustrates a simplified but provocative model of this challenge and specifies the key approaches that may be successfully used.

	High Contextual Low	
High	Appealing to sophisticated markets with sophisticated products Much information needs to be imparted High risk-high return products	Appealing to less sophisticated markets with limited incomes Both information and interaction are required High risk but lower return products
Complexity	Appealing to sophisticated markets with less sophisticated products More interaction than information needed Low risk-medium to low return products	Appealing to less sophisticated markets with limited incomes More interaction than information is needed Low risk but higher return products
Low		

Figure 10.2 Challenges of marketing people in global markets

Figure 10.2's first dimension is the high-context and low-context dichotomy originally introduced by Hall (1976). This is a critical way of categorizing and differentiating cultures. In a low-context culture, messages are explicit and words carry the key portion of the information that is imparted. By contrast, high-context cultures pay less attention to the information communicated through written or verbal efforts, and much more attention is paid to the context of communications such as the backgrounds, interpersonal relations and surrounding societal values. In high-context cultures, an individual's handshake is more critical than the written documents and attorneys that are so crucial in low-context environments. A high-context bank loan, for instance, is based not on detailed financial statements as in low-context cultures, but on the standing of the individual (Keegan, 1989; Samli, 1995). Even though theory allows this clear differentiation, the international marketer cannot choose one side or another. Rather, the work has to reflect varying expectations and cultures around the globe. Therefore, the persona offered by the international marketer must be cognizant of differences and reflective of local conditions. In terms of appeals, communications and visual cues, the international marketer has to develop a greater flexibility than ever before.

The second dimension of Figure 10.2 is the level of complexity of the goods and services offered in global markets. On one hand, very complex, high-tech products are being offered such as computers and IT products. On the other hand, basic remedies such as aspirin or basic apparel such as shirts or underwear form the strong demand foundation of a society. The basic differences of goods and services in terms of their complexity will necessarily modify the marketer's efforts to communicate with prospective buyers:

- The upper left quadrant, where high complexity meets low context, offers the greatest challenge and the most substantial returns. Marketing people have to be very informed about the products and services, and have to be ready to encounter new conditions at every turn.
- The upper right quadrant indicates offering sophisticated products to less sophisticated markets with a substantial cultural memory. Here, marketers need to be more informed and make decisions regarding a fit for a high-context culture. The gradual development of conditions may mitigate risk, but also leads to lower returns.
- The lower left quadrant deals with marketing people who are functioning in sophisticated markets with less sophisticated products. Their focus must be the creation of new images, particularly in light of the likelihood of severe competition, which will affect the return on investment.
- Finally, the lower right quadrant describes marketing people's role as appealing to less sophisticated markets and offering less complex products. Typically, such markets are less wealthy. This situation calls for an increase in interactions on the part of marketers.

As can be seen, the responsibilities and challenges of marketing people are likely to increase critically. It is certainly expected that they will play a more strategic role in implementing their companies' strategic objectives.

The challenges of the decision makers

Our discussion thus far has emphasized primarily the field workers and sales representatives functions in the four transitional eras. It is necessary to look at the critical decisions that are made by chief international marketing executives. Their challenge has been increasing and growing in complexity. In Figure 10.3, we present four critical challenges that today's international decision makers are facing. These four areas are global branding, strategizing, overcoming cultural complexities, and developing a global vision:

1. *Global branding:* today's international marketing decision maker will be challenged to identify bottom of the pyramid opportunities and complexities (Prahalad, 2005). According to Prahalad (2005) and Samli (2004), there are many emerging markets that are in need of many different products and services. Developing global umbrella brands and achieving their acceptance by different global markets is a necessary but complex undertaking (Wood et al., 2008).
2. *Strategizing:* constantly increasing global competition necessitates the development of generic strategies. Such strategies might be catering to the firm's present and future competitive advantage; however, these generic strategies will have to be adapted to regional and local markets. Here, the marketing decision maker is challenged more then ever before to become familiar with critical differences in local and regional markets and then apply their generic strategies to these markets, with an understanding that their differences are completely understood and dealt with (Solberg and Durrieu, 2008).

3. *Overcoming cultural complexities:* although inherent in the two challenges above, this challenge needs explaining. Without identifying the cultural underpinnings that prevail in a market, the international marketing decision maker will not be successful in implementing international strategies. Because of the complexities that exist among different cultures, today's international marketing decision maker has to be a combination of sociologist, psychologist and anthropologist. If the international decision maker successfully understands the cultural underpinnings, they will be able to adjust their strategic thinking accordingly (Darley and Blankson, 2008).

4. *Developing a global vision:* as the world becomes more interlinked and the opportunities, as well as the challenges, become greater, the international marketing decision maker must develop a futuristic vision that will not only explain the immediate differences in world markets but also the emerging needs in newly developing niche markets. Thus the international marketing decision maker will have a vision of a near and a far future. Having a vision in this case is not sufficient; the international decision maker will be forced to fuel innovations for these new ideas and new products in these emerging new markets (Roll, 2008).

Figure 10.3   The challenge of international decision makers

Conclusions

Marketing is a social science. It is a people business and marketing people carry out an important social activity. On a global level, the emphasis of marketing may vary, but marketing work is instrumental in delivering an improved quality of life. Differentiating marketing by generational changes allows an analysis of the changing role of marketing people. The marketer's role as a crucial decision maker is likely to continue to grow in terms of challenges as well as opportunities.

On a global level, differences in values carry the potential for divisiveness, while similarities are likely to encourage collaboration. Values themselves are learned behaviour, shaped by society and experience. Every time international marketers make an international transaction, the linkages of goods, services, ideas and communications make a contribution to a growing proximity of value systems (Czinkota, 2005). As life's experiences grow more international and more similar, so do values. And this, perhaps, is the greatest role and contribution of international marketers to the world, attesting to their importance. Their activities contribute to the aligning of global values, which is likely to make it easier for countries, companies and individuals to build bridges between themselves and improve life and living conditions.

Issues for further discussion

1. Has the 'coincidence period' ended in all countries?
2. Will 'creative conflicted collaboration' result in more friction in global society? What should be the main considerations of marketers in the context of the bottom of the pyramid?
3. As product quantity and diversity increases, how do you see the issue of high and low context changing?

CASE STUDY

Damar International

Damar International, a fledgling firm importing handicrafts of chiefly Indonesian origin, was established in Burke, Virginia, a suburb of Washington, DC. Organized as a general partnership, the firm is owned entirely by Dewi Soemantoro, its president, and Ronald I. Asche, its vice president. Their part-time, unsalaried efforts and those of Soemantoro's relatives in Indonesia constitute the entire labour base of the firm. Outside financing has been limited to borrowing from friends and relatives of the partners in Indonesia and the US.

Damar International estimates that its current annual sales revenues are between $20,000 and $30,000. Although the firm has yet to reach breakeven point, its sales revenues and customer base have expanded more rapidly than anticipated in Damar's original business plan. The partners are generally satisfied with results to date and plan to continue to broaden their operations.

Damar International was established to capitalize on Soemantoro's international experience and contacts. As the daughter of an Indonesian Foreign Service officer, Soemantoro spent most of her youth and early adulthood in Western Europe and, for the past 18 years, has resided in the US. Her immediate family, including her mother, now resides in Indonesia. In addition to English and Malay, Soemantoro speaks French, German and Italian. Although she has spent the past four years working in information management in the Washington area, first at MCI and currently for Records Management Inc., her interest in importing derives from the six years she spent as a management consultant. In this capacity, she was frequently called on to advise clients about importing clothing, furniture and decorative items from Indonesia. At the urging of family and friends, she decided to start her own business. While Soemantoro handles the purchasing and administrative aspects of the business, Asche is responsible for marketing and sales.

Damar International currently imports clothing, high-quality brassware, batik accessories, woodcarvings and furnishings from Indonesia. All these items are handcrafted by village artisans working in a cottage industry. Damar International estimates that 30% of its revenues from the sale of Indonesian imports are derived from clothing, 30% from batik accessories and 30% from woodcarvings, with the remainder divided equally between brassware and furnishings. In addition, Damar markets in the eastern US sell comparable Thai and Philippine handcrafted items imported by a small California firm. This firm in turn markets some of Damar's Indonesian imports on the west coast.

Most of Damar's buyers are small shops and boutiques. Damar does not supply large department stores or retail chain outlets. By participating in gift shows, trade fairs and handicraft exhibitions, the firm has expanded its customer base from the Washington area to many locations in the eastern US.

In supplying small retail outlets with handcrafted Indonesian artefacts, Damar is pursuing a niche strategy. Although numerous importers market similar mass-produced Indonesian items chiefly to department stores and chain retailers, Damar knows of no competitors that supply handcrafted artefacts to boutiques. Small retailers find it difficult to purchase in sufficient volume to order directly from large-scale importers of mass-produced items. More importantly, it is difficult to organize Indonesian artisans to produce handcrafted goods in sufficient quantity to supply the needs of large retailers.

Damar's policy is to carry little if any inventory. Orders from buyers are transmitted by Soemantoro to her family in Indonesia, who contract production to artisans in the rural villages of Java and Bali. Within broad parameters, buyers can specify modifications of traditional Indonesian wares. Frequently, Soemantoro cooperates with her mother in creating designs that adapt traditional products to American tastes and the specifications of US buyers. Soemantoro is in contact with her family in Indonesia at least once a week by telex or phone to report new orders and check on the progress of previous orders. In addition, Soemantoro makes an annual visit to Indonesia to coordinate policy with her family and maintain contacts with artisans.

Damar also fills orders placed by Soemantoro's family in Indonesia. The firm, in essence, acts as both an importer and an exporter despite its extremely limited personnel base. In this, as well as with its source of financing, Damar is atypical. The firm's great strength, which allows it to fill a virtually vacant market niche with extremely limited capital and labour resources, is clearly the Soemantoro family's nexus of personal connections. Without the use of middlemen, this single bicultural family is capable of linking US retailers and Indonesian village artisans and supplying products that, while unique, are specifically oriented to the US market.

Damar's principal weakness is its financing structure. There are limits to the amount of money that can be borrowed from family and friends for such an enterprise. Working capital is necessary because the Indonesian artisans must be paid before full payment is received from US buyers. Although a 10% deposit is required from buyers when an order is placed, the remaining 90% is not due until 30 days from the date of shipment FOB Washington, DC. Yet the simplicity of Damar's financing structure has advantages. To date, it has been able to operate without letters of credit and their concomitant cost and paperwork burdens.

One major importing problem has been the paperwork and red tape involved in US customs and quota regulations. Satisfying these regulations has occasionally delayed the fulfilment of orders. Furthermore, because the Indonesian trade office in the US is located in New York rather than Washington, assistance from the Indonesian government in expediting such problems has at times been difficult to obtain because of Damar's limited personnel. For example, an order was once delayed in US customs because of confusion between the US Department of Commerce and Indonesian export authorities concerning import stamping and labelling. Several weeks were required to solve the problem.

Although Damar received regulatory information directly from the US Department of Commerce when it began importing, its routine contact with government is minimal because regulatory paperwork is contracted to customs brokers.

One of the most important lessons that the firm has learned is the critical role of participating in gift shows, trade fairs and craft exhibitions. Soemantoro believes that the firm's greatest mistake was not attending a trade show in New York. By connecting with potential buyers, both through trade shows and 'walk-in scouting' of boutiques, Damar has benefitted greatly from helpful references from existing customers. Buyers have been particularly helpful in identifying trade fairs that would be useful for Damar to attend. Here, too, the importance of Damar's cultivation of personal contacts is apparent.

Similarly, personal contacts offer Damar the possibility of diversifying into new import lines. Through a contact established by a friend in France, Soemantoro is currently planning to import handmade French porcelain and silk blouses.

Damar is worried about sustained expansion of its Indonesian handicraft import business because the firm does not currently have the resources to organize large-scale cottage industry production in Indonesia. Other major concerns are potential shipping delays and exchange rate fluctuations.

This case study is taken, with permission, from Czinkota, M. and Ronkainen, I. (2010) International Marketing *(9th edn), Cincinnati: Thomson.*

Questions

1 Evaluate alternative expansion strategies for Damar International in the US.
2 Discuss Damar's expansion alternatives in Indonesia and France and their implications for the US market.
3 How can Damar protect itself against exchange rate fluctuations?
4 What are the likely effects of shipment delays on Damar? How can these effects be overcome?

References

Czinkota, M.R. (2005) 'Freedom and international marketing'. *Thunderbird International Business Review*, 47(1): 1–13.

Czinkota, M.R. and Samli, A.C. (2007) 'The remarkable performance of international marketing in the second half of the twentieth century'. *European Business Review*, 19: 316–31.

Czinkota, M.R., Ronkainen, I.A. and Moffett, M.H. (2011) *International Business* (8th edn). Hoboken, NJ: Wiley.

Darley, W.K. and Blankson, C. (2008) 'African culture and business markets: Implications for marketing practices'. *Journal of Business and Industrial Marketing*, 23(6): 374–83.

Drucker, P.F. (1999) *Management Challenges for the 21st Century*. New York: Harper Business.

Farmer, R.N. (1987) 'Would you want your granddaughter to marry a Taiwanese marketing man?' *Journal of Marketing*, 51: 114–15.

Friedman, T.L. (2006) *The World is Flat*. New York: Farrar, Straus and Giroux.

Global Business Policy Council (2000) *Globalization Ledger*. Washington DC: A.T. Kearney.

Hall, E.T. (1976) *Beyond Culture*. New York: Anchor Press/Doubleday.

Hauk, J.G. (1965) 'Research in personal selling', in G. Schwartz (ed.) *Science in Marketing*. New York: John Wiley & Sons.

Keegan, W.J. (1989) *Global Marketing Management*. Englewood Cliffs, NJ: Prentice Hall.

Kosenko, R. and Samli, A.C. (1985) 'China's four modernizations program and technology transfer', in A.C. Samli (ed.) *Technology Transfer*. Westport, CT: Quorum Books.

Kotler, P. and Keller, K.L. (2006) *Marketing Management*. Upper Saddle River, NJ: Pearson/Prentice Hall.

Lewis, H. III and Richardson, J.D. (2001) *Why Global Commitment Really Matters*. Washington DC: Institute for International Economics.

Prahalad, C.K. (2005) *There is a Fortune at the Bottom of the Pyramid*. Boston, MA: Wharton School Publishing.

Roll, M. (2008) 'Visionary CEOs: Leader of the brand'. *Brand Strategy*, July, 40–3.

Samli, A.C. (1995) *International Consumer Behavior*. Westport, CT: Quorum Books.

Samli, A.C. (2004) *Entering and Succeeding in Emerging Countries*. Mason, OH: Thomson/Southwestern.

Solberg, C.A. and Durrieu, F. (2008) 'Strategy development in international markets: A two tier approach'. *International Marketing Review*, 25(5): 520–43.

Stiglitz, J.E. (2006) *Making Globalization Work*. New York: W.W. Norton.

Wood, V.R., Pitta, D.A. and Franzak, F.J. (2008) 'Successful marketing by multinational firms to the bottom of the pyramid: Connecting share of heart, global umbrella brands and responsible marketing'. *Journal of Consumer Marketing*, 25(7): 419–29.

11
Processes: the way forward

Kirsti Lindberg-Repo

Learning outcomes

At the end of this chapter, readers should be able to:

1. Understand the need of evolving processes as the customer has become global.
2. Understand the evolution of the world economy and the face of changing processes.
3. Understand the method of building strong processes and how value becomes the core concept of process innovation.
4. Identify the different kinds of processes.
5. Comprehend the various ways in which processes can be aligned to meet changing consumer needs.

Key points:

- The increasing importance of value as the generator of organic growth necessitates the need for managing, delivering and co-creating value more efficiently and effectively than competitors.
- Customer needs in this new marketplace are becoming more niche as consumers take more intelligent decisions supported by a variety of new tools.
- Value is a central motivator for customers' enduring brand connection and the holistic value experienced by current customers is perhaps a more sustainable competitive advantage than product or service features or benefits.
- Adaptive challenge presents itself in combinations of speed and complexity that are simply unprecedented.
- Revolving the company processes around customers keeps the company close to the focal point and then adaptation and flexibility are easy to achieve.
- The idea behind enabling customer purchase is that the firm has to be dynamic in relocating its processes, in order to strike the 'right chord' in the customer's mind.
- Reconfiguring builds dynamic capabilities to help the firm to integrate, build and reconfigure internal and external competences to address rapidly changing environments.

Introduction

Global forces are creating relentless market disruption, shorter strategy cycles and rapid obsolescence. This tumult creates a stream of adaptive challenges for the firm and increases the risk of personal and organizational failure. The new paradigm is based on combining interdisciplinary activities, with an emphasis on continuous improvement with adequate flexibility (Roy, 2005). According to Konosuke Matsushita of Matsushita Electric Industrial Co.:

> Business is now so complex and difficult, the survival of firms so hazardous in an environment increasingly competitive and fraught with danger, that their continued existence depends on the day-to-day operations of Business Process and mobilization of every ounce of intelligence.

Processes are groups of logically related decisions and activities required to manage or run the business. These can be thought of as similar to Porter's 'technologically or economically distinct activities' that create value. At the highest level, these might be marketing, production, sales and so on (Dhar, 1992).

The processes followed by an organization offering a product or service to its consumers influence the growth of the organization as the external members of the supply chain and the end user are influenced by the organization's processes. Flexibility in processes motivates customers and consumers to deal with the company in future dealings as well. Processes have an effective role to play in the output received by the companies from the marketing mix, in terms of return on investments made by them.

Rise of global customers drives the need to evolve processes

Emerging preferences of global customers

Today, the global customer has reached beyond the borders of distance and time towards a realm of experiencing a true value proposition. Marketers and brand managers work hard to provide a seamless customer experience. The availability and accessibility of a plethora of products and services is the norm of the day. Possessing a technological edge or a product or a service is no longer the basis of competition, the bar has risen to a higher and more abstract level of experiential management.

Glancing behind

Looking back, one can clearly see that human civilization has survived on the wings of globalization ever since the silk route (a network of trade routes that crossed Europe and Asia from the Mediterranean coast to India and China in ancient times and the Middle Ages) was envisioned to enhance business relations and cultural exchanges between East and West. It was one of the first steps that human beings took to make a global footprint by opening up new avenues of availability at the global level. The trading of spices and eventually the start of the Industrial Revolution were propelled by

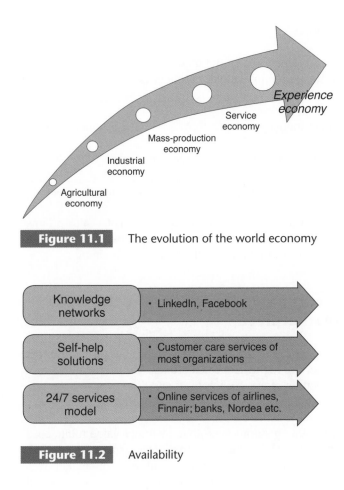

a new paradigm of accessibility – an uninterrupted supply chain of resources to the factories of northern Europe (Figure 11.1).

Figure 11.1 The evolution of the world economy

Figure 11.2 Availability

Snapshot of the present

This is an era of unparalleled variety and alternatives. The global customer has an abundance of options and choices. 'Availability is only a click away' as the customer is now positioned on an online front, equipped as never before with tools of technology and gears of purchasing power. Today, products and services are both *available*, that is, the product or service exists, and *accessible*, that is, the customer knows it exists.

Availability has reached new paradigms, as shown in Figure 11.2.

The increasing importance of value as the generator of organic growth emphasizes the need for managing, delivering and co-creating value more efficiently and effectively than competitors.

Customer experience forms the new focus

Customer needs in this new marketplace are becoming more niche as consumers take more intelligent decisions supported by a variety of new tools.

Starbucks, the US-based coffee shop, comprises a value architecture that is geared to the modern lifestyle in global metropolitan areas, and as well as serving coffee, it creates an ambiance that fills customers with a sense of community as well as caffeine. Starbucks' phenomenal growth is down to its unique way of managing its value creation processes and continuously innovating new value areas.

As we move towards the 'experience economy', it does not limit itself to Starbucks, it is rapidly permeating all professional fronts. The all-pervasive media, technical knowledge and increased information-gathering capabilities and avenues are stimulating customer knowledge and alertness.

Emergence of newer markets

Customer experience is being streamed across the globe, resulting in a new professional mindset, conscious of the global marketplace. This is especially true of the IT and ITES (IT enabled services) industry:

- Emergence of the entire BPO industry in India for a 24/7 business model for the companies of the West
- Emergence of IT service industry in India for developing online self-help solutions.

The need is to continuously innovate and upgrade one's skills to satisfy the insatiable customer of today.

The communicated value proposition must lead to the perception of a value promise among customers that is in line with the firm's value delivery capacities and intentions. If this alignment is lacking, favourable value fulfilment will not emerge.

Foundation of building strong processes is to know the value brands carry in a global marketplace

Building and properly managing brands in the global marketplace has turned out to be the number one challenge for several highly respected brands. The problem that most often arises is how brands, seen as major corporate assets as they stand for price competition and a loyal customer base, can keep up their value offering in the eyes of customers and other stakeholders. This has become the central task for several Nordic brands as well, to manage the value generation so that customer value fulfilment is achieved. The scope of branding in Nordic countries ranges from global superbrands, such as IKEA, Nokia, Volvo, H&M, Bang & Olufsen, to a multitude of smaller, well-known brands, such as LEGO and Finnair. These companies represent globally acknowledged brands that constantly try to address customer's value fulfilment.

Value is the core concept of process innovation

The increasing importance of value as the generator of organic growth emphasizes the need for managing, delivering and co-creating value more efficiently and effectively than competitors. The concept of value also drives the debate among academic researchers and marketing practitioners. The Nordic School of marketing, originated in the 1980s, acknowledges that value is not delivered to customers but co-created with customers in each step of the value process. Only in this way can customer value be created. In 2004, the American Marketing Association launched a new definition of marketing, and further updated it in 2008. It emphasizes the concept of customer value as the cornerstone of marketing actions (Grönroos, 2007).

Value is a central motivator for customers' enduring brand connection and the holistic value experienced by current customers is perhaps a more sustainable competitive advantage than product or service features or benefits. Hence, both scholars and practitioners need to gain more insights of what is valuable in the branding process and

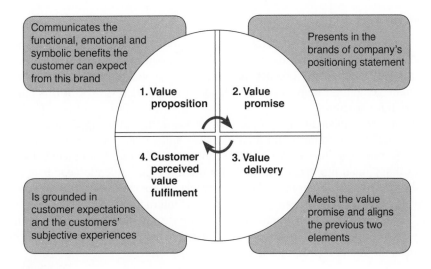

Communicates the functional, emotional and symbolic benefits the customer can expect from this brand

Presents in the brands of company's positioning statement

1. Value proposition

2. Value promise

4. Customer perceived value fulfilment

3. Value delivery

Is grounded in customer expectations and the customers' subjective experiences

Meets the value promise and aligns the previous two elements

Figure 11.3   Dimensions of value

how the brand can be made more valuable for customer fulfilment to be achieved. The company's view of developing processes should revolve around four important value dimensions, as shown in Figure 11.3.

Value proposition

According to Aaker (1996), value proposition carries out the strategic vision of the company, clarifies the identity of the brand and what the company aims to achieve with its brand. Value proposition should, in a persuasive way, communicate the functional, emotional and symbolic benefits the customer can expect from this brand. In order for the value proposition to be effective, the brand identity must be adopted throughout the company and linked to an organization's internal culture and values (Hatch and Schultz, 2002). Being clear about what the brand stands for will help to create word-of-mouth brand awareness. Brand visibility and brand experience are central parts of the brand-building process that is grounded in the value proposition.

Value promise

At first glance, value proposition and value promise have several similar features. A brand is essentially a marketer's promise to deliver predictable product or service performance. Consequently, a brand promise is the marketer's vision of what customers will expect the brand to be and do for them (Kotler and Keller, 2006).

Hence, the true value and future prospects of the brand rest with consumers, their knowledge about the brand and their likely response to marketing activities as a result of this knowledge. The value promise is implicitly or explicitly present in the company's positioning statement. It represents how the marketer wants customers and prospects to think and feel about the brand. These thoughts and feelings should stand out in contrast to competitors' offerings and motivate customers or prospects to want to try a given brand.

Value delivery

A demanding value promise needs great execution. According to Kotler and Keller (2006), delivering value means substantial investment in infrastructure and capabilities, market research and forecasts into the future. A well-planned customer relationship management strategy, and the software to support this, also forms part of the delivery infrastructure.

Finnair, the Finnish airline company, which is strongly growing its business in Asia, seeks to deliver value partly through websites and service call centres and partly by creating a service culture that tries to be consistent at all touch points in delivering the values that Finnair promises in its global marketing communication campaigns – 'Take the shortcut to Asia'. In services, the delivery takes place in interactions with customers and value is what customers experience in these interactions. As for any service-based firm, these customer–firm interactions, or service encounters, are dominant value delivery touch points for Finnair as well. These touch points also reveal if the company practises the values it promotes in its value proposition.

Value fulfilment

Value has become a strong competitive asset. The top marketing companies pay attention to their customers' value perceptions. From the brand value perspective, value fulfilment can be seen as a result of consistent value processes, where the different parts (value proposition, value promise and value delivery) all are distinct dimensions, but at the same time they are interrelated and connect to customers' value fulfilment. In this chapter, value fulfilment is a concept similar to customer-based brand equity, that is, the differential effect that brand knowledge has on consumer responses to the marketing of that brand. Customer-based brand equity occurs when consumer responses to marketing activity differ, depending on whether consumers know or do not know the brand (Keller, 2007). However, value fulfilment extends the concept further and points out the distinct levels of value processes that ensure the development of value fulfilment more effectively and efficiently.

Value fulfilment can be perceived from several perspectives, the stakeholder perspective, including public opinion, shareholders and employees, or the subjective consumer perspective. Value fulfilment follows from an alignment of all three parts of the brand value process. When such an alignment is achieved, the firm's strategic vision will be carried out in the marketplace in a coherent and consistent way.

For example, in general, customers have a unified and globally consistent perception of what IKEA stands for and how IKEA is different from its competitors. For children who value LEGO, the company does not represent toys but pieces of Lego, and children become value creators when they play with them.

Need to adapt to changing global scenario

It is important for companies to adapt to the ever-changing world around them. A number of Nordic companies have developed successful brands, due to their ability to renew themselves and develop superior long-term performance. For a firm to create and manage a well-defined brand value process, the parts or dimensions of the process outlined in this chapter can be used as a guideline. When doing so, it is important to align the four parts of the process with each other. The *communicated value proposition* must lead to a *perception of a value promise* among customers that is in line with the firm's *value delivery capacities and intentions*. If this alignment is lacking, a favourable *value fulfilment* will not emerge.

Adaptive challenge presents itself in combinations of speed and complexity that are simply unprecedented. If an organization must learn each time it responds to an adaptive challenge, the learning implications of the global age are breathtaking. The ultimate source of adaptive capacity, renewal and competitiveness is the ongoing ability of an organization to learn and apply its knowledge. This capability precedes and underlies innovation, execution and adaptive or pre-emptive response (Clark and Gottfredson, 2008). Organizations must undergo new learning cycles to prepare for new competitive cycles, constantly retooling in order to maintain competitiveness. But most organizations struggle to endure the competitive pressure. To secure and sustain competitive advantage, continuous innovation is a must. The mantra in the age of globalization is *innovate or perish*. But there has been a paradigm shift in the manner in which organizations innovate these days.

We need to evolve processes because economies evolve

From goods to service economy and now as services are commoditized, firms have to look not only at innovation in products but also every service offering or rather every customer touch point (Figure 11.4).

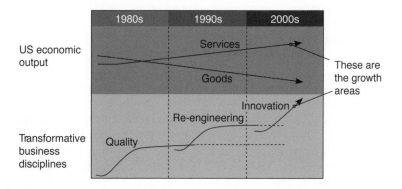

Figure 11.4   Services and innovation as current sources of growth

A lack of strategy and process capabilities indicates a fundamentally flawed approach to innovation – an approach where companies indulge in multiple, one-off activities that have little or no strategic foundation. Unstructured chaos is bound to lead to haphazard results.

Once management takes the time to lay down a strategy and process for innovation, they are committing to it. They're defining innovation, establishing metrics and goals,

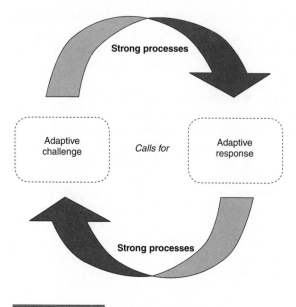

Strong processes

Adaptive
challenge

Calls for

Adaptive
response

Strong processes

Figure 11.5 Adaptive challenge calls for
adapted response
Source: Adapted from Clark (2007)

assigning ownership, and charting out a path for shepherding ideas through the pipeline. But having these capabilities in place means that these managers are now accountable for innovation and, more importantly, accountable for the successes and failures that follow. Many of our clients and partners have noticed this trend – this fundamental fear of commitment and accountability. At the end of the day, managers aren't willing to put their livelihood on the line for something they don't quite understand (Figure 11.5).

According to Hammer and Champy (1993), a successful business process re-engineering (BPR) implementation is one that yields expected improvements in productivity and quality. The success of any BPR implementation can be measured on the following parameters:

- process time reduction
- process cost reduction
- quality output
- employee adaptability to the new process
- responsiveness to customer needs.

How can we collaborate with our customers to co-create superior value? Business process redesign (or, simply, process redesign) approaches have become popular in organizational circles, particularly since the emergence of the BPR movement in the early 1990s (Hunt, 1991; Hammer and Champy, 1993; Reijers, 2003). In spite of being touted as a new and revolutionary idea, it can be argued that process redesign has a long history, dating back to Taylor's (1911) scientific management movement.

Processes can be:

- operational
- real time
- rapidly evolving, easy to change
- learning – more data makes them 'smarter'
- customer-centric
- demonstrably compliant
- cost-effective
- business driven.

Mapping customer journey to process evolvements is the key to success

Customer-centricity is the key and hence we propose a model that maps the customer-buying journey as the input to the evolement process (Figure 11.6).

The ultimate value driver is the customer. Revolving company processes around customers keeps the company close to the focal point and then adaptation and flexibility are easy to achieve. It's like being close to your friend so that you can be most receptive to their preferences and reach out as soon as they are in need. This model uses the customer journey as the core and the 7Rs of process evolve at each stage of the journey. The central premise is to leave no gap at any point of the customer-buying process.

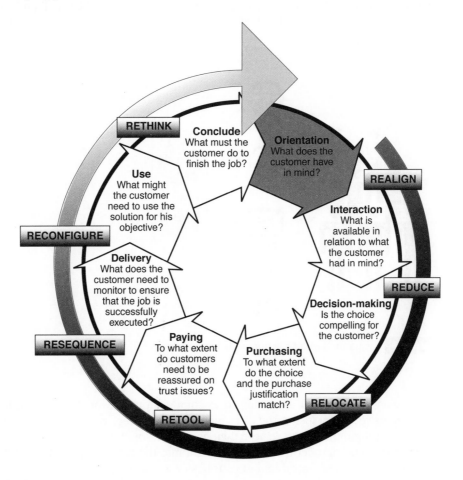

Figure 11.6　Mapping customer journey to process evolvements

Step 1: shift from transaction to interaction

Realign processes

Moments of interaction with the customer will teach the company about customer preferences. This gives the company an opportunity to realign its processes in accordance with these preferences and provide the customer with innovative and flexible processes.

Interact with the customer

As a first step, a good marketer will often talk to their customers (Figure 11.7). They will ask customers about their perceptions of these upcoming challenges. Do customers see these new products or services as beneficial? Are they evaluating them? Are they considering changing? Do they believe they will migrate to these new solutions in the next 6, 12 or 24 months?

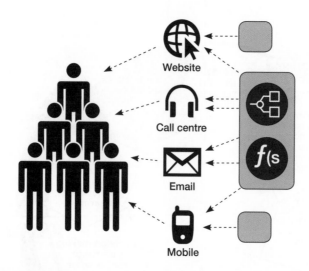

| Figure 11.7 | Channels of interaction with the customer |

Equally as important as talking to existing customers would be talking to those customers you either lost, those you cannot seem to attract, or (and these are often the most important) those who achieve their goals with solutions you don't provide. These non-customers can offer tremendous insight into the solution 'just over the horizon' that can be a tremendous threat to your business (Hartung, 2000).

Engage stakeholders (customers, suppliers, employees)

In today's business climate, there are tremendous opportunities for innovation, yet companies are struggling with the challenge of satisfying their customers and achieving sustainable, profitable growth. This managerial dilemma is caused by the barrage of emerging industries and technologies, and accelerating globalization. All these rapid changes set the stage for an expanded role for customers. In this new environment, the customer is no longer a passive recipient of products passed through an entrenched value chain, instead customers are now active co-creators of value.

In this new model, companies have a greater opportunity to work with their customers (and their customers' customers) to generate value above and beyond what each can build individually. The key change in this new environment is that companies can no longer say: 'Here's our product, take it or leave it.' Instead, companies are employing early and continuous customer input to tailor the product, as well as the entire bundle of products and services surrounding it. This customer-centric approach produces an overall 'experience' that's more responsive to customer needs.

A classic example of co-creation is the pioneering work of Federal Express in establishing online tracking, which has since been copied by other shippers. In the old days, giving a package to a shipper was like putting it in a black hole. You trusted it would arrive, without ever being part of the process. With FedEx online tracking, the paradigm changed – the consumer is involved and can now see where their package is at every step of the journey, from drop-off point to ultimate delivery.

One of the biggest hurdles in co-creation is changing the mindset of those within the company. Whether they're engineers, marketers or CEOs, most corporate managers view the world as revolving around the company. And they see their job as harnessing the resources of the company, to meet their definition of customer needs and extract the value they believe customers gain from their company's products. Instead, managers need to experience the business like the customer does. Whether it's seeing the issues customers face when shipping a product, driving on the road or having a pacemaker fitted, the key is understanding what customers feel and what would add value to their experience.

Step 2: aid decision making

Developing processes to reduce uncertainties

Possibly the most challenging concept in marketing deals with understanding why buyers do what they do (or don't do). But such knowledge is critical for marketers, since having a strong understanding of buyer behaviour will help shed light on what is important to the customer and also suggest the important influences on customer decision making (Figure 11.8). Using this information, marketers can create marketing programmes that they believe will be of interest to customers (knowthis.com).

As you might guess, factors affecting how customers make decisions are extremely complex. Buyer behaviour is deeply rooted in psychology, with a dash of sociology thrown in just to make things more interesting. Since every person in the world is different, it is impossible to have simple rules that explain how buying decisions are made. For marketers, it is important to understand how consumers treat the purchase decisions they face.

If a company is targeting customers who feel a purchase decision is difficult, their marketing strategy may vary greatly from a company targeting customers who view the

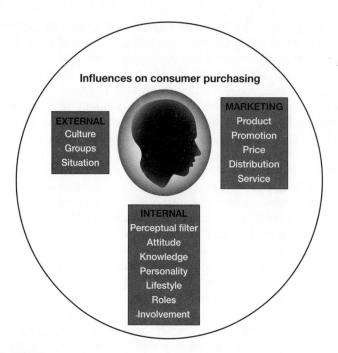

Figure 11.8   Influencing consumer purchasing

purchase decision as routine. In fact, the same company may face both situations at the same time; for some the product is new, while other customers see the purchase as routine. The implication of buying behaviour for marketers is that different buying situations require different marketing efforts.

Step 3: facilitate purchase

Relocate to reach the customer

The idea behind enabling customer purchase is that the firm has to be dynamic in relocating its processes, not only literally but figuratively, in order to hit the 'hot spot' in the customer's mind. There are various ways in which a firm can achieve this. In many cases, the solution chosen by the consumer is the same as the product whose evaluation is the highest. However, this may change when it is actually time to make the purchase. The 'intended' purchase may be changed at the time of purchase for many reasons:

• the product is out of stock
• a competitor offers an incentive at the point of purchase, for example a store sales-person mentions a competitor's offer
• the customer lacks the necessary funds, for example, their credit card doesn't work

- members of the consumer's reference group take a negative view of the purchase, for example a friend is critical of the purchase.

Marketers whose product is most desirable to the consumer must make sure that the transaction goes smoothly. For example, internet retailers have worked hard to prevent consumers from abandoning their online purchase, that is, online shopping carts, by streamlining the checkout process. For marketers whose product is not the consumer's selected product, last chance marketing efforts may be worth exploring, such as offering incentives to store personnel to 'talk up' their product at the checkout queue. Hence the key is to have processes that avoid any deficit on the firm's side to service the customer at the point of purchase.

Step 4: enable trust in payments

Retool the processes to equip the customer

Today's customers are accustomed to self-service. Yet for many sophisticated products and/or products sold through channel partners, it's often not easy for customers to start the transaction online.

To convince the customer, it is imperative that the information and advice must be credible, and the source must be trustworthy. The need for trust applies equally to the human and the software system, but the latter has the greater challenge. An internet-delivered software adviser cannot provide the face-to-face cues of trustworthiness that a human can. However, although a software adviser may have no initial reputation for trust (based on past experience), such an image can be built over time by personal usage, word-of-mouth recommendations or public endorsements, for example by consumer-oriented magazines' endorsement of the system's knowledge and interest-edness (Russo, 2002).

Try to implement this four-point strategy for retooling or arming your customer for a better tomorrow (Seybold, 2006):

1. Improve the search ability and quality of information on your website(s).
2. Make it easy and safe for customers to transact online.
3. Give customers easy online access to their transactions, information, profiles and projects.
4. Make it as easy as possible for customers to select and buy your products.

Step 5: assure safe delivery

Resequence for successful execution

For years, consultants have been telling their clients to break down the isolated silos within their companies and integrate them for added efficiencies, increased profitability and better customer service. Driven by competitive markets that punish companies that have poor customer service, inefficient operations and excess inventory, these companies are embracing new leaner, demand-driven processes in their businesses.

At the same time, manufacturers and service providers are realizing they need a new kind of senior executive to manage previously isolated silos such as manufacturing, warehousing, transportation and so on. C-level managers (CEOs, CFOs and so on) are seeking new solutions to meet this challenge.

The supply chain manager has the potential to provide these solutions and, in doing so, move the supply chain manager from the 'backroom to the boardroom' (Srivastava er al., 1998).

Step 6: make it useful

Reconfigure to match their needs

Business processes can be reconfigured to create and capture value (Chesbrough and Rosenbloom, 2002). Reconfiguring builds dynamic capabilities to help the firm to integrate, build and reconfigure internal and external competences to address rapidly changing environments (Teece et al., 1997). Like Vargo and Lusch (2008), Normann (2001) shifted the focus of the offering from an output to a process of value creation and perceived the firm as an organizer of this process, with the customer as a co-producer, rather than a receiver of value. He also argued that offerings are 'frozen knowledge', similar to Vargo and Lusch's contention that the basis of exchange is applied operant resources (service) and suggested that the 'dematerialization' of resources increases their 'liquidity', which allows increased 'density' for value creation. Thus, he suggested that firms need to 'reframe business' – rethink the logic of value creation – to reveal opportunities in reconfiguring the value constellations of which they are part.

Step 7: seal the deal: conclude

Rethink to close any value gaps

The process is not finished here, the firm needs to continuously monitor itself in the shape of the following model (Figure 11.9) to make sure that the business processes cover the critical aspects of:

- capturing the target market segment
- creating a unique value proposition
- championing the value chain
- determining the profit mechanism
- leveraging on the value network
- devising competitive strategy.

Covering all these parameters can only ensure the deal for the organization.

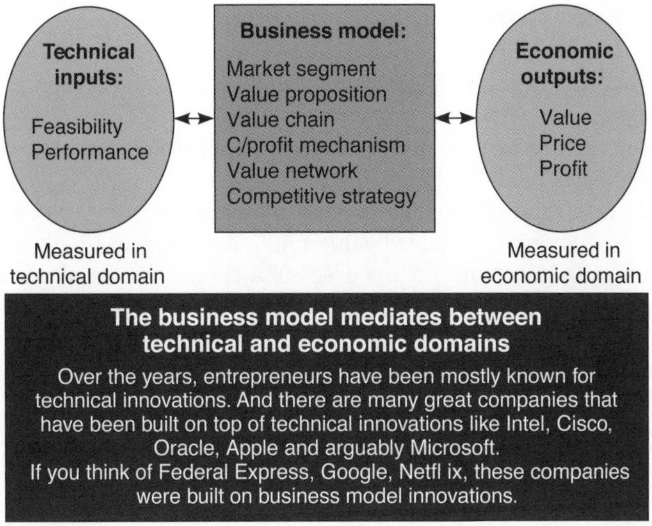

The business model mediates between
technical and economic domains

Over the years, entrepreneurs have been mostly known for
technical innovations. And there are many great companies that
have been built on top of technical innovations like Intel, Cisco,
Oracle, Apple and arguably Microsoft.
If you think of Federal Express, Google, Netfl ix, these companies
were built on business model innovations.

Figure 11.9   Technical and economic outputs of a business model

To rethink, companies need to shift from a closed innovation mindset to an open innovation mindset through creating new ventures out of internal technologies – taking internal knowledge out to the external market.

For implementing the above processes, a data survey indicates the following:

1. *Minimal investment required*: Focusing on ideas is a quick, low-investment way to jumpstart an innovation programme and show momentum. Many idea-specific activities can be done in small teams and at any level of the organization. It's also easy to quantify and show the results of these activities (number of ideas generated, number of people involved in innovation, number of 'experiments' in development).

2. *A need for momentum:* Successes in idea capabilities provide quick wins that teams can showcase both internally and externally to shape employee and marketplace perceptions. The power of perception is important in the innovation world, when innovation is perceived to be part of someone's work, it becomes a more integral part of the way things are done.

3. *Little management commitment required:* Idea capabilities require less senior management involvement than strategy and process capabilities. Idea-shaping activities (brainstorming, selecting incremental ideas to go to market, rewarding innovation efforts) can start and grow anywhere within an organization, but strategy and process-building activities (setting organizational vision, defining metrics, setting programme governance) require leadership involvement, support and commitment.

Issues for further discussion

1. Imagine that you are a hotel manager. Explain how you would design a seamless customer experience and why.
2. Analyse the value architecture of Google in terms of customer experience, availability and accessibility.
3. Developing processes should revolve around value proposition, value promise, value delivery and customer perceived value fulfilment. Explain briefly what these are and how you would develop the processes of a shoe store, an airline company or a local restaurant.
4. Describe a global customer. Then choose a global company and draw up a picture of how the changing needs of global customers have modified the company strategy and processes.

CASE STUDY

Seagate

Background

When Seagate was founded in 1979, its hard disk drives helped create the PC revolution. Today, the company is helping to revolutionize the way we live, work and play by enabling the growth of the internet, putting the world's information at your fingertips. Storage technology, Seagate's core business, has become the centre of the new computing architecture. Seagate's position as the world's largest manufacturer of disk drives, magnetic disks and read-write heads puts it at the heart of today's 'information-centric' world.

Seagate, one of Dell's largest customers in purchasing dollars, stepped forward to evolve its manual procurement process to an electronic procurement process through Ariba and its electronic commerce business solutions. Seagate approached Dell to move to a business-to-business (B2B) connection, which would enable it to purchase Dell products over the internet through the Ariba-based applications. Dell had also integrated to Ariba Services Network, so the timing and fit worked well.

Challenge

Most buyers start out the B2B connection by having their suppliers put together product information for purchasing into spreadsheets and other file formats. The files are then transferred to the customer by email, FTP (file transfer protocol) or by faxing the documents. Ariba allows for the use of CIF (catalog interchange format) as a method for buyers to electronically send their product information or 'catalogs' by exporting data from the spreadsheets and uploading these items into Ariba in the CIF format. This is how Dell started with Seagate. In this way, the customer can select the items intended for purchase from the supplier's catalogue and place the order either by email, fax or XML (eXtensible Markup Language).

While there were benefits to the new system of purchasing, managing content using CIF has a downside. Catalogue information on the products was difficult to maintain as spreadsheets and other files were passed back and forth between Seagate and Dell many times to ensure accuracy and product availability. The CIF load process required special human interaction from both Dell and Seagate just to load the catalogue. Dell could not deliver pictures of third party items with

CIF, which would give the customer the ability to review products more thoroughly. CIF file description fields were limited to 256 characters. And finally, Dell still received an emailed product order that had to be printed and rekeyed into the Dell order system, adding time and possible errors to the process.

Solution

Seagate decided to move to 'Punchout' with Dell (an Ariba supplier hosted solution), which allows Seagate end users to shop on Dell's catalogue, pull back the order requisition into their e-procurement system, submit the electronic order in XML and receive a purchase order acknowledgement that confirms each order.

This solved many problems created by the previous CIF setup. This allows the Dell sales team to manage the catalogue so any technology or pricing changes can be updated instantly. Seagate no longer has the burden of catalogue maintenance on its side. The system ties back to Dell's existing online information so images and product descriptions are current and automatically shown to the Seagate shopper with no more limitations on product description. Best of all, fewer resources were required to manage the product catalogues at both Seagate and Dell. Seagate orders are entered automatically into Dell's ordering system, eliminating additional time and possible order entry errors.

Seagate was also using American Express for its payment of catalogue orders. By using Ariba, items purchased from the various suppliers would be combined into one payment from the American Express system. By using an e-procurement solution with Dell, Seagate could use the Ariba order link number to tie purchase orders back to the American Express payment system. This assists and speeds up the reconciliation process for tying the purchase orders to the invoices as paid.

Results

Seagate says that the use of this e-procurement arrangement has done many things to improve and optimize its ordering processes. With 'Punchout', Dell hosts the catalogue, which is up to date, more accurate and available for Seagate's shoppers and buyers to access. Seagate can also contact its Dell account team for any immediate modifications.

This solution also streamlines the payment system because the use of Ariba, and using American Express in the background, helps to speed invoice payment and reconciliation processes. This helps combine the payment process into fewer billing statements and means that Dell does not have to send as many invoices.

Anne Farren, senior procurement manager at Seagate, is pleased with the new process. Approximately 80% of Seagate's orders to Dell now go through the Ariba 'Punchout' catalogue.

Questions

1. How can you partner with different available channels to improve your processes?
2. What is the way forward to evolve processes in the ever-changing consumer scenario?
3. How can top management be involved in shaping the organization's processes to the benefit of both employees and consumers?
4. How can customer feedback and opinions be used to add value to a firm's existing processes?

References

Aaker, D. (1996) *Building Strong Brands*. New York: The Free Press.

Chesbrough, H. and Rosenbloom, R.S. (2002) 'The role of the business model in capturing value from innovation: Evidence from Xerox Corporation's technology spin-off companies'. *Industrial and Corporate Change*, 11(3): 529–55.

Clark, T. and Gottfredson, C. (2008) *In Search of Learning Agility*, available online at http://www.elearningguild.com/content.cfm?selection=doc.1054.

Clark, T.R. (2007) *Epic Change: How to Lead Change in the Global Age*. San Francisco, CA: Jossey-Bass.

Dhar, V. (1992) A Value-chain Based Process Model to Support Business Process Reengineering, IBM Technical Report 17221 (#77966), February.

Grönroos, C. (2007) *Service Management and Marketing: Customer Management in Service Competition* (3rd edn). Chichester: John Wiley and Sons.

Hammer, M. and Champy, J. (1993) *Reengineering the Corporation: A Manifesto for Business Revolution*. New York: HarperBusiness.

Hartung, A. (2000) *Beating the Marketer's Dilemma: Using The Phoenix Principle™ to Overcome Customer Lock-in*.

Hatch, M.J. and Schultz, M. (2002) 'The dynamics of organizational identity'. *Human Relations*, 55(8): 989–1017.

Hunt, S.D. (1991) *Modern Marketing Theory: Critical Issues in the Philosophy of Marketing Science*. Cincinnati, OH: South-Western Publishing.

Keller, K.L. (2007) *Strategic Brand Management: Building, Measuring, and Managing Brand Equity*. Upper Saddle River, NJ: Prentice Hall.

Kotler, P. and Keller, K.L. (2006) *Marketing Management*. Upper Saddle River, NJ: Pearson/Prentice Hall.

Normann, R. (2001) *Reframing Business: When the Map Changes the Landscape*. Chichester: Wiley.

Reijers, H.A. (2003) *Design and Control of Workflow Processes: Business Process Management for the Service Industry*. Berlin: Springer-Verlag.

Roy, T. (2005) *Business Process Re-engineering: An Effective Management Tool*, available online at http://papers.ssrn.com.

Russo, J. (2002) Aiding Purchase Decisions on the Internet, International Conference on Advances in Infrastructure for Electronic Business, Education, Science, and Medicine on the Internet, L'Aquila, Italy, 21–26 January.

Seybold, P.B. (2006) *Outside Innovation: How Your Customers Will Co-Design Your Company's Future*. New York: HarperCollins.

Srivastava, R., Shervani, T. and Fahey, L. (1998) 'Market-based assets and shareholder value: A framework for analysis'. *Journal of Marketing*, 62(1): 2–18.

Taylor, F.W. (1911) *The Principles of Scientific Management*. New York: Harper and Brothers.

Teece, D.J., Pisano, G. and Shuen A. (1997) 'Dynamic capabilities and strategic management'. *Strategic Management Journal*, 18(7): 509–33.

Vargo, S.L. and Lusch, R.F. (2008) 'Service-dominant logic: Continuing the evolution'. *Journal of the Academy of Marketing Science*, 36(1): 1–10.

12

Export market-oriented processes and export performance: quadratic and moderated relationships

Mark J. French and John W. Cadogan

Learning outcomes

At the end of this chapter, readers should be able to:

1. Understand export market-oriented (EMO) behavioural processes, and their potential role in shaping export success.

2. Discuss and debate the differential impact that EMO behavioural processes may have on cash flows and profits.

3. Discuss the managerial implications of EMO behavioural processes, identifying how EMO behaviour can be leveraged for enhanced success.

4. Identify gaps in knowledge, and discuss aspects of the relationship between EMO behavioural processes and export success that are in need of further elaboration.

Key points

- Market orientation is a core tenet of international marketing strategy. It is defined as the implementation of the marketing concept and is seen as a source of sustainable competitive advantage that will result in long-term superior performance.

- Export market orientation involves the organizational behaviour processes of generating information on export markets, disseminating that information, and responding to it.

- Empirical research predominantly views the relationship between a firm's level of EMO processes and export performance as monotonically increasing. Marketing practitioners are often recommended to increase their firm's market orientation on the assumption that the benefits are always the same whatever the starting point.

- The literature outside exporting suggests that the EMO processes–performance relationship could be nonlinear. Diminishing returns, for example, imply that marginal increases in EMO process investment will lead to decreasing marginal benefits.

- Export market environments are often different from the domestic market environment, and each export market may be different from another. Contingency theory indicates that the environment may affect the EMO processes–performance relationship.

- Different performance measures capture different dimensions of a firm's performance. Profit-based measures capture the revenues and costs of a firm and may have a different relationship to EMO processes than sales-based measures of performance.

- An empirical study of New Zealand exporting firms supports a nonlinear EMO processes–export performance effect for profit performance and a linear relationship for sales performance. Both relationships are contingent on market dynamism.

Introduction

We examine the relationship between export market-oriented (EMO) behavioural processes and export success using data collected from 292 exporters. We hypothesize that this relationship will be U-shaped and our study findings confirm this. However, extrapolation of our findings indicates that when environmental conditions are dynamic, the relationship between EMO processes and export success may become an inverted U-shaped one.

Background

The search for managerially controllable factors that contribute to export performance continues, building on decades of empirical investigation (Aaby and Slater, 1989; Zou and Stan, 1998; Katsikeas et al., 2000; Sousa et al., 2008). In this field, a topic receiving increasing attention is export market orientation (Sousa et al., 2008), with researchers seeking to determine whether there is a positive linear relationship between the extent to which exporting firms adopt and implement market-oriented processes and export performance (Sundqvist et al., 2000; Kwon and Hu, 2000; Rose and Shoham, 2002; Akyol and Akehurst, 2003; Beaujanot et al., 2006; Murray et al., 2007; Racela et al., 2007). Implicit in these studies is the notion that the returns accruing from market-oriented processes are consistent, no matter how market oriented the firm is already. As a result, there are calls for exporters to seek to increase their market orientation by investing in the development of enhanced market-oriented processes (Rose and Shoham, 2002).

Yet increasing a firm's market orientation in its export markets (referred to hereafter as export market-oriented [EMO] processes) and maintaining high EMO process levels is expensive (Slater and Narver, 1994), and recommendations that exporters should continuously enhance their EMO processes are grounded in the assumption that the benefits of market-oriented activities do not operate under a law of diminishing returns. However, empirical research addressing possible nonlinear relationships between EMO processes and export performance is scarce, making it hard to draw conclusions about whether the relationship between market orientation and export performance is linear or nonlinear. In this study, therefore, we investigate the following questions:

1. Is there a linear monotonic increasing relationship between EMO processes and export performance? And is this relationship consistent across all environmental conditions firms may face?
2. Alternatively, is the relationship between EMO processes and export performance quadratic? And does market dynamism play a role in shaping the relationship between EMO processes and export success?

In order to examine these issues, the next section provides the theoretical underpinnings of EMO processes, and presents a model of potential quadratic and moderated relationships between EMO processes and export success. Following this, the methods used to asses the hypotheses are outlined, the results are explained, implications for scholars and managers are discussed, and future research avenues are presented.

Conceptual model

EMO processes

The marketing concept is an organizational culture, a set of values and beliefs that place the customer at the heart of the business's thinking about strategic direction, tactical manoeuvres and competitive response. Firms that translate the marketing concept into practice are 'market oriented', and market orientation, it is argued, is a source of sustainable competitive advantage (Kohli and Jaworski, 1990). Jaworski and Kohli (1993, 1996) go on to operationalize market orientation as a set of behavioural processes. Specifically, they define market orientation as consisting of three core elements – market intelligence generation, dissemination and responsiveness. Importantly, Cadogan and Diamantopoulos (1995) (see also Diamantopoulos and Cadogan, 1996) show that the generic processes underpinning market orientation are directly transferable to an exporting context, and as a result, Cadogan et al. (1999, p. 690) conclude that 'the basic nature of the [market orientation] construct is not changed as a result of changing the setting in which it is applied'. Cadogan et al. (1999) go on to define export market orientation as consisting of export market intelligence generation, dissemination and responsiveness.

Export market-oriented firms generate intelligence on export customers' current and future needs and wants, as well as about the forces that shape customers' preferences and opinions, for example export market competitors, foreign government regulations and cultural trends. This information is then disseminated to export decision makers, and across business functions to maximize its value. The export market-oriented business then responds rapidly to this information, in order to shape the actions of customers and players in the firms' current and future export markets.

Thus, market-oriented exporters are reactive to export market intelligence, and will use the information they generate from their monitoring activities to help select export markets, identify what customers in those export markets value, and deliver that value to them. However, EMO processes are not purely reactive, since a reactive stance is only one aspect of market orientation. EMO processes are also proactive, focusing on developments and influences beyond the current export customers. Often, the seeds of ideas for export product innovations are internal to the firm (employees coming up with new ideas). Market-oriented exporters may thus be ahead of the market in terms of identifying customers' emerging expectations, but nevertheless, they will refine their ideas using intelligence generated from the export marketplace.

Benefits of EMO processes

What, then, are the benefits of EMO processes? There are two potential classes of benefit that we consider here: export sales and export profits. Researchers looking at the benefits of market orientation in exporting firms tend to make no distinction in their theories about how market orientation may shape export sales and export profits. Certainly, EMO processes should enable firms to develop products and services that export customers value, and to communicate this value to the export markets they operate in (Cadogan et al., 2003). Similarly, firms with more developed EMO processes are more likely to choose more effective export partners (for example distributors) when they are looking for ways of managing their export channels (Beaujanot et al., 2006). Accordingly, linear relationship between market orientation and export sales perform-ance are proposed or sought after in the literature (Cadogan et al., 2002a, 2003; Rose and Shoham, 2002). Furthermore, since export sales performance is believed to be a driver of export profitability, researchers also expect that there is an indirect link between EMO processes and export profits (Cadogan et al., 2002a, 2003). Finally, researchers also argue that market orientation has a direct positive linear relationship with export profits; for example, by capitalizing on current market needs and using industry foresight to identify latent needs, firms with EMO processes can reap the profit benefits associated with higher export market shares, a greater utilization of capacity, export customer loyalty, and the ability to charge premium prices. Accordingly, it is argued that 'market-oriented firms should also exhibit increased export profitability and positive changes in export profitability' (Rose and Shoham, 2002, p. 219).

The following null and alternative hypotheses summarize these arguments:

H1Null: There is no relationship between EMO processes and export sales performance
H1Alternative A: There is a positive linear relationship between EMO processes and export sales performance
H2Null: There is no relationship between EMO processes and export profit performance
H2Alternative A: There is a positive linear relationship between EMO processes and export profit performance

U-shaped relationships

However, empirical findings from beyond the exporting literature indicate that the relationship between EMO processes and export performance may not be linear. Indeed, in their seminal work on market orientation, Narver and Slater (1990) suggest that market-oriented processes may not be effective for firms that do not fully embrace market orientation. Narver and Slater's (1990, p. 28) logic is that firms with low levels of market orientation:

> perceive that increasing their market orientation could be substantially costly and thus unattractive … To increase its market orientation, a … business must be consistent and pervasive in adapting all of its systems to … create customer value … [Some businesses] will be tentative in adopting a market orientation. They will initiate some of the appropriate steps, but will not undertake them in sufficient magnitude or with sufficient persistence or quality.

Narver and Slater (1990, p. 28) go on to argue that firms with low levels of adoption of market-oriented processes are highly internally focused: 'businesses lowest in market orientation, that is, the most internally oriented businesses, may be very consistent and efficient in what they do'. These businesses, perhaps by being successful in achieving a low-cost strategy, can achieve profit success through the generation of high sales volumes (Narver and Slater, 1990). Firms that have high levels of adoption of market-oriented processes are also likely to have profit success, since they can reap the rewards associated with the creation of superior customer value.

Narver and Slater (1990) argue that a problem exists for firms that adopt mid-range levels of market-oriented processes, since these tentative adopters of market-oriented processes do not have a sufficient internal focus to achieve suitably low costs, and so do not compete effectively against the firms with very low levels of market-oriented processes. Furthermore, in these mid-range firms, the market-oriented processes are not sufficiently developed to be able to consistently create superior value for customers, relative to the highly market-oriented businesses that excel at creating superior customer value. As a result, Narver and Slater (1990) propose that the relationship between market orientation and profitability may well be U-shaped.

It is interesting to note that Narver and Slater's (1990) logic applies most strongly to profit performance. Indeed, Narver and Slater say very little about the effect of market-oriented processes on sales. However, it seems that Narver and Slater's logic makes good sense in terms of sales performance also. For instance, by focusing on internal efficiencies, firms with low levels of market orientation generate profits by stimulating sales (that is, profits require large sales volumes). Similarly, firms that are highly market oriented can identify new markets and new sales opportunities and, through the creation of superior value, are best placed to identify and respond to market and sales opportunities. Once more, it can be argued that mid-range market-oriented firms are at a disadvantage.

As a result, and extending this logic to the specific case of exporting firms, the following alternative hypotheses are presented:

H1Alternative B: There is a U-shaped relationship between EMO processes and export sales performance (formally, there is a positive quadratic relationship between EMO processes and export sales performance)

H2Alternative B: There is a U-shaped relationship between EMO processes and export profit performance (formally, there is a positive quadratic relationship between EMO processes and export profit performance)

Environment as moderator

What influence, if any, does the environment play in terms of shaping the relationship between EMO processes and export success? Several studies look to identify environmental moderators of the relationship between EMO processes and export performance, with equivocal results. For instance, Cadogan et al. (2002b), Kwon and Hu (2000) and Rose and Shoham (2002) show that environmental factors are not significant moderators of the relationship between market orientation and export success. On the other hand, Cadogan et al. (2002a) and Cadogan et al. (2003) both show that environmental conditions are significant moderators of the relationship between EMO processes and export performance. For instance, Cadogan et al. (2003) demonstrate that under low levels of turbulence, the relationship between EMO processes and export sales efficiency performance is strong and positive, but becomes less positive under more turbulent conditions.

In this respect, Cadogan et al. (2002a) argue that a weakening in the positive relationship between EMO processes and export success is likely to occur as the export environment becomes more dynamic. This is because, they argue, EMO processes are most efficient when the environment is fairly stable. In these market conditions, customers' needs and wants are fairly easy to monitor and predict, and changes in the environment can be dealt with in fairly standard ways. In very dynamic export markets, however, EMO process development and maintenance can be costly, and the benefits accruing from market-oriented responses, in terms of sales and profits, are less certain. As a result, firms that invest in the development of EMO processes in highly dynamic markets may find that the export market intelligence they generate has a short 'shelf life', and that even rapid dissemination and response to changes occurring in their export markets is unsuccessful, as export customer preferences evolve in unpredictable ways. Ultimately, these firms may be better off, both in terms of sales and profits, by adopting lower levels of EMO processes.

In light of this logic, and given the fact that there is some empirical evidence to justify this conclusion, in this study, it is expected that the greater the market dynamism in the export markets faced by firms, the weaker the relationship between EMO processes and export performance. As a result, the following alternative hypotheses are proposed:

H1Alternative C: The positive linear relationship between EMO processes and export sales performance becomes weaker the greater the degree of export market dynamism

H2Alternative C: The positive linear relationship between EMO processes and export profit performance becomes weaker the greater the degree of export market dynamism

H1Alternative D: The positive quadratic relationship between EMO processes and export sales performance becomes weaker the greater the degree of export market dynamism

H2Alternative D: The positive quadratic relationship between EMO processes and export profit performance becomes weaker the greater the degree of export market dynamism

Research method

The sample

In order to shed light on these research questions, data obtained from a mail survey of exporting firms were used. The sample consisted of 853 companies randomly selected from Profile Direct's complete listing of 1,022 New Zealand exporting firms with 50 or more employees. For each firm, the key informant (the export manager, the marketing manager or the CEO) was contacted by telephone in order to establish whether the firm was eligible to be sent a questionnaire, to correct contact details, and determine whether the key informant would agree to cooperate in the study. In total, 438 of the 853 companies contacted proved to be ineligible, either because the firm had never exported, no longer exported, or because the firm was listed more than once.

Of the remaining 417 eligible companies, 45 firms indicated that they did not wish to participate in the study, either because they were time constrained or because company policy precluded them from providing data to external bodies. Those firms agreeing to participate in the study were mailed a questionnaire, together with explanatory materials. Nonrespondents were mailed a reminder card seven days after the initial mailing. A further seven days later, a second pack containing a questionnaire and explanatory materials was mailed out to the remaining nonrespondents. In total, 292 completed questionnaires were returned.

Measurement and measure assessment

The constructs in the model were all measured using established measuring instruments. Cadogan et al.'s (1999) measures of export market orientation served as the basis for measuring EMO processes. The scales capture the extent to which firms generate information about their export markets, disseminate this information to key individuals in the exporting company, and respond to the export market intelligence in a timely manner. Export sales performance and export profit performance were captured using measures developed by Cadogan et al. (2002a, 2005). The export sales performance questions capture respondents' degree of satisfaction with their firms' performance in terms of export sales volumes, export market shares, export market entry programmes, and sales growth relative to industry norms. The export profit performance measure captures the firm's degree of satisfaction with its export profits over the last three years, and assesses the overall profitability of the firm's exporting operations during the last financial year. Finally, export market dynamism was measured using a scale developed by Jaworski and Kohli (1993), modified to account for the exporting context. The items capture the extent to which changes are occurring in firms' export markets in terms of customers' preferences and needs. All the measures are presented in the Appendix.

Prior to model testing, the measures were assessed for unidimensionality, convergent and discriminant validity, and reliability. All analyses were undertaken using LISREL 8.72, using the covariance matrix as input, and maximum likelihood estimation procedure. Specifically, the items were all entered simultaneously into a confirmatory factor analysis model. The measurement model fit was adequate (see Table 12.1), since, although the chi-square statistic was significant, the remaining fit heuristics all indicate a good to excellent fit. All items load significantly on their respective factors. Subsequently, the composite reliability (an alternative to Cronbach's alpha) was calculated for each scale, together with the average variance extracted. In all cases, the composite reliability exceeded 0.60, and the average variance extracted exceeded 0.50 in the majority of cases. These results indicate that, for each set of scale items, the items tend to converge on a common theme, and thus display convergent validity.

Table 12.1 Model fit indices, correlation coefficients and measurement descriptive information

Model fit	$\chi 2$ (df)	RMSEA	CFI	NNFI	GFI
Measurement model	362.99 (215)	.049	.96	.96	.90
Structural model	67.96 (32)	.062	.96	.92	.96

Correlations	1	2	3	4	5	6	7	8	9	10	11
1. Generation	–										
2. Dissemination	.29	–									
3. Responsiveness	.40	.30	–								
4. EMO processes	.76	.72	.76	–							
5. Market dynamism (MD)	.20	.05	.02	.12	–						
6. EMO processes squared	–.01	.02	–.01	.00	–.09	–					
7. MD squared	–.04	.00	.02	–.01	.00	–.03	–				
8. EMO processes x MD	–.05	.05	–.01	.00	.00	.14	.35	–			
9. EMO processes squared x MD	.11	.10	.14	.15	.00	.00	–.05	.16	–		
10. Export sales performance	.31	.21	.33	.38	.04	–.03	.03	.07	.06	–	
11. Export profit performance	.09	.12	.15	.16	–.08	.10	–.04	.08	–.04	.45	–
CR	.78	.89	.76	.81*	.81	–	–	–	–	.79	.79
AVE	.48	.59	.52	.53*	.42	–	–	–	–	.50	.66
Mean	4.32	5.25	4.80	4.79	3.84	.00	.00	.00	.00	5.80	.00
Standard deviation	1.19	1.21	1.19	.89	1.10	1.07	1.00	1.00	1.00	1.51	.91

Key: RMSEA: root mean square error of approximation; CFI: comparative fit index; NNFI: non-normed fit index; GFI: goodness of fit index; *: average across three constituent scales

To assess discriminant validity, for each pair of multi-item reflective scales, the average variance extracted for each scale was compared with the square of the correlation between the scales. In each case, the average variance extracted exceeded the square of the correlation between scales, and this indicates that the scales discriminate from each other (Table 12.1). In summary, we can be confident in the unidimensionality of the measures used in the study.

Model-testing strategy

Having confirmed that the measures are adequate for model-testing purposes, LISREL 8.72 was also used to assess the hypotheses. In essence, the approach adopted was a path analysis with quadratic and product interaction terms. The first step involved creating single observed scores for the latent constructs involved in the hypothesized quadratic effect (that is, EMO processes) and product interaction effect (that is, market dynamism). Single indicants are recommended for use with quadratic and interaction-based structural models as a way of reducing model complexity (Ping, 1995; Jöreskog and Yang, 1996). To create a single score for EMO processes, single scores were first created for each of the three individual export market information processing behaviours of generation, dissemination and responsiveness, by averaging across the respective scale's items. The single scores for export market information generation, dissemination and responsiveness were then summed for each exporter, and divided by three, resulting in a score that reflects the composite of each firms' EMO processes. A single score was created for export market dynamism by simply averaging across the scales' five items for each firm.

Of course, given that the analysis calls for the creation of quadratic and interaction terms, multicollinearity may be a problem when model testing. As a result, after creating the quadratic and interaction terms, but prior to testing the model, Little et al.'s (2006) recommended procedure for orthogonalizing observed interaction and quadratic terms was followed. It is these orthogonalized values that are used in the subsequent analysis and reported in the correlation matrix (Table 12.1).

To test the model, we simultaneously estimated the following two equations using the LISREL package, where EMO = export market-oriented processes, MD = market dynamism, γs are intercepts and slope estimates, and the δs are residual variances.

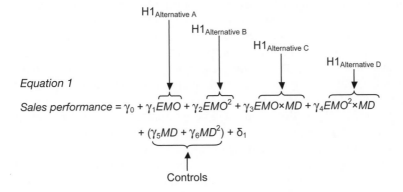

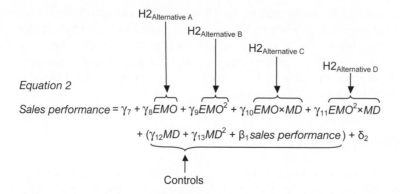

Since the quadratic and product interaction terms have been orthogonalized, the variables were all entered straight into the structural model (the use of nested or hierarchical entry is not necessary in this situation), and for specification purposes, a number of control variables were included in the models. The fit for the structural model was satisfactory (see Table 12.1). That is, although chi-square was significant at 5%, the other standard fit heuristics indicate that the model fits the data quite well. Accordingly, we use the results of the structural model to assess the hypotheses.

Results and discussion

Table 12.2 provides the path estimates and t-values for the structural model. For export sales performance, only one alternative hypothesis returns a significant result. Specifically, EMO processes are significant predictors of export sales performance ($\gamma = 0.40$, $p<0.05$), whereas neither EMO processes squared ($\gamma = -0.04$, ns), nor EMO processes × export market dynamism ($\gamma = 0.08$, ns), nor EMO processes squared × export market dynamism ($\gamma = -0.01$, ns) significantly contribute to variance in export sales success. Accordingly, H1Null is rejected in favour of H1Alternative A: that is, there is a positive and significant linear relationship between the extent to which firms put in place EMO processes and export sales performance. Furthermore, EMO processes explain a satisfactory 16% of variation in the export sales performance measure.

With respect to export profit performance, two of the hypothesized alternative paths are significant, and the model explains 38% of export profit performance. Specifically, EMO processes squared is a significant predictor of export profit performance ($\gamma = 0.10$, $p<0.05$), as is EMO processes squared × export market dynamism ($\gamma = -0.10$, $p<0.05$), while neither EMO processes ($\gamma = -0.04$, ns) nor EMO processes × export market dynamism ($\gamma = 0.07$, ns) are significant predictors of export profit success. Since H2Alternative B is nested within H2Alternative D, these findings indicate that H2Null is rejected in favour of H2Alternative D.

Importantly, H2Alternative B can only be interpreted in context of the significant finding for H2Alternative D. That is, although the results indicate that there is a U-shaped relationship between EMO processes and export profit performance (that is, in accordance with H2Alternative B, there is a positive quadratic relationship between EMO processes and export profit performance), the results further show that the posi-

		Unstandardized path estimate	Standardized path estimate	t-Value a
Table 12.2 Standardized and unstandardized path estimates: export sales and export profits as dependent variables				
Hypothesized paths				
H1Alternative A	EMO processes → export sales performance	1.96	0.40	6.54
H1Alternative B	EMO processes squared → export sales performance	–0.14	–0.04	–0.69
H1Alternative C	EMO behaviour × export market dynamism → export sales performance	0.32	0.08	1.26
H1Alternative D	EMO behaviour squared × export market dynamism → export sales performance	–0.03	–0.01	–0.14
H2Alternative A	EMO behaviour → export profit performance	–0.04	–0.04	–0.65
H2Alternative B	EMO behaviour squared → export profit performance	0.07	0.10	1.80
H2Alternative C	EMO behaviour × export market dynamism → export profit performance	0.05	0.07	1.06
H2Alternative D	EMO behaviour squared × export market dynamism → export profit performance	–0.08	–0.10	–1.68
Control paths				
	Export market dynamism → export sales performance	–0.17	–0.05	–0.86
	Export market dynamism squared → export sales performance	–0.05	–0.01	–0.19
	Export sales performance → export profit performance	0.12	0.61	7.27
	Export market dynamism → export profit performance	–0.06	–0.09	–1.53
	Export market dynamism squared → export profit performance	–0.04	–0.06	–0.95

Notes: a: critical value ($\alpha = 0.05$) = 1.645 (because all hypotheses are directional, we used one-tailed tests); export sales performance: squared multiple correlation = 0.161; export profit performance: squared multiple correlation = 0.379

tive quadratic relationship between EMO processes and export profit performance becomes weaker the greater the degree of export market dynamism (in accordance with H2Alternative D).

It is instructive to examine the results for the export profit performance aspect of the model using surface plots. Figure 12.1a provides the surface plot for export profit performance with EMO processes and export market dynamism as predictors.[1] The plot is restricted to show the surface only for values of EMO processes and market dynamism in or near the range of scores actually observed in the dataset. As the plot shows, under the lowest levels of observed export market dynamism (that is, at the back edge of Figure 12.1a), the U-shaped curve falls steeply and rises steeply: thus, firms low in EMO processes and firms high in EMO processes perform very well in terms of profits, whereas firms with moderate levels of EMO processes are less successful. This finding directly mirrors the relationship that Narver and Slater (1990) predicted would be observed between market orientation and profit performance.

Under very high levels of export market dynamism (that is, at the front edge of Figure 12.1a), although the U-shaped curve is still apparent, the steepness of the curve has diminished, in accordance with H2Alternative D. An implication of this finding is that changes in EMO processes will have a less dramatic influence on export profits when firms are operating in highly dynamic markets. For example, an increase in EMO processes from a value of 6 to a value of 7 will produce a more marked increase in export profits in firms operating in less dynamic export markets.

Figure 12.1b is an extrapolation of the data. It uses the parameter estimates obtained for the export profit performance model to draw a surface plot beyond the range of observable EMO process and market dynamism values. Of course, we must be careful drawing conclusions from this extrapolation because only a portion of the surface drawn in Figure 12.1b is based on real data from exporters – that is, only the high-lighted section of Figure 12.1b is based on real data (the area that corresponds to Figure 12.1a). Nevertheless, it is interesting to see what the model parameters predict will happen to the relationship between EMO processes and export profits under extreme conditions (both in terms of EMO processes and market dynamism). Perhaps most interestingly, the model predicts that as market dynamism increases, the U-shaped relationship between EMO processes and export profit performance will first flatten off, and then under extremely high levels of market dynamism, the relationship will become an *inverted* U-shaped one.

This prediction finds some empirical support in the export literature. In a study of Chinese export agents, Cadogan and Cui (2004) find that the extent to which agents are market oriented has an inverted U-shaped relationship with a general measure of export

1. To obtain the plots, the analysis was rerun using the raw (unorthogonalized) data. The results of the hypothesis testing are not substantively different using the raw data (only the values of the model coefficients are affected; neither the sign nor the significance of the coefficients change), and its use allows for more intuitive plotting of the data. That is, observed values of EMO proc-esses and market dynamism can be plotted, and a more realistic picture of where minima and maxima occur can be obtained. This would not be the case using the orthogonalized data, since the quadratic and product interactions have been transformed to eliminate shared variance with the EMO processes and market dynamisms variables.

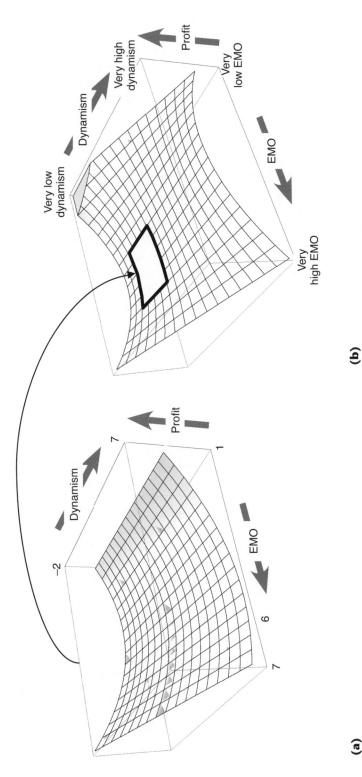

(a)
The relationship between EMO processes and export profit performance across the observable range of values in the sample

(b)
The relationship between EMO processes and export profit performance extrapolated beyond the observable range of values in the sample

Figure 12.1 The relationship between EMO processes and export profit performance under differing levels of market dynamism

performance. They argue that, as a result, there is an optimal level of EMO behavioural processes that exporters should aspire to. Now, while the findings of the current study are diametrically opposite to those reported by Cadogan and Cui (2004) (in the current sample, a U-shaped relationship was obtained), the extrapolation of the current study findings (see Figure 12.1b) indicates that if exporting firms operate in very dynamic markets, an inverted U-shaped relationship with profit performance may exist.

Conclusions

This study of exporting firms' EMO processes develops a complex model predicting how EMO processes and market dynamism interact to shape export sales and export profits. The results show that increases in EMO processes always lead to enhanced export sales performance. However, when it comes to the role that EMO processes have in shaping profit performance, the findings also show that increases in EMO processes are most beneficial for exporters who have already made considerable investment in market orientation in their export operations, and are least beneficial for exporters who have yet to invest in export market orientation. For the latter group of businesses, incremental (small) increases in EMO behaviour may lead to reduced profits, since the investments are insufficient to allow these firms to compete (via the creation of superior customer value) with their more market-oriented competitors. The findings add weight to Narver and Slater's (1990) logic, which argues that market orientation's relationship with profit performance is not a linear function, but is U-shaped.

For export managers, the results of the study are interesting. We can conclude that exporters should either have very high levels of market orientation in their export operations, or they should have very low levels of export market orientation, and should instead focus on an internal orientation (Narver and Slater, 1990). Firms stuck in the middle need to make the decision as to whether to invest in developing strong EMO processes, in order to be assured that they can create superior value for customers (relative to competitors), or whether to strip away the costs that a mid-range level of market orientation brings with it (for example market monitoring costs and market response costs), and focus on other activities and orientations.

These decisions are further complicated by the fact that market dynamism also shapes the relationship between EMO processes and profit performance. In the sample used in this study, under lower levels of market dynamism, EMO processes are strongly associated with export profit performance, whereas under higher levels of market dynamism, EMO processes are more weakly associated with export profit performance. In fact, using the results obtained for Equation 2, and extrapolating beyond the observable range of scores for EMO processes and market dynamism, it can be seen that under *very* high levels of market dynamism, the relationship between EMO processes and export profit performance may become an inverted U-shaped one. Interestingly, recommendations to export managers operating in extremely dynamic export markets would revolve around the identification of their firm's optimal level of EMO processes, and making recommendations to them about how to achieve this level.

There are clear future research requirements arising from this study's findings. First, there is a need to replicate the study to determine whether the findings are sample specific. In this respect, researchers should seek to generate samples of firms operating in many diverse market conditions, for example exporters operating in high-tech sectors or businesses operating in very stable environments. The objective should be to generate samples that maximize variance in terms of market dynamism as well as maximizing variance in terms of EMO processes. The results of this study indicate that EMO processes are less effective at higher levels of market dynamism. However, in order to make firmer recommendations to export managers, there is still a need to determine under what conditions, if any, the relationship between EMO processes and export profit performance is an inverted U-shaped one. Consequently, future researchers should look to reassess the model identified in this study using samples of exporters operating in extremely dynamic markets.

Second, there is a need to assess more carefully the relationships between EMO processes and export performance under other environmental conditions, for example competitive intensity or environmental munificence. The current study incorporates only a single facet of firms' export environments, yet it may be that different elements of the export environment shape the relationship between EMO processes and export success in different ways. Accordingly, a more holistic treatment of the export market environment is required.

Third, research in the new product development research domain indicates that new product success has complex nonlinear relationships with market orientation (Atuahene-Gima et al., 2005). In this study, only export sales and export profit performance are examined. Since it may be that the success of new products in export markets is a function of export market orientation, future researchers should look to determine whether findings generated within the non-export new product development literature also hold in the exporting context.

Last, although a proactive market orientation is implicit in the definition of export market orientation (Cadogan et al., 1999), current measures of EMO processes tend to focus on reactive elements of EMO processes. There is certainly a need to develop new measures that capture this proactive aspect to export market orientation. Similarly, research in non-export settings indicates that proactive market orientation also has a complex nonlinear relationship with aspects of business success (Tsai et al., 2008), and so there is a pressing need to determine what the situation is for exporters in this respect.

Issues for further discussion

1. How market oriented should exporters strive to be in their export markets?
2. How easy is it for management to develop and change EMO behaviour? Is it easier for firms to be market oriented in their domestic operations? Why?
3. Will firms always be market oriented to the same extent in their export and domestic marketing activities? Why? Why not?
4. Other than those studied in this research, what other factors may have an impact on the relationship between EMO behavioural processes and export success?

Export market orientation

Organizations today are more global in nature, and their export orientation can take different forms, ranging from organizations exporting home country products to organizations positioning themselves directly in different countries. Financial services can be a 'domestically located export' (Lewis, 2005), in the sense they relate to home-grown products adapted locally at the point of distribution, or 'intrafirm exports' (Roberts, 1999) demonstrating establishment of their operation within a particular market (either polycentrc or regiocentric), or they can be ethnocentric or geocentric in the provision of host products internationally. Leveraging export investment benefits are not fully charted for each of these strategies.

In recent years, intrafirm exports have become the focal target for the exponential growth in global trade. This has had implications for the behaviour of firms, such as job creation, infrastructure build and market growth at local and global levels and particularly in areas of risk management. However, there can be different outcomes where relationships between growth, market size and export orientation are either strong or weak (Adams and Hall, 1993). Where the markets are weak, it may be difficult to leverage a strong performance from export investment strategies.

Furthermore, there are individual country effects that can destabilize the benefits of export investment, particularly in areas where there are political and economic concerns. Evidence shows that in such areas there is an inclination by domestic firms to consider inward trade rather than outward orientation, partly as there is less knowledge, confidence and understanding of the export market and partly because governmental constraints push towards domestic trade build-up. To reduce the shock factor and marginalize political and economic turbulence effects, it has been determined that focus should initially be given to increasing domestic competition, while seeking to diversify exports and enhance the outward orientation of local industries (Collier et al., 1999; Azam et al., 2000).

Organizations undertaking export investment strategies have to consider their risk threshold level and management of risk performance. Export investment strategies consider the level of risk appetite for innovating new products tailored to specific markets. For example, the growth of early reserve back paybacks on insurance policies in developing countries meant increasing the organizational risk appetite to reach out to professional groupings nationally. Growth trends and reserving policies are critical within these countries.

Export investment involves higher risk (Begley, 1995; Das and Teng, 2001; Keh et al., 2002) and higher risk taking (Oviatt et al., 2004; Fernandez and Nieto, 2005). Obviously, size and experience enables higher risk-taking behaviour and higher organization risk appetite thresholds. Export markets are more volatile and difficult to control than domestic markets as they can vary by political, economic and social differences. Furthermore, the speed of market dynamics can increase the risk for the exporting organization. For example, a developing country that is exporting may have less governance in place than the importing country and will therefore need to invest more to ensure that governance standards are being met. Thus it becomes necessary to increase the risk appetite of a firm and take more risks when exporting than when doing business alone in domestic or regional markets. So it can be expected that companies that have better export performance would also have a higher level of risk appetite and risk-taking capacity.

From the above discussion, it needs to be noted that the export investment has brought about a new phase in organizational marketing, involving new forms of knowledge transfer within the three aspects of organizational behaviour: renewed organizational risk appetite, increasing resource capacity, and scanning and managing environmental risk:

- *Organizational risk appetite* considers the innovation appetite of the company and the level of risk the organization is willing to tolerate.
- *Resource capacity* is the availability of risk capital to enable export investment.
- *Environmental risk* is the risk prevalent in a particular market, in addition to that prevalent in the global market.

New learning skills need to be developed for adaptation to new environments. The greater the organization's innovativeness and adaptability, the greater the likelihood of performance success (Autio et al., 2000). Aaby and Slater (1989) observed that organizations that have an international vision, positive perception and attitudes towards exports, are willing to take risks and with the resource capacity to invest in exporting were likely to fare better in terms of performance and competitive edge.

Organizations operate in a highly competitive environment and hence export investment is an attractive option to many. Export performance represents an important indicator of performance measuring the success of financial service organizations in their export operations.

There are, however, barriers to export investment:

1. The advent of global corporate governance rules has put significant pressure on the need for accountability and transparency.
2. Exporting is a relatively new form of business for many financial service providers, and so it is difficult for firms to benchmark their export performance.
3. It is not necessarily easy for firms to understand how best to determine the appropriate level of export investment – or degree of internationalization.
4. The management of export fraud, which includes the misdescription of products, quantity declaration fraud, under/overvaluation fraud, off-record transaction fraud (hence nonaccountable) and so on.
5. There are technical barriers to trade, which Becker (1997) explains, albeit in the context of agricultural exports, as: 'widely divergent measures that countries use to regulate markets, protect their consumers, and preserve natural resources (among other objectives), but which can also be used to discriminate against imports in order to protect domestic industries'.

This case study was developed by Jyoti Navare.

Questions

1. What factors need to be taken into consideration when firms decide on the extent to which they should engage in exporting operations?
2. To what extent is organizational behaviour affected by export investment strategies?
3. What are the key barriers to, and issues shaping, the success of an export market-oriented strategy in firms' export operations.
4. Is there a link between investing in export activities and being export market oriented?

Appendix

Scale items

Export Market Intelligence Generation Behavioural Processes (7-point scale with very strongly disagree/very strongly agree anchors)
1. In this company, we generate a lot of information concerning trends (for example regulations, technological developments, political, economic) in our export markets.
2. We constantly monitor our level of commitment and orientation to serving export customer needs.
3. We periodically review the likely effect of changes in our export environment (for example regulation, technology).
4. We generate a lot of information in order to understand the forces which influence our overseas customers' needs and preferences.

Export Market Intelligence Dissemination Behavioural Processes (7-point scale with very strongly disagree/very strongly agree anchors)
1. Too much information concerning our export competitors is discarded before it reaches decision makers. R
2. Information which can influence the way we serve our export customers takes forever to reach export personnel. R
3. Important information about our export customers is often 'lost in the system'. R
4. Information about our export competitors' activities often reaches relevant personnel too late to be of any use. R
5. Important information concerning export market trends (regulation, technology) is often discarded as it makes its way along the communication chain. R

Export Market Responsiveness Behavioural Processes (7-point scale with very strongly disagree/very strongly agree anchors)
1. If a major competitor were to launch an intensive campaign targeted at our foreign customers, we would implement a response immediately.
2. We are quick to respond to significant changes in our competitors' price structures in foreign markets.
3. We rapidly respond to competitive actions that threaten us in our export markets.

Export Market Dynamism (7-point scale with not at all/to an extreme extent anchors)
1. Our export customers' product preferences change quite a bit over time.
2. New export customers tend to have product-related needs that are different from those of our existing export customers.
3. Our export customers tend to look for new products all the time.
4. Our export customers tend to have stable product preferences. R
5. We are witnessing changes in the type of products/services demanded by our export customers.

Export Sales Performance

1. How does your average annual export sales growth/decline compare to the industry average? (10-point scale with poor/outstanding anchors).
2. How satisfied are you with your performance, over the past 3 years, in terms of your export sales volume? (10-point scale with very dissatisfied/very satisfied anchors).
3. How satisfied are you with your performance, over the past 3 years, in terms of your export market share? (10-point scale with very dissatisfied/very satisfied anchors).
4. How satisfied are you with your performance, over the past 3 years, in terms of your rate of new market entry? (10-point scale with very dissatisfied/very satisfied anchors).

Export Profit Performance

1. How satisfied are you with your performance, over the past 3 years, in terms of your export profitability? (10-point scale with very dissatisfied/very satisfied anchors).
2. During the last financial year, how profitable has exporting been? (10-point scale with very unprofitable/very profitable anchors).

References

Aaby, N.-E. and Slater, S.F. (1989) 'Management influences on export performance: A review of the empirical literature 1978–88'. *International Marketing Review*, 6(4): 7–26.

Adams, G. and Hall, G. (1993) 'Influences on the growth of SMEs: An international comparison'. *Entrepreneurship & Regional Development*, 5: 73–84.

Akyol, A. and Akehurst, G. (2003) 'An investigation of export performance variations related to corporate export market orientation'. *European Business Review*, 15(1): 5–19.

Atuahene-Gima, K., Slater, S.F. and Olson, E.M. (2005) 'The contingent value of responsive and proactive market orientations for new product program performance'. *Journal of Product Innovation Management*, 22(6): 464–82.

Autio, E., Sapienza, H.J. and Almeida, J.G. (2000) 'Effects of age at entry, knowledge intensity and imitability on international growth'. *Academy of Management Journal*, 43: 909–24.

Azam, J.-P., Calmette, M.-F., Loustalan, C. and Maurel, C. (2000) *Domestic Competition and Export Performance of Manufacturing Firms in Côte d'Ivoire*. WPS/2000/1. Centre for the Study of African Economies, University of Oxford.

Beaujanot, Q.A., Lockshin, L. and Quester, P. (2006) 'Delivering value: Market orientation and distributor selection in export markets'. *Advances in International Marketing*, 16: 111–38.

Becker, G.S. (1997) *Agricultural Exports: Technical Barriers to Trade*, CRS Report to Congress, October.

Begley, T.M. (1995) 'Using founder status, age of firm and company growth rate as the basis for distinguishing entrepreneurs from managers of smaller businesses'. *Journal of Business Venturing*, 10(3): 249–63.

Cadogan, J.W. and Cui, C.C. (2004) 'Chinese export agents' adoption of export market-oriented behaviours: Measurement and performance relationship'. *Journal of Asia Pacific Marketing*, 3(2): 21–37.

Cadogan. J.W. and Diamantopoulos, A. (1995) 'Narver and Slater, Kohli and Jaworski and the market orientation construct: Integration and internationalization'. *Journal of Strategic Marketing*, 3(1): 41–60.

Cadogan, J.W., Cui, C.C. and Li, E.K. (2003) 'Export market-oriented behavior and export performance: The moderating roles of competitive intensity and technological turbulence'. *International Marketing Review*, 20(5): 493–513.

Cadogan, J.W., Diamantopoulos, A. and de Mortanges, C.P. (1999) 'A measure of export market orientation: Scale development and cross-cultural validation'. *Journal of International Business Studies*, 30(4): 689–707.

Cadogan, J.W., Sundqvist, S., Salminen, R.T. and Puumalainen, K. (2002a) 'Market-oriented behavior: Comparing service with product exporters'. *European Journal of Marketing*, 36(9/10): 1076–102.

Cadogan, J.W., Diamantopoulos, A. and Siguaw, J.A. (2002b) 'Export market-oriented activities: Their antecedents and performance consequences'. *Journal of International Business Studies*, 33(3): 615–26.

Cadogan, J.W., Sundqvist, S., Salminen, R.T. and Puumalainen, K. (2005) 'Export marketing, interfunctional interactions, and export performance'. *Journal of the Academy of Marketing Science*, 33(1): 520–35.

Collier, P., Gunning, J.W. and Associates (1999) *Trade Shocks in Developing Countries*, vol.1: *Africa*, vol. 2: *Asia and Latin America*. Oxford: Oxford University Press.

Das, T.K. and Teng, B.-S. (2001) 'Strategic risk behaviour and its temporalities: Between risk propensity and decision context'. *Journal of Management Studies*, 38(4): 515–34.

Diamantopoulos, A. and Cadogan, J.W. (1996) 'Internationalizing the market orientation construct: An in-depth interview approach'. *Journal of Strategic Marketing*, 4(1): 23–52.

Fernandez, Z. and Nieto, M.T. (2005) 'International strategy of small and medium family business: Some influential factors'. *Family Business Review*, 18(1): 77–89.

Jaworski, B.J. and Kohli, A.K. (1993) 'Market orientation: Antecedents and consequences'. *Journal of Marketing*, 57(3): 53–70.

Jaworski, B.J. and Kohli, A.K. (1996) 'Market orientation: Review, refinement, roadmap'. *Journal of Market Focused Management*, 1(2): 119–35.

Jöreskog, K. and Yang, F. (1996) 'Non-linear structural equation models: The Kenny–Judd model with interaction effects', in J. Marcoulides and R. Schumacker (eds) *Advanced Structural Equation Modeling*. Hillsdale, NJ: Erlbaum.

Katsikeas, C.S., Leonidou, L.C. and Morgan, N.A. (2000) 'Firm-level export performance assessment: Review, evaluation, and development'. *Journal of the Academy of Marketing Science*, 28(4): 493–511.

Keh, H.T., Foo, M.D. and Lim, B.C. (2002) 'Opportunity evaluation under risky condition: The cognitive processes of entrepreneurs'. *Entrepreneurship Theory and Practice*, 27(2): 125–48.

Kohli, A.K. and Jaworski, B.J. (1990) 'Market orientation: The construct, research propositions, and managerial implications'. *Journal of Marketing*, 54(2): 1–18.

Kwon, Y.C. and Hu, M.Y. (2000) 'Market orientation among small Korean exporters'. *International Business Review*, 9(1): 61–75.

Lewis, N. (2005) 'Code of practice for the pastoral care of international students: Making a globalising industry in New Zealand'. *Globalisation, Societies and Education*, 3(1): 5–47.

Little, T.D., Bovaird, J.A. and Widaman, K.F. (2006) 'On the merits of orthogonalizing powered and product terms: Implications for modeling interactions among latent variables'. *Structural Equation Modeling*, 13(4): 497–519.

Murray, J.Y., Gao, G.Y., Kotabe, M. and Zhou, N. (2007) 'Assessing measurement invariance of export market orientation: A study of Chinese and non-Chinese firms in China'. *Journal of International Marketing*, 15(4): 72–80.

Narver, J.C. and Slater, S.F. (1990) 'The effect of a market orientation on business performance'. *Journal of Marketing*, 54(4): 20–35.

Oviatt, B.M., Shrader, R.C. and McDougall, P.P. (2004) 'The internationalization of new ventures: A risk management model', in M.A. Hitt and J.L. Cheng (eds) *Theories of the Multinational Enterprise: Diversity, Complexity, and Relevance*. Amsterdam: Elsevier.

Ping, R.A. Jr (1995) 'A parsimonious estimation technique for interaction and quadratic latent variables'. *Journal of Marketing Research*, 32(3): 336–47.

Racela, O.C., Chaikittisilpa, C. and Thoumrungroje, A. (2007) 'Market orientation, international business relationships and perceived export performance'. *International Marketing Review*, 24(2): 144–63.

Roberts, J. (1999) 'The internationalisation of business service firms: A stages approach'. *The Service Industries Journal*, 19(4): 68–88.

Rose, G.M. and Shoham, A. (2002) 'Export performance and market orientation: Establishing an empirical link'. *Journal of Business Research*, 55(3): 217–25.

Slater, S.F. and Narver, J.C. (1994) 'Does competitive environment moderate the market orientation-performance relationship?' *Journal of Marketing*, 58(1): 46–55.

Sousa, C.M., Martínez-López, F.J. and Coelho, F. (2008) 'The determinants of export performance: A review of the research in the literature between 1998 and 2005'. *International Journal of Management Reviews*, 10(4): 343–74.

Sundqvist, S., Puumalainen, K., Salminen, R.T. and Cadogan, J.W. (2000) 'The interaction between market orientation, industry environment, and business success: Evidence from an exporting context'. *Australasian Journal of Marketing*, 8(1): 55–69.

Tsai, K.-H., Chou, C. and Kuo, J.-H. (2008) 'The curvilinear relationships between responsive and proactive market orientations and new product performance: A contingent link'. *Industrial Marketing Management*, 37(8): 884–94.

Zou, S. and Stan, S. (1998) 'The determinants of export performance: A review of the empirical literature between 1987 and 1997'. *International Marketing Review*, 15(5): 333–56.

13

The dematerialization of marketing in a global economy

Adrian Palmer

Learning outcomes

At the end of this chapter, readers should be able to:

1. Recognize the importance of services to modern developed economies.

2. Appreciate the interrelatedness of tangible goods and intangible services.

3. Appreciate differences in buying processes for services compared with goods, especially with regard to perceived risk.

4. Understand the impact of the internet on the 'dematerialization' of marketing.

5. Understand the consequences of the dematerialization of marketing for global distribution via the internet.

Key points

- Services now dominate modern Western economies.

- 'Service dominant logic' suggests that all marketing is based on service benefits, and goods act in a secondary, supporting role to services.

- Consumers increasingly seek a range of hedonistic benefits from the goods and services they consume, rather than purely utilitarian benefits.

- Customer experience management has emerged as a holistic integrator of the tangible and intangible benefits that consumers perceive.

- The internet has blurred the distinction between reality and virtual reality – in many situations, internet experiences have become the dominant reality.

Introduction

This chapter explores the role of physical evidence in the product offer. It is suggested that while physical evidence is often crucial to the marketing of apparently intangible services, the general role of physical evidence within the total product offer has tended to decline over time.

Physical evidence has been at the heart of traditional marketing. Visit a traditional fruit and vegetable market in any part of the world and buyers will be interested primarily in one thing – the quality of the goods on offer, and whether they represent value for money by satisfying their needs better than goods from competing stalls. Physical evidence was everything.

Traditional markets, based on physical products, still exist, but the trend in Western developed economies has been to augment the basic product on offer with a range of services. So, British and American buyers of fruit and vegetables now buy most of their produce in supermarkets, and their choice about what to buy and where to buy it is based on a range of issues that have less to do with the physical evidence. Can I be sure that the item of produce will be in stock on a Saturday afternoon? Can I trust this supermarket to select only the best produce? Does it offer a no quibble guarantee if the produce is bad? Can I pay with my credit card? Do I get loyalty reward points for buying my fruit and vegetables at the supermarket? Does it offer a home delivery service? In fact, many supermarket shoppers will be quite happy to buy a bag of potatoes without even looking at them, in contrast to the situation of a street market in a less developed economy where the buyer would need to critically examine the goods, and would expect little else by way of additional services from the supplier.

This apparent dematerialization of marketing can be related to a model of the changing focus for competitive differentiation between companies. Christopher et al. (1991) presented a model by which the dominant basis for market-based competitive advantage has evolved, noting that during the 1950s and 60s, firms in manufacturing-dominated economies used tangible product qualities to gain competitive advantage. As the development of tangible bases for differentiation reached a plateau from the 1970s, the focus for differentiation moved to services. In turn, services, which began as a differentiator eventually became generic and from the 1980s, the quality of ongoing relationships became a new differentiator (Christopher et al., 1991). The authors illustrate this evolution with reference to the car industry where services such as finance, warranties and insurance were used to differentiate otherwise increasingly generic tangible offerings from the 1970s. In turn, services became generic, leading to the development of relationship marketing strategies. But what happens if relationships themselves become generic, and all companies operating in a product area and targeting similar groups of customers have similar patterns of relationship development activity? By extending Christopher et al.'s model, experience may be a differentiator in markets where relationships have ceased to be a point of competitive differential advantage (Figure 13.1).

The growth of services

There is little doubt that the services sector has become a dominant force in many national economies. Within the 27 EU countries, services (including public administra-

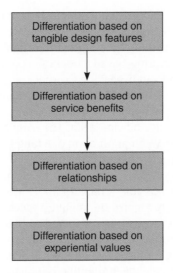

Figure 13.1   Evolution of the dominant basis for differentiation
Source: Based on Christopher et al. (1991)

tion) accounted for 71.7% of total value added in 2007 (Eurostat, 2008). However, there is continuing debate about the relationship between goods and services. Some analysis has seen goods and services as being quite distinct (Rathmell, 1974; Lovelock, 1981). The early services marketing literature emerged out of the much longer established literature on goods marketing.

In practice, it can be difficult to distinguish services from goods, for when a good is purchased, there is nearly always an element of service included. Similarly, a service is frequently augmented by a tangible product attached to the service. In this way, a car may be considered to be a good rather than a service, yet cars are usually sold with the benefit of considerable intangible service elements, such as a warranty or a financing facility. On the other hand, a seemingly intangible service such as a package holiday includes tangible elements in the purchase, for example use of an aeroplane, the hotel room and transfer coach. In between is a wide range of products that are a combination of tangible good and intangible service. A meal in a restaurant is a combination of tangible goods (the food and physical surroundings) and intangible service (the preparation and delivery of the food, reservation service and so on). Lovelock and Gummesson (2004) are among many who have pointed out that many services are, in fact, tangible rather than intangible, separable rather than inseparable, homogeneous rather than variable and durable rather than perishable. For example, on the subject of variability, there are some non-service industries – such as tropical fruits – that have difficulty in achieving high levels of consistent output, whereas some service industries such as car parks can achieve a consistent standard of service in terms of availability and cleanliness and so on. Similarly, many tangible goods share the problem of intangible services in being incapable of full examination before consumption. It is not normally possible, for instance, to judge the taste of a bottle of wine in a supermarket before it has been purchased and (at least partially) consumed. Services marketers have learned a lot from marketing activities in the goods sectors and vice versa.

The debate about the factors that distinguish or unite goods and services was crystallized in an article by Vargo and Lusch (2004), which talked about a new 'service dominant logic' of marketing. They argued that marketing was originally built on a goods-centred, manufacturing-based model of economic exchange developed during the Industrial Revolution, but in seeking to broaden its scope to include services, it has been constrained by the language and models of manufactured goods. Factory metaphors have frequently been applied to services, using such terms as inputs, processing, outputs and productivity (Goodwin, 1996). The early phases of service research deliberately drew parallels between production of a tangible good and delivery of an intangible service. Early articles placed consumers in the factory, as contributors to production processes (Lovelock and Young, 1979) or as potential bottlenecks to be processed as quickly as possible (Chase, 1978). However, factory metaphors fail when marketers are forced to recognize the unique aspects of human consumers as inputs to a service production process, as compared to inanimate inputs. The latter can be inventoried in a warehouse for months at a time, whereas customers can become dissatisfied after waiting for just a few minutes in a queue. Vargo and Lusch argue that the characteristics that have been identified as distinguishing services from goods – intangibility, inseparability, heterogeneity and perishability – only have meaning from a manufacturing perspective, and do not in themselves distinguish services from goods. They suggest that advances made by service academics can provide a foundation for a more service dominant view of all exchanges.

A fundamental part of Vargo and Lusch's (2004) argument is that the customer is always a co-creator of value, rather than merely the target of selling and the passive recipient of a firm's efforts. This idea of co-creation is crucial to understanding the manner in which both goods and service exchanges take place. As an example, even the most basic agricultural products must be made accessible to the consumer by means of service-type activities, and decisions must be made about how, when and where the product will be exchanged, and the role in this exchange to be played by producer and consumer. In effect, Vargo and Lusch (2004) argued that the focus of marketing (the dominant logic) has moved from the product (goods and/or services) to what the product does for the consumer, from the consumer's point of view.

From goods to service to experience

The traditional function of goods has been to satisfy basic human needs. A hundred years ago in Britain or America, nearly all food bought for consumption would have been evaluated, primarily on the basis of a means-end analysis, which matched the nutritional value of the food with the needs and resources of the buyer. Millions of people throughout the world still live in an environment where they can dream of no more than food that is safe and available for them to eat. Today, food buyers in Western developed economies typically place much less emphasis on the basic nutritional elements, and more on the augmented product values. In terms of Maslow's hierarchy of needs, they have moved from satisfying basic physical needs to higher order self-actualization needs (Maslow, 1943). To many people, the experience of consuming the food has become as important as the underlying nutritional value of the food. Recent articles in both academic and practitioner journals have indicated the importance of experiential values of consumption. Food is not defined in terms of its basic nutritional characteristics, but in terms of the environment in which it is consumed and the higher order needs that it is associated with, typically social acceptance, excitement, novelty, curiosity, experimentation and so on. But what do we mean by the experience of consuming a product?

Hedonistic definitions of customer experience imply a variety of stimuli that create value for consumers. The effects of individual stimuli have been extensively researched, for example:

- the physical setting of a service encounter (Grove et al., 1992; Gupta and Vajic, 2000)
- customer-focused product design with expected levels of quality (Price et al., 1995)
- the service delivery processes (Harris et al., 2001)
- aspirational and utilitarian brands (De Chernatony and McDonald, 2003)
- supporting relationships (Gummesson, 1997).

The challenge for the development of a customer experience construct is to integrate a typically diverse array of stimuli in order to assess the trade-offs that are entailed in creating value for consumers. Stimuli present in a customer experience are typically interactive and it has been pointed out by Csikszentmihalyi (1988) that the manner in which these stimuli are combined and sequenced is important in defining consumer experience.

The literature indicates a drift away from an essentially utilitarian view of experience towards definitions based more on the hedonistic properties of a product. Thus, Schmitt, B. (1999, p. 26) stated that experiences 'provide sensory, emotional, cognitive, behavioural and relational values that replace functional values'. A more all-embracing definition of customer experience is provided by Gupta and Vajic (2000, p. 34), who state that 'an experience occurs when a customer has any sensation or knowledge acquisition resulting from some level of interaction with different elements of a context created by the service provider'. Other authors have sought to broaden the concept of customer experience, sometimes with seemingly circular definitions, for example 'total customer experience emphasizes the importance of all contacts that a consumer has with an organization and the consumer's holistic experience' (Harris et al., 2003). However, such broad definitions take us back to an early understanding of experience as being the transformation of products into value as perceived by the consumer.

The development of a customer experience construct may be informed by the work of Sheth et al. (1999), who argue that a combination of three factors help shape a consumer's attitude to a product:

1. *Stimulus characteristics:* people perceive a stimulus differently according to its sensory characteristics and information content. Stimuli that differ from others around them are more likely to be noticed (Solomon, 1999).
2. *Context:* in perceiving stimuli with a given set of characteristics, individuals will also be influenced by the context of the stimulus (Biswas and Blair, 1991).
3. *Situational variables* in which the information is received, including social, cultural and/or personal characteristics: perceptions are greatly influenced by individual characteristics, including prior experience with a particular product or service offering.

The role of emotions has been noted as a distinguishing feature of customer experience, and a stimulus that has a positive affective outcome for one consumer may have a negative outcome for another consumer with a different emotional predisposition (Oliver, 1997). As well as being an antecedent to a consumer-based definition of customer experience, emotions can also be an outcome. It has been noted by O'Shaughnessy and O'Shaughnessy (2003) that what people get emotional about is indicative of what they consider to be particularly important.

Using physical evidence for product evaluation

If we now return to the subject of relatively 'pure' services, the problem remains of being able to evaluate them thoroughly prior to consumption. Unlike goods, which can often be examined before purchase, services must generally be consumed before a full evaluation can be made. The importance of physical evidence in the purchase process decision is based on the type of product in question. A longstanding classification of products and their evaluation processes is based on whether they are characterized by search, experience or credence qualities (Darby and Karni, 1973). Consumers are able to evaluate search qualities prior to purchase, for example the appearance of fruit. Experience qualities can only be evaluated after the purchase is made, for example the taste of the fruit, while credence qualities cannot typically be evaluated and demand a high level of trust in the seller's statements, for example whether the fruit was ethically produced.

The intangible nature of a service means that potential customers are unable to judge a service before it is consumed, thereby increasing the perceived riskiness inherent in a purchase decision. Credence qualities may be particularly high, and consumers' evaluation of competing service offers may be based on the trustworthiness of the seller, implying a high level of risk where the credentials of the seller are not known. An important element of marketing planning is to reduce this level of perceived risk by offering tangible evidence of the nature of the service. This evidence can take a number of forms. At its simplest, a brochure can describe and give pictures of important elements of the service – a holiday brochure gives pictorial evidence of hotels and resorts for this purpose. The appearance of staff can give evidence about the nature of a service – a tidily dressed ticket clerk for an airline gives some evidence that the airline operation as a whole is likely to be run with care and attention. Buildings are frequently used to give evidence of service nature. Towards the end of the nineteenth century, railway companies outbid each other to produce the most elaborate station buildings. For people wishing to travel from London to Scotland, a comparison of the grandeur of the three competing railway terminals in London's Euston Road could give some clue about the ability of each railway to get passengers safely and speedily to their destination. Today, accountants often use similar principles for their offices – a bright, impressive entrance to the public parts of their building, while staff may work in less salubrious surroundings. A clean, bright environment used in a service outlet can help reassure potential customers at the point where they make a service purchase decision. For this reason, fast-food and photo processing outlets often use red and yellow colour schemes to convey an image of speedy service. However, in a globalized marketplace, it can be difficult to know what physical evidence will work in different markets. Colours, for example, are notorious for having differing meanings in different cultures.

Physical evidence in an internet environment

The issue of physical evidence becomes even more complex in an internet environment. There is evidence that transactions carried out through the medium of the internet are associated with high levels of perceived risk (Soopramanien and Robertson, 2007). This isn't surprising, because in an internet exchange, the bases on which a buyer can judge the trustworthiness of a seller are reduced. Some of the senses that are used for evaluating a product are not available, most notably the senses of touch and smell. Instead of being able to actually touch and feel goods on offer, the buyer has to make do with a visual, two-dimensional representation. It is harder for individuals to assess a seller's trustworthiness in the absence of cues that are normally present in face-to-face interactions, for example facial expressions, emotions, posture and gestures. It has been noted that up to 93% of the meaning of all conversations comes from nonverbal communication (Mehrabian, 1971). There are also many high-involvement goods where buyers feel more comfortable being able to see and feel the goods before they commit to a purchase. The failed internet clothes retailer boo.com encountered the reality that many people would probably find it much easier and more reassuring to try on clothes in a shop rather than relying on a computer image.

How do companies overcome the problem of lack of physical evidence in an internet environment? Research suggests that the most appropriate solution is contingent on the type of product being offered and the characteristics of the buying situation. Where the characteristics of a product are widely known and are evaluated for their search qualities, a seller may need to do very little, other than list the product on its website. A standard product such as a DVD or an electrical item produced by a known branded manufacturer will probably not require much effort on the part of the seller to establish the credentials of the product. The product is widely available and can be easily specified in terms of what the customer will receive. Furthermore, there is evidence that for commonly available goods, consumers switch between online and offline sources in their research and evaluation processes (Rosenbloom, 2007). A buyer's search may begin on the internet, but any doubts about the product may be resolved by visiting a local shop in order to inspect the goods. Such a secondary inspection may be undertaken to fulfil the perceived lack of knowledge about crucial physical details that cannot be portrayed on a web page, for example the texture of materials used in construction. At other times, further research offline may be needed in order to convince the buyer that they are making the correct choice and to overcome the possibility of future cognitive dissonance. Sometimes of course, the evaluation process may be triggered in an offline retail setting, and the evaluation process then transfers online where the buyer can see product reviews and compare prices between different retailers.

Sellers who use the internet to sell physical products that are assessed on the basis of their experience qualities face greater difficulties. How can you actually experience something physical through the medium of a graphical representation on a computer screen? Faster internet connections, improved software and improved performance of PCs have greatly improved the quality of images that can be transmitted, improving the ability of a buyer to inspect the physical characteristics of a product online. Facilities such as the ability to zoom in or rotate an image are a great improvement on previous static representations. Where evaluation is based on visual aesthetics, for example works of art, thumbnail images can allow the buyer to rapidly research and compare alternatives, according to predetermined criteria.

Can the layout of a website seek to recreate the physical environment of an offline retailer? A customer can quickly identify the difference between, say, a budget grocery retailer such as Lidl, and a more upmarket one such as Waitrose. The uncluttered, spacious and visually attractive appearance of the latter contrast with the brash, cramped appearance of the former. The appearance of the latter sends out a message of sophistication, high service levels, matched by high prices, in contrast to the focus on discounts and no-frills service provision of the former. Can such analogies be drawn in an internet environment?

A number of studies have sought to extend the principles of Bitner et al.'s (1990) original 'servicescape' model to online environments. Many such approaches have used Bitner et al.'s stimulus-organism-response model, initially developed by Mehrabian and Russell (1974). But what are the electronic equivalents of stimuli such as store atmosphere, layout, smells and the body language used by staff during the service encounter? Web-based stimuli are much narrower in their scope than those typically encountered in a face-to-face encounter. Smell and body language, for example, are just two of the cues that have been difficult or impossible to emulate in an online environment. Many studies have therefore focused on the content and design of a website.

Shih (1998) developed the concept of 'telepresence', defined as the extent to which a website visitor feels the real presence of the company behind the website. The quantity and quality of sensory information have been described as their 'vividness' and the level of interaction with the product as 'interactivity' components of telepresence (Steuer, 1992; Shih, 1998). To what extent did the website provide all the information that a visitor was looking for, and how vividly did the required information stand out from other information that was of no interest? Did the imagery used create liking for the organization or specific products? Fiore et al. (2005) noted that telepresence is affected by how closely the quality and quantity of simulated sensory information corresponds with the sensory information available during interactions in a real-life environment.

There is evidence that a strong telepresence has a positive impact on online consumer responses (Klein, 2003; Fiore et al., 2005). Klein (2003) reported that telepresence positively affected consumers' beliefs and attitudes towards the product represented. The mechanisms were further explored by Fiore et al. (2005), who observed that a high level of telepresence induced consumer response indirectly by facilitating utilitarian product evaluation and by creating hedonistic experiences.

Bitner et al. (1990) talked about 'approach behaviour' in their discussion of real-life servicescapes. Approach behaviour for an online service provider may be facilitated by a number of measures. A strong offline presence would reassure many individuals that the company is a real one, and helps to provide reassurance that they could go to speak to somebody in person if necessary. Simply having a local contact address and telephone number may reassure some people. In addition, many companies have adopted industry association standards to certify their security and privacy credentials, such as VeriSign. These specify standards for the manner in which the company deals with customers and handles their information. Where such schemes are backed by specific industry sector associations, they may provide some recompense against deviant members. In a study of the banking sector, Yousafzai et al. (2005) found that banks that displayed a security policy, a privacy policy and a statement of compliance with banking codes on their websites were more likely to be trusted than those which did not.

Where an online service provider has no real-life presence, and has no local facilities that can be checked out, the task of establishing credibility with new customers is particularly difficult. A high level of advertising, both offline and online, may eventually bring about familiarity in the eyes of potential customers, on the basis that a company with an ability to communicate so widely is likely to be around long enough to deliver its promise. Unfortunately, there have been many cases of sham online companies that have set up in business with enticing offers, but have rapidly disappeared without trace. Some have been set up to obtain customers' personal information, which was then used fraudulently, after the company had disappeared.

From the preceding discussion, it may be presumed that the internet is particularly good at selling search goods where physical evidence can be evaluated offline or, to a certain extent, from online visual representations. However, there is an argument that the internet is particularly good at selling those physical goods that are evaluated more on the basis of their credence qualities rather than their search or experience qualities. The internet offers far greater opportunities than are typically present in a physical retail environment for establishing these credence qualities. As an example, a retailer selling a shirt in a shop with a distinctive selling proposition of being produced in an ecologically sound way has very little opportunity of presenting a proposition to buyers as to why their shirt is ecologically sound, and the benefits to the buyer of choosing this shirt, rather than one that is less ecologically sound. The space available on the product itself, or in the surrounding shelf space is, in reality, likely to preclude the development of a comprehensive message. By contrast, the internet environment can offer the possibility of communicating much more comprehensive information to buyers, in an interactive manner which satisfies individuals' differing levels of curiosity or need to establish credence qualities (Klein, 1998). There is some evidence that when such extrinsic information is provided in an internet sales environment, it can have more impact on buyer behaviour than intrinsic details about physical characteristics, even where these characteristics are portrayed graphically (Degeratu et al., 2000).

From physical reality to virtual reality

The progress of internet development now allows much more realistic three-dimensional representations of reality than had previously been thought imaginable. The term 'virtual reality' has been used to describe attempts to simulate physical reality in a virtual environment. There has been much discussion of 'hyperreality', in which there is a blurring of the distinction between the real and the unreal. Indeed, when a virtual reality is established as a benchmark, it can itself become a new reality (Baudrillard, 1993). It has been noted that in a postmodern society, individuals have focused on signs and symbols to such an extent that these have become more significant to them than the underlying properties they stand for. Miller and Real (1998, p. 30) noted that 'we live in a world where the image or signifier of an event has replaced direct experience and knowledge of its referent'.

Virtual environments combine fact and fantasy. The representation of products can go some way to simulating physical reality, but can also allow fantasy about the physical product in use. Holbrook (1986) proposed a consciousness-emotion-value model of the consumption experience, in which consciousness includes not only cognitions or beliefs about consumer products, but also a variety of mental events such as fantasy or imagery created by exposure to a stimulus. Jasper and Quellette (1994) found that where an individual was able to imagine themselves wearing an item of clothing, their frequency and total expenditure was increased.

Recent advances in computer graphics and internet download speeds have allowed companies to communicate messages in three-dimensional, interactive, collaborative virtual environments. A striking recent application of this emerging technology is seen in the Second Life social network site (www.secondlife.com). Second Life is a shared online simulation that allows individuals to create a lifelike version of themselves through the medium of an avatar. They can then live a virtual life, meeting other avatars, either of real or imaginary people. They can also buy goods and land with a virtual currency. As an example, a small private island might cost $1,500, plus monthly land fees of $200 or so. As in reality, prime sites have attracted a lot of interest, and individuals and dealers have traded land, so that the community meeting places have become expensive, while cheaper land is available in relatively inaccessible areas of this virtual environment. Second Life was created in 2003 by Linden Lab, and by September 2008, the virtual community had a 'population' of 15 million, although it is not clear how many of these are consistent, long-term users. The company reported that in January 2008, 'residents' spent 28,274,505 hours 'in world', so on average about 38,000 residents were logged on at any particular moment.

Some would argue that the distinction between virtual reality and physical reality is becoming increasingly blurred. In Second Life, individuals can buy virtual clothing for their avatar, and third party traders market virtual clothing using emotional appeals similar to those made by real-life clothing companies. Individuals can also pay to change the physical appearance of their avatar. The following statement from the blog of a Second Life resident illustrates the interplay between virtual reality and physical reality:

> after a few months of running around looking like a newbie I forked out $10 and went shopping. First thing that caught my eye was a Nehru suit – black of course. Next stop shoes – leather and etched steel – just what the doctor ordered. Then I decided that my skin was bothering me and that my hair just wasn't hanging the way I wanted it. So I bought a face job and a new style (complete with 'blood' colouring). The whole process was very simple – probably too easy. I can see how people become addicted to the way in which they look (I've heard some saying they own more SL clothing than they do in their real life).

It is not just physical reality that has an effect on virtual reality whereby individuals use their models of an ideal physical world applied to a virtual environment. Virtual clothes have crossed over to the physical world, and in this example, 'Nehru' suits that were popularized in virtual reality became a fashion accessory in real life.

Conclusion

This chapter started with a traditional street market selling a basic commodity product that buyers needed to inspect carefully, and ended up in virtual reality, where the whole concept of physical evidence becomes complex to understand. A buyer at the traditional street market is probably focused above all else on the functional benefits of the vegetables they are able to buy. Physical evidence was all important in giving a competitive advantage to a seller – if apples or carrots appeared to be in poor condition, a sale would be lost to another seller who could demonstrate a better quality of vegetables. With further developments in society's wealth, and rising expectations, marketing has adapted. Physical evidence is still important, but increasingly has become augmented with service benefits. Utilitarian benefits have been supplemented with experiential benefits.

What of the future? Can the apparently diminishing role of physical evidence that has been suggested in this chapter be sustained? Increases in wealth might suggest that we will continue to place a value on service and the experiential benefits associated with physical products. But it must not be forgotten that these higher order benefits will be diminished if the underlying physical product is of poor quality. Fruit and vegetables may increasingly be purchased for the service and experiential benefits that accompany them, but if they are, in fact, mouldy and inedible, much of these higher order benefits will be lost. The issue of sustainability of ecological resources must also be considered. One scenario for the future is a world in which natural resources become increasingly scarce, and transport more expensive in real terms. In such a scenario, physical evidence may again become the focus for much more marketing.

Issues for further discussion

1. What will be the effects of changing cultural and demographic trends on an apparent preoccupation with service and experience rather than the core physical product?
2. What will be the impact of future concerns about the use of scarce ecological resources on the transition reported in this chapter from a focus on goods to a focus on services and experience?
3. To what extent, and in what circumstances, can virtual reality systems provide a substitute for physical evidence in the product offer?
4. How do the principles of 'service dominant logic' relate to the apparent dematerialization of marketing?

CASE STUDY

Selling a dream: marketing Spain as a tourism destination

It used to be said that the toughest training ground for a budding marketer was to work at one of the fast-moving consumer goods companies such as Procter & Gamble – in such a fiercely competitive market, you would need to use all your skills and expertise to keep your brand in a strong market position. But more recently, it can be argued that an even more challenging environment for a marketer to cut their teeth on is the increasingly important field of destination marketing. Look through any Sunday newspaper supplement, and it is quite likely that you will see plenty of advertisements enticing you to take a holiday in exotic sounding places. Destination marketing is now a huge, competitive business. A visit to the annual World Travel Market in London will find hundreds of local, regional and national destination marketers jostling with each other to persuade tour operators to include their destination in tourist itineraries, rather than other destinations. But if you thought that selling a packet soup or a new variety of yogurt was difficult, how much more difficult would it be when you are selling a faraway dream, rather than an actual physical product?

Tourist destinations are full of physical evidence – beaches, bars, shops, hotels and public infrastructure such as roads and public open spaces. However, selling the bundle of physical evidence to buyers who have never previously visited a destination is a complex task that is being taken on by destination marketing organizations. Potential visitors may have seen a destination on TV and had their appetite whetted, but as we all know, cameras can be selective and not show the complete physical reality. There have been countless stories of hotels that have shown pictures in their brochures of sun-drenched swimming pools, but missed out the building site opposite or the noisy airport just a short distance away.

The main problem facing destination managers is that they typically have very little control over the 'product' that the consumer receives. The experience of staying in one of the destination's hotels, drinking at its bars and coffee shops or visiting its shops is dependent upon the activities of organizations over which the destination manager has vey little, if any direct control. There is also a problem when a destination manager has to address the interests of different stakeholders who may have quite different views about what an area should look like. Very often, those promoting tourism would like to emphasize the quaint and old in developing an image for their area. On the other hand, those promoting inward investment may want to suppress any physical evidence that suggests 'olde worlde' charm, instead preferring images associated with modernity and the latest technology. Ireland is just one of many countries that has faced this dilemma – should its brand image reflect the traditional image of a simple, rural country with slightly quirky ways, or a high-tech country with an increasingly ethnically diverse population? A further group of stakeholders are the inhabitants themselves – how do they want to be portrayed? Many attempts at creating abstract brand identities for tourist destinations have met with ridicule from local people who do not recognize the physical reality represented by the brand image.

Many experts in destination marketing agree that Spain has overseen the most successful implementation of a destination marketing programme. Key to this success was a tourism marketing campaign launched in 1982 on the occasion of the football World Cup held in Spain. The campaign used Joan Miró's sun design to symbolize the modernization of Spain. This logo has since become Spain's tourism logo.

Overseeing the brand is the Instituto de Turismo de España (TURESPAÑA), an administrative unit of the Spanish central government. Key to TURESPAÑA's strategy has been the development of a brand communication strategy that highlights the unique and differentiating elements which a visit to Spain would provide, compared with other competing destinations. The brand values of Spain have particularly focused on the way of living and the general lifestyle in Spain, the cultural traditions of Spain and the size and diversity of the country.

Many commentators agree that Spain has developed and executed one of the most successful examples of national tourism destination marketing. The advertising guru Wally Olins (1999) noted how until just a few decades ago, Spain was seen as an isolated, backward, poor country on the fringes of Europe. The reality of Spain has changed, and today it is a modern, vibrant, prosperous and democratic country. The branding campaign has reflected the reality of Spain's new position in Europe. But it can be difficult to tell which was cause and which was effect. Much of the change in the perception of Spain has occurred beyond the domain of tourism management, for example the Barcelona Olympics of 1992 and the Seville International Exhibition put the country on the map in many people's minds. The growth, privatization and globalization of Spanish companies such as Repsol, Telefonica and Union Fenosa have made many people aware that Spain is now an economic powerhouse. The restoration of Spain's major cities, including Barcelona, Valencia and Bilbao, inspired confidence among visitors that this was no longer a backward country.

But destination brand management for Spain still faces problems. Within Europe, changing perceptions of Spain have matched the changing physical and economic reality. However, in the US, the brand image of Spain tends to be confused with that of Latin American countries, where Spain has a historical influence. In Asia and Africa, it is claimed that Spain is largely unknown, and indistinguishable from other European countries.

The marketing of Spain as a tourism destination has succeeded where many other countries have failed. Other countries have tried to promote an image that does not reflect physical reality, or identified particularly indistinctive aspects of a brand. Many new countries have emerged during the past two decades in central and Eastern Europe, but the brand development in many of these has had little impact because of the lack of truly distinctive positioning which has value in the minds of potential tourists. Many attempts at destination branding have failed because of the often conflicting demands of tourism marketers to position their brand on the basis of a country's history, while those responsible for inward investment want to drop these images as quickly as possible and portray their country as thoroughly modern. A great achievement of the Spanish tourism branding campaign has been to incorporate many modern icons, such as the Guggenheim Museum in Bilbao, into the brand image, without having to rely exclusively on outdated images of flamenco dancing.

Based on the Instituto de Turismo de España (TURESPAÑA) website http://www.tourspain.es/en/HOME/ ListadoMenu.htm.

Questions

1. What are the principal ways in which a tourist marketing organization can reassure potential visitors about the quality of services and facilities available at the destination?
2. What are the challenges facing a destination marketing organization as it seeks to provide consistent standards of facilities within a resort?
3. How can the portrayal of a destination using virtual reality systems help or hinder the task of destination marketing?

References

Baudrillard, J. (1993) *The Transparency of Evil: Essays on Extreme Phenomena.* London: Verso.

Biswas, A. and Blair, E.A. (1991) 'Contextual effects of reference prices in retail advertisements'. *Journal of Marketing,* 55(3): 1–12.

Bitner, M.J., Booms, B.H. and Tetreault, M.S. (1990) 'The service encounter: Diagnosing favourable and unfavourable incidents'. *Journal of Marketing,* 54(1): 71–84.

Chase, R.B. (1978) 'Where does the customer fit in a service operation?' *Harvard Business Review,* 56(6): 137–42.

Christopher, M., Payne, A. and Ballantyne, D. (1991) *Relationship Marketing: Bringing Quality, Customer Service and Marketing Together.* Oxford: Butterworth-Heinemann.

Csikszentmihalyi, M. (1988) 'The flow experience and its significance for human psychology', in M. Csikszentmihalyi and I.S. Csikszentmihalyi (eds) *Optimal Experience: Psychological Studies of Flow in Consciousness*. Cambridge: Cambridge University Press.

Darby, M.R. and Karni, E. (1973) 'Free competition and the optimal amount of fraud'. *Journal of Law and Economics*, 16(4): 67–88.

De Chernatony, L. and McDonald, M. (2003) *Creating Powerful Brands*. Oxford: Butterworth-Heinemann.

Degeratu, A.M., Rangaswamy, A. and Wu, J. (2000) 'Consumer choice behaviour in online and traditional supermarkets: The effects of brand name, price and other search attributes'. *International Journal of Research Marketing*, 17(1): 55–78.

Eurostat (2008) *Eurostat Yearbook 2008: Europe in Figures*. Luxembourg: Eurostat European Commission.

Fiore, A.M., Kim, J. and Lee, H. (2005) 'Effect of image interactivity technology on consumer responses toward the online retailer'. *Journal of Interactive Marketing*, 19(3): 38–53.

Goodwin, C. (1996) 'Moving the drama into the factory: The contribution of metaphors to services research'. *European Journal of Marketing*, 30(9): 13–36.

Grove, S.J., Fisk, R.P. and Bitner, M.J. (1992) 'Dramatizing the service experience: A managerial approach', in T.A. Swartz, D.E. Bowen and S.W. Brown (eds) *Advances in Services Marketing and Management*, vol. 1. Greenwich, CT: JAI Press.

Gummesson, E. (1997) 'Relationship marketing as a paradigm shift: Some conclusions from the 30R approach'. *Management Decision*, 35(3–4): 267–73.

Gupta, S. and Vajic, M. (2000) 'The contextual and dialectical nature of experiences', in J.A. Fitzsimmons and M.J. Fitzsimmons (eds) *New Service Development: Creating Memorable Experiences*. Thousand Oaks, CA: Sage.

Harris, K., Harris, R. and Baron, S. (2001) 'Customer participation in retail service: Lessons from Brecht'. *International Journal of Retail and Distribution Management*, 29(8): 359–69.

Harris, R., Harris, K. and Baron, S. (2003) 'Theatrical service experiences: Dramatic script development with employees'. *International Journal of Service Industry Management*, 14(2): 184–99.

Holbrook, M.B. (1986) 'Emotions in the consumption experience: Toward a new model of consumer behaviour', in R.A. Peterson, W.D. Hoyer and W.R. Wilson (eds) *The Role of Affect in Consumer Behavior: Emerging Theories and Applications*. Lexington, MA: Heath.

Jasper, C.R. and Quellette, S.J. (1994) 'Consumers' perception of risk and the purchase of apparel from catalogs'. *Journal of Direct Marketing*, 8(2): 23–36.

Klein, L.R. (1998) 'Evaluating the potential of interactive media through a new lens: Search versus experience goods'. *Journal of Business Research*, 41(3): 195–203.

Klein, L.R. (2003) 'Creating virtual product experiences: The role of telepresence'. *Journal of Interactive Marketing*, 17(1): 41–55.

Lovelock, C.H. (1981) 'Why marketing management needs to be different for services', in J.H. Donnelly and W.R. George (eds) *Marketing of Services*. Chicago: American Marketing Association.

Lovelock, C.H. and Gummesson, E. (2004) 'Whither services marketing? In search of a new paradigm and fresh perspectives'. *Journal of Service Research*, 7(1): 20–41.

Lovelock, C.H. and Young, R.F. (1979) 'Look to consumers to increase productivity'. *Harvard Business Review*, 57(3): 168–78.

Maslow, A. (1943) 'A theory of human motivation'. *Psychological Review*, 50(4): 370–96.

Mehrabian, A. (1971) 'Nonverbal betrayal of feeling'. *Journal of Experimental Research in Personality*, 5(1): 64–73.

Mehrabian, A. and Russell, J.A. (1974) *An Approach to Environmental Psychology.* Cambridge, MA: MIT Press.

Miller, G. and Real, M. (1998) 'Post modernity and popular culture', in A.A. Berger (ed.) *The Post-Modern Presence.* London: Sage.

Olins, W. (1999) *Trading Identities: Why Countries and Companies are Taking on Each Others' Roles*. London: Foreign Policy Centre.

Oliver, R.L. (1997) *Satisfaction: A Behavioural Perspective on the Consumer.* London: McGraw-Hill.

O'Shaughnessy, J. and O'Shaughnessy, N.J. (2003) *The Marketing Power of Emotion.* Oxford: Oxford University Press.

Price, L., Arnould, E. and Tierney P. (1995) 'Going to extremes: Managing service experiences and assessing provider performance'. *Journal of Marketing*, 59(2): 83–97.

Rathmell, J.M. (1974) *Marketing in the Service Sector.* Cambridge, MA: Winthrop.

Rosenbloom, B. (2007) 'Multi-channel strategy in business-to-business markets: Prospects and problems'. *Industrial Marketing Management*, 36(1): 4–9.

Schmitt, B. (1999) *Experiential Marketing: How to Get Customers to Sense, Feel, Think, Act and Relate to Your Company and Brands*. New York: Free Press.

Sheth, J.N., Mittal, B. and Newman, B.I. (1999) *Customer Behaviour: Consumer Behaviour and Beyond*. New York: Dryden Press.

Shih, C.-F. (1998) 'Conceptualizing consumer experiences in cyberspace'. *European Journal of Marketing*, 32(7/8): 655–63.

Solomon, M.R. (1999) *Consumer Behaviour* (4th edn). Englewood Cliffs, NJ: Prentice Hall.

Soopramanien, D.G. and Robertson, A. (2007) 'Adoption and usage of online shopping: An empirical analysis of the characteristics of "buyers", "browsers" and "non-internet shoppers"'. *Journal of Retailing and Consumer Services*, 14(1): 73–82.

Steuer, J. (1992) 'Defining virtual reality: Dimensions determining telepresence'. *Journal of Communication*, 42(4): 73–93.

Vargo, S.L. and Lusch, R.F. (2004) 'Evolving to a new dominant logic for marketing'. *Journal of Marketing*, 68(1): 1–17.

Yousafzai, S.Y., Pallister, J.G. and Foxall, G.R. (2005) 'Strategies for building and communicating trust in electronic banking: A field experiment'. *Psychology & Marketing*, 22(2): 181–201.

14

Physical evidence as an asset in nation brand equity

Keith Dinnie

Learning outcomes

At the end of this chapter, readers should be able to:

1. Understand the key features of the nation-branding paradigm.

2. Appreciate the importance of public–private sector partnerships as a core component of a nation-branding strategy.

3. Acquire the ability to apply the services marketing concept of physical evidence to the context of nation brand equity.

4. Gain awareness of the diverse range of tangible manifestations of nation brand equity.

Key points

- Nation branding is a relatively new area of academic study, and is rooted to some extent within the established field of international marketing.

- It is critical for nations to proactively manage their reputations, rather than passively be branded by external third parties.

- The major objectives of nation branding normally focus on export promotion, investment attraction and tourism promotion.

- A collaborative, stakeholder approach is required for optimal outcomes in a nation-branding strategy.

- The concept of brand equity can be applied in the context of nations as well as product and corporate brands.

- The tangible, physical evidence of nation brand equity includes branded exports, the diaspora, brand ambassadors, and embassy buildings and cultural institutes.

- A high level of heterogeneity prevails in the management by different nations of their physical evidence.

Introduction

This chapter considers the concept of physical evidence and applies it in a novel setting, that of the self-presentation of nation brands. To achieve this, I consider physical evidence as an asset in nation brand equity and focus on how nation brands possess and manage physical evidence in international markets in terms of their branded exports, diaspora, brand ambassadors, embassy buildings and cultural institutes.

Nation branding: key features of an emerging paradigm

Nation branding represents an emerging paradigm that is conceptually related to international marketing, although distinctly interdisciplinary in nature, drawing as it does on fields as diverse as international business, international relations, public diplomacy, public administration and sociology, among others. As nation branding is still in an emergent phase, its interdisciplinary foundations are as yet weakly established and much work remains to be done in solidifying the field's intellectual base. In terms of contemporary practice, nations display a similarly tentative grasp of how to 'do' nation branding, with some nations defaulting to an ill-considered reliance on expensive one-off advertising campaigns rather than a comprehensive long-term strategy. Some well-established concepts in the field of international marketing – such as the need to balance standardization versus adaptation of product and service offerings in international markets – have yet to penetrate the mindsets of many countries' embassy networks, despite an overall increasing trend towards the introduction of private sector commercial techniques into public sector agencies.

The key features of nation branding include:

- the prevalence of public–private sector partnerships
- a focus on managing the nation's reputation rather than passively allowing events to conspire in creating potentially negative perceptions
- a wide range of objectives that encompass the desire to improve the nation's performance primarily, although not exclusively, in terms of export promotion, tourism and inward investment
- a highly politicized context within which nation branding strategy is crafted.

These issues, and the ways in which they intersect with established issues and concepts within international marketing, will now be considered.

Prevalence of public–private sector partnerships

The prevalence of public–private partnerships in nation branding derives from the need to serve an extremely diverse and wide-ranging spectrum of stakeholders. On their own, the public sector or the private sector would be incapable of rising to the challenges inherent in developing a nation-branding strategy. Government must play an important, if not leading, role in nation branding in order to ensure that the strategy and its benefits accrue to society as a whole rather than to narrow sectoral interests. On the other hand, the private sector plays an equally crucial role in providing market expertise that is not necessarily present within public sector agencies. Many countries have demonstrated templates for public–private sector partnerships. One of the most high profile such partnerships can be seen in the India Brand Equity Foundation (IBEF), a public–private partnership between the Indian government's Ministry of Commerce and Industry and the Confederation of Indian Industry. The stated aim of the IBEF (2008) is to effectively present the India business perspective and leverage business partnerships in a globalizing marketplace. While much of the IBEF's work is grounded in economic policy, for example in the setting up of special economic zones as a means to liberalize the trade and investment environment in India, it is interesting to note that as an organization, IBEF has given itself a name drawn from the field of branding rather than from the more conventionally referenced fields of economics and international trade. This is one reflection of a growing awareness around the world on the part of both governments and business organizations regarding the need to integrate the techniques of branding into all levels of a country's strategic decision making.

Further examples of nation branding executed through public–private partnerships include campaigns run by nations such as Brazil, Iceland and France (Dinnie, 2008). In the case of Brazil, a significant challenge was found to reside in the powerful and positive yet limited imagery associated with that country. Existing perceptions of Brazil as a vibrant and dynamic country, based on hedonic associations such as carnival, samba music, football and beaches, engendered much goodwill towards Brazil but contributed nothing to Brazil's desired positioning as a provider of high-quality IT services and products. To remedy this image deficit, a public–private partnership was established in order to generate global recognition of the Brazilian IT industry, particularly in the USA, the world's largest consumer of IT products. A different type of challenge faced Iceland in that country's efforts to develop its nation brand. For Iceland, a key challenge was to raise the country's profile within the North American market, specifically in order to increase the demand for Icelandic products and also to encourage tourism from North America to Iceland. Within the overall framework of the 'Iceland Naturally' campaign, the Icelandic government's Ministry of Foreign Affairs and Ministry of Communication collaborated with private sector actors including Icelandair, Iceland Spring Natural Water, Blue Lagoon and 66° North, among others. An equally broad coalition of public–private sector partners was assembled by France in its campaign titled 'The New France'. The objectives of the campaign were threefold:

1 to raise France's economic profile among five leading target investment countries – the USA, the UK, Germany, Japan and China
2. to improve foreign investor opinions of France to attract new business and increase inward investment
3. to create solid relationships with foreign investors for long-term dialogue.

To achieve these objectives, a multitude of stakeholders came together, including the Invest in France Agency, the national tourist office Maison de la France, the Ministry of Foreign Affairs, the French Economic Mission, and key individual experts such as Pierre Dauzier, communications expert and ex-president of advertising company Havas.

244 O   STRATEGIC INTERNATIONAL MARKETING

Managing the nation's reputation

Reputation management has become a well-established field over the past decade, largely through the work of the Reputation Institute (www.reputationinstitute.com) and through the platform for scholarly and practitioner research that is provided by journals such as *Corporate Reputation Review* and *Corporate Communications: An International Journal*. To date, reputation management has prevailed largely in the domain of corporations. However, the governments of many nations are becoming more interested in the importance of attempting to manage their country's reputation, allied to the realization that managing a nation's reputation in the digital age of instantaneous global communication demands a different approach to that offered by traditional diplomacy. Further fuelling governments' interest in the way that their nations are perceived has been the recent proliferation of indexes that claim to offer league tables of nation brands.

By far the most widely quoted such index is the Anholt-GfK Roper Nation Brands Index, which claims to be a unique barometer of global opinion and a cost-effective, comprehensive system for measuring and managing national reputation worldwide. Other indexes are now produced, which use different methodologies but which claim to provide a similar service, namely the ranking of different countries according to how positive or negative their reputation is. Branding consultancy FutureBrand, for instance, publishes its annual 'Country Brand Index' in partnership with Weber Shandwick, and advertises this index as including rankings and trends as well as country brand analytics, travel motivations and insights into the challenges and opportunities within the world of travel, tourism and country branding. The most recent arrival on the country reputation index scene is the East West Global Index 200, produced by consultancy East West Communications. This index differs from the Anholt and FutureBrand indexes in that it is based not on survey questionnaire data but on coverage of countries in international media vehicles. The publicity generated by the standings obtained by different countries from indexes such as the above three has led governments to become acutely aware of the issue of country image perceptions.

Although many governments recognize the need to manage their country's reputation, there is scant evidence that sound, systematic long-term strategies have been put in place to achieve this aim. On a tactical level, some noteworthy examples of crisis management are provided by Avraham and Ketter (2008), who postulate a range of message-focused strategies to protect a nation's reputation when it is in crisis. These proposed strategies include:

- disregard for/partial acknowledgement of the crisis
- full acknowledgement of the crisis and moderate coping measures
- full acknowledgement of the crisis and extreme coping measures
- disengagement from the place's main characteristics.

The broader potential role of public relations in managing country reputation is as yet underresearched.

Nation-branding objectives: export promotion, tourism and inward investment

The clear link between nation branding and international marketing becomes most apparent when one considers the three major objectives of nation branding, namely, export promotion, tourism and inward investment. Most international marketing textbooks cover exporting and inward investment in detail as market entry or market development options (see Ghauri and Cateora, 2005; Muhlbacher et al., 2006; Czinkota and Ronkainen, 2006), while tourism has utilized marketing and branding techniques at state level to such an extent that for many countries the national tourist organization has, for better or worse, been the country's de facto nation-branding agency.

The relative importance of export promotion, tourism and inward investment will be contingent upon each individual country's unique circumstances; however, a common challenge faced by all nations is how to coordinate the activities of the country's export promotion agency, national tourism office and inward investment agency. Linkages between these three functions remain largely unexploited and therefore potential synergies remain unrealized. The 'siloitis' that can afflict multinational corporations also afflicts state agencies that should be working collaboratively but which, in reality, may jealously guard their own turf and actively reject a cooperative approach. For example, the nation branding of one European country has been hampered by the refusal of the powerful tourism office and government tourism minister to participate in any collaborative nation-branding activities with other agencies such as export promotion and inward investment (personal communication from the head of the country's nation-branding team); similarly, in another European country, the nation-branding strategy only took a partially inclusive approach and actively excluded the nation's export promotion agency, an extraordinarily small-minded and short-sighted act based on political and personal power plays (personal communication from a member of the country's nation-branding committee).

Highly politicized context of nation branding

In addition to the internal politics that characterize any organization, a key feature of nation branding lies in the extremely high level of public scrutiny that accompanies any nation-branding activity, particularly when public money is being spent. Journalists, commentators of various ilks and vocal members of the general public tend to latch onto any nation-branding expenditure as being an irresponsible waste of taxpayers' money. Scorn is heaped most vociferously on the allocation of expenditure to initiatives such as slogans, logos and advertisements, all of which tend to be perceived – often correctly – as crass, superficial and unworthy of funding when compared to apparently more pressing and deserving causes such as hospitals, schools and so on. No country appears to be immune to this phenomenon. Everywhere that a publicly funded nation-branding initiative is announced, there is an instant outcry against it. In order to defuse this hostility, governments need to clearly communicate the rationale for the initiative and its intended beneficial outcomes. Too often, governments only do this on a reactive basis after the wave of criticism engulfs them, instead of taking a more proactive approach and securing buy-in and support for the strategy in its early phases. The most spectacular example of this was the Blair government's ill-fated 'Cool Britannia' campaign in the late 1990s, which engendered such a frenzy of hostility that the campaign was allowed to fade away, with the UK government subsequently retreating to the quieter waters of 'public diplomacy' and away from the stormier seas that accompany the more provocative term, 'nation branding'.

Having reviewed the key features of nation branding, we will now turn to the concept of brand equity and its application to the field of nation branding.

Brand equity and nation brand equity

The concept of brand equity can be approached from two broad perspectives. While both perspectives are concerned with examining the value of a brand, the first approach focuses on the value of a brand in terms of customer perceptions, whereas the second approach seeks to attribute a financial value to a brand. As the financial valuation approach to brand equity is of limited relevance to nation branding, this section will look exclusively at the first approach to brand equity, an approach which has been advocated most notably by Keller (1993). Keller addresses the value of a brand through the concept of 'customer-based brand equity', which is predicated upon the strength, favourability and uniqueness of the brand associations that consumers hold in their minds towards a brand. Keller claims that the following benefits may be obtained through building customer-based brand equity:

- greater loyalty
- less vulnerability to competitive marketing actions and crises
- larger margins
- more elastic response to price decreases
- more inelastic response to price increases
- greater trade cooperation and support
- increased marketing communication efficiency and effectiveness
- possible licensing opportunities
- more favourable brand extension evaluations.

The brand-building tools that, according to Keller, allow a brand to achieve such benefits include:

- choosing brand elements such as brand name, logo, symbol, character, packaging and slogan
- developing effective marketing programmes
- the leveraging of secondary associations such as the company behind the brand, country of origin, channel of distribution and so on.

The consumer perspective on brand equity is also adopted by another major authority on branding, David Aaker (1991, p. 15), who defines brand equity as:

a set of brand assets and liabilities linked to a brand, its name and symbol, that add to or subtract from the value provided by a product or service to a firm and/or that firm's customers.

Drawing on the consumer perspective on brand equity advocated by Keller and Aaker, a model of asset-based nation brand equity (Figure 14.1) has been developed in order to extend the brand equity concept beyond its product origins and into the realm of nation brands (Dinnie, 2008). Nation brand equity (NBEQ) is shown in the model to comprise two main dimensions: internal assets and external assets. Internal assets are further categorized into 'innate' assets and 'nurtured' assets. External assets are categorized into 'vicarious' assets and 'disseminated' assets.

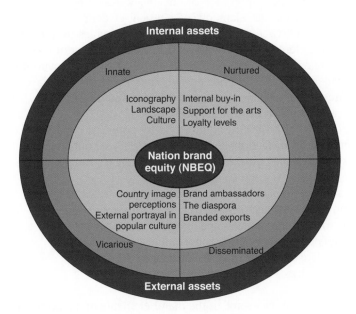

Figure 14.1   Asset-based model of nation brand equity

A holistic nation-branding strategy will seek to build and manage the full range of assets shown in Figure 14.1. However, for the purposes of our examination of physical evidence as an asset in NBEQ, we will focus our attention on the tangible manifestations of the nation brand in international markets and therefore limit our consideration of NBEQ to the assets shown as external, disseminated assets. These assets include brand ambassadors, the diaspora and branded exports. To this indicative list of disseminated assets, we will add embassy buildings and cultural institutes, to reflect in its fullest sense the concept of physical evidence derived from the services marketing literature to which we will now turn.

Physical evidence

A detailed treatment of physical evidence is provided by Zeithaml et al. (2006), who devote a chapter in their book specifically to the topic of physical evidence and the servicescape. Within the services marketing literature, there has been extensive research into physical evidence, yet the topic has barely been broached within the context of nation branding. We will therefore consider the essence of the physical evidence concept within its original domain of services marketing, before going on to extend the concept to the domain of NBEQ.

Zeithaml et al. (2006, p. 317) contend that 'because services are intangible, customers often rely on tangible cues, or physical evidence, to evaluate the service before its purchase and to assess their satisfaction with the service during and after consumption', and hence the importance of effectively designing physical, tangible evidence. The authors divide the elements of physical evidence into those directly associated with the servicescape and then all the other tangibles used by the service company. Servicescape elements are categorized into facility exterior elements, such as exterior design, signage, parking, landscape and surrounding environment, and facility interior elements, such as interior design, equipment, signage, layout and air quality/temperature. Other tangibles comprise business cards, stationery, employee dress, brochures, web pages and virtual servicescapes.

Given the importance of physical evidence and its potential impact on consumer choice, consumption and satisfaction, Zeithaml et al. (2006) set out some guidelines to assist companies in developing a coherent physical evidence strategy:

- recognize the strategic impact of physical evidence
- blueprint the physical evidence of service
- clarify strategic roles of the servicescape
- assess and identify physical evidence opportunities
- be prepared to update and modernize the evidence
- work cross-functionally.

The following section outlines some of the major elements of nation brands' physical evidence in international markets, and suggests ways in which nation brands can manage the different manifestations of their physical evidence in a strategic manner, as advocated by Zeithaml et al. in the context of service organizations.

Physical evidence as an asset in NBEQ

Many elements of physical evidence may contribute to perceptions of a nation brand. Country image perceptions can be influenced by an infinite number of factors, many of which are beyond the control of those involved in developing and implementing nation-branding campaigns. Controlling the behaviour of every citizen, for example, is an impossibility even though from a branding point of view, it would be preferable if a country's citizens refrained from engaging in antisocial behaviour such as criminal activity, which, when committed in a foreign country, will often attract a higher level of media attention than the same criminal activity committed by a domestic citizen.

Widescale and frequent football hooliganism by England football fans during the 1980s, for example, attracted vast media attention and tarnished the country's image in many countries. But despite the large number of uncontrollable elements in a nation brand's physical evidence, there exists considerable scope for managing other elements of physical evidence as part of a coherent overall strategy. In this light, we will now consider four key elements of physical evidence that form part of a nation's brand equity: branded exports, the diaspora, brand ambassadors, and embassy buildings and cultural institutes (see Figure 14.2).

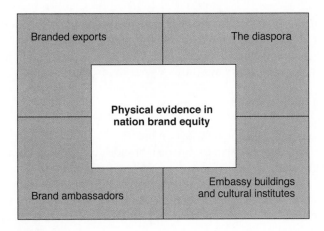

Figure 14.2 Physical evidence in nation brand equity

Branded exports

The symbiotic relationship between brands and their country of origin has, to date, been studied overwhelmingly from a unidirectional perspective. That perspective is the impact of country of origin on consumer choice, preference, belief, attitude, perception and so on. The country of origin literature on the topic is vast (for reviews of the literature, see Peterson and Jolibert, 1995; Al-Sulaiti and Baker, 1998; Verlegh and Steenkamp, 1999; Dinnie, 2004; Usunier, 2006). Much less studied has been the other dimension of the brand–country of origin relationship, which is the impact of the export brand image on the image of the brand's country of origin. For example, one may conjecture that the prestige and high-quality image of the Sony corporate brand has enhanced the image of Japan, its country of origin. But has this effect materialized in the case of Nokia and Finland? It is far less certain that consumers associate Nokia with Finland to anywhere near the same extent that they associate Sony with Japan.

There are several issues at play here. One is that for some corporate and product brands, there are advantages in being perceived as global rather than parochial. This can be observed in sectors such as high-tech goods, where Nokia appears to downplay its Finnish origins. Similarly, but perhaps to a lesser extent, Korean corporate super-brands such as Samsung and Hyundai do not appear to emphasize their Korean origin in their branding. In cases such as these, there is a creative and entrepreneurial challenge facing national governments regarding how to harness the potential country image enhancement that could be derived from a clear association with stellar corporate brands, which, for their own well-grounded strategic reasons, do not wish to be closely associated with their country of origin. Another issue concerns the paucity of empirical research into the extent to which export brand image influences overall country image; this lack of research means that the debate on the relationship between export brand image and overall country image is often based on speculation rather than data. A further issue is that coordinated, strategic efforts to enhance the relationship between the image of export brands and the image of the nation brand remain relatively rare.

One of the few examples of a coordinated approach in this regard can be seen in the case of the Leading Brands of Spain Forum, an initiative of the leading Spanish brands in collaboration with Spain's Public Administration. Founded in 1999, the Forum has consolidated its role in the following ways (http://www.brandsofspain.com):

- it has grown from 17 to more than 70 members
- it has fostered involvement by the competent public authorities
- it has generated momentum for the new law on brands
- it has promoted the new support plan for Spanish brands developed by the Spanish Institute for Foreign Trade
- it has certified key individuals from civil society as Spain Brand Honorary Ambassadors (Seve Ballesteros held the role and Rafael Nadal is one of the current crop)
- it proposes and develops public support for the internationalization of Spanish companies and brands
- it organizes annual information and educational events and publishes prestigious publications in which members participate actively.

Any brand that wishes to join the Leading Brands of Spain Forum must meet certain criteria, for example the brand or its image must be Spanish and have an excellent reputation as well as having achieved a certain level of internationalization. As stated on its website (http://www.brandsofspain.com/info/foro/), its mission is:

- Be the leading spokesperson for Spanish brands, to institutions and key audiences: the administration, the business community, academia, the media, etc.
- Operate as a support platform for Spanish brands going international.
- Promote the optimum legal, economic and fiscal framework to allow Spanish brands to grow and develop in Spain and abroad.
- Be a forum for discussion and knowledge on brands, their value and development as a key element for the competitiveness of Spain's economy.
- Promote, alongside the public administration, the Spain brand as a brand which adds value to Spanish companies and institutions operating abroad.

The final point in this list represents a clear commitment on the part of member brands to contribute to the promotion not only of their own individual brands, but also to the enhancement of Spain's nation brand. In this way, prestigious Spanish brands work in a collaborative fashion with the relevant public authorities to create a win–win situation, whereby the improving image of individual Spanish brands enhances Spain's nation brand, and, reciprocally, the improving image of Spain's nation brand casts a benign halo effect over brands with a Spanish origin. Brands from many different sectors participate in the forum. This diversity of brands can be expected to help strengthen the Spain brand image as a good country from which to buy exports, rather than allowing the narrow perception of Spain to continue as being highly ranked as a tourism destination but not for anything else. Consumers in international markets are becoming increasingly familiar with Spanish export brands as one element of the Spain brand's physical evidence through brands such as Movistar (telecommunications), Santander (financial services), Zara (fashion), Iberdrola (energy), *El Pais* (media) and Real Madrid and FC Barcelona (sports).

The diaspora

The economic importance of diasporas in terms of remittances sent by migrants back to the home country has been well documented (see for example Kuznetsov and Sabel, 2006). Indeed, some less developed countries rely heavily on such remittances for poverty alleviation. However, diasporas can also be considered as a key element of a nation brand's physical evidence in a similar way that a company's employees are considered to be a key element of an organization's physical evidence. Any interaction between a foreign citizen and a member of a country's diaspora represents a 'moment of truth', in that the encounter will be direct, personal, probably unscripted and therefore perceived to be more authentic than any scripted, paid-for advertising or branding communications that the nation brand may have invested in. What, then, can countries do in order to leverage their diasporas as a key element of reputation-building physical evidence?

Various strategies for initiating diaspora networks and activity have been proposed by Marks (2006, p. 184), whose suggestions are made in the context of South Africa's diaspora networks but which may also be applied to other nations. These strategies include:

- provide ongoing, long-term financial support for existing diaspora networks, bearing in mind that such networks will take time to bear fruit and often require dedicated human resources to ensure that they run efficiently
- develop a combination of virtual (internet-based) and relationship-based networks
- use university alumni associations as the entry point into existing overseas networks.

Such principles could usefully be adopted by any country. The specifics of creating a diaspora network are examined by MacRae and Wight (2006), who focus on Scotland's GlobalScot diaspora network, which emphasizes targeted membership and a clear value proposition. Members of the network are required to:

- be influential and active in a key sector, that is, a sector agreed to be a priority for Scotland's economic development
- have a strong affinity with Scotland
- be based in a target location, that is, predominantly one in which Scottish Development International has a presence
- be motivated and able to participate.

A diaspora network such as GlobalScot, which has a membership of around 800 influential and motivated businesspeople, represents an extremely valuable asset in a nation brand's equity, as well as being a key element of the nation brand's physical evidence, particularly within the corporate world, which may be more resistant to conventional marketing communications messages than general consumer markets.

Brand ambassadors

While nations have historically appointed an official ambassador to each of their embassies worldwide, it is unusual for that individual to have a high profile among the general public of the host country. Traditional diplomacy involves diplomats talking to other diplomats and host country government officials, although the relatively recent rise of 'public diplomacy' has generated a trend towards a higher level of engagement and communication between a country's diplomats and the population of the country to which they have been posted. Even so, the role of an official ambassador remains low key compared to the role played by 'brand ambassadors' in the commercial sector. When a brand adopts a brand ambassador, that ambassador may be either a celebrity or a member of the company with the depth of knowledge and range of social skills necessary to effectively represent, and to some extent embody, the brand. Just like any company, a country that appoints a brand ambassador will do so in order to provide the brand with a human face and to make an emotional connection with target audiences. However, the same risks that are faced by companies are also faced by countries that appoint a brand ambassador, with the chief risk being that the individual brand ambassador may behave in an inappropriate manner or become engulfed in a personal scandal that could, by extension, damage the brand that they are representing.

Great care needs to be taken therefore in the appointment of nation brand ambassadors. Ideally, a set of criteria should be drawn up to ensure that there is a good fit between the characteristics or personality of the nation brand and the individual brand ambassador. Given the multidimensional nature of nation brands, it would be appropriate for nations to appoint a wide range of nation brand ambassadors, each of whom is selected to project a specific facet of the nation brand, rather than to appoint one individual who, however popular or well known, cannot be expected to embody every dimension of the nation brand. Once the nation brand ambassadors have been identified, resources need to be allocated to enable those individuals to make an impact in their respective fields. This argument is not, however, accepted by some governments, which do not value the potential contribution to enhancing nation brand image that is offered by soft power techniques such as cultural nation brand ambassadors. For example, Schneider (2007, p. 154) advocates the use of music as an effective form of soft power, while regretting the lack of funding that has been made available by the US government in recent years for such activities:

> Although jazz is widely recognized to have been an extremely effective tool for diplomacy, its presence has dramatically declined from its heyday during the 1960s when the State Department toured Ellington, Armstrong and Brubeck and their bands for weeks at a time, sending them to countries all over Africa, Asia and the Middle East, as well as to the Soviet Union and Eastern Europe. Today, the greatly

diminished annual budget of US$840,000 for the Jazz Ambassadors programme funds concerts by eight jazz quartets.

The recent election of Barack Obama as US president may herald the beginning of a new era of well-resourced US public diplomacy, particularly as Joseph S. Nye, the foremost authority on soft power, has been acting as a foreign policy adviser to the newly elected president.

Embassy buildings and cultural institutes

In a similar way to nation brand ambassadors, embassy buildings and cultural institutes provide a tangible cue to target audiences who otherwise may have few other tangible means of forming perceptions regarding a nation brand. The quality of service provided by embassies and consulates in processing visas and other administrative items may impact upon perceptions of the nation brand. At a more strategic level, some countries have invested heavily in the development of international networks of cultural institutes as a means of enhancing their country image and establishing goodwill through educational and artistic programmes and events. Such institutes include the British Council, the Goethe Institute and, more recently, the Confucius Institutes established by the Chinese government, of which there are 316 in 94 countries and regions. These cultural institutes may play a role in softening and humanizing the image of nations that might otherwise appear as imperialistic and militaristic.

Issues for further discussion

1. What are the implications of the symbiotic relationship between the image of a country's branded exports and a country's nation brand image?
2. How can countries identify and map out the full range of physical evidence that nation brands have at their disposal in international markets, beyond the four elements that have been discussed in this chapter: branded exports, diaspora, brand ambassadors, embassy buildings and cultural institutes?
3. What strategies do different countries use regarding the activation of diaspora networks as an important component of their nation brand's overall strategy?
4. How can appropriate processes be established to ensure a rigorous, systematic approach to recruiting and managing nation brand ambassadors?

CASE STUDY

Physical evidence as nation brand equity in Tokyo, Japan

The following observations on physical evidence as nation brand equity are drawn from an ongoing series of research projects initiated by the author in January 2008 in Tokyo, Japan. The city of Tokyo merits selection as the locus of attention, given the size of the Japanese economy and the important role played by Japan in international relations. A considerable amount of physical evidence as nation brand equity is deployed in Tokyo by many countries. We will now consider certain elements of physical evidence possessed and managed in Tokyo by four countries: Canada, the Czech Republic, the UK and China.

Canada

Canada is one country that has taken the strategic decision to use its embassy building not just for conventional diplomatic purposes, but also as a tool for enhancing its country image. In a video interview broadcast on itvjapan.com (MacArthur, 2008), Peter MacArthur of the Canadian Embassy comments that:

> the Canadian embassy was built largely to showcase Canadian business and our scientific and technological strengths as well … It is very much a landmark building and it helps shine the image of Canada here in Japan.

MacArthur states that every year around 15,000 Japanese businesspeople flow through the embassy, attending events such as product launches, demonstrations, seminars and other networking events. Possessing an iconic building in which to run these events may be regarded as a shrewd investment in what MacArthur describes as 'a complex, large, premium market such as Japan', where the establishing and nurturing of face-to-face personal relationships are critical for foreign enterprises seeking to enter the Japanese market. The Canadian Embassy in Tokyo may be viewed as an enactment, at nation rather than firm level, of Bitner's (1992, p. 63) proposition that 'perceptions of the servicescape influence how people categorize the organization; thus, the environment serves as a mnemonic in differentiating among firms'.

Czech Republic

Another nation that leverages its embassy facility in Tokyo as a reputation-building asset is the Czech Republic, through the housing within the embassy of the Czech Centre, part of a network of institutions promoting Czech culture abroad. The Czech Centre organizes a series of cultural events on an ongoing basis, including photography exhibitions, book launches and Czech language lessons. In 2008, the centre hosted a launch party and accompanying exhibition for the book, *Corporate Identity in the Czech Republic* (Richtr and Zaruba, 2008). This initiative allowed Tokyo residents to experience in tangible form, through the book and exhibition photographs, a spectrum of contemporary Czech design that would otherwise have remained inaccessible. Essays in the book include:

- a short history of corporate design
- forms of corporate design and visual communication
- corporate identity and graphic design in the 1990s.

The bulk of the book comprises brief cases of the use of design by Czech brands such as Komercni Bank, Skoda, Czech Telecom, Hotel Josef and Zentiva, among many others. When considering the design work used by the city of Prague, Richtr and Zaruba (2008, p. 155) answer their own rhetorical question regarding the appropriateness of applying graphic design techniques to places of all kinds:

> Should large complex social organisms like towns, counties, provinces and their institutions really have their own visual style? Many examples from around the world show that in the

21st century, the visual identities of such entities increasingly do act on new inspiration from beyond the tradition of heraldry.

Although the application of design to nation brands is a relatively recent phenomenon, a substantial body of work has built up that demonstrates the importance of design in the strategic management of corporate brands (Cornelissen and Elving, 1999; Balmer and Greyser, 2002; Melewar and Karaosmanoglu, 2006).

The UK

In terms of leveraging branded exports as a key element of physical evidence within overall nation brand equity, the UK and Scotland in particular have benefited from a successful and popular annual whisky event, 'Whisky Live'. Run in various cities worldwide, in 2007 in Tokyo, this event attracted over 3,700 people during the day who enjoyed a huge variety of whisky, live music, 21 masterclasses, cigars, chocolates, haggis 'and most of all the camaraderie that whisky brings' (www.whiskylive.com/japan/). Although organized by private sector companies, with a narrow sector focus, the event potentially creates a positive halo effect over the Scotland nation brand, as well as over the nation brands of the other whisky-producing nations that are represented such as Japan and the US. The importance of food and drink as an authentic and powerful element of a nation's culture, and thereby as a key asset of nation brand equity, has been realized by a surprisingly limited number of countries, and in the future, it is to be expected that many more nations will adopt strategic approaches to managing their food and drink culture as important elements of physical evidence among their other nation brand equity assets.

China

As a further manifestation of physical evidence, the strategic importance of cultural institutes has been embraced enthusiastically by the Chinese government, which funds an international network of Confucius Institutes. The mission of the institutes is to promote the Chinese language and culture in host countries. As such, this represents an important attempt by China to increase its previously low level of soft power (Huang and Ding, 2006). There are currently 10 Confucius Institutes in Japan, although they do not appear to have gained a high level of recognition. This may in part be due to the policy of locating the institutes within the existing buildings of host country universities, rather than using standalone buildings, as is frequently done by other cultural institutes such as the British Council. In this respect, the importance of a building as physical evidence may be underlined – without an unambiguous physical presence, it may be more challenging to fully leverage cultural institutes as an asset in nation brand equity.

Questions

1. How does Canada integrate physical evidence into its nation-branding strategy within Japan?
2. In what ways does the Czech Republic combine tangible and intangible elements of its nation brand equity in Japan?
3. What is the contribution of the Whisky Live event to the nation branding in Japan of the UK and Scotland?
4. How significant an element of China's nation brand equity is represented by that country's network of Confucius Institutes?

References

Aaker, D. (1991) *Managing Brand Equity*. New York: The Free Press.

Al-Sulaiti, K.I. and Baker, M.J. (1998) 'Country-of-origin effects: A literature review'. *Marketing Intelligence & Planning*, 16(3): 150–99.

Avraham, E. and Ketter, E. (2008) *Media Strategies for Marketing Places in Crisis: Improving the Image of Cities, Countries and Tourist Destinations*. Oxford: Butterworth-Heinemann.

Balmer, J.M. and Greyser, S.A. (2002) 'Managing the multiple identities of the corporation'. *California Management Review*, 44(3): 72–86.

Bitner, M.J. (1992) 'Servicescapes: The impact of physical surroundings on customers and employees'. *Journal of Marketing*, 56(2): 57–71.

Cornelissen, J. and Elving, W.J. (2003) 'Managing corporate identity: An integrative framework of dimensions and determinants'. *Corporate Communications: An International Journal*, 8(2): 114–20.

Czinkota, M.R. and Ronkainen, I.A. (2006) *International Marketing*. Mason, OH: South-Western/Thomson Learning.

Dinnie, K. (2004) 'Country-of-origin 1965–2004: A literature review'. *Journal of Customer Behaviour*, 3(2): 165–213.

Dinnie, K. (2008) *Nation Branding: Concepts, Issues, Practice*. Oxford: Butterworth-Heinemann.

Ghauri, P. and Cateora, G. (2005) *International Marketing* (2nd edn). Maidenhead: McGraw-Hill.

Huang, Y. and Ding, S. (2006) 'Dragon's underbelly: An analysis of China's soft power'. *East Asia*, 23(4): 22–44.

IBEF (India Brand Equity Foundation) (2008) 'India: Foreign Direct Investment. The Policy and Regulatory Framework', http://www.ibef.org, accessed 11 December 2008.

Keller, K.L. (1993) 'Conceptualising, measuring and managing customer-based brand equity'. *Journal of Marketing*, 57(1): 1–22.

Kuznetsov, Y. and Sabel, C. (2006) 'International migration of talent, diaspora networks, and development: Overview of main issues', in Y. Kuznetsov (ed.) *Diaspora Networks and the International Migration of Skills: How Countries Can Draw on Their Talent Abroad*. Washington, DC: WBI Development Studies.

MacArthur, P. (2008) Video interview, http://www.itvjapan.com/cccj.asp?id=1, accessed 10 July 2008.

MacRae, M. and Wight, M. (2006) 'A model diaspora network: The origin and evolution of Globalscot', in Y. Kuznetsov (ed.) *Diaspora Networks and the International Migration of Skills: How Countries Can Draw on Their Talent Abroad*. Washington, DC: WBI Development Studies.

Marks, J. (2006) 'South Africa: Evolving diaspora, promising initiatives', in Y. Kuznetsov (ed.) *Diaspora Networks and the International Migration of Skills: How Countries Can Draw on Their Talent Abroad*. Washington, DC: WBI Development Studies.

Melewar, T.C. and Karaosmanoglu, E. (2006) 'Seven dimensions of corporate identity: A categorisation from the practitioners' perspectives'. *European Journal of Marketing*, 40(7/8): 846–69.

Muhlbacher, H., Leihs, H. and Dahringer, L. (2006) *International Marketing: A Global Perspective* (3rd edn). London: Thomson Learning.

Peterson, R.A. and Jolibert, A.J. (1995) 'A meta-analysis of country-of-origin effects'. *Journal of International Business Studies*, 26(4): 883–900.

Richtr, M. and Zaruba, A. (eds) (2008) *Corporate Identity in the Czech Republic 1990–2007*, Czech Republic.

Schneider, C. (2007) 'Culture communicates: US diplomacy that works', in J. Melissen (ed.) *The New Public Diplomacy: Soft Power in International Relations*. Basingstoke: Palgrave Macmillan.

Usunier, J.-C. (2006) 'Relevance in business research: The case of country-of-origin research in marketing'. *European Management Review*, 3: 60–73.

Verlegh, P.W. and Steenkamp, J.-B. (1999) 'A review and meta-analysis of country-of-origin research'. *Journal of Economic Psychology*, 20: 521–46.

Zeithaml, V.A., Bitner, M.J. and Gremler, D.D. (2006) *Services Marketing: Integrating Customer Focus Across the Firm* (4th edn). New York: McGraw-Hill International.

15

Future directions in international marketing: the decade ahead

Richard Fletcher and Tendai Chikweche

Learning outcomes

At the end of this chapter, readers should be able to:

1. Appreciate that the decade ahead will involve major changes in how international marketers need to operate in order to be successful.

2. Identify future trends that will need to be taken into account in identifying and doing business in international markets.

3. Understand issues in conducting market research that impact on a complete understanding of non-Western markets.

4. Focus on how to identify the drivers of consumer purchase decision making in non-Western markets.

5. Specify how firms need to modify their offerings to appeal to consumers in non-Western markets.

6. Recognize the importance of the bottom of the pyramid (BOP) market to the future of international marketing.

Key points

- The growth markets of the future in international marketing will lie in non-Western countries.

- Applying etic approaches will provide indications as to how like Western markets non-Western markets are rather than the actual drivers of decision making in those markets. For this, an emic approach is required.

- Theories of international marketing derived from research in Western markets are unlikely to capture the drivers of consumer decision making in non-Western markets.

- These non-Western markets are likely to require a much greater degree of adaptation of traditional approaches on the part of firms.
- These new growth markets contain greater extremes of wealth and greater diversity of market segments than found in traditional Western markets.
- Growth areas in such markets are most likely to come from those at the bottom of the pyramid rather than from the upper and middle-class sectors.

Introduction

There are a number of future trends in international marketing that will manifest themselves more fully in the decade ahead. These include ethnic and economic groupings replacing the nation state as a segmentation variable, the BRIC (Brazil, Russia, India and China) nations replacing the triad nations (North America, Europe and Japan) as international growth locations, the disappearance of economic rationalism, an increasing focus on the negative impacts of globalization and an increasing questioning of the relevance of Western-derived theories and practices in international marketing for forging profitable links with the growth markets in the developing world. To illustrate these trends, the chapter focuses on one of the greatest opportunities for growth in international marketing. It is an opportunity that hitherto has been largely ignored and involves two-thirds of the world's population, that is, the market at the bottom of the pyramid (BOP). The techniques that will be needed to successfully engage with this market will be explored in detail and illustrated by recent research conducted in Zimbabwe.

Future directions

In the decade ahead, a number of trends will manifest themselves and probably change the approach currently adopted in international marketing. Over the years, the focus of international marketing has been on identifying and segmenting markets whose consumers have a capacity to consume, who respond to traditional integrated marketing communications and who can pay a sustainable price for the product, where access to the product is readily available and support structures exist that can enhance the purchase. This business model has shaped the business of multinational corporations (MNCs) and small and medium-sized enterprises in the developed world and in many developing countries. Generations of students have been subjected to the concept that marketing strategy, both domestic and international, depends on the 4Ps of product, price, place and promotion. Implicit in the 4Ps is the concept of a somewhat passive consumer who can be manipulated by the firm. More recently, this notion has been called into question and marketing concepts such as relationships, networks, service dominant logic, customer relationship management and corporate social responsibility combine to add new dimensions to the exchange process. Not only are these dimensions likely to become more important in the decade ahead but they have the effect of shifting the decision-making focus increasingly from firms to consumers. These factors are highly relevant in international marketing where exchange takes place across borders and involves two or more environments with different economic, political, legal and cultural drivers.

Traditionally, the basis for segmentation in international marketing has been the nation state. This is a limited basis for segmentation, however, as nation states are mostly political creations with little concern for cultural differences within their boundaries or ethnic divisions. In fact, there are often greater similarities as far as the drivers of purchasing are concerned between members of an ethnic group that cross national boundaries, such as the Armenians or Kurds, than between different nations. As an example, the Chinese in Singapore, Indonesia and Malaysia have more in common than the Malays, Chinese and Indians within Malaysia. A future trend is likely to be that groups that cross nations will replace national boundaries as the major segmentation variable in international marketing as the barriers between nation states diminish.

In recent decades, the engines of growth in international marketing were considered to lie in the developed triad nations. In the decade ahead, this will no longer be the case as China challenges the US for the number one economic position in the world and the growth engines switch from developed to developing nations such as the BRIC group. These countries have within them wide disparities in income between groups and regions and large numbers living at subsistence levels.

For decades, approaches in international marketing have been underpinned by economic rationalism, based on the concept that business knows best and the government should 'keep its hands off'. The advice has been that market orientation was the only rationale to pursue and the collapse of communism showed that other countries were eager to follow suit. In these circumstances, protectionism had no place and the free flow of trade should be unrestrained. Public sector enterprises were sold off and thus governments in the developed world reduced their debt levels. This approach may not work in the BRIC markets, all of which have, to a greater or lesser extent, a history of socialism and major government involvement in commercial activities, which may well reduce the attractiveness to them of approaches based on economic rationalism.

Globalization has also heavily influenced international marketing in recent years, not only being viewed as inevitable but also as being good for business and for the country. This was because it led to greater efficiencies by enabling countries to focus on what they do best and created cheaper goods by outsourcing/offshoring elements of production and the wider value chain to low-cost countries. Little attention was given to the downside of globalization. Korten (1999) showed that although financial assets had risen sharply and GDP had risen to a lesser extent due to globalization, the net beneficial output had, in fact, fallen and social capital had fallen even further. Of course, globalization was championed by the developed countries who stood to benefit most from it. Fletcher (2000) showed how globalization had a negative impact on developing countries with respect to each element of the marketing mix. If the developing nations have missed out because of globalization, will they embrace it as they become the powerhouses of the future?

Recent events have shown that international marketing is susceptible to circumstances in the environment beyond the control of the international marketer. Few anticipated the 2008/9 subprime crisis and the resulting recession. It has led to governments of developed economies bailing out firms to an extent not seen before and becoming shareholders in the process. This has resulted in record levels of government debt, massive government intervention to stimulate the economy, an upsurge in governments sponsoring 'buy local' campaigns and favouring a return to protectionism (naturally disguised). These sudden changes challenge the trends outlined above and are likely to impact on international marketing and markets in the decade ahead.

The trends noted above will also call into question the relevance in the decade ahead of international marketing theories and practices developed in the West. How well will they apply to emerging markets in the developing world? To date, little thought appears to have been given to the fact that theories developed in the West may not be relevant to other countries, and that to truly cater for the needs of such markets, and the whole of these markets as opposed to just the westernized elite, it may be necessary to develop theories and models from within those markets themselves based on the values that exist within such markets. This will involve adopting an *emic* approach, which is culture or group specific, as opposed to the etic approach of applying existing theories to the new emerging markets. The *etic* approach is likely to reflect how similar these markets are to Western markets rather than the actual drivers that operate within these markets as the *emic* approach does. To capture such markets in the decade ahead, it will be necessary to do more than continue to offer, with only minor modifications, the same products, accompanied by the same pricing structures, distribution strategies and promotional support packages as offered in existing traditional developed markets.

Approaches by developed countries to international marketing leave them exposed, given the trends noted above. Firms in developed countries have tended to focus first on other developed countries as they were easier to understand and do business with. From a supply side perspective, the psychic distance was less, and from a buyer perspective, the country of origin effect was smaller. However, growth in such countries averaged only 3% compared with double or three times that rate in developing countries (Aggarwal, 2006). When firms from developed countries focused on developing country markets, the focus was on business-to-business activities and on upper and middle-class consumers – people more like us. This approach ignored those within the developing country at the bottom of the pyramid. This BOP segment, which crosses national boundaries, will be a major source of growth in international marketing in the decade ahead. However, it will require a change in the mindset of international marketers if its potential is to be realized. This chapter is devoted to the BOP, its potential, its unique characteristics, how to research it, how its consumers behave and how firms should react to its potential.

The opportunity at the BOP

According to Aggarwal (2006), the BOP constitutes a market valued at US$13,500bn a year. Examples of BOP markets include countries in sub-Saharan Africa, South Asia, East Asia and non-resource rich countries in Latin America and the Caribbean. South Asia is home to half the world's poor population, while East Asia has countries such as Bangladesh, China, India and Indonesia, which are home to many poor consumers (World Bank, 2008). This segment is forecast to grow to 6 billion in 40 years' time (Prahalad and Hart, 2002), largely because the majority of the world's population growth takes place within this group. Hammond et al.'s (2007) study on the BOP presents aggregate data for four developing regions – Africa, Asia, Eastern Europe and Latin America – based on surveying 110 countries for which household survey data were available. Their study focused on analysing market composition in terms of income and expenditure and outlined the actual size and potential of BOP markets. For example, Asia has a population of 2.86 billion people, of which 83% are BOP consumers, with a total income of US$3.47 trillion (£2.08 trillion), of which 42% of the purchasing power belongs to BOP consumers (Hammond et al., 2007). Africa's BOP market is worth US$429bn (£260bn), the BOP consumer is the dominant consumer in the region and population growth is forecast to be highest in this region between 2005 and 2050 compared to other regions with BOP markets. The study also measured and outlined the size of the BOP market by sectors such as health (US$158bn – £95bn), housing (US$332bn – £200bn), energy ($433bn – £260bn) and food (US$895bn – £537bn). The study shows that while BOP consumers' incomes are low, there is still a sustainable amount of spending by these consumers, 'low income is not no income' and the huge numbers in these markets add up to create a viable market (Hammond et al., 2007). For several years, visionaries such as Prahalad (2005) and Mahajan and Banga (2006) have been arguing that due to 'tunnel vision', international business has ignored the BOP market. With a few notable exceptions such as Unilever and Bata, this group have been largely overlooked by so-called global firms because they are difficult to reach out to, are often beyond the rule of law, have a majority of people who live at subsistence levels, have high mortality rates due to increased susceptibility to disease, often have no fixed abode, live in regions plagued by instability and are located in countries often described as economic 'basket cases'. The reality, however, is that even the most extreme 'basket case' countries contain people who buy, consume, eke out an existence and are 'economic beings'. Although the individual purchasing power among this BOP group may be miniscule, collectively it is significant. Given current global circumstances, firms dependent on international business can no longer afford to ignore this segment of the global market, as growth in developed country markets declines and that in developing countries increases. Advocates of catering to this market argue that the challenges in serving it do not just lie in the literal numbers of people in the market but in the distinct challenges of reinventing Western models of doing business to fit the local needs and requirements of this vast market (Prahalad and Hart, 2002; Mahajan and Banga, 2006; Viswanathan et al., 2008). Applying Western models will only reveal a limited percentage of the driving forces underlying consumer and firm behaviour at the BOP, as these models ignore the driving forces that are unique to the BOP. It is argued that companies that develop strategies that take into account the local market's unique conditions and do not stereotype the market based on Western approaches are likely to succeed in exploring the potential that exists at the BOP (Khanna et al., 2005). The BOP market is not one huge homogeneous entity, but has unique needs and system requirements, which companies need to understand so as to adapt their business models to facilitate effective engagement with the BOP.

The nature of the market at the BOP

The variables that make this market different from that in developed countries can be categorized as either environmental or individual. In some cases, the impact of these variables is totally different at the BOP, and in other cases the variables are much more important at the BOP compared to developed country markets.

Environmental variables at the BOP

Culture is central to different consumer behavioural patterns in developed and developing markets. There has been limited research on the application and comparison of consumer behaviour across divergent cultures such as the West and BOP markets (de Mooij, 2004). Different cultures, such as those to be found at the BOP, are shaped by different beliefs, attitudes, norms and values, which have an impact on consumer behaviour in these environments. Scholars like Craig and Douglas (2005), Fletcher and Fang (2006) and D'Andrea et al. (2006) advocate an emic approach to studying culture, which acknowledges the cultural differences and uniqueness that exist in markets. While etic research by Hofstede (1991) and Trompenaars and Hampden-Turner (1997) highlights the cultural differences between emerging and developed markets, it treats developing markets (those with large BOP groupings) as countries having national cultural groups, with no distinctions being made between the various ethnic groups within these countries. It ignores the fact that the nation state contains within it different categories of consumers, each of which is likely to have different customs, tastes and value orientations that are bound to impact on their product choices (Fletcher and Melewar, 2001). Different cultures view products differently and this can affect the way people buy and use products.

The social class structure that is assumed by researchers in general is the Western model based on income, which cannot be universally applied, given the different characteristics and make-up of different markets (Usunier, 2000). Chikweche and Fletcher's (2008) classification of the Zimbabwean BOP into four tiers – urban, diluted urban who were formerly middle class, rural working in urban locations, and rural – invalidates the universalization of social class. Gilbert and Kahl (1982) identified a number of variables other than income that can be used to determine social class – occupation, personal performance, interactions, possessions, value orientations and class consciousness – of which occupation was regarded as the best. However, occupation may not necessarily be the best indicator of social class in BOP markets, where unemployment levels are often very high, for example in Zimbabwe it is 80%. This points to the need to broaden the indicators for social class beyond occupation in such environments. People are not permanently confined to social classes as there is room for individuals to move from one social class to another. Zimbabwe has, for example, witnessed high levels of social mobility, which have resulted in the creation of the 'diluted urban' group – one of the most important influences of consumer decision making (Brown, 1979).

The make-up of the family and the role it plays in individuals' lives are different across markets, particularly in the context of Western compared to BOP markets. Western markets are likely to adopt the concept of a nuclear family, which focuses on the immediate group of father, mother and siblings, while at the BOP, the concept of an extended family made up of the nuclear family plus other relatives is likely to be dominant. Although families use products, individuals usually buy these products and have to make the purchase decision. It is possible to have multiple roles and multiple actors per purchase and this is particularly relevant at the BOP when it comes to buying products such as food and personal hygiene products. The role of children as part of the family is an important influence in consumer decision making. In the West, children of all ages can influence parents as to what to buy and are perceived to be influential in the purchase decision (Kim and Lee, 1997). In the context of the BOP, the role of children is likely to be different from that in Western markets. At a young age, because of limited disposable income and the importance of each purchase, children are unlikely to be involved or even influence the decision process. Older children play a different role and become responsible for buying their parents basic food and personal hygiene products – often due to the death of a parent from war or HIV/AIDS.

Social networks at the BOP form the basis of how people relate to each other and to the environment outside their communities. Trust and the creation and retention of long-term relationships are part of the social fabric of communities in BOP markets (Kuada and Sorenson, 2000). Family and kinship play an important role in the creation and maintenance of this trust among the communities who live and operate in a variety of formal and informal networks that cover different aspects of their social and business life (Michailova and Worm, 2003). Thus there is an emphasis on relationships and sharing information in these communities (Fafchamps, 2000). Research by Burt (1987) and Marshall and Gitosudarmo (1995) confirmed the influence of opinion leaders in BOP communities on consumer decision making, whereby the community is likely to take a lead from community leaders as to which products to buy when trying new products. McPherson et al. (2001) used the concept of homophile to illustrate 'that contact between similar people is likely to take place at a higher rate than among dissimilar people and this influences the information they share'. This is the case at the BOP. Unilever India's strategy for Annarpurna iodized salt is an example of the importance of tapping into networks in BOP markets. By developing the Shakti programme, which used women's self-help groups in communities to sell and distribute the company's products, Unilever was able to successfully penetrate the rural salt market (Ahmad et al., 2004; Rangan and Rajan, 2006).

Individual variables at the BOP

The individual variables are age, gender, rural or urban location, size of dwelling, degree of uncertainty and turbulence in the environment, nature and adequacy of infrastructure and the extent of the informal economy. While these variables may be found in all markets, the significance of age, gender and location is different at the BOP.

The age demographic is different at the BOP, because whereas populations are ageing in the West, the median age is much younger in developing countries. According to the World Bank (2007), nearly half the world's population is less than 25 years old and 90% of these live in developing countries. Gender is also an issue in many BOP groupings, as women in general have less opportunity to speak out, to directly influence purchasing decisions and possibly participate in market research. It is likely that their influence on purchasing decisions may be more indirect than in the West. Nonetheless, their opinions will need to be obtained and this will require a sensitive approach to ensure that the responses obtained reflect their espoused views rather than 'acceptable' views. Rural versus urban location reflects a trend of migration from country to town. On a global basis, 2007 marked the first time that the urban population exceeded the rural population. At the BOP, however, there are the complicating factors, such as large numbers of breadwinners working in the city to support a family in the village

The impact of dwelling size, turbulence, infrastructure and the informal economy is greater at the BOP than in developed country markets. Purchasing behaviour is often influenced by the size of the dwelling and the number of occupants per dwelling. In developed countries, dwelling sizes are usually much larger and the number of occupants fewer; for example, in the US, the average dwelling is 2,200 sq ft – 26 times larger than the average dwelling in Africa (Mahajan and Banga, 2006). Countries where those at the BOP are most likely to reside are also more likely to be subject to turbulent change and those at the BOP are least likely to be able to do anything to influence the consequences, protect their interests or seek legal remedy. This creates a mindset of having 'portable assets' (for example money or jewellery rather than property) and a 'just in time' philosophy on purchases, resulting in the purchase of goods for immediate consumption rather than storage. In developing countries, infrastructure is often inadequate and unreliable and this can have an impact on consumer decision making. BOP consumers are more likely to be inconvenienced by infrastructure shortcomings, as the upper/middle classes in these countries can often 'buy' their way around the problem by sinking their own bore wells or installing their own power generators. This infrastructure inadequacy poses challenges to those wishing to serve the BOP and will require product design innovation (for example solar powered units) to avoid existing infrastructure problems.

A final issue influencing consumer decision making at the BOP is the size of the informal economy, as this may well influence their purchasing behaviour and consumption patterns. Unlike the informal economy at the top of the pyramid, which is driven by the desire to avoid paying taxes, the informal sector at the BOP often exists because of the expense of registering commercial activities due to archaic rules (Hart, 2007), a lack of enforcement of regulations, breakdown of law and order and corruption in general. Given that 80% of employment in India, Pakistan, Indonesia and Philippines is in the informal economy and that in India only 3% of the population pays income tax (Mahajan and Banga, 2006), it is likely that many in the BOP are outside the formal economy. This creates an unwillingness to discuss activities related to the informal economy, which in turn increases the likelihood that activities in the BOP sector will not be fully represented in published secondary data. As shown by Chikweche and Fletcher (2008), these environmental and individual variables will impact on the conduct of research at the BOP.

Researching the BOP

The nature of the market at the BOP creates a number of unique challenges when conducting research. These include theoretical considerations such as data definition and equivalencies, constructs, measurement and sampling. They also involve practical considerations such as social issues, a lack of familiarity with research among BOP subjects, and the attitude of BOP respondents to the conduct of research. These factors will impact on the design of research at the BOP, including what can and cannot be researched, the impact of poor infrastructure on the conduct of research, and issues related to local languages and dialects. Also relevant are issues related to the collection and evaluation of data at the BOP, for example the reliability of secondary information, operational considerations, selection of respondents, quality of responses, and the credibility of the researcher as far as the respondent is concerned. Accessing suitable respondents at the BOP is a major issue, namely accessing the networks to which they belong, discovering the actual unit of decision making, and understanding the social power structure that operates in respondents' lives.

Equivalence challenges

Issues of construct (including conceptual and definitional equivalence), sampling and measurement equivalence have been highlighted as deeper issues that need to be considered when conducting research at the BOP (Van de Vijver and Leung, 1997; Steenkamp and Baumgartmer, 1998; Craig and Douglas, 2005). The absence of measurement scales relevant to the BOP makes it difficult to conceptualize constructs (Green and White, 1976). Hence, in Zimbabwe, it became necessary that managers and BOP consumers defined the constructs to ensure that the research was going to measure what it was meant to measure. Concept equivalence is at risk with research at the BOP because of the wide cultural disparity between researchers and respondents. This is likely to be more important at the BOP, as cultural concepts tend to be more deeply embedded among 'lower orders' of society and researchers are more likely to come from a more educated sector of society where cultural concepts are more likely to have been modified by Western influences. As an example of this, the BOP is a fairly new and 'unknown' concept in the mindset of marketing executives in Zimbabwe. Hence there was a challenge to define the concept and the constructs that were to be measured. In most firms, the executives defined and referred to the BOP as the mass market but on reflection they agreed that they were serving this market but knew little about it and its intricacies and divisions. The same was encountered with consumers when it came to defining concepts such as social networks – their understanding and categorization of networks was different from the way the companies defined and viewed these networks.

Information gathering and data collection challenges

Obtaining primary and secondary data in international markets is often a difficult task. It is even more difficult at the BOP due to the embeddedness of cultural differences, lack of the rule of law, greater dependence on the informal economy and policy-induced shocks in the environment. The first of the challenges related to data definition and collection issues. Often, BOP markets typically do not have readily available documented secondary data such as census reports and industry updates. The definition and classification of data may complicate undertaking research at the BOP. The unavailability and falsification of data by governments are common problems and governments in BOP markets are often accused of falsifying statistics in order to attract investment and donors. In Zimbabwe, there are many parallel data compilation processes undertaken by different groups with different motives.

The second of these challenges relates to selecting respondents. Selection can be by various means using geographical and administrative indicators, such as available census data (Weiss, 2005). However, in Zimbabwe, an ethnographic approach, where the researchers actually lived with potential respondents, helped identify the respondents. Visits to rural areas and high-density urban areas enabled the researchers to draw on the expertise of local leaders on how best to approach the issue of recruiting an appropriate sample. For example, social interactions after church services gave the researchers an insight into the profiles of target respondents before inviting them to participate in the consumer interviews. In the case of the companies, social interaction and networking between the chief researcher and marketing personnel in the companies enabled the researcher to gain insights into the potential of companies for use as case studies.

The third of these challenges was that of access and trust. Access to potential respondents for the administration of questionnaires and conduct of interviews can be affected by the different traditions and cultural norms. In some BOP markets in Asia and Africa, access is likely to be difficult due to general mistrust of strangers and unwillingness to discuss issues that might be perceived to be personal and taboo (Napier et al., 2004). Religion is likely to play a key role in most BOP markets, with the exception of those in former communist states. A lack of knowledge of local customs and norms of target respondents in BOP markets can provoke negative reactions from the locals, which in turn can hinder getting them to fully participate in the data collection process. Researchers will be faced with the challenge of adapting their own behaviour so that the behaviour exhibited is perceived as culturally appropriate by the target sample for the research. In Zimbabwe, access to respondents was found to be a major challenge. Personal introductions and social networking were critical in enabling the researchers to gain access to consumers and companies. A knowledge and understanding of local norms and customs assisted the chief investigators and research assistants to gain access to local consumer respondents. In the case of the companies, personal networking by the chief researcher enhanced easy access to the firms.

The fourth challenge was the credibility of the researcher in the eyes of the BOP-based respondents (Yeung, 2004; Daniels and Cannice, 2004). The importance of networking and personal introductions was confirmed in the consumer interviews and the company case studies. Access and general cooperation were experienced in interviews where the researchers had been introduced at church services or at community meetings. The same applied to the case studies, where the chief researcher expanded on his personal network in the industry through references from credible people such as managing directors of the leading MNCs in the sector. A person's nationality can evoke negative and positive opinions resulting from respondents' perception of the country of origin of the researcher (Tsang, 1998; Wilkinson and Young, 2004). This was evident in the research in Zimbabwe where the social class of the chief researcher and the research assistants had varying impacts on the conduct of research.

The fifth challenge was having researchers whose personal characteristics were acceptable and compatible with those of the respondents. Key personal characteristics for consideration were age and gender. People in different cultures have different associations with age terms such as 'young' and 'old'. These can have different meanings and mental mapping in the minds of potential research respondents. The perceived distance in age between the interviewer and the respondent may result in a refusal to respond to questions. Managers may misinterpret young age for inexperience and this can create a level of inequality in terms of power and influence in the interview situation (Michailova and Worm, 2003). Gender may also provide different challenges for researchers in BOP markets. In African BOP markets where the social standing of women is not necessarily the same as that of men, there may be some reluctance by respondents to be interviewed by women. On the other hand, female respondents might not be comfortable being interviewed by male researchers especially on issues that are perceived to be the domain of women. Although these factors apply in most international marketing research, they are especially important at the BOP due to culturally determined factors being more deeply embedded. While age has been mentioned as a factor for consideration, in the Zimbabwean context, it proved to be critical to have a balanced age group of research assistants who could appeal to a broad age demographic and not just the elderly group.

A final challenge was obtaining truly espoused opinions. In Zimbabwe, the use of qualitative flexible interview protocols and local research assistants assisted in improving the quality of responses. Michailova and Worm (2003) argue that there are greater chances of resentment towards the recording of interviews at the BOP due to the culture of suspicion and mistrust of strangers. The experience in Zimbabwe demonstrated that the majority of individual respondents were somewhat anxious when asked for permission to record the interviews, particularly the over 45, rural-based BOP consumers. Refusal to allow the recording of interviews was common when interviews were carried out at or after community functions such as church services. When the location changed to individual homesteads, respondents were more relaxed and not only felt more confident about allowing the recording of interviews but also provided more in-depth responses. The recording of interviews was not a problem with company executives.

It was important to schedule the timing of the interviews in a convenient way for the respondents. At times, it was impossible to have a one-on-one interview without some people lingering around even though they would not be participating in the interview process. Hence, field note taking was a major additional method of recording information. About 24% of the interviews were conducted with consumer respondents after social events such as church services or community meetings such as women's clubs' meetings. About 10% of consumer interviews were conducted at respondents' places of work. The scenario was significantly different with the interviews with company executives for the case studies. At times, meetings were cancelled at the last minute and in most of the cases appointment times were not strictly adhered to. The researchers had to wait patiently for respondents to create free time even though there was a confirmed appointment time. Given the fast pace at which things change in the risky and uncertain Zimbabwean environment, executives have to think on the spot and execute decisions without delay, as failure to do so can cost the company a lot of money. The executives themselves were cognizant of this issue and at least 45% of the interviews took place at locations other than their offices – in places such as sports clubs or over drinks.

Operational considerations

Cultural issues are at the centre of academic discussion on international cross-cultural research (Hofstede, 2001; Davies and Fitchett, 2004; Fletcher and Fang, 2006), hence the need to validate or invalidate the conceptual mindset that researchers have about these challenges in the context of the BOP. Sumner and Tribe (2004) have argued that it is problematic to transpose generic social science concepts and methods from Western developed markets to underdeveloped markets such as at the BOP, where the collective perception of reality prevails over the individual perception. While the collective perception towards reality was prevalent in BOP markets where consumers have been exposed to extreme economic shocks such as in Zimbabwe, the research discovered differences across age groups in their appreciation of the need for a collective perception to life. Younger consumers, especially those born after independence in 1980 and who largely reside in high-density urban areas, tend not to have a lot of respect towards collective decision making. Unlike the older generation whose collectivism was due to induction into collectivism from the preceding generations and the liberation struggle, the younger generation viewed life from a more individual perspective. However, the situation changes slightly with the rural BOP consumers.

Another consideration is whether the attitude towards research at the BOP is the same as in developed countries or among the upper and middle classes in developing countries. Hofmeyer et al. (1994) argue that tradition and cultural sensitivities such as reluctance to take part in interviews and general mistrust of strangers are some of the common problems likely to be faced by researchers in BOP markets. The other key culturally influenced research issue is the attitude towards research itself at the BOP. There is a large difference between academic culture and business culture, in the sense that managers at the BOP are often not familiar with the rigours of academic culture and do not place the same value on research as academic researchers. This is likely to be more prevalent in markets at the BOP, given the low levels of collaboration between the private sector and academia in developing countries. While broadly speaking this is true in Zimbabwe, there is some indication of a gradual change in this attitude.

In developed countries, the study of networks in marketing has mostly been in the business-to-business context, whereas at the BOP, networks are extremely important in the business-to-consumer context. Although networks are important in most international marketing activities, it is argued that relationships and networks are more influential at the BOP, due to lack of government and other support programmes and greater levels of uncertainty and unanticipated shocks in the environment. In business activities at the BOP, informal social networks take on a particular significance in the light of political uncertainty, ethnic clustering, and the absence of the rule of law (Fletcher and Fang, 2006).

As previously noted, communities live and operate in a variety of formal and informal networks that cover different aspects of their social and business life (Michailova and Worm, 2003). The research undertaken in Zimbabwe provides insights into how social networks impact on conducting research in these markets. There are two types of networks:

1. *Traditional networks* are largely driven by geographic location, common traditions and norms. The most common traditional networks were village development groups, burial societies and collective labour groups. They are likely to fit into the traditional community hierarchy systems of chiefs, village heads and kraal heads. These are common in rural areas in Zimbabwe where communal living, tradition and group norms are more common.

2. *Modern social networks* are based on semi-commercial or subsistence-oriented activities. While these are common in both the rural and urban BOP environment, they were more common in the urban areas where they were used as a key mechanism for survival. The key networks are women's community clubs, savings clubs, buying clubs, vending clubs, cross-border associations, church groups and residents' groups. Their focus is on empowering members through the provision of loans and access to products from distribution channels.

Language and translation play an important role when undertaking research at the BOP. Various scholars have provided insights into the importance of language in international cross-cultural research, citing its impact on conducting field work, the design of research instruments, and access to sample populations (Hofmeyr et al., 1994; Kasse-Grisar, 2004; Marschan-Piekkari and Reis, 2004; Wilson, 2004). High levels of illiteracy and poor educational facilities in most African BOP markets further compound the problem of language (Hofmeyr et al., 1994). The actual wording of the instruments needs to be culturally sensitive to the target respondents at the BOP. The deployment of local researchers in Zimbabwe, who were not only fluent in the local language but also fully understood the cultural and language sensitivities of the target respondents in BOP markets, helped address any language complexities.

Weaknesses in and/or the unavailability of infrastructure necessary for conducting research at the BOP pose a key challenge for researchers (Daniels and Cannice, 2004), which can influence the research design and the field work. Weak postal services can hinder the use of postal questionnaires and can have a negative impact on the sampling frame, since surveys would be restricted to convenience sampling because of the absence of details such as proper street addresses that researchers can use. Poor and expensive telephone network systems in Asian and African BOP markets can hinder effective communication during the research phase as with interviews. Unreliable transport networks combined with the sparse geographic conditions (such as the isolation of villages) can hinder researchers' access to target respondents. This was the case in Zimbabwe, where natural and policy-induced forces have resulted in the destruction of basic infrastructure such as roads and telecommunications.

Methodology

To further explore the influence of environmental and individual variables on purchasing at the BOP, a study was undertaken in Zimbabwe. Zimbabwe is a country where at least 85% of the population live on less than US$2 (£1.20) a day (Consumer Council of Zimbabwe, 2007; UNDP, 2008), self-employment accounts for 60–70% of income, infrastructure is totally inadequate, risk and uncertainty are the norm and where there are adverse political, economic and natural shocks, such as rampant inflation, persistent drought and frequent economic structural adjustment programmes such as land reform. A mixed methods approach was employed as it exposes researchers to opportunities to utilize multiple sources of information to gain new insights and understand more about business phenomena (Axin et al., 1991; Tesch, 1992). The use of this approach is likely to produce some concepts that do not fit existing theories or models. Empirical data were collected from BOP consumers using qualitative consumer interviews to establish the drivers of their purchasing behaviour. The focus was on the purchase of fast moving consumer goods (FMCG), specifically food and personal hygiene items, as these account for the bulk of purchases at the BOP and 65% of BOP purchases in the case of Zimbabwe. Informants were asked a set of questions using an interview guide, which covered general classification questions and those relating to the drivers of purchasing decision making. A total of 65 BOP consumers were interviewed – 23 from the urban BOP, 14 from the diluted urban BOP who had formerly been middle class, 16 from the BOP segment of rural breadwinners working in urban areas, and 12 rural BOP consumers. These in-depth interviews were supplemented with interaction of researchers with BOP consumers at 16 social network gatherings such as women's community clubs, self-help group meetings and church meetings. In addition, the researchers stayed in the accommodation of the members of one of each of the four BOP groups and accompanied them on purchasing activities in the formal and informal sector so as to observe actual purchasing behaviour. Empirical data were also collected from firms manufacturing FMCG in Zimbabwe. There were four case studies – two on subsidiaries of MNCs, one on a large local FMCG producer and one on a medium-sized FMCG manufacturer. These four firms accounted for 72% of the production of food, drinks and personal hygiene goods in Zimbabwe. The interviews for the case studies were supplemented by archival material and observations of the interactions between firms and consumers that took place when the researchers accompanied the firms' personnel on visits to the formal and informal market sectors.

Consumer behaviour at the BOP

Culture impacts on the behaviour of consumers. It is for this reason that developed country models of consumer behaviour need to be modified when doing business in developing countries. Different tastes, customs and habits are likely to result in different preferences. The impact of consumer behaviour at the BOP is discussed in detail in a paper by Chikweche and Fletcher (2010).

Understanding consumer purchase influences in BOP marketplaces

There have been a limited number of studies conducted in BOP markets that discuss factors that influence purchase. This is a research stream that takes a broad perspective to understanding consumer behaviour in BOP markets (Viswanathan, 2007; Sridharan and Viswanathan, 2008; Viswanathan et al., 2009). To date, their studies in South India are the only ones that attempt to investigate the factors that influence subsistence consumers to buy products. Another key study in Bangladesh focused on the impact of social networks on the livelihoods of subsistence consumers (Purvez, 2003).

Value and appeal of the offer

The basic concern for consumers in BOP marketplaces is to satisfy physiological needs in the best way possible. This may not just be a matter of price as is often assumed. The results from the study carried out in South India by Viswanathan et al. (2009) indicated concerns for fairness, product quality and the right price as important influencers for these consumers. This could be indicative of common concerns in subsistence markets and description may take different forms, given the different circumstances consumers face in their environments. The value and appeal of the offer was reflected in the ability of the offer to satisfy physiological needs and products being available for purchase when required. The interviewees indicated that consideration for meeting basic physiological needs was paramount in making a decision to buy products such as food and personal hygiene items. However, while there was a basic need to buy food to prevent hunger and soap in order to be clean, there was variation in the type and mix of the products that were purchased to meet these needs. Examples highlighted by interviewees included buying soya chunks instead of meat, using cheaper forms of cooking oil to cook or using washing bar soaps for bathing. Affordability was an important element in this connection. The interviewees highlighted the fact that product availability was not guaranteed in Zimbabwe, especially through the formal channels of distribution. This resulted in the consumers giving availability virtually equivalent ranking to physiological needs and price of products.

Income and consumer spending

Income and consumer spending are related to affordability, which involves income distribution and its impact on the consumer. Engel's law (see Houthakker, 1957) attempts to generalize consumer spending patterns across markets using Western markets as a basis. However, circumstances might be different in BOP markets, as evident from the studies in Bangladesh and South India, and needs are not universal especially in the context of BOP versus Western markets where there are different levels of income. In Zimbabwe, there has been a major decline in real income, which has resulted in more consumers spending the majority of their income on food, transport and other basic needs that are affected by hyperinflation (UNDP, 2008). The assumption that consumers are driven by a rational quest to maximize utility may not apply in Zimbabwe, where income alone was unlikely to be the only influence on consumers' buying behaviour, given the existence of other constraints. Affordability of products emerged as a key purchase influencer.

Social networks

In the context of BOP markets, the role of social networks has also been studied in a variety of disciplines such as economics, medicine and sociology (Woodcock, 1996; Cattell, 2001; Wood, 2003). Individual consumer behaviour has been found to be influenced by participation in social networks, which helps shape the psychological make-up of consumers so that they conform to group expectations and norms (Chakravarti, 2006; Sridharan and Viswanathan, 2008; Viswanathan et al., 2009). For example, social networks were found to be a key component of consumers' lives in Bangladesh (Rangan and Rajan, 2005) and South India (Viswanathan, 2007). In Zimbabwe, consumers were found to be active in a number of social networks, such as self-help groups, as a way of diversifying their income source and as a source of employment (Barr, 2004; Ersado, 2006). In rural areas, these were initiated by nongovernmental organizations such as CARE International as a way of empowering the peasant farmers. Social networks are a vehicle for information dissemination as word of mouth has been found to be influential in determining purchases. This is important in BOP markets in general where consumers tend to have a collectivist approach to life and form social networks which are a key conduit for survival in their environment in subsistence markets (Purvez, 2003; Michailova and Worm, 2003; Kirchgeorg and Winn, 2006).

In Zimbabwe, at least four out of five interviewees indicated they were active in some form of social network that influenced their purchase. Most of the informants acknowledged the importance of familial and kinship networks (family, friends and neighbours) as the first port of call for information on products. Both informal and formal networks across the groups were identified as having an important role in determining whether to buy or not to buy a product. The common networks based on social activities were women's community clubs, buying clubs, religious groups, burial societies and nongovernmental organizations. The buying clubs are an extension of community clubs where women formed groups based on their area of residence to pool their meagre financial resources and then approach companies to be allowed to buy groceries in bulk at discounted prices. The self-help groups cover a broad spectrum of activities such as self-employment projects (for example sewing, crocheting, knitting clubs, carpentry, livestock-rearing schemes), and buying clubs, whose main goal is to encourage residents to engage in self-sustaining livelihood projects to help them cope with the economic shocks. Membership was drawn from unemployed men, women and retrenched semi-skilled tradespeople

Environmental challenges

BOP consumers are exposed to a variety of environmental challenges that can influence their purchase decision. There is a well-documented stream of literature on the impact of economic, political, social, human and natural factors on subsistence consumers' livelihoods (Nwanko, 2000; Ersado, 2006; Loayza et al., 2007; Johnson et al., 2007; Kauffman et al., 2008). Examples of hazards include corruption, lack of income, unemployment and hyperinflation. These were confirmed in the studies in Bangladesh and South India, where there was a prevalence of 'uncertainty, complexity and lack of control' of the day-to-day activities in subsistence markets (Purvez, 2003; Viswanathan, 2007). In Zimbabwe, there has been a continual decline in GDP, unemployment levels exceed 80% and it has the world's highest inflation rate (Coorey et al., 2007; Hanke, 2008). Corruption levels are also deemed to be very high, exposing consumers to varying incidences of corrupt practices from politicians, public servants and suppliers of products (Kauffman et al., 2008). Other factors include the influence of government and politicians in the terms of competition and how the market functions, whereby the government determines when, where, how much and how products are sold. This results in shortages, thereby forcing consumers to buy often, not because they need the products, but because they are available.

Family role

The family constitutes one of the most important influences on consumer decision making (Brown, 1979). In subsistence markets such as Zimbabwe, the concept is of an extended family made up of the nuclear family as well as other relatives and this is likely to be dominant (Bracking and Sachikonye, 2006; Zimbabwe Government, 2006). Traditionally, women are in charge of buying household staples in subsistence markets.

This was evident in the study in South India by Viswanathan (2007), who highlighted the fact that the husband delegates the role of buying household products to the wife. The same applied in Zimbabwe, where traditionally women are also in charge of buying household staples (Mazzeo, 2006; Gweru and Zinyama, 2007). The role of children in consumer decision making in subsistence markets will be different from that of their counterparts in Western markets who are likely to influence choice of products and brands (Kim and Lee, 1997; Zimbabwe Government, 2006; MPOI, 2007).

The results in Table 15.1 are a summary of the factors that influenced subsistence consumers in Zimbabwe when making purchases of food and personal hygiene products. Those that relate to the review of the literature include the perceived value and appeal of the offering in terms of catering for physiological needs in a climate of uncertain availability of goods. Other factors found in this research, but not discussed in the literature review, include the role of new product introductions, the effect of different forms of promotion, and the issue of convenience as reflected in package sizes and shopping location. The three most important influencers overwhelmingly identified by our interviewees were physiological needs, uncertain product availability and price. Our interviewees indicated that these three influencers were interlinked and dependent on each other, such that they evaluated them jointly when making purchases, hence all three score 93%.

Table 15.1 Key purchase influencers and their components

Core purchase drivers	Components	Overall ranking % preference
Physiological needs	Hunger Personal hygiene Acceptable performance	93
Uncertainty of product availability	Product shortages Black market Speculation No option	93
Price	Income availability Market distortions Hard currency pricing	93
Peer and social networks	Source of information Source of product access	81
Family	Family roles	78
New products	Cheaper alternatives Product performance	64
Firms' promotion activities	Direct marketing Branding In-store promotions General above the line promotion	58

Core purchase drivers	Components	Overall ranking % preference
Environmental hazards	Economic Political Literacy levels Consumer rights	54
Convenience	Location and availability of channel Product size Multipurpose use	53

Manifestations of consumer behaviour in BOP markets

New/alternative products

The interviewees mentioned that the availability of new or alternative products to meet their needs, such as fridge-free margarine, multipurpose soap, animal fat-based cooking oil and flavoured soya chunks, was an important influencer on their purchasing. The new fridge-free margarine was created for subsistence consumers who do not have access to refrigeration, but unlike traditional margarine, it has a higher salt content. Alternative products were selected by consumers with availability and afford-ability in mind. Interviewees indicated that they always made an effort to look for new or alternative products in the marketplace as part of their purchase decision-making process for products.

Firms' promotion activities

Promotional activities and branding were cited as important influencers of purchase, although their role was becoming less important. Interviewees indicated that they used to pay a lot of attention to promotional activities through media such as newspa-pers, radio and TV but this has changed. Regular electricity cuts and the costs of purchasing TVs, PCs and newspapers were cited as reasons for the diminishing role of media-based promotions on their purchases. However, respondents did indicate their interest in and appreciation of direct marketing activities such as in-store sampling and promotional road shows as sources of information on products.

Convenience

The economic situation in Zimbabwe also reduced the impact of convenience as a consumer decision-making influence. The depth of store-keeping units or sizes was identified as an important influencer of purchase. Interviewees highlighted the link between product size, price and available income. Limited disposable income prevented interviewees from buying products in large sizes. They now resorted to buying single servings of products, since these were cheaper and addressed their immediate needs. Interviewees also indicated a preference for buying products at their local shops where they had a relationship with the shopkeeper and could get credit facilities, instead of travelling distances to buy products. However, the different dynamics of product availability in their market diminished the importance of location convenience.

Importance of the BOP segment to firms' business

Table 15.2 shows the contribution of the BOP to firms' turnover. In terms of importance, there was consensus that the segment was important to the business and growth prospects of all four firms and, in terms of turnover, it accounted for an average 59% of total contribution.

Table 15.2   Turnover contribution and growth prospects of the BOP market

Indicator	Firm A	Firm B	Firm C	Firm D
Turnover contribution (%)	86	56	68	47
Importance of BOP segment	Main segment	Key unknown segment	Strategic segment	Key segment
Growth prospects	High	High	High	High

Marketing mix issues

The discussion of consumer purchase decision making suggests that BOP markets provide distinct marketing challenges to firms either serving these markets or intending to enter these markets. Firms need to vary each element of the marketing mix when attempting to tap the potential of the BOP segment in developing countries. Various authors have criticized the marketing mix model, highlighting its limitations in addressing issues such as the importance of relationships and services marketing (Kotler, 1984; Shultz, 2001). However, the model is still the trusted conceptual framework of marketing practitioners Hence the use of the 4Ps model in this study, since food and personal hygiene products were used for the study. The four elements of the marketing mix – product, price, distribution (place) and promotion – are reviewed in the context of the BOP and the modifications that may be required to accommodate the issues that pertain to operating at the BOP.

Product

A key challenge BOP firms face is providing the right products to meet BOP consumers needs. Their ability to do so can be influenced by different macro-environmental constraints that firms face such as the economic, political and infrastructure challenges common at the BOP (Nwanko, 2000; Johnson et al., 2007; Ndulu et al., 2007). For example, government policies can reserve certain categories of goods for local indigenous firms, ban some products for health reasons or stipulate standard sizes for some consumer products (Dunning, 1997). These policies have the potential to shape the interactions between firms and consumers. BOP consumers are faced with the challenge of gaining access to affordable products, a challenge that can be met by manufacturers changing their conventional methods of serving the segment by enhancing product accessibility and affordability (Ndulu et al., 2007). While this will require a paradigm shift in the business models used in developed markets, it will allow international executives to understand these markets better and be able to put into place systems that can facilitate consumption of these products and services, thereby facilitating exchange interactions between the two. The nature of the product is important at the BOP and can determine how a company can effectively serve the BOP market (Viswanathan, 2007; Viswanathan et al., 2008). Companies often have to assess the importance of using particular products and then add some value through product innovation to enhance access and consumption of the product by consumers.

In the four case studies in Zimbabwe, firms acknowledged the importance of changing their conventional methods of providing products for the BOP segment and agreed it was necessary to enhance product accessibility and affordability by assessing their degree of essentiality and potential for value added. Product availability and accessibility were enhanced by the development of new affordable products that took the degree of essentiality into consideration. Table 15.3 provides a summary of the initiatives by the four companies to enhance product accessibility.

Table 15.3 Product initiatives by the four firms

Firm A	Firm B	Firm C	Firm D
Local FMCG producer	Medium-sized FMCG manufacturer	MNC subsidiary	MNC subsidiary
Single portion of meat substitute soya chunks	Single portion of cooking oil substitute using pork and beef dripping	Fridge-free margarine	Meat substitute soy mince
Single serve soya-based cooking oil		Multipurpose soap bar	Single portion of relish aids
		Single portion of washing powder	Sugar and powdered milk mixture

Pricing

Pricing is considered to be the most challenging task for marketing managers at the BOP, especially in MNCs (Austin, 1990). Research by London and Hart (2004) found that MNCs usually tried to impose their pricing formulae on developing country markets with little success at the BOP. Macro-environmental challenges such as government intervention have the potential to determine the pricing strategies used by firms at the BOP. Governments use price controls to ensure the affordability and access of products to consumers at the BOP (Ndulu et al., 2007; Kauffman et al., 2008). Firms therefore need to devise pricing strategies specifically for the BOP and price the offering in a way that takes into account the unique circumstances faced by BOP consumers. Dramatic cost reductions are often necessary to achieve this. The technique should be based on low margins and high volumes. This may involve taking the goods or services, reducing them to their bare essentials and offering them on a massive scale. It also involves ways of making the offering cheap enough to be affordable to this larger, poorer market. According to Anderson (2005), apart from low price points, this requires minimum marginal costs, deskilling of associated servicing requirements so non-experts can deliver them, and the use of local entrepreneurs. Creating affordability may require repackaging and recovery of costs so that the upfront cost of access is reduced for potential consumers with little or no disposable income. This might be achieved by charging a small upfront payment and a monthly usage fee, instead of selling the product outright. This will insert a performance promise into the transaction as the monthly fees will continue only as long as the product performs.

In the four case studies in Zimbabwe, firms acknowledged the need to strike a balance between low income and high value consciousness of BOP consumers so as to provide a product these consumers could afford and gain access to. Firms C and D stated that they received directions from head office on their pricing strategies – in particular in the area of margin management. In firms A and B, there was evidence that they aligned their margins to the dictates of the market, which is now dominated by the BOP segment. Firms A and B had already been using the high-volume, low-margin strategy as a competitive tool to take market share from the two MNCs. Another cost reduction strategy used by all the firms was packaging modification. On average, packaging constituted the majority of costs for these firms' products, largely because the packaging materials were imported. Where practical, the firms substituted imported packaging with local packaging, and as result, firms A and B claimed they achieved overall savings of between 13% and 33% on some products.

Distribution

The physical accessibility to products and services remains a key challenge for consumers and firms at the BOP markets (Austin, 1990). BOP consumers' access to products is often hindered by the weak distribution infrastructure that is common in these markets, while weak supporting infrastructure, such as storage facilities, telecommunications and transport, makes firms' distribution channels longer and more expensive (Nwanko, 2000; Fay and Morrison, 2005). Consumers and firms often have to make use of formal and informal distribution channels to enhance their interactions (Mahajan and Banga, 2006; Viswanathan, 2007). This has resulted in the development of informal distribution systems that are often linked to social networks in the communities and in some instances are state controlled (De Soto, 2000; Viswanathan et al., 2009). Distribution at the BOP may need to involve networks built on existing relationships. This is illustrated in the preference at the BOP for shopping at small shops as relationships are a significant determinant of purchase and ad hoc credit is provided. Finally, at the BOP, these informal channels can coexist with authorized channels and provide a lower priced entry strategy. Such informal channels can also provide value-creating services that are not catered for by authorized channels (Rubesch, 2005). At the BOP, companies often have to make use of local community networks as distribution systems to enhance consumers' access to products in situations of shortages, infrastructure shortcomings or unofficial marketing channels.

In the study in Zimbabwe, there was evidence of the use of formal and informal channels of distribution to access products by consumers at the BOP. The main formal channels include family-owned local grocery shops, supermarkets and wholesalers, and the informal channels include tuckshops and open market stalls. All four firms acknowledged using informal channels as a key distribution channel for their products to those at the BOP, although firms A and B were more active in using informal channels. All the firms cited informal channels as being critical to their distribution strategy due to their links with the BOP consumers' social networks. However, all the firms still utilized formal distribution channels for the BOP, although they indicated this was changing in line with the consumer trend to buy products from the informal sector where they were more readily available. The issue of stringent price control inspection in formal channels was cited as a reason for their decreasing importance in distribution, although this varied among the firms. There was evidence in three of the firms of the emergence of franchises linked to social networks, such as women's community groups and buying clubs, which became distribution agents for the companies.

Promotion

Affordability and accessibility of promotional media is a key issue for consideration for companies penetrating the BOP market (Fletcher and Melewar, 2001). Firms are likely to face problems of a lack of adequate communication infrastructure in some BOP markets, while BOP consumers face the challenge of accessing information from firms through above the line media such as newspapers, radio and TV, which are often unaffordable or not available on a reliable basis due to electricity cuts (Loayza et al., 2007). Many at the BOP live in 'media dark' zones, where they do not have access to the print media due to illiteracy, and limited or no access to the radio, TV and the internet. Research by Thomas (1996) stresses that unique and innovative promotion methods will be necessary to communicate with potential BOP customers. Thomas illustrates this by citing 'wokabaut' (walkabout) marketing in the highlands of Papua New Guinea, where promotion is by a troupe of actors going from village to village performing plays from the back of a truck that promote products, supplies of which have been previously augmented at the little shops along the dirt roads that link the villages. In Africa, the use of road shows as a promotional tool has become widespread as a vehicle for firms to reach out to BOP markets. These are conducted at social gatherings where products are introduced to the community through drama and musicals. Fletcher (2006) conducted studies on the differences in promoting to the upper/middle classes and those at the BOP in Vietnam, Thailand and Sri Lanka. He took a standard communications model (Griffin, 1994) and respondents were asked a number of questions regarding 'sender', 'medium', 'receiver', 'interference' and 'feedback' issues. He found that different messages, content and media were required for each group.

In Zimbabwe, all four firms mentioned that they used a diverse set of communication channels to interact with consumers. There was evidence of a bias by the firms towards below the line activities for interacting with consumers such as product demonstrations. These were mainly conducted at women's clubs in the residential areas of BOP consumers as an alternative to above the line activities such as TV advertising. The various forms of communication used and their contribution to the firms' integrated marketing communication channels are outlined in Table 15.4.

Table 15.4   International marketing communications activities targeted at the BOP

Activities	Firm A	Firm B	Firm C	Firm D
Above the line	Minimal radio Minimal print	Outdoor Minimal print	Television Print Radio	Minimal radio Minimal print
% of budget	21	18	38	28
Below the line	Wet sampling Women's clubs	Mobile advertising Wet sampling Women's clubs	Wet sampling Women's clubs Churches	Road shows Wet sampling Women's clubs Churches Schools
% of budget	79	82	62	72

The firms noted that marketing expenses across all BOP categories had been drastically reduced in response to the harsh economic environment. They indicated that they now pursued innovative and cost-effective methods of communicating with their customers. Firm D had initiated the concept of community road shows where they conducted plays to dramatize their products, either demonstrating how the products were used and their advantages or introducing new products. All the firms indicated that they used the social networks for demonstrating their products and gaining feedback from consumers.

Implications for creating a strategy for BOP markets

These findings confirm previous findings by Prahalad (2005) and Viswanathan et al. (2008) but provide more insights on the product extensions that manufacturers can implement in order to adapt their product strategy. The study also reinforces the notion that by virtue of their resources base, MNCs tend to take the lead in product development with their wide product mix as suggested by Austin (1990). While scholars like Mahajan and Banga (2006) and Prahalad (2005) have highlighted the importance of product innovation and the use of single portions as key product mix modifications necessary at the BOP, it is necessary to link to degree of essentiality of products with consumer needs.

The study reinforces the importance of macro-environmental constraints, such as inflation, on how firms devise their product pricing strategies. It provides new insights on the need for firms to strike a balance between low income and high value consciousness on the part of consumers so as to provide a product that meets the market's needs. This will require a nominal price that will be offset by the large volumes of business that make up for the loss of margin. The study demonstrates how the constraints faced by MNC subsidiaries at the BOP resulted in their adoption of a more flexible approach towards pricing by using a low-margin, high-volume strategy. The study has reinforced justification for increased marketing to the BOP as advocated by early proponents of the concept such as Prahalad and Hart (2002). It demonstrates the importance of the segment to firms' turnover. Findings also highlight new ways of cost reduction that firms can use to enhance product affordability such as packaging substitution.

The influence of social networks as a means of interaction between consumers and firms is confirmed in the study in Zimbabwe where social groups are important at the BOP. While previous studies by Barr (2004), Kirchgeorg and Winn (2006) and Michailova and Worm (2003) have focused on the influence of social networks on BOP consumers' livelihoods, the study in Zimbabwe provides new insights into how social networks, such as buying clubs and women's clubs, have become key conduits for firms to distribute their products to BOP consumers As a result, firms are switching to informal channels where possible. These informal channels are difficult for government to supervise as far as price controls are concerned. Not only do these networks enable firms to minimize the negative impact of the distribution challenges that are common at the BOP, but they also enable consumers to gain access to products and provide employment and business ownership opportunities for marginalized consumers, especially women.

Given the challenges of communicating with BOP consumers, findings from the study confirm firms' shift to below the line direct marketing activities as a strategy to cope with the constraints of affordability and accessibility of promotional media and enhance their communication with BOP consumers. The study also provides new insights into the use of social networks as a way of enhancing this direct marketing approach to BOP consumers and highlights examples of new forms of direct marketing such as the road shows and mobile product sampling units.

Conclusion

The research in Zimbabwe confirms the view that it is necessary for managers wishing to do business in BOP markets to develop separate marketing strategies for these markets. To successfully access BOP markets requires tailored approaches rather than a global approach. This is because those in BOP markets have not been exposed to developed country influences. The marketing mix adopted for offerings aimed at the BOP will need to be tailored to existing cultural differences and take into account local conditions. Approaches to BOP consumers will need to capitalize on existing relationships and employ those who are insiders in the local networks. Offerings to the BOP segment will require a deep understanding of the local environment and involve a bottom-up approach resulting from identifying, leveraging and shoring up the existing social infrastructure. Strategies might include:

- The creation of a unique business model tailored to the local market that is both culturally sensitive and economically feasible.
- The identification of consumers' real needs and product adaptation to meet these needs in a way that creates opportunities for local participation.
- The development of tactics to overcome the infrastructure problems faced by BOP consumers.
- Detailed research into each BOP market, its needs and its characteristics and tailoring the research to the BOP market environment.
- Collaboration with nontraditional partners in the market so as to gain expert knowledge of the existing social infrastructure.

References

Aggarwal, R. (2006) 'Business strategies for profitable sales to the poor: How free enterprise can fight poverty', in S.C. Jain and S. Vacani (eds) *Multinational Corporations and Global Poverty Reduction.* Cheltenham: Edward Elgar.

Ahmad, P.S., Gorman, M.E. and Werhane, P.H. (2004) 'Hindustan Lever Limited and marketing to the poorest of the poor'. *International Journal of Entrepreneurship and Innovation Management*, 4: 495–511.

Anderson, C. (2005) 'Long tail vs bottom of the pyramid', 22 March, http://longtail.typepad.com/the_long_tail/2005/03/.

Austin, J. (1990) *Managing in Developing Countries: Strategic Analysis and Operating Techniques*. New York: Free Press.

Axin, W.G., Fricke, T.E. and Thornton, A. (1991) 'The micro demographic community study approach: Improving survey data by integrating the ethnographic method'. *Sociological Methods and Research*, 20(2).

Barr, A. (2004) 'Forging effective new communities: The evolution of civil society in Zimbabwean settlement villages'. *World Development*, 32(10): 1753–6.

Bracking, S. and Sachikonye, L. (2006) *Remittances, Poverty Reduction and the Informalisation of Household Wellbeing in Zimbabwe*, Working Paper Series 45. Global Poverty Research Group.

Brown, J.W. (1979) 'The family and consumer decision making: A cultural view'. *Academy of Marketing Science Journal*, 7(4): 335–45.

Burt, R.S. (1987) 'Social contagion and innovation: Cohesion versus structural equivalence'. *American Journal of Sociology*, 92(6): 1287–335.

Cattell, V. (2001) 'Poor people, poor places, and poor health: The mediating role of social networks and social capital'. *Social Science and Medicine*, 52(10): 1501–16.

Chakravarti, D. (2006) 'Voices unheard: The psychology of consumption in poverty and development'. *Journal of Consumer Psychology*,16(4): 360–76.

Chikweche, T. and Fletcher, R. (2008) Undertaking Research at the Bottom of the Pyramid: From Theoretical Considerations to Practical Realities. Proceedings of the Conference of the Consortium for International Marketing and Research, Rio de Janeiro, Brazil, 17–21 June.

Chikweche, T. and Fletcher, R. (2010) 'Understanding factors that influence purchases in subsistence markets'. *Journal of Business Research*, 63(6): 643–50.

Consumer Council of Zimbabwe (2007) *Economic Update*. Harare.

Coorey, S., Clausen, J.R., Funke, N. Munoz, S. and Ould-Abdallah (2007) *Lessons from High Inflation Episodes for Stabilizing the Economy in Zimbabwe*, Working Paper, WP/07/99. Washington, DC: IMF.

Craig, C.S. and Douglas, S.P. (2005) 'Beyond national culture: Implications of cultural dynamics for consumer research'. *International Marketing Review*, 23: 322–42.

D'Andrea, G., Ring, J., Lopez-Aleman, B. and Tengel, A. (2006) 'Breaking the myths on emerging consumers in retailing'. *International Journal of Retail & Distribution Management*, 34: 674–87.

Daniels, J.D. and Cannice, M.V. (2004) 'Interview studies in international business research', in R. Marschan-Piekkari and C. Welch (eds) *Handbook of Qualitative Research Methods for International Business*, Cheltenham: Edward Elgar.

Davies, A. and Fitchett, J.A. (2004) 'Crossing culture: A multi-method enquiry into consumer behaviour and the experience of cultural transition'. *Journal of Consumer Behaviour*, 3(4): 315–30.

De Mooij, M. (2004) *Consumer Behaviour and Culture Consequences for Global Marketing and Advertising.* Thousand Oaks, CA: Sage.

De Soto, H. (2000) *The Mystery of Capital: Why Capitalism Triumphs in the West and Fails Everywhere Else.* London: Bantam Press.

Dunning, J.H. (1997) *Multinational Enterprises and the Global Economy.* Wokingham: Addison-Wesley.

Ersado, L. (2006) *Income Diversification in Zimbabwe: Welfare Implications from Urban and Rural Areas*, Policy Research Working Paper No.3964. Washington, DC: World Bank

Fafchamps, M. (2000) 'Ethnicity and credit in African manufacturing'. *Journal of Development Economics*, 10: 108–41.

Fay, M. and Morrison, M. (2005) *Infrastructure in Latin America: Recent Developments and Key Challenges*, Report No. 32640-LCR. Washington, DC: World Bank.

Fletcher, R. (2000) 'The impact of globalization on national sovereignty: An Australian perspective'. *Journal of Current Research in Global Business*, 2(2): 95–103.

Fletcher, R. (2006) International marketing at the bottom of the pyramid: A three country study. Conference of the Consortium for International Marketing and Research, Istanbul, 26–30 May.

Fletcher, R. and Fang, T. (2006) 'Assessing the impact of culture on relationship creation and network formation in emerging Asian markets'. *European Journal of Marketing*, 40: 430–46.

Fletcher, R. and Melewar, T.C. (2001) 'The complexities of communicating with customers in emerging markets'. *Journal of Communications Management*, 6: 9–23.

Gilbert, D. and Kahl, J.A. (1982) *The American Class Structure: A New Synthesis*. Homewood, IL: Dorsey Press.

Green, R.T. and White, P.D. (1976) 'Methodological considerations in cross-cultural consumer research'. *Journal of International Business Studies*, 7(2).

Griffin, T. (1994) *International Marketing Communications*. Oxford: Butterworth-Heinemann.

Gweru, S. and Zinyama, T. (2007) Gender, education and development. Background paper to the Zimbabwe human development report on gender and human development: unlocking the gender paralysis in development (a win-win situation). Poverty Reduction Forum, Ministry of Public Service, Labour and Social Welfare, UNDP.

Hammond, A.L., Kramer, W.J., Katz, R.S. et al. (2007) *The Next Four Billion.* Washington, DC: World Resources Institute and International Finance Corporation.

Hanke, S.H. (2008) *Zimbabwe: Hyperinflation to Growth.* Harare: Imara Holdings.

Hart, S. (2007) *Capitalism at the Crossroads: Aligning Business, Earth, and Humanity.* Upper Saddle River, NJ: Pearson Education.

Hofmeyer, K., Templar, A. and Beaty, D. (1994) 'South Africa: Researching contrasts and contradictions in a context of change'. *International Studies of Management and Organisation,* 24(1–2).

Hofstede, G. (1991) *Cultures and Organizations.* London: HarperCollins.

Hofstede, G. (2001) *Culture's Consequences: Comparing Values, Behaviours, Institutions and Organizations across Nations.* Thousand Oaks, CA: Sage.

Houthakker, H.S. (1957) 'An international comparison of household expenditure patterns: Commemorating the centenary of Engel's Law'. *Econometrica,* 25(4).

Johnson, S., Ostry, J. and Subramanian, A. (2007) *The Prospects for Sustained Growth in Africa: Purchasing and Constraints,* Working Paper No 07/52. Washington, DC: IMF.

Kasse-Grisar, K. (2004) 'The role of negative personal experiences in cross-cultural case study research: Failure or opportunity', in R. Marschan-Piekkari and C. Welch (eds) *Handbook of Qualitative Research Methods for International Business.* Cheltenham: Edward Elgar.

Kauffman, D., Kraay, A. and Mastruzzi, M. (2008) *Governance Matters VII: Aggregate and Individual Governance Indicators, 1996-2007.* Washington, DC: World Bank.

Khanna, T., Palepu, K. and Sinha, J. (2005) 'Strategies that fit emerging markets'. *Harvard Business Review,* 83(6): 63–76.

Kim, C. and Lee, H. (1997) 'Development of family triadic measures for children's purchase influence'. *Journal of Marketing Research,* 34: 307–21.

Kirchgeorg, M. and Winn, M.I. (2006) Sustainability marketing for the poorest of the poor'. *Business Strategy and the Environment,* 15: 171–84.

Korten, D.C. (1999) The dark side of globalization: Financial and corporate rule. Proceedings of the Annual Meeting of the Academy of International Business, Charlestown, SC, 22–24 November.

Kotler, P. (1984) *Marketing Management: Analysis, Planning and Control* (5th edn). Englewood Cliffs, NJ: Prentice Hall.

Kuada, J. and Sorenson, O.J. (2000) *Internationalization of Companies from Developing Countries.* New York: International Business Press.

Loayza, N., Ranciere, R., Serven, L. and Ventura, J. (2007) 'Macroeconomic volatility and welfare in developing countries'. *World Bank Economic Review,* 21(3).

London, S.L. and Hart, T. (2004) 'Reinventing strategies for emerging markets: Beyond the transitional model'. *Journal of International Business Studies,* 35: 350–70.

Mahajan, V. and Banga, K. (2006) *The 86% Solution: How to Succeed in the Biggest Market Opportunity of the 21st Century.* Upper Saddle River, NJ: Wharton School Publishing.

Marshall, R. and Gitosudarmo, I. (1995) 'Variation in the characteristics of opinion leaders across cultural borders'. *Journal of International Consumer Marketing,* 8: 5–22.

Marschan-Piekkari, R. and Reis, C. (2004) 'Language and languages in cross-cultural interviewing', in R. Marschan-Piekkari and C. Welch (eds) *Handbook of Qualitative Research Methods for International Business*. Cheltenham: Edward Elgar.

Mazzeo, J. (2006) *Summary of Findings from CARE's Household Livelihood Security Assessment*. Harare, Zimbabwe: CARE

McPherson, M., Lovin, S. and Cook, J.M. (2001) 'Birds of a feather: Homophily in social networks'. *Annual Review of Sociology*, 27: 415–44.

Michailova, J.A. and Worm, V. (2003) 'Personal networking in Russia and China: Blat and guanxi'. *European Management Journal*, 21: 509–19.

MPOI (2007) Survey Findings on the State of Zimbabwe's Economy and People's Survival Strategies. Unpublished report commissioned by the National Endowment for Democracy, July.

Napier, N.K., Hosley, S. and Nguyen, T. (2004) 'Conducting qualitative research in Vietnam: Ethnography, grounded theory and case study research', in R. Marschan-Piekkari and C. Welch (eds) *Handbook of Qualitative Research Methods for International Business*. Cheltenham: Edward Elgar.

Ndulu, B.L., Chakraborti, L.L., Ramachandran, L.V. and Wogin, J. (2007) *Challenges of African Growth, Opportunities and Constraints, and Strategic Directions*. Washington, DC: World Bank.

Nwanko, S. (2000) 'Assessing the marketing environment in sub-Saharan Africa: Opportunities and threats analysis'. *Marketing Planning and Intelligence*,18: 144–513.

Prahalad, C.K. (2005) *The Fortune at the Bottom of the Pyramid*. Upper Saddle River, NJ: Wharton School Publishing.

Prahalad, C.K. and Hart, S.L. (2002) 'The fortune at the bottom of the pyramid', *Business Strategy*, 1(14): 2–14.

Purvez, S.A. (2003) 'Making use of mediating resources: Social network of the extreme poor in Bangladesh'. Dhaka, Bangladesh: IMEC.

Rangan, K.V. and Rajan, R. (2006) 'Unilever in India: Hindustan Lever's project Shakti – marketing FMCG to the rural consumer'. *Harvard Business Review*, 9: 505–56.

Rubesch, E. (2005) Incorporating informal channels into market entry strategy for emerging markets. Proceedings of Conference of the Australian and New Zealand Marketing Academy, Perth, 5–7 December.

Schultz, D.E. (2001) 'Marketers: Bid farewell to strategy based on the old 4P's'. *Marketing News*, 35(2): 7.

Sridharan, S. and Viswanathan, M. (2008) 'Marketing in subsistence economies'. *Journal of Consumer Marketing*, 25(7): 1–24.

Steenkamp, J.-B. and Baumgartner, H. (1998) 'Assessing measurement invariance in cross-national consumer research'. *Journal of Consumer Research*, 25(1): 78–90.

Sumner, A. and Tribe, M. (2004) The nature of epistemology and methodology in development studies: What do we mean by rigour? Paper for DSA Annual Conference, Bridging Research and Policy, Church House, London, 6 November.

Tesch, R. (1992) *Qualitative Research: Analysis, Types and Software Tools*. New York: Palmer Press.

Thomas, A.O. (1996) 'Advertising to the masses without mass media: The case of wokabaut marketing', in D.W. Johnson and E. Kaynak (eds) *Marketing to the Third World*. London: Haworth Press.

Trompenaars, F. and Hampden-Turner, C. (1997) *Riding the Waves of Culture: Understanding Cultural Diversity in Business.* London: Nicholas Brealey.

Tsang, E.W. (1998) 'Mind your identity when conducting cross-national research'. *Organisation Studies*, 19(3): 235–50.

UNCTAD (United Nations Conference on Trade and Development) (2008) *The Least Developed Countries Report.* Washington, DC: UN.

UNDP (United Nations Development Programme) (2008) Comprehensive Economic Recovery in Zimbabwe: A Discussion Document. Harare: UNDP.

Usunier, J.C. (2000) *Marketing Across Cultures* (3rd edn). Harlow: Pearson Education.

Van de Vijver, F.J. and Leung, K. (1997) 'Methods and data analysis in comparative research', in J.W. Berry, Y.H. Poortinga and J. Pandey (eds) *Handbook of Cross-Cultural Psychology*, vol. 1, *Theory and Methods*. Boston: Allyn Bacon.

Viswanathan, M. (2007) 'Understanding product and market interactions in subsistence marketplaces: A study in South India', in M. Viswanathan and J.A. Rosa (eds) *Product and Market Development for Subsistence Marketplaces: Consumption and Entrepreneurship Beyond Literacy and Resource Barriers*. London: Elsevier.

Viswanathan, M., Sridharan, S. and Ritchie, R. (2008) 'Marketing in subsistence marketplaces', in C. Wankel (ed.) *Alleviating Poverty Through Business Strategy*. Basingstoke: Palgrave Macmillan.

Viswanathan, M., Sridharan, S. and Ritchie, R. (2009) 'Understanding consumption and entrepreneurship in subsistence marketplaces'. *Journal of Business Research*, 63: 535–7.

Weiss, J. (2005) 'Experiences with poverty targeting in Asia: An overview', in J. Weiss (ed.) *Poverty Targeting in Asia*. Cheltenham: Edward Elgar.

Wilkinson, I. and Young, L. (2004) 'Improvisation and adaptation in international business research interviews', in R. Marschan-Piekkari and C. Welch (eds) *Handbook of Qualitative Research Methods for International Business*. Cheltenham: Edward Elgar.

Wilson, E.M. (2004) 'An outsider in India', in R. Marschan-Piekkari and C. Welch (eds) *Handbook of Qualitative Research Methods for International Business*. Cheltenham: Edward Elgar. 421-438.

Wood, G. (2003) 'Staying secure, staying poor: The Faustian bargain'. *World Development*, 31(3): 455.

Woodcock, M. (1998) 'Social capital and economic development: Toward a theoretical synthesis and policy framework'. *Theory and Society*, 27(2): 151–208.

World Bank (2007) *Population Issues in the 21st Century: The Role of the World Bank.* Washington, DC: World Bank.

World Bank (2008) *World Economic and Financial Surveys, Regional Economic Outlook, Sub-Saharan Africa*. Washington, DC: World Bank.

Yeung, H. (2004) 'Getting the ear of the minister', in R. Marschan-Piekkari and C. Welch (eds) *Handbook of Qualitative Research Methods for International Business*. Cheltenham: Edward Elgar.

Zimbabwe Government (2006) *Poverty Assessment Study Report*. Harare.

Conclusion

Richard Fletcher

As we embark upon the second decade of the new millennium, international marketing practitioners and academics alike face a number of unprecedented changes and challenges. These relate not only to the market being served, but the 7Ps of international marketing – namely the offering, its communication, its pricing and its distribution. In the international domain, they also relate to the people involved, the processes employed and physical evidence, such as the nature of the export marketing environment – all aspects that are articulated in depth in the individual chapters that make up this book.

These contemporary changes and challenges reflect the fact that the markets we cater for are no longer the same as was the case in the first decade of this millennium. Future growth in international markets is less likely to be found in Western developed country markets, as the four fastest growing markets are now all in the developing world – Brazil, Russia, India and China – the so-called BRIC markets. Other markets in the developing world are also experiencing considerable growth. These growth markets are markets where different cultures, different political systems, and different ethical practices confront the established norms of international marketing. These are also markets where the traditional Western approach of catering for those market segments that are 'more like us' is likely to be increasingly irrelevant, as their growing middle classes are different to the middle classes in the West, and an increasing percentage of real growth is likely to come from catering to the masses at the bottom of the pyramid.

These changes and challenges suggest that the academic community needs to take a close look at current theories that guide the practice of international marketing as have the authors of the chapters in this book. For the most part, these theories were developed in the West and based on large-scale surveys that measured average performance. This quantitative approach reflected past performance and practices due to delays between the gathering of data and publication of the results. This approach also ignored or averaged out the outliers, which are indicators of change and future developments. This approach is difficult to apply in developing country growth markets due to the unavailability of data on which to base sampling techniques, the reliability of existing statistical information, a lack of experience by respondents in answering questionnaires, and an unwillingness to express individual opinions when they conflict with group norms.

In these circumstances, a qualitative approach is to be preferred so as to understand current behaviour and predict future trends in developing country markets. Such techniques could include focus groups, case studies, ethnographic observations and experiments. These techniques with an etic focus are more likely to reflect the circumstances in the growth markets of the future than the more traditional approach of applying Western-based etic instruments, which effectively only measure the degree to which these developing country growth markets resemble the Western markets in which the instruments were developed and ignore the unique features of such growth markets and the drivers of such growth.

Even when using preferred qualitative techniques, there will be a need to incorporate cultural factors into the recording and scoring of responses as these impact on the willingness to participate, the representative nature of the sample and the nature of the response given. This suggests that to cater for these growth markets of the current millennium, if international marketing academics are to be relevant to the practice of international marketing, there is an urgent need to devise theories from within these growth markets based on qualitative techniques with an emic focus.

The products we need to offer to capture growing international markets will no longer be the same as far as the manufacturing sector is concerned. Offshoring and outsourcing blur the traditional distinctions of country of origin, and the concept of service dominant logic calls into question what it is that should be offered to international customers. Technical innovation mandates that firms no longer offer the finished product overseas but rather focus on offerings containing those elements of the value chain in which their distinctive competence is greatest.

Communication with customers in growth markets is likely to require a paradigm shift from above the line promotion based on advertising, as widespread literacy can no longer be assumed or the continued affordability of instruments to receive above the line advertising messages such as computers and TVs. Instead, international marketers will need to hone their skills in below the line promotional methods such as village theatre, in-store promotion and 'word of mouth' marketing. They will also need to adopt an approach to customer relationship management that reflects local expectations as opposed to corporate norms.

Strategies for entering and extending distribution channels in developing country growth markets will also need to be reviewed. The existence and acceptability of the same distribution channel structure as in Western markets can no longer be assumed, and new channels with a focus on individual ethnic, regional and socioeconomic groups will need to be located and accessed. Particular challenges exist in the selection and appointment of intermediaries and local partners, as, on the one hand, it is essential they have 'insider' status and, on the other, their ethical behaviour and performance have the potential to backfire on the overall image of the company.

Pricing approaches should be based on long-term considerations rather than short-term gains and structured in a way that creates mutual dependence between buyer and seller, so as to safeguard against opportunistic behaviour by competitors. Prices should be set on a local rather than a global basis. A pricing approach built around the creation of obligation and dependency accords better with the cultural drivers prevailing in most developing country growth markets.

In operating in these developing country growth markets, it is important to appreciate the people factor and understand the different nature of the relationship between employer and employee that exists in such markets and the obligations of each to the other, the expectations of a long-term relationship, and the welfare implications of this mutual dependency. Failure to research and appreciate the implications of the differences in this relationship compared to the West will impact adversely on relationships with intermediaries and the effectiveness of activities in developing country growth markets.

For most international marketers, involvement in developing country growth markets is but part of their overall global involvement, and processes will need to be put in place to integrate all the firms' operations and, in the process, take individual variations into account, so as to deliver maximum returns not just to shareholders but also to all the firms' stakeholders regardless of where they are based.

This may well require the development of new strategies in relation to building global brand equity, a greater focus on those elements of the value chain where the firm has the greatest competitive advantage in each market where it operates, and an integration of these so as to maximize the delivery of value. In this respect, a greater understanding of the environmental variables in each international market will be required, a local focus on the application of corporate social responsibility will be needed, and a willingness to make modifications to accommodate these environmental variables will be essential if global competitiveness is to be achieved.

Index

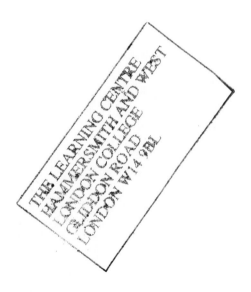